THE WILSON ERA
ESSAYS IN HONOR OF
ARTHUR S. LINK

Arthur S. Link

THE WILSON ERA

ESSAYS IN HONOR OF
ARTHUR S. LINK

Edited by

John Milton Cooper, Jr.
University of Wisconsin–Madison

and

Charles E. Neu
Brown University

HARLAN DAVIDSON, INC.
ARLINGTON HEIGHTS, ILLINOIS 60004

Library of Congress Cataloging-in-Publication Data

The Wilson era : essays in honor of Arthur S. Link / edited by John Milton Cooper, Jr., Charles E. Neu.
    p.   cm.
    Includes bibliographical references.
    ISBN 0-88295-877-1 (cloth). — ISBN 0-88295-872-0 (pbk.)
    1. Wilson, Woodrow, 1856–1924.   2. United States—Politics and government—1865–1933.   3. Progressivism (United States politics)   4. League of Nations—United States.   5. Link, Arthur Stanley—Bibliography.   I. Link, Arthur Stanley. II. Cooper, John Milton.   III. Neu, Charles E.
E762.W55   1991
973.91'3'092—dc20   90-46386
                                                                       CIP

Manufactured in the United States of America
95 94 93 92 91 1 2 3 4 5   MG

In Memory of Harlan Davidson

CONTRIBUTORS TO THIS VOLUME

John Milton Cooper, Jr., William Francis Allen Professor of History at the University of Wisconsin–Madison, is the author of *Walter Hines Page: The Southerner as American, 1855–1918* (1977), *The Warrior and the Priest: Woodrow Wilson and Theodore Roosevelt* (1983), and *Pivotal Decades: The United States, 1900–1920* (1990).

Dewey W. Grantham, Holland N. McTyeire Professor of History at Vanderbilt University, is the author of *Hoke Smith and the Politics of the New South* (1958), *The Regional Imagination: The South and Recent American History* (1979), and *The Life and Death of the Solid South: A Political History* (1988).

William H. Harbaugh, Langbourne M. Williams Professor of American History at the University of Virginia, is the author of *Power and Responsibility: The Life and Times of Theodore Roosevelt* (1961) and *Lawyer's Lawyer: The Life of John W. Davis* (1973).

Thomas J. Knock, assistant professor of history at Southern Methodist University, wrote his dissertation at Princeton on "Woodrow Wilson and the Origins of the League of Nations" (1982).

Richard W. Leopold, William Smith Mason Professor of History, emeritus, Northwestern University, is the author of *Robert Dale Owen: A Biography* (1940), *Elihu Root and the Conservative Tradition* (1954), and *The Growth of American Foreign Policy* (1962).

Ralph B. Levering, associate professor of history at Davidson College, is the author of *American Opinion and the Russian Alliance, 1939–1945* (1976), *The Kennedy Crises: The Press, the Presidency, and Foreign Policy* (1983), and *The Cold War, 1945–1987* (1988).

William A. Link, associate professor of history at the University of North Carolina at Greensboro, is the author of *A Hard Country and a Lonely Place: Schooling, Society, and Reform in Rural Virginia, 1870–1920* (1986).

John M. Mulder, President of Louisville Presbyterian Theological Seminary, is the author of *Woodrow Wilson: The Years of Preparation* (1978).

Charles E. Neu, professor of history at Brown University, is the author of *An Uncertain Friendship: Theodore Roosevelt and Japan, 1906–1909* (1967), *The Troubled Encounter: The United States and Japan* (1975), and "The Rise of the National Security Bureaucracy" in Louis Galambos, ed., *The New American State: Bureaucracies and Policies since World War II* (1987).

Steven J. Ross, associate professor of history at the University of Southern California, is the author of *Workers on the Edge: Work, Leisure, and Politics in Industrializing Cincinnati, 1788–1890* (1985).

George B. Tindall, Kenan Professor of History at the University of North Carolina at Chapel Hill, is the author of *The Disruption of the Solid South* (1972), *The Emergence of the New South, 1913–1945* (1967), and *The Ethnic Southerners* (1976).

CONTENTS

FOREWORD

ONE of the continuing treasures of my life has been a deepening friendship with Arthur and Margaret Link and their family that began forty years ago. Following service as a bomber pilot in World War II, I enrolled at Northwestern University as a graduate student in American history. It was in those postwar years that I came under the influence of three great professors of American history—the late Ray Allen Billington, Richard W. Leopold, and Arthur Link. These men opened my mind and stirred my heart with the drama of the American story.

Arthur Link suggested the dissertation topic that I was to research and write and later publish as a book—the bitter and bloody Colorado coal strike of 1913–1914 culminating in the Ludlow Massacre. It was my good fortune to be Professor Link's first full-scale dissertation student, and I owe to him not only an excellent topic, but the careful and firm direction that enabled me to complete the dissertation and the doctoral degree while rearing a family and teaching full-time.

The ancient Roman, Quintilian, once defined an orator as "a good man speaking well." If I may paraphrase Quintilian, I would describe Arthur Link, the historian, as "a good man teaching and writing history well." He has always given his students the best of which he was capable, and his students have reciprocated by quality learning and enriching his life.

The first volume of his epic biography of Woodrow Wilson carries these words in the preface: "To my wife, Margaret Douglas Link, I owe the greatest debt of all. She has been my own best critic in all matters relating to this book. . . ." Those words were written at Princeton on October 21, 1946.

A decade later, writing the preface to his second Wilson volume, on

March 25, 1956, at Northwestern University, Professor Link referred to his "colleague and collaborator, Professor Richard W. Leopold," to whom he dedicated the book.

It is one important measure of Arthur Link's creativity that he has keenly understood and fully utilized the stimulus and enrichment of his family, his colleagues, and his students. I'm highly gratified to count myself among those who have benefited from his teaching, his writing, and his friendship. What follows are the more carefully distilled findings and thoughts of those who have similarly benefited from the inspiration, scholarship, and friendship of Arthur Link.

GEORGE MCGOVERN

INTRODUCTION

WHEREVER he has gone in his life and career, Arthur S. Link has left in his wake tales that seem legendary. Some years ago, Dewey W. Grantham recalled that when he entered graduate school at the University of North Carolina in 1946, fellow students remembered Arthur "with considerable awe and a little envy as an intellectual phenomenon. They spoke of his incredible drive and prodigious memory, while recalling his feat of assimilating the twenty-seven volumes in the American Nation Series in the space of a few weeks." More recently, Robert R. Palmer, who was Arthur's faculty colleague at Princeton, commented on his phenomenal output of books and articles, especially in the 1950s. "It wasn't human," Palmer said. "He must have had God on his side." Such tales could be multiplied with observations from his tenure at Northwestern, his service as Harmsworth Professor at Oxford, and his editorship of *The Papers of Woodrow Wilson.*

What all these tales have in common is that they are not legends. They are true. Arthur Link has wrought all the feats recounted in these tales and more. His career stands as a unique achievement among American historians in the twentieth century. He has combined conviction, industry, concentration, perseverance, breadth, and brilliance to create an extraordinary body of work and to exert a powerful influence in his discipline and in the entire world of scholarship. He is an original in whom the reality exceeds all efforts at embellishment.

Most of the tales about Arthur Link dwell on his awe-inspiring industry. That is probably because this is the quality in him that his professional associates can most readily understand, even as we fall so short of matching it. Yet few among us appreciate the source from which this industry springs. If in his awesome, sustained productivity Arthur appears to hark back to such predecessors as Samuel Eliot Morison and Allan Nevins, it is because in critical respects he does resemble them more than he does his own contemporaries or later generations of historians. Both his convictions, which stem from his religious faith, and his concentration, which is unforced and unshakable, set him apart in 1950, much less in 1990. In a century when educated Americans have either abandoned or cloaked their religious beliefs in embarrassed silence, consider how this most distinguished professor at a leading university closes his entry in *Who's Who in America:* "I have no thoughts on life that do not stem from my Christian faith. I believe that God created me to be a loving, caring person to do His work in the world. I also believe that He called me to my vocation of teacher and scholar." In other words, Robert Palmer was right: he has had God on his side.

Arthur's sense of being a humble instrument of divine will underlies not only his industry but also, in two senses, his concentration. His faith supplies the serenity to surmount momentary discouragements and even physical and emotional pain to get on with the job. It also furnishes an unshakable belief in the importance of what he has chosen to do. In an age when many historians have rejected "mere biography," political history, and narrative history itself, Arthur has ignored these trends within the profession and has remained true to his original vision. He has spent nearly half a century studying the life and times of Woodrow Wilson and creating an authentic, comprehensive record of Wilson's writings. He has focused his attentions largely on a single half century in a single nation, all the while brushing aside the usual topical identifications of diplomatic, political, or social history as sterile pigeonholes. We do not know whether Arthur shares Wilson's admiration for Rudyard Kipling's poem "If," but he has certainly pursued his life's work with a single-minded intensity, and with an unfeigned unconcern for intellectual fashion.

The results of this life's work encompass more than tremendous output and elegant exposition—either of which would suffice to make a great reputation. Impressive breadth and deep insight also characterize his published work. In American history, he has made major contributions to political, diplomatic, educational, Southern, and African-American history. Abroad, his work has illuminated the histories of France, Germany, Great Britain, and Russia, as well as the whole continent of Europe and the international system. His interpretations of American politics and foreign policy have influenced two generations of students and historians, while his monumental labors as editor of *The Papers of Woodrow Wilson* have stimulated and recast the study of an entire epoch of American and world history.

In addition to his writings, Arthur's personal influence has extended around the world and across the decades among both historians and their subjects. For nearly forty years, at Northwestern and Princeton, he has inspired undergraduates and trained a distinguished line of doctoral students, who have worked in a variety of fields. In those years he has likewise unfailingly aided and guided scholars of all nationalities and persuasions and at every stage in their careers. Few historians in this century have exerted so much influence in so many ways. As one of Arthur's students, Stephan A. Oxman, remarked, "We are all the beneficiaries of these gifts, working their way over many lives during many years in many different ways. We have all come together to honor our benefactor . . . and to rejoice that in our lives we have had such a friend and teacher as this."

This volume of essays is meant to honor Arthur Link's great and multifaceted work and influence and to suggest something of his qualities as a teacher and scholar. The idea for this volume first glimmered in the spring of 1986. After consulting a few people, we invited the scholars who are represented in this volume to contribute papers. We adopted only two principles of selection. First and foremost was quality. We sought contributions that would honor Arthur by approaching the standards of research, analysis, and writing that he has set in his own work. Second was breadth. We solicited essays that would illuminate the breadth of Arthur's work, interests, and influence. The contributors include, therefore, historians who have and have not been his students and faculty colleagues, whose interests range far and wide, and whose birthdates span almost half a century. It is our hope that in both quality and variety these contributions come close to emulating the example of the man who has inspired us all.

On May 11–12, 1989, we held a conference at Princeton in Arthur's honor. At that conference commentators examined and criticized these papers, the authors responded, and they and other participants in the conference engaged in discussion. All the papers have been revised in light of those comments and discussions. May we thank all those who participated in the conference and particularly those who served as commentators: O. Vernon Burton, Kendrick A. Clements, Justus D. Doenecke, Gerald N. Grob, Robert C. Hilderbrand, Walter Licht, Daniel T. Rodgers, Klaus Schwabe, Betty Miller Unterberger, and Kurt Wimer. The conference also featured two dinners at which friends and students of Arthur's spoke. At the first dinner, William T. McCleery recalled the wit and wisdom of Woodrow Wilson, and Andrew J. Davidson recalled Arthur's long, close association and friendship with his late father, the publisher Harlan Davidson. At the second dinner, two of his former students recounted their early and lasting associations with Arthur. One was Stephen A. Oxman, who studied with Arthur as an undergraduate at Princeton and who is now an investment banker. The other was George McGovern, who wrote his dissertation at Northwestern under Arthur's direction, and who has contributed a foreword to this volume. May we thank them for adding such fine notes of personal and intellectual appreciation.

As with any such project, especially one involving a conference and a book, the contributors behind the scenes have made the production possible. For financial and institutional contributions, may we thank Harlan Davidson, Inc., Princeton University, Princeton University Press, the University of North Carolina Press, and the Papers of Woodrow Wilson. For conference arrangements and other assistance may we thank Margaret Douglas Link, Manfred F. Boemeke, David W. Hirst, and Cynthia S. Horr. For prolonged and cheerful clerical assistance, may we thank the staffs of the Department of History, Brown University, and the Department of History, University of Wisconsin–Madison, particularly Karla Cinquanta, Cherrie Guerzon, Karen Delwiche, and Anita Olson. For unfailing encouragement and editorial skill, may we thank Andrew J. Davidson, Angela Davidson and Maureen Gilgore Hewitt. Every one of you should feel a deep, generous pride for his or her hand in a labor of love.

JOHN MILTON COOPER, JR.
Madison, Wisconsin

CHARLES E. NEU
Providence, Rhode Island
February 1, 1990

PART I
THE MAKING OF A HISTORIAN

George B. Tindall

THE FORMATIVE YEARS

"By something like an historical accident, Thomas Woodrow Wilson was born a Virginian," Arthur Stanley Link wrote at the start of his first book, *Wilson: The Road to the White House*. When Link wrote that, the parallel in his own life must have crossed his mind.

Born August 8, 1920, in New Market, Virginia, no more than forty miles from Wilson's native Staunton, Link was the child of parents who had come from the tip of West Virginia's eastern panhandle, from around Shepherdstown—to which they often returned during Link's youth to visit his grandparents and where he remembers spending long summer days devouring books from the little public library: "every Tom Swift book, *The Three Musketeers*, Jules Verne, the sort of thing boys would read."

Arthur's father was pastor of a Lutheran church in New Market, where a younger sister, Elinor, would be born, and had served earlier in Strasburg, where two older siblings were born, John William, Jr., and Elizabeth. Link's first childhood memory, however, is of moving, sometime in 1923, from New Market to Danville, where he remembers the home address, 55 Holbrook Avenue, which his mother drummed into the children, the bridge across the Dan River, going to kindergarten. He remembers, too, the move in early 1927 from there to Mount Pleasant in Cabarrus County, North Carolina, where he would grow up. A man named Luther Lipe came up and drove the family down in a touring car—about two weeks later there was a "huge snow."

Looking back, he found Mount Pleasant "about as idyllic a place to grow up as it's possible to conceive." A village of about a thousand in his youth, much of it unchanged since the nineteenth century, the place regarded itself as something of a cultural center with a small

7

private academy for boys and another for girls, whose faculties leavened the area with college graduates, some with an M.A. The town had two small cotton mills at either end, the Tuscarora and James mills.

People commonly knew each other. Crime was so rare that the town never had a policeman and the Links habitually left the door unlocked. Arthur does remember one crime of passion when a man found another man in bed with his wife, and just cut the other man's throat. There was never an indictment. "But that was high crime," Arthur says, "and very respectable crime, but otherwise there was no crime."

Everybody was poor, the richest being the owners of the mills, whose family income probably did not exceed $10,000 a year. The average family income in Mount Pleasant was probably $800, but there was enough to eat. The Links, like many others, kept a cow— which Arthur milked on occasion—and chickens and pigs. Arthur worked the family garden and mowed the lawns at the church and parsonage plus about an acre in between and above—all because his older brother had had a rheumatic heart attack at age ten. The same brother, ironically, later joined the 82nd Airborne in World War II.

Behind the house, Arthur remembers nothing but fields and forest, meadows dappled with Indian paintbrush, where he used to run free with friends from school. "I didn't realize it, but in many ways it was like the garden of Eden, I suppose." The town had at its center a couple of stores, but for "serious shopping" or for movies, an optional sport, and the courthouse and the oratory on court days, one had to go nine miles west to Concord, the county seat.

Link remembers relatively little sense of social stratification in the town, and little sense of anonymity. Everybody knew everybody else. The sharpest lines were between the mill and town children, and between blacks and whites. In keeping with small-town Southern custom, Arthur knew many blacks, including three or four playmates who were often in the Link home up until about age twelve to fourteen. But aside from separate schools and churches, there was little Arthur remembers in the simple society of Mount Pleasant which served as a reminder of racial segregation.

The few blacks in town worked largely as artisans; few were servants because few whites had the means to hire them. Arthur remembers fondly one black friend who was always called Mr. Shankle; because he had a car, he would drive the kids in town to band concerts in Concord or Albemarle. An old black man born a slave and known as Uncle Sandy survived in Arthur's youth. On his birthday the school children would take him presents and Uncle Sandy would come out

and sing them a song: "Run, nigger, run, or the patterol'll get you"—
a reference to militia slave patrols lost on the schoolchildren of a
later day.

Arthur's father, he recalls, was friendly with a couple of local black
ministers, had them over to the house and brought them in the front
door to the living room or to his study to study and discuss theology.
He was close also to the minister of a black mission just down the road,
supported by the theologically conservative Missouri Synod of Lu-
therans. The Links themselves adhered to the Eastern or Old Lutheran persuasion. The Reverend Link was also a kind of social
worker among blacks and, when they were sick, took them off to Duke
Hospital on occasion or to Barber-Scotia, a junior college for black
women in Concord.

When the family moved to Mount Pleasant, Arthur went directly
from the Danville kindergarten to the first grade of a small elementary school that met, at first, in an old frame building in the northern
part of town—with a potbellied stove for heat, a well with a bucket
and dipper, and outdoor facilities. After two or three years, however,
the school moved into quarters abandoned by the girls' academy when
it closed. Seventh grade brought a transfer to a consolidated school,
which housed both elementary and secondary grades, eleven in all.
School terms geared to the cotton culture ran in the summer from
about mid-July to the end of September, the "lay-by term" (when cotton was left to ripen in the hot weather), then let out six weeks for
cotton-picking.

The secondary curriculum consisted chiefly of old-fashioned basics,
including mathematics, English, French, and history—four years
starting with the ancient world, on through medieval and modern European, English and American, taught by Miss Ruth James who had
attended the woman's college in Greensboro and whose family owned
one of the Mount Pleasant mills. The English teacher was a man with
an M.A. from Columbia and work toward a Ph.D. at the University of
North Carolina in Chapel Hill; the French teacher, just out of Chapel
Hill, was "fresh and vigorous and young." The English teacher was
known as Major Webster (although he had been a sergeant in World
War I) and apparently was the teacher who most excited young Link's
interest in books—books of history as well as literature. And the Link
family took three newspapers which the young man devoured: the
Charlotte Observer, the *Charlotte News*, and the *Concord Tribune*.

Somewhere along the way, the young man from the country town
had conceived an ambition to get a Ph.D. in history and become a
college professor. Exactly how remains as much a mystery to him as to
anybody else. The nearest thing to a role model apparently was Major

Webster. "I don't know how I got that in my head," Link said in response to a direct question. "I knew there were such, and I knew all
they did was study history and that's what I wanted to do, so that's why
I wanted to be a college professor." Some college professors, as well as
ministers, had passed through the parsonage, probably people interested in Lutheran youth groups. Arthur had visited two campuses:
Wittenberg College, he remembered, to see his brother graduated in
1934, and the Woman's College of the University of North Carolina in
Greensboro, where he and his father had taken sister Elizabeth. He
had never visited Davidson, which was located only a few miles beyond Concord.

Until his final year in high school, there remained an unspoken assumption that he would attend Lenoir-Rhyne, a Lutheran college at
Hickory. "I knew as much about Chapel Hill as I knew about Berkeley
and Santa Barbara in those days." There was no thought of Chapel
Hill until the spring of 1937, when his father offered to drive him over
for a look at the University of North Carolina and encouraged him to
consider it as the best place he could afford to go. It was the first time
young Arthur had ever been east of Greensboro, and Chapel Hill impressed him from the start: "Big buildings and huge campus and I
said, 'Now this is where I want to go.'" Little thought was given to
nearby Davidson: "Fine reputation. Couldn't afford. . . . Never occurred to me I could get a scholarship. Never heard of them. And
Daddy wasn't all that worldly wise either."

But money was running low. Two of the Link children had already
gone to college. His father had cashed in his life insurance. Arthur
had to make his own way and could best do that at Chapel Hill. So he
applied and gained admission—and a $75 tuition scholarship, at the
in-state rate. One of the elder Link's friends was a vice-president at
Cannon Mills in nearby Kannapolis, and through him Arthur got a
summer job as a sweeper in a spinning room: eight hours a day at 22.5
cents an hour. Largely from this, Arthur managed to save $100, and
with another $100 from his father, in September he entered the uni-
versity and took up residence in Aycock Dormitory.

He remembers the first sense of what it meant to a "country boy"
going to Chapel Hill in those days: "The grandeur and romance and
glory of it and intellectual excitement of that place. Intellectual freedom. Anything went. I mean it could be anything. Didn't matter.
People were very accepting in their tolerance. . . . I remember the
first two or three days. I'd just roam the campus and look at the buildings and all those books, like a banquet to me in those days, and the
excitement of scholarly minds and bright people and bright undergraduate students." Oral tradition on the campus still preserves a

story of this strange young man standing around and staring at buildings, a story which may date from his senior year when the buildings became the subject of his honors thesis.

The institution which would shape Link's career had itself been shaped into a university for the most part during his lifetime. And, as mentioned, Link himself would chronicle the physical shaping of its campus in his senior honors thesis, "A History of the Buildings at the University of North Carolina." The first state university to open its doors to students, in 1795, UNC had remained for more than a century essentially a small liberal-arts college. It emerged as a genuine university during the years of Link's youth.

President Harry Woodburn Chase (1919–1930), a professor of psychology, had presided over the decade characterized in the title to Part IV of Link's senior thesis, "The State Builds a University, 1921–1929." In his inaugural address, "The State University and the New South," on April 28, 1920, the New England-born Chase had set forth an agenda that foretokened the university's emergence during the interwar years: "To one who looks long at the currents that now flow freely through Southern life, there comes the growing conviction that here there now begins a great new chapter, not only in the history of this section, but in the history of America. For here, as nowhere else, are now at work those great creative impulses that have made America possible."

Certainly in Chapel Hill the creative impulses were loosed during the years of expansion which followed. New construction during the decade of Chase's presidency, mostly to the south and east of the old campus, set off a colonial revival in Chapel Hill architecture several years before the restoration of Williamsburg began to popularize the style more widely. The most important of all the new buildings was in the neoclassical style, however, a new university library dedicated in 1929 with space for about 400,000 volumes and special collections.

A climate of creativity prevailed, especially around the Carolina Playmakers, the university press, and the new sociological empire of Howard Odum—all focused on Southern themes. These and other stirrings in the village amounted to a minor renaissance. The aspect of this renaissance that touched the young Arthur Link most directly was the school of Regionalism that Odum had developed. The Regionalists produced no single manifesto to compare with the Nashville Agrarians' *I'll Take My Stand*, but their chief works were Rupert B. Vance's *Human Geography of the South* (1932) and Odum's *Southern Regions of the United States* (1936). Both were comprehensive surveys of the South: inventories of human and physical resources, agriculture and industry, institutions and folkways. Fundamentally, Southern Regionalism was a concept of the "Problem South," a region with short-comings but potentialities that called for rational planning. It was also a more manageable frame of reference than the whole country for study, uniting the physical and social sciences with the humanities. For a season Regionalism was all the rage, the subject of undergraduate courses across the country, one of which Arthur Link had with the guru himself.

In the Department of History, to which Arthur was drawn from the first, there was in 1937 no "public intellectual" like Odum, but several historians of stature among their professional colleagues. J. G. de Roulhac Hamilton, at the University since 1907, had recently left the classroom to give full time to the Southern Historical Collection, which he founded in 1930, but his presence was still felt around the department in Saunders Hall, as was the presence of R. D. W. Connor, who had left in 1936 to become the first archivist of the United States.

Chairman in 1937 was Albert Ray Newsome, recognized especially for his work at the state historical commission and for three consecutive terms, 1936–1939, the first president of the Society of American Archivists. The most popular lecturer probably was Hugh T. Lefler, colonialist and professor of state history, who enlivened classes with his store of anecdotes and his biting wit. In 1935 the department brought in from New York University Howard K. Beale, known then chiefly for *The Critical Year* (1930), an economic interpretation of Reconstruction which reflected the pervasive influence of Charles A. Beard in those days. Fletcher M. Green, who would become Link's mentor, had just returned the previous year from an appointment at Emory to cover the courses on the South previously taught by Hamilton.

Frank P. Graham, former professor of history, had succeeded Chase as president of the university in 1930. Long active in public causes of uplift and human rights, Graham (according to historian Francis B. Simkins) "signed enough liberal manifestoes to put the South in the reformer's paradise." But his liberalism, Jonathan Daniels noted, was "rooted deep in his Presbyterian soul in a Calvinistic righteousness and right doing." What was important for North Carolina, however, was that the sense of moral mission was "devoted to the cause of the free mind and the free school." Graham also had a phenomenal memory for faces and names, and an outgoing personality which brought to his support many conservatives.

At the outset Graham faced the enormous tasks of keeping the university afloat through the lean years of depression and guiding it through consolidation with its sister schools, North Carolina State in Raleigh and the Woman's College in Greensboro. The onset of the

Great Depression brought a lull in new building in the early 1930s, but New Deal projects, especially Public Works Administration (PWA) projects set off a new wave of expansion in the late 1930s that by the end of Arthur Link's undergraduate career had added thirteen more buildings and remodeled others at relatively little cost to the state. The projects just about completed the plan laid out twenty years before, designed to stabilize the university at a level of about 4,000 students—although another war and postwar expansion would in turn render that figure out of date.

Throughout all this the creative spirit remained alive in the faculty, and the expansion begun under Chase was revived with the help of New Deal programs. Graham, who had close relations with Franklin and especially Eleanor Roosevelt, was increasingly called away for advice and tasks in the New Deal and defense efforts. When in residence, however, he observed open house for students on Sunday evenings. As an undergraduate Link went to the sessions, which he found lively and interesting. Graham was a national figure and the conversations were animated. Arthur's student friend Lewis Williams recalls Graham greeting guests and, with his phenomenal memory for names, introducing each to everyone else in the reception hall. He recalls also that he and Arthur gloried in Graham's persistent defense of academic freedom and freedom of speech.

The feelings of awe and wonder with which Link first greeted the place in 1937 had to yield to the need to make his own way. It was not something new to him since he never had an allowance but had raised money from the garden, held rummage sales, and managed to have a dollar or so a week. An expert typist (he had learned in a high-school class), he got a job working in the campus YMCA, making about $18.50 a month. Somehow a job turned up tutoring football players, not in history but in psychology, at 50 cents an hour. He was able to supplement that by typing dissertations and student papers. The activities in Aycock dorm proved as habitually nocturnal and noisy then as now, and he would flee to the library for the quiet in which to study. Link was finding his way, getting organized, learning how to do things, when a severe setback struck in the first, or Fall Quarter: pain in the side, an appendectomy at Watts Hospital in Durham. A week there and then a week at home. Because of the setback, the next quarter proved to be his worst, with a D in algebra, and C's in freshman French and physical education.

After the freshman year, however, the undergraduate record was all A's, except for a B in the required hygiene course. Link settled into a busy schedule that left little spare time between studies and earning his keep. Classes usually filled three or four hours a day, reading and studies six to eight—a long day aside from the odd jobs. Yet, as he recalled later, a dollar went further in those years. His room cost about $60 a year, and meals at the student cafeteria in Swain Hall (affectionately called "Swine Hole" by generations of students, until a new dining hall opened in 1940), came to about 15 cents for breakfast, lunch maybe 18-20 cents, and dinners always 25 cents, the "student special": entree, two vegetables, bread, dessert, drink. One could go through, Link estimated—room, board, everything—for $300, and he always made it, with a little spending money left over.

Link's horizons were broadening in spite of the grind. In the spring of 1939 he followed up an advertisement posted outside the student aid office and found congenial employment for the summer as a guide at the New York World's Fair. It was his first trip to the city, although five years earlier, at the age of fourteen, he had persuaded his mother to let him go to the Chicago World's Fair. He signed on as a baggage boy with a bus tour leaving from Hickory and went off with $10. At the New York fair he pushed wheeled vehicles around the fairgrounds, two visitors at a time, for about $25 a week. He "felt like Tom Wolfe in New York," he testified later, with something of the same sense of the "billion-footed city" that Wolfe had had. Working five days a week left him two days in which to get acquainted with the city. He visited museums and theaters, haunted the docks where he went through the *Ile de France* and saw the *Carinthia* arriving on her maiden voyage. "We didn't make much money," he wrote Fletcher Green, "just a lot of good experience."

There was little time for frivolity or for becoming a "big man on campus," but Arthur found or made time for a few activities, principally the Glee Club and the Dialectic Society, one of two student debating societies almost as old as the university. On behalf of the Di he led an unsuccessful effort to raise $5000 to buy Thomas Wolfe's papers (but nonetheless read every word that Wolfe published). He was also active in the YMCA, and briefly on the staff of *The Daily Tar Heel*. The Link family was somewhat musical (the older brother and younger sister majored in music) and beginning as a sophomore Arthur sang baritone with the Glee Club for three years. The group practiced weekly and undertook some "tough things": a lot of Bach, including the *St. Matthew Passion* and *Christmas Oratorio*. They also sang with the North Carolina Symphony and made spring trips across the state and into Tennessee, Georgia, Alabama, Virginia, and Washington, DC, one year, singing to alumni groups, church groups, and at other colleges.

The Dialectic Society, however, became the most absorbing extracurricular activity. It was a congenial group of about forty or fifty people, including a young woman, Jenny Wells Newsome, daughter of the head of the history department, so "super intellectual" that she frightened Arthur (surely a rare achievement among his contemporaries) but also gifted with "a lot of Southern charm." The Di and its sister group, the Philanthropic Society, both founded in 1795, the year the university opened, preserved the formal traditions of nineteenth-century debating societies. Members of the Di addressed each other as Senator, of the Phi as Representative.

Arthur, an active high-school debater, joined the Di as a freshman and stayed with it throughout his undergraduate career, much of the time as either clerk or parliamentarian and in the Spring Quarter of his senior year as president. In his junior year he served as chairman for a debate with the Phi on a possible third term for Franklin D. Roosevelt. The Di, supporters of the third term, won. Under Link's presidency some damaged portraits in the Di hall were restored, including one of former member James K. Polk by Thomas Sully. Link also found the society's old diploma plate and had special diplomas printed for the members. He also had special keys designed for the Di and the debate team.

The team's chief activity was debating current issues, which more and more focused on issues of war and foreign policy. War had erupted in Asia the summer before Link entered UNC and in Europe at the beginning of his junior year. At the time, Link's instincts were anti-war, perhaps the more so because of his exposure to revisionist views on World War I. Actually his concern went back to little Mount Pleasant, where the Nye Committee's inquiry into the wartime profits of bankers and munitions makers, the "merchants of death," had been a chief topic of conversation for several years. Still, Link harbored the belief then common, at least in his part of the world, that if the United States had only joined the League of Nations, World War II might never have happened. Link recalls that he read Walter Millis's *The Road to War* (1937) as a sophomore or junior, and Charles C. Tansill's *America Goes to War* (1938) as a junior or senior, both revisionist books on World War I.

Albert Ray Newsome, chairman of the history department, the faculty member with whom Link became personally closest, he described as "kind of obsessed" with staying out of war. Early in his sophomore year, shortly after the Munich Agreement, Senator Link spoke in favor of a resolution approving the policy of the Chamberlain government in Britain. The resolution was approved on the principle that the policy kept the peace. In the spring of 1939 he spoke in favor of a resolution, which the Di adopted, to support a campus peace movement. In 1940 he opposed a third term for President Roosevelt on the basis of constitutional tradition and fear that Roosevelt would lead the country into war. Later he consistently opposed Roosevelt's foreign policies which led the country closer to war, although by his last quarter in the spring of 1941 he had begun to see the real prospect of a war with Japan. In continuing to supply "the fighting forces of the Mikado," he said, "We seem to be feeding the dog that is most likely to turn and bite us in the back." If a Japanese move into the Dutch East Indies and the Philippines threatened American vital interests, then the United States would have to fight.

Link had joined the Di in part because it seemed a good place to meet people. During his freshman year, he became a close friend of two fellow Senators. In Lewis J. Williams of Lewisville, North Carolina (near Winston-Salem), he found a kindred spirit with whom he shared "a bond of poverty." Both were working their way through and in their senior year shared a basement room on Gimghoul Road, across from the Newsomes, in the home of William F. Thrall, an English professor with whom Arthur had a course in Elizabethan literature. Lew and Arthur paid for their keep by chauffeuring Mrs. Thrall, tending the furnace, and mowing the grass. One summer they paid for their keep in Swain Hall by securing the building at night.

The third member of what they took to calling "the Triumvirate" was Carrington Gretter, a physically handicapped student from Connecticut who got about with two canes. Link was often the volunteer when Gretter needed help carrying his books and with other chores around the campus. The bond among the three, aside from their compatibility, was a shared interest in current events and history. Link and Gretter majored in history, Williams in political science.

The academic program, of course, remained central in Link's interests. Science courses interested him at first—he flirted with the idea of taking up medicine—and he remembers fondly having psychology his first semester with English Bagby, which led to his tutoring football players in the subject, botany under John Couch, a specialist in mushrooms, and zoology under "a great old man," Henry Van Peters Wilson. He continued his high-school French for two years, topped off with an informal, noncredit course in conversational French. In his sophomore year Link first encountered Fletcher Green, who would become his mentor, in a year-long survey of American history, using the John D. Hicks survey text, at that time new. At this point he formed a great respect for Green, although he found him a somewhat forbidding figure. A course in historical geography and one in economic theory provided brief encounters with those fields.

By the junior-senior years his program focused almost completely on history, political science, and English. The history, moreover, was altogether American, except for a course in modern Europe taught by Mitchell B. Garrett and one in the social history of the Roman Empire. For colonial history, with Hugh Lefler, he read the classic works by Andrews and Osgood. He had American diplomatic history with Cecil Johnson, his instructor in freshman social science. For diplomatic history Johnson used a new textbook by Thomas A. Bailey. Link had courses in the Federal and Middle Periods with Albert Ray Newsome, whom he found "probably the best lecturer I ever knew. Perfectly organized. Perfectly."

Reading for honors with Fletcher Green, he went through all the original American Nation Series and a large quantity of sources on the South. Then he wrote his huge honors thesis on the buildings of the campus, the idea for which originated with the superintendent of buildings and grounds, P. L. Burch. Fletcher Green proposed Link for the project, which served a double purpose of permitting him to finish his undergraduate program with highest honors while being paid for the project by the National Youth Administration.

"A History of the Buildings at the University of North Carolina" traced the growth of the campus from 1793 to 1941 and, including the bibliography, ran 292 pages in length. For an undergraduate thesis it was monumental (actually longer than Link's M.A. thesis would be), and although unrelated to Link's later work it provided a challenging apprenticeship in research. There is still a steady demand for the paper in the North Carolina Collection at the university.

During his senior year Link had the Civil War–Reconstruction course with Howard K. Beale, a curious bundle of contradictions, lavish prodigality and narrow scrimping, liberal impulses and ingrained snobbery, a man with a gift for putting noses out of joint, a running adventure in culture shock for countless Southerners and not a few fellow Yankees. One theory among history students at the time had it that Beale's mother had been frightened by Henry Adams during her pregnancy. It was at Beale's home that young Link first learned how to eat an artichoke. Erudite but disorganized, Beale was at his best in a seminar or as editor of a student manuscript. Generous to students he befriended, he took Arthur and a couple of others along to the 1940 meeting of the Southern Historical Association in Charleston, and upon arrival sent Arthur in to inquire about prices in bed and breakfast places—on the theory that somebody with a Southern accent could get a better rate than he.

The next spring Beale decided that Arthur just had to go to Harvard for his graduate work and persuaded him to make application. In the spring, however, another opportunity presented itself in the form of a fellowship in Chapel Hill and Link decided to accept it—

partly because by the spring of 1941 the new draft law had created a new expectation. Better to stay put than relocate for just a few months. Beale insisted that by withdrawing his Harvard application Link had blown a chance at a fellowship there. Having invited Link up to visit his summer home in Thetford, Vermont, that summer, Beale withdrew the offer on the grounds that after Link declined Harvard there was doubt that he would be socially acceptable. Relations were not patched up until about the time Arthur went to Princeton on his first appointment a few years later, which presumably rendered him socially acceptable.

The opportunity that held Link in Chapel Hill came in a research assistantship offered by sociologist Rupert Vance, who had recently agreed to write the tenth and final volume of the LSU History of the South series. Presumably Vance had asked Fletcher Green for a recommendation.

And so Link was launched on what he would later call "the craziest graduate career of anyone who'd ever gone through graduate school," a career during which he was away from Chapel Hill most of the time after his first year. His early start in the 1941 summer school proved serendipitous—good Presbyterians might say providential—for in a class with a visiting professor Link found his calling. Chester Macarthur Destler, then between jobs at Georgia Southern and Connecticut Colleges, taught a course in recent American history. Destler is best remembered for his work on Henry Demarest Lloyd and American radicalism, but he piqued Link's interest that summer with his admiration for Woodrow Wilson and the Wilson policies. Link, his curiosity aroused, began to read Ray Stannard Baker's biography, completed only a few years earlier, and then the rest of the existing Wilson literature.

Thus fortified, he plunged into a master's thesis, which he completed that academic year as "The Wilson Movement in the South: A Study in Political Liberalism," 218 pages, bibliography and all. The thesis, like the dissertation that would grow from it, was focused more on Southern history than on Wilson the man. At the time, Link testifies, he was "much more interested in Southern political history than . . . I was in Wilson," interested mainly in the onset of progressivism.

Link was, after all, living and working on the campus where the Southern Regionalist movement flourished. He knew Koch, Paul Green, and Couch well. During his senior year, hoping to add a new dimension to his historical knowledge, he began to take courses in sociology. With Howard Odum he had a course on regional problems and planning and with Guy B. Johnson one on social anthropology. In the summer of 1941 he took Rupert Vance's course in population and that fall had Vance for social theory and Johnson for race relations. During the first two quarters of that year he finally picked up Fletcher Green's courses on the Old South and the New, plus his seminar in Southern history and "Studies in the South," a course built around primary sources.

In this year of immersion in Southern studies, Link increased his already enormous respect for Fletcher Green. The real impact, he recalled nearly five decades later, came in the seminar, in Green's "emphasis on sources and his refusal to generalize, saying, 'What's your evidence for that?'" Also, he testified, Green's respect for historical truth. "There was a certain integrity about this fellow. Drummed into me was this emphasis on the use of sources and meticulous care in writing history, which always made me nervous about writing history." Ever since, he has said, "I never write anything or do any historical work without thinking of Fletcher looking over my shoulder and thinking: This was right; this was wrong. I never had that feeling about my other teachers."

What is more, Arthur had a desk on the fourth floor of Alumni Hall, in which the Regionalists and the Institute for Research in Social Science had their quarters. And he was immersed in gathering materials for Vance on the recent South. He did papers for Vance on Senator George W. Norris, Southern congressmen, the Muscle Shoals controversy, the antievolution controversy, the Federal Reserve Board, and the agricultural depression of 1920–1921. He put together a bibliography on the recent South and clipped newspapers and magazines. He also became deeply attached to the Vances and played bridge with them every week.

Arthur's first year as a graduate student was fortuitous in another sense. On the fourth floor of Alumni Hall there were four desks, Arthur, of course, at one and three women at the others. One of them was Margaret McDowell Douglas, an Agnes Scott graduate, an M.A. candidate in sociology, and a graduate assistant to Guy B. Johnson—a "gofer" as she recalls it. Link remembers that they first met on the steps of Alumni at the end toward Old East on October 12, 1941— Columbus Day elsewhere but University Day in Chapel Hill, the anniversary of the date on which the cornerstone for Old East was laid in 1793. That Arthur remembers the date they met suggests that something implanted it in his memory right away, but Margaret was then "going heavily" with another young man. They nevertheless became, as Arthur put it, "very good friends."

Before the academic year was out, sometime early in 1942, Howard Odum was playing the role of Cupid. He urged Arthur to look again at Margaret Douglas, this marvelous woman. He did, and when she broke up with her boyfriend, Arthur took the romantic offensive. All the while, Odum was working on Margaret to take more notice of Arthur.

But circumstances were to separate them for yet a while, circumstances in which Odum once more had a hand. Odum had suggested to Arthur that he apply for a Rosenwald Fellowship for the following year, 1942–1943. Link got it. His application strikingly reveals the influence of the Regionalism which surrounded him. The project was "An evaluation of the South's place in the New Freedom: the contribution of Southern leaders to the New Freedom, its Southern roots; and the effect of the New Freedom upon the development of the South." Recent studies of regionalism at Chapel Hill, Vanderbilt, and elsewhere, he argued, had given "too little attention to the political aspect of history and the problem of leadership in cultural and regional development. My purpose is to fuse the historical approach with the regional approach in an analysis of the South's contribution to the New Freedom, utilizing the various regional studies as a background to a political interpretation of the period."

He began by relating his subject to a political current then running strong—the conservative rebellion against the New Deal, which, he said, "prompts a comparison with the Wilson period during which the nation carried out . . . an extensive program of reform." "It seems," he complained, "that the conventional idea is that the South has since the early days of Calhoun been conservative and reactionary." The literature of the Wilson period neglected the regional connection because it neglected the domestic program in favor of the war policies. "For instance, Colonel House, the reformer, has been obscured by House the diplomat. Yet, House did some of his greatest work in a distinctly Southern reform experiment in Texas."

These premises in turn generated a torrent of questions. If Southern political leaders were so conservative, why were they in the vanguard of reform? Out of sheer party loyalty or awareness they were taking part in a liberal movement? To what degree did the war wreck the New Freedom and prevent its development in the South? How did the New Freedom affect Southern attitudes toward prohibition and women's suffrage? He appended an outline of chapters, the first three of which would incorporate the M.A. thesis, down through the election of 1912, the remainder of which would cover the New Freedom and the South. "I shall be preparing myself as well as possible," he concluded, "for future work in the South." He seems to have been up to what a number of his contemporaries were up to: the effort to find a usable liberal past in Southern history.

Letters of reference from sociologists and historians were unanimously enthusiastic. Howard Odum pronounced Link's work "first-class," the candidate "persistent" and gifted with a "fine capacity to turn out a large amount of work." Rupert Vance dubbed him "the most promising young historian to become interested, of his own initiative, in the regional approach developed at North Carolina." His proposal showed "the insight and historical imagination we expect of a mature scholar." Guy B. Johnson foresaw "a real contribution to the field of social history."

Fletcher Green had "observed him closely since he first attracted my attention in his Sophomore year by his almost photographic memory, his wide reading and general knowledge, his clear cut and incisive questions and analyses, his ability to select the salient and significant facts, and by his intellectual curiosity." The favorable impressions had been strengthened by continuing contacts and by his honors paper, which demonstrated abilities to dig up data, synthesize, and interpret them "in a way that few undergraduate students I have taught could do." Albert Ray Newsome, who had gotten to know Link "as thoroughly as I ever knew any student," wrote that as an undergraduate "he had, and achieved graduate standards of work." From the time he entered college he had headed directly and seriously for the Ph.D.

One jarring note, however, appeared in the letters of the two historians, who seemed to be taking care to cover their flanks. "His youth, brilliance, enthusiasm, and achievement do not make for popularity with his fellow graduate students," Newsome wrote, "but I do not think that he has any serious personality defect or social ineptitude which more experience will not take care of." Green testified that "he does seem to rub other students the wrong way by 'parading' his superior knowledge; but this is a mark of youth, and will, I am confident, give way before age and experience." Fellow students have testified to this quality as well. Bennett Wall remembers: "Every new day in the library was a revelation to Arthur who became somewhat insistent on sharing his discoveries with us." But "he was tracked to do Wilson and all hell could not stop him." Echoes of such reactions lingered to be picked up by graduate students who entered soon after Link left.

Rosenwald fellowship in hand, Arthur left for a summer and fall of research mainly in Washington, where he became once more the roommate of Lew Williams, who took a job with the Library of Congress which Arthur had put him on to. Arthur held to Fletcher Green's injunction "that you are expected to exhaust as nearly as possible all available sources for a doctoral dissertation. In early July he wrote Green that he was consuming wholesale lots of newspapers. By October, he was able to write William Haygood of the Rosenwald Fund from Chapel Hill. He had covered some fifty-one Southern newspapers (in thirteen states) plus the *New York Times*, numerous secondary works, and some manuscript collections. He was frustrated by the discovery that the bulk of the Wilson papers and all the papers of several other worthies had been moved to a more secure locale for the duration of the war.

Meanwhile, he had an interview with old Senator Thomas P. Gore, whom he found to be bitterly anti-Wilson, and dropped in at Richmond and Charlottesville to see various papers. In Charlottesville he met historian Richard Heath Dabney, Wilson's friend at the university, "who had forgotten everything" but was "still a treat," and had a long talk with Oscar W. Underwood, Jr. Later he touched base with Francis B. Simkins in Farmville, Virginia, to discuss "Pitchfork Ben" Tillman, whose biography Simkins was then working on.

When he got back to Chapel Hill in late October, he promised Green, he would be devoting his "entire energies" from then until Christmas to learning German. But in November he was off on another research trip, first to Yale (where he was "entirely overwhelmed by the beauty and grandeur of the new campus") for the E. M. House papers and Harvard for the Walter Hines Page papers, a collection which started after Link's period but which he nonetheless mined for future reference. On the way back he dropped in at the New York Public and Columbia University libraries and visited the Wilson Foundation Library where he found a few pamphlets he had not seen before. By December 1942, he was already at work on a first draft of the dissertation.

Through the year Arthur anxiously awaited a call from the draft board. He had drawn a high number, he informed William Haygood of the Rosenwald Fund in April 1942, and had received no call as yet. Meanwhile, he tried to get into the navy and the air corps, but was turned down because of nearsightedness. On August 11, 1942, he had a preliminary physical, which turned up a very fast pulse, a heart murmur, and a leaking heart. This led to a classification of 1-B. Back in Chapel Hill for the Winter Quarter 1943, he took a course on World War I and its background with Mitchell Garrett, only his third course in any other than American history.

Then, in February, came a call from James W. Patton, history department chairman at North Carolina State College in Raleigh, to go to teach in the Army Student Training Program (ASTP) beginning March 1, 1943. Green and Odum both agreed with Link's feeling that this was a clear opportunity to serve the war effort and at the same time get some needed teaching experience. In Raleigh, he took a room in the home of Lillian Parker Wallace, a nineteenth-century European historian who taught at Meredith College, and began teaching army students "some measure of European history." To Albert Ray Newsome he wrote, "I want to tell you how much I am enjoying my work, I never dreamed before that teaching . . . could give one such stimulation and inspiration. I guess we are extremely fortunate in having as students boys who are unusually intelligent and interested."

Soon after he arrived there, the call finally came in April for induction into the army at Camp Croft, near Spartanburg, South Carolina. "It was quite an experience," he wrote William Haygood shortly afterward, "for the fellows in our group (or a large part of them) were true characters for sociological study." When he got there the army doctors put him in 4-F "finally, as they said." The problem this time was that a mild case of polio when he was eighteen months old had left him with one leg two inches shorter than the other and thus with one shoulder slightly lower than the other.

Arthur has confessed to having had no ambition to join the infantry, but with his older brother in an airborne division that fought through the Italian campaign with heavy casualties, he agonized for the duration over the possibility of taking up some kind of war work. But there was always another step just ahead in his chosen career. He pushed on with the dissertation, and not long after the Camp Croft visit had three copies of a second draft out to friends for criticism.

Soon he was pressing Fletcher Green to schedule the award of his degree for 1944. Green demurred, however, and after talking with Newsome, laid down the law in a letter of May 27, 1943: "I feel that you are too good a man to cut corners in getting the degree, and this full year should be taking courses, and not mere technical registration. If you feel you cannot go to Chicago or Harvard next year, then you should return to the University of North Carolina and take a full course load covering as much of European history as possible." Green rejected also the alternatives of taking courses in Chapel Hill while continuing to teach in Raleigh or taking the degree in 1944 and then attending classes up north, which would put him in an anomalous position with fellow students.

Link, needing the support of a salary, continued to teach at State through the year 1943–1944, an experience he found gratifying, since the students in the ASTP by his testimony were a select group who had a motivation to learn about modern Europe and the background to the war. Link, fortunately, had just taken such a course himself, only his second in modern European history.

The experience cemented friendships with other Chapel Hill doctoral candidates Bennett Wall and Buck Yearns, who were teaching in the program. Wall, however, remembers that he and Arthur sometimes grated on each other and that their arguments often got dogged, determined, and loud, although Patton seemed to enjoy having "the two wild men from Chapel Hill"—up to a point.

During that year, too, Link met another young historian, John Hope Franklin, and his wife Aurelia, and the encounter led to a lifelong friendship. Franklin, two years out from a Harvard Ph.D., was teaching at St. Augustine's College (an Episcopal school for blacks) in Raleigh in the spring of 1943. The University of North Carolina Press had just published his first book, *The Free Negro in North Carolina.* Chairman Patton one day mentioned the presence in town of a bright young scholar at St. Augustine's whom he had met at professional meetings. Link sought him out, and took along a visiting historian, Francis B. Simkins. The Franklins lived in a dormitory, which was the site of both home and office at the time, and Simkins opined to Arthur in his unique plosives: "Patton is too prudent. Patton is too prudent. He won't visit in a Negro's house."

Whatever the truth about that, Link felt awkward that he could not reciprocate for want of a home of his own. He and Franklin visited on each other's campuses, however, but by fall Franklin had moved to North Carolina College (now North Carolina Central University) in Durham. Ben Wall testified that he never saw any hint of racism in Link. Link himself remembered no formal lessons in living Jim Crow when he was growing up. His father would argue with racists, he remembered, but did not buck the system. Active in the campus YMCA, Arthur had attended interracial conferences in Greensboro, at Elon College, and elsewhere, and had gone to a couple of YMCA summer conferences at Blue Ridge, North Carolina, one of the places where the Y's student secretary, Willis D. Weatherford, had pioneered the Southern interracial movement.

Blocked in the effort to complete his doctorate in 1944, Link turned back to the Rosenwald Foundation, which had declined to renew his previous grant. He proposed to do three months of research and writing at the Library of Congress and nine months of course work, writing, and research at Columbia University, taking courses with Allan Nevins and Henry Steele Commager and in European history. During this time he anticipated completing "The South's Place in the Birth of the New Freedom," the working title of the dissertation for which he already had a draft.

Fellowship in hand, before the end of May 1944, Arthur had been to New York to arrange housing for the fall and was in Princeton, where he had worked through the Wilson material, and was commuting to Trenton for New Jersey newspapers and state archives. After his summer in Washington, where he finally had access to the Wilson papers which had returned from hiding, he took a job in Chapel Hill teaching navy V-12 candidates during July and August. From Chapel Hill on August 4, 1944, he wrote Fletcher Green, "I finished my dissertation today." This proved to be, as always in such projects, a preliminary stage of completion. Further revisions would be called for. In September Arthur left for New York via West Virginia and Washington, where he saw the new movie, "Wilson." "Hollywood," he complained, "seems to be congenitally incapable of making a historical movie completely accurate." In New York he took up residence at the International House on Riverside Drive and entered Columbia, where he began a year-long seminar on the recent United States with Commager (Nevins was away on leave), a course on the Soviet Union with George Vernadsky, and another on nineteenth-century British social history with Bart Brebner. But three-fourths of his time, he confessed, he spent in research and writing on "my Wilson study."

His research interest had taken a new turn. He had become fascinated by the rapid rise of Wilson from university president to governor and president, and began to plan a scholarly book à la Kerney—that is, like journalist James K. Kerney's *The Political Education of Woodrow Wilson* (1926), covering the ten years from the start of his Princeton presidency in 1902 to the presidential election of 1912. And through the year of his residency at Columbia he was working on that project in Commager's seminar, all the while polishing up chapters of the dissertation, and sending them up to Fletcher Green at Harvard, where Green was visiting professor for the year.

Commager in those days had a fearsome reputation at Columbia, something like Green's at Chapel Hill. Both were demanding and sometimes regarded as overbearing in their probing demands for verification. Commager had some eight or ten thousand volumes in his office and, as Link has described the procedure, when a student cited a reference, "The book would come down he would—whish!—'I don't see that on this page.' Well, that put the fear of God into them." Link's fellow students he found less stimulating, possibly because their ranks had been depleted by the draft. "I may be wrong," he wrote Fletcher Green soon after classes got under way, "but it seems to me that most of the graduate students here are woefully ignorant of the basic facts of American history." None of the others in the seminar knew who Alton B. Parker was.

Arthur often worked past midnight in Butler Library and walked across a park between Riverside Church and International House to his room, without any concern that he might be in danger of street violence. Living in New York was "a great experience," he wrote to Mrs. William Haygood. "People of all races and nationalities live together amicably and ought to present something of a working example of social democracy." During the war there were shortages, but nothing to cause real hardships. And one could never exhaust the cultural resources of the city, he thought. He visited museums and galleries, sometimes with his younger sister Elinor, who was a voice student in her second postgraduate year at Manhattan School of Music.

That December Arthur had his first encounter with the Metropolitan Opera. His older brother John, home for hospitalization and recuperation after eighteen months in Italy with the airborne regiment (that had taken casualties of 300 percent of its original numbers), got tickets for Arthur and Elinor. He was so late that only the most expensive seats were left, in the middle of the golden horseshoe. "That was quite an experience, wasn't it," he wrote back to Ray Newsome in Chapel Hill, "going to the opera for the first time and sitting in a box." He cannot now remember which opera it was, probably because, thoroughly hooked, he went to about two dozen more that year, though not in such luxury. After one experience with a seat on the side, where he could not see a thing, he learned to use standing room, and once or twice a week went downtown early to get a place where he could lean on the rail.

Somewhere in these busy years, young Arthur had found or made the time for one of his greatest achievements, to woo and wed Margaret Douglas of Davidson. During the year of Arthur's first Rosenwald, 1942–1943, she had completed her M.A. in sociology. Then, during Arthur's year at North Carolina State, the courtship continued mostly by correspondence between Raleigh and Charlotte, where Margaret was teaching at Queens College. For Christmas, 1944, the Link family was home, except for his brother, who was back in the army hospital. Arthur wrote Fletcher Green soon afterward: "My girl was just as I had hoped and, as you know, we are engaged." The wedding was set for June.

For the remainder of the academic year Arthur continued on his set course, polished up his dissertation draft and finished a draft of the Wilson study, meanwhile submitting to journals articles extracted from the dissertation. Of these the most important was one based on chapter VII of his dissertation, "The Progressive Movement in the South" in the *North Carolina Historical Review* (1946), an early milestone in the study of Southern progressivism.

In January 1945, concerned about talk of legislation to mobilize 4-Fs for war work, Arthur toyed with the idea of making his contribution by taking a job in the Dallas office of the Commission on Fair Employment Practices (FEPC), but by spring an academic job search was actively in progress, leading to some exchanges with Washington, Michigan State, and Rollins College, among others. Three of the contacts led to offers, all from institutions in or near New York: Sarah Lawrence, Columbia, and Princeton. Arthur remembers that on a visit to Sarah Lawrence he was told that teachers there had to be mentors, personal friends, advisers, and counselors of the young ladies. In the spring of 1945, he was still twenty-four. "And that scared the life out of me and I caught the next train back to New York and that was that."

The Columbia and Princeton offers came at about the same time. The position came about because Professor Clifton R. Hall had just died, and the department needed a twentieth-century historian. Arthur was drawn to Columbia, which had a strong department and was prepared to offer a somewhat higher salary, but he anticipated faster advancement at Princeton. In any case, although he had enjoyed New York, he wrote to Fletcher Green, "I like the small, college-town atmosphere of the place (it is much like Chapel Hill) infinitely better than the city; and I think Margaret will be happier at Princeton." And Princeton was within reach of New York in any case. Surely the Wilsonian connection also had something to do with the decision.

During that busy year Link submitted to Datus C. Smith, Jr., director of the Princeton University Press, the draft of what would become *Wilson: The Road to the White House.* The reworking of the first volume was carried on through 1945 and into the fall of 1946, when the book went to press. It was published in April 1947, but before then, at Smith's suggestion, Arthur was already referring to it as the first in a series of volumes rather than a solitary work. The level of detail given to the years 1902–1912, as it happened, would dictate a similar level of detail in what would follow.

The student days were drawing to an end with the Chapel Hill commencement in June. It was the sesquicentennial year of the University of North Carolina. The wedding was moved up to an earlier date than originally planned because Margaret's brother, Captain John M. Douglas, would be home. Arthur and Margaret were married June 2, 1945, at the Davidson Presbyterian Church in Davidson, where her father was professor emeritus of physics. Professor Douglas offered one parting admonition to his daughter: "Be careful of Arthur's time, for he is a young man with a future." Arthur was back in Chapel Hill for his final examinations about the 12th and took Margaret over to dinner with the Franklins in Durham afterward. Commencement was in Memorial Hall on a very hot June 25. That night the young couple took a sleeper north from Raleigh.

The following morning they arrived in Princeton in time to lay in groceries and have their first meal in their temporary home at 7 Cleveland Lane (they moved in September to a small second-floor apartment at 75 Patton Avenue). "When you come to see us," Arthur wrote to Fletcher Green the next day, "we shall be able to offer you the choice of any one of five or six bedrooms and, I believe, five baths." Arthur had a "fine commodious office" at 108 Dickinson, all to himself, with "a spacious desk, desk-chair, large bookcase, copious maps on the wall, lamp, and eight extra chairs (for use in preceptorials)." Army students who had been expected in July were unable to come until August, and he looked forward to a light load for the coming month.

The letter to Fletcher Green closed: "At this, the end of my student days at Chapel Hill, I want to tell you again how greatly I appreciated, and do appreciate, your guidance and encouragement. Your scholarship and knowledge have always been a stimulus to me."

Notes

Footnotes for this paper seem unnecessary since the sources are relatively few and either fairly obvious or mentioned in the text. The richest single source, especially for Link's early life, was an interview with Arthur Link (with Margaret joining in part of the time) in Montreat, North Carolina, August 8–9, 1989. The most informative written source was the Link file in the Julius Rosenwald Foundation Papers, photocopies of which the Fisk University Library kindly supplied me. These papers include applications, recommendations, and Link's correspondence with Dr. and Mrs. Haygood regarding his activities. The Fletcher Melvin Green Papers in the Southern Historical Collection are rich in exchanges with Link as are the letters of Green and Albert Ray Newsome in the University of North Carolina Archives, copies of which the departmental secretary kept in departmental records. The University Archives also preserve incomplete minutes of the Dialectic Society.

The North Carolina Collection at Chapel Hill has files of the UNC student yearbook, the *Yackety Yack*, and the student newspaper, *The Daily Tar Heel*, which include occasional references to Link, particularly related to his activities in the Dialectic Society at Chapel Hill. It also houses copies of Arthur Link's senior honors thesis, his M.A. thesis, and his Ph.D. dissertation, as well as other printed materials at least peripherally relevant. The UNC General Alumni Association has a small file of items pertaining to Link.

Two university histories by Louis Round Wilson provide useful information about the milieu into which Link moved in Chapel Hill: *The University of North Carolina, 1900–1930: The Making of a Modern University* (Chapel Hill: The University of North Carolina Press, 1957) and *The University of North Carolina Under Consolidation, 1931–1963 History and Appraisal* (Chapel Hill: The University of North Carolina Consolidated Office, 1964). Daniel J. Singal's *The War Within: From Victorian to Modernist Thought in the South, 1919–1945* (Chapel Hill: The University of North Carolina Press, 1982) offers two chapters on the intellectual renaissance in Chapel Hill, especially on the University Press and the Southern Regionalists.

Among people helpful to me in doing this paper, William Link pointed to a number of sources, most important of which turned out to be the Rosenwald Papers. Mrs. Frances W. Saunders supplied a useful sketch from which to begin in her article, "From Campus Penury to Literary Heights," in the *Carolina Alumni Review*, 76 (Fall, 1987): pp. 57–62. A number of Link's contemporaries shared information with me or read and commented on the draft paper, or both. These include Lewis J. Williams of Dayton, Ohio, one of the Chapel Hill "triumvirate," John Hope Franklin of Durham, North Carolina, Bennett H. Wall of Athens, Georgia, Allen J. Going of Tuscaloosa, Alabama, and J. Carlyle Sitterson, William S. Powell, and James R. Caldwell of Chapel Hill, North Carolina. Margaret and Arthur Link also were kind enough to go over the draft and save me from numerous errors.

Richard W. Leopold

ARTHUR S. LINK
AT NORTHWESTERN
THE MATURING OF A SCHOLAR

ARTHUR S. Link spent eleven years at Northwestern University, a relatively short span in a long and distinguished career. But it was, as he wrote in October 1959, a critical period in his development, one in which he came to maturity as a scholar and teacher. Almost thirty years later he said he was grateful to Northwestern for giving him the opportunity to strike out on his own, in a way that he could never have enjoyed if he had remained at Princeton in 1949 as one of seven assistant professors.

I first met Link at the Mayflower Hotel in Washington, where the American Historical Association was assembled in December 1948. We were introduced by E. Harris Harbison. Link's name was known to me as early as April 1947 when the Princeton University Press published his 570-page *Wilson: The Road to the White House*. Three months later, in a letter to Thomas J. Pressly, whom I had taught at Harvard and who was then on the Princeton faculty, I expressed surprise that Link was still an instructor. If a blizzard had not paralyzed all rail traffic out of New York on December 26, 1947, I might have seen Link for the first time in Cleveland, where he read a paper before the American Historical Association on "Biographical Reinterpretations of Recent American History."

In December 1948 I had more than a passing interest in this youthful looking southerner, born in Virginia in 1920 but reared in North Carolina and armed with three degrees from Chapel Hill. I had just gone to Northwestern as the third full-time Americanist. The other two, both professors, were Chairman Tracy E. Strevey, born in 1902, with a Chicago doctorate of 1930, and Ray A. Billington, born in 1903, with a Harvard doctorate of 1933. Strevey had been at Northwestern since 1935, teaching the sophomore survey, advanced lecture course on recent American and constitutional history, and graduate seminars. Billington had arrived in 1944 and lectured regularly on intellectual and frontier history and occasionally on the American Revolution, as well as giving graduate seminars. As an associate professor, born in 1912, with a Harvard doctorate of 1938, I was to teach diplomatic history, conduct graduate seminars, and share in the sophomore survey which would now be divided between Strevey, Billington, and myself. Strevey's resignation, three months after my acceptance, to become dean at Southern California left me with two-thirds of the survey and the department with a desire to find an established scholar who might possess Strevey's interests.

Link, it was believed at first, was not that person. He had been made an instructor at Princeton in 1945, the year he received his doctorate, and had been promoted to assistant professor in 1948. Despite one major book, several articles in leading journals, appearances at professional meetings, and a one-semester appointment at The Institute for Advanced Study, he lacked the prestige and experience initially sought by both the department and the university. He had not met any member, although Gray C. Boyce, the new chairman, had listened to his paper at Cleveland. In October 1948 the department recommended at the professional level, first David M. Potter and then Samuel H. Brockunier. The former declined an offer when Yale unexpectedly advanced him to professor; the latter was vetoed by both President Franklyn B. Snyder and Simeon E. Leland, dean of the College of Liberal Arts. It was then decided to defer action until after the meeting of the American Historical Association in late December and a further scrutiny of younger men. In this category were Link, who was invited on November 22 to teach in the 1949 summer session, and Richard Hofstadter, an assistant professor at Columbia.

At Washington Link impressed everyone, but the Princeton system, which kept junior faculty from giving their own courses, continued to count against him. Except for apprentice teaching in a wartime program at North Carolina State and sharing a graduate seminar at the Woodrow Wilson School at Princeton, Link's classroom experience had been confined to precepting in the courses of his senior colleagues. When Hofstadter was also eliminated because of a false rumor that Columbia was promoting him, the department chose Bell I. Wiley, a proven scholar and a veteran teacher, fourteen years older than Link. But Snyder again insisted that Northwestern could do better; while Leland, listening to Jacob Viner, a former Chicago colleague then at The Institute for Advanced Study, urged the historians to reconsider Link. Informants at Princeton stressed anew Link's scholarly ambition and capacity for work. He was reputed to be the only historian seen in the library on Sundays. (If I had known then how paramount a role religion plays in Arthur's life, I would have been even more impressed.) Sensing that Snyder wanted someone from a prestigious institution and knowing Leland's preference, the department invited Link for an interview.

Two days before he arrived on February 17, 1949, I wrote Frederick Merk that I did not know how deep was Link's interest or whether he might come as an assistant professor, an associate professor, or a professor. I had reason to be puzzled, for I later learned that the conversation with Dean Leland went something like this.

Dean: Professor Link, we very much want you at Northwestern.
Link: Thank you, sir.
Dean: We are prepared to go well beyond your Princeton salary.
Link: That is very generous of you.
Dean: As to rank, it might be best, since you have just been promoted to assistant professor, to come at that rank but at a very high salary; but if you insist, we are ready to make you an associate professor.
Link: Thank you. Again you are generous. I shall be happy to consider an appointment as associate professor.

Link took back to New Jersey an offer of associate professor at $5,500, half again as much as his Princeton salary. Officials there met part of that increase but did not promise an early promotion or the same independence in teaching. After some inconclusive talk about an appointment at The Institute for Advanced Study, where Edward Mead Earle was already his staunch supporter, Link accepted Northwestern's terms on March 10, 1949.

His decision surprised and delighted me. On March 21 I wrote Arthur M. Schlesinger: "I felt Princeton would not let him go, that it would feel compelled to jump him over the heads of his less distinguished seniors." To Pressly I said less discreetly on April 21: "I was surprised as I could be when Old Nassau let us steal Link away. Despite his youth and teaching inexperience and whatever other defects there may be, Link appears to the outside world a much brighter luminary than Persons, Isely and Crowl combined."

The department that Link joined was small, congenial, professionally oriented, outstanding in teaching, and quite new. Of the other ten members, seven had arrived since 1944. There were three professors, three associate professors, two assistant professors, and two instructors. Five were Europeanists, one a Latin Americanist, and one a specialist on England. A fourth Americanist, on a term appointment, was replaced as an instructor by Clarence L. Ver Steeg, born in 1922, with a Columbia doctorate of 1950, in that year. The much larger department that Link left in 1949 consisted of six professors, three associate professors, seven assistant professors, and five instructors.

Link quickly endeared himself to his colleagues. At some sacrifice to his research he kept a commitment, made before he came for an interview, to teach in the summer of 1949. He agreed to defer until 1950–51 a Guggenheim fellowship he had received right after accepting the Northwestern appointment. To my relief he took over the first quarter of the sophomore survey, which Billington had given in 1948–49, although Link's specialty was the twentieth century, thus allowing me to repeat in 1950 and thereafter the two quarters I had been forced to work up after Strevey resigned. One sensed immediately that Link tied his career to the prestige of the Northwestern History Department. Freed from a subordinate status in the hierarchical Princeton setting, he spoke his mind on appointments, curriculum, and placement. He never shirked a teaching or committee assignment, and his regular attendance at professional meetings was a boon to graduate students seeking jobs. Not the least of the satisfactions his presence brought was his wife, the former Margaret McDowell Douglas, a graduate of Agnes Scott and daughter of a revered professor at Davidson. Despite a growing family, Margaret was not only a charming hostess but also a skilled critic and proofreader whose talents benefited Arthur and his colleagues.

At Northwestern Link taught no more and no less than other members of the department. Until 1955 his load was outrageously heavy by today's standards. He regularly lectured for one quarter in the sophomore survey, for two quarters in the upperclass history of the South, and for three quarters in the advanced history of America since the 1890s. He also offered each year a two-quarter graduate seminar. In his first five years he taught, too, four times in the summer session and four times in the extension work on the Chicago campus. The birth of his second child in 1950, his third in 1951, and his fourth in 1954 help explain his taking on these additional burdens.

While at Northwestern, Link compiled a scholarly record that few, if any, historians of his age or of any age could match. He published four major books and completed the manuscript of a fifth. He co-edited and contributed to two editions of a volume designed for classroom use. He wrote five articles and at least eleven book reviews for leading journals. He profited from a year's leave of absence three times. In 1950–51 he held a Guggenheim fellowship. In 1954–55 he was a member of The Institute for Advanced Study. In 1958–59 he was the Harold Vyvyan Harmsworth Professor of American History at Oxford. On all three occasions Northwestern gave generous financial support.

Link arrived in Evanston with a good start on the second volume of the Wilson biography. After teaching in the summer of 1949, he spent ten days in research at Chapel Hill. The next summer found him in New Haven, Cambridge, New York, and Philadelphia, examining the House, Polk, Page, and other collections. In September 1950 he settled with his family in Arlington for a year's work in the Wilson papers and other riches in the Library of Congress and in the State Department records in the National Archives. He devoted evenings and weekends, when those depositories were closed, to a volume for Prentice-Hall which, in April 1951, he and I agreed to edit. By then, or soon thereafter, he contracted to write two other books, one for Harper's *The New American Nation Series*, the second a textbook for Alfred A. Knopf. Also while near Washington, he joined five other scholars in a one-day conference at The Institute for Advanced Study, arranged by Earle, to discuss a draft of George F. Kennan's Walgreen Lectures. In the second volume of his *Memoirs* in 1972 Kennan thanked Link for his criticism on that occasion. Link returned to Evanston in September 1951 with enough material to complete all three projects and to organize the second Wilson volume.

Problems in American History appeared in April 1952, one year after it had been conceived. A book of 929 pages, it contained twenty problems aimed at the survey course in United States history. Eighteen contributors plus the editors dealt with issues within their expertise. They were a young group, fifteen of them were forty years old or younger, but one soon to be leaders in their fields. Richard N. Current, Fred Harvey Harrington, Thomas LeDuc, Rodman W. Paul, Kenneth M. Stampp, and I were born in 1912; Stow Persons in 1913; John Hope Franklin and Oscar Handlin, in 1915; Frank Freidel, in 1916; Link, in 1920; Ver Steeg, in 1922; and Charles G. Sellers, in 1923. As coeditor, Link typed most of the correspondence; as contributor, he constructed a model for others to follow. To this sideshow he brought efficiency, good humor, and an ability to soothe hurt feelings. He undertook the enterprise partly to meet course needs at Northwestern and partly to provide for an expanding family. On April 20, 1952, I wrote Billington: "At times Arthur seems to think our fortune is made; at others he is not so certain."

Next came *Woodrow Wilson and the Progressive Era, 1910–1917*, released in January 1954. A book of some 340 pages and the first in the series, it was written between September 1951 and June 1952. All or part of the manuscript was read by Margaret and by ten other scholars, including editors Henry Steele Commager and Richard B. Morris, Charles Seymour, Earle, and three Northwestern colleagues—Billington, Leopold, and Howard F. Cline. Link spent the summer of

1952 constructing a bibliographical essay of 100 typed pages and fretting over Commager's slowness in reading chapters. If he does not move more quickly, Link wrote me on June 22, I will be "in a terrible fix, with nothing to do for the rest of the summer." That unlikely prospect soon dissipated with Commager's helpful suggestions. By February 1953 Link could sign the preface; by mid-December he inscribed copies for his colleagues.

The acclaim that greeted *Woodrow Wilson and the Progressive Era* left little doubt that the young author had become the leading authority on Wilson. Based upon prodigious research—a description of the manuscript collections used required four pages of small type—it established the benchmark for later writers on such matters as Wilson's swing to progressivism, "missionary diplomacy," and the submarine controversy with Germany. Among the laudatory reviewers were Merle Curti, D. W. Brogan, John M. Blum, Walter Johnson, William E. Leuchtenburg, Eric F. Goldman, and Earle. Even the *Chicago Tribune* spoke of its "marked impartiality." Link's own estimate was modest. He called it a synthesis of his research for the next three volumes of the biography (they would eventually grow to four), an outline of a more detailed story of the first Wilson administration.

He turned next to the twentieth-century textbook. Even as the Harper volume moved slowly into print and while teaching full-time, Link completed by June 1953 a manuscript of about 75,000 words, two-thirds of the projected work. By August 1954, after two more summers of teaching plus the regular year, he had carried the draft to the end of the Truman administration and had revised the whole after obtaining comments from specialists. Max Beloff, Blum, Freidel, Margaret, and I read the entire typescript; Billington, Franklin D. Scott, Roger F. Hackett, Ernest Samuels, and William Miller perused substantial portions. Entitled *American Epoch: A History of the United States since the 1890's*, the profusely illustrated 783-page volume, replete with original maps, was published in late April 1955 and immediately began its long life as the pre-eminent work in its field.

This impressive record caused Dean Leland to report in August 1954 that Link was the "most promising" member of the most distinguished department in the college. Fifteen months earlier, in a letter supporting Link's application for a year at the Institute for Advanced Study, I predicted to Earle (who needed no persuading) that Arthur would become "one of the most productive scholars of his generation." Very wisely his senior colleagues moved to insure Link's promotion at the end of his initial five-year appointment, even though it would jump him over two associate professors who had joined the faculty in 1946 and 1947. An informal agreement in June 1953 became an official recommendation on October 5. Neither Boyce's letter to the dean nor the report of the *ad hoc* committee has survived, but the latter's lavish praise can be read in my communication of April 30, 1954, as acting chairman to the absent Boyce. The body created to advise the dean raised no questions, while Leland asserted that he had never read "more favorable letters from so prominent a group of scholars" outside the university. Mindful of the glowing reviews then appearing of *Woodrow Wilson and the Progressive Era*, the full professors unanimously declared Link to be eligible for promotion to that rank, and the Board of Trustees approved on June 13, 1954.

By then plans were in place to write the second Wilson volume at the Institute for Advanced Study. The family arrived in Princeton on September 10, 1954. After a couple of weeks of additional research in Trenton and Jersey City, Link began writing on October 13. But before he completed a draft in May 1955, he faced the first of two emotion-draining decisions affecting his ties with Northwestern.

A fortnight after Link arrived at the Institute, Jeter A. Isely died of a heart attack. A former colleague at Princeton, Isely had been promoted to assistant professor a year earlier than Link and had since advanced to associate professor. On October 9, 1954, I wrote Link saying he must not be pressed into temporary service and he must make it known that he was "out of bounds" for the future. On the thirteenth Link gave me assurances on the first point and said he was "very dubious" about any permanent offer. His promotion, he believed, probably put him beyond anything Princeton could do. The next three months seemed to bear out his belief, but in January Boyce learned that his counterpart, Joseph R. Strayer, had asked Link whether he would consider rejoining his old department. Although it was rumored that Strayer had also approached Freidel of Stanford and Current of Illinois, the senior professors in Evanston took no chances. On January 31, 1955, they recommended that Link's salary for 1955–56 be raised to $8,000, and he was so informed. Still, uncertainty prevailed as Freidel first accepted and then rejected a Princeton offer so that he could accept one from Harvard. On February 4 I wrote Link: "What is new on the Princeton appointment? Has Freidel been confirmed? I am told that they may be wanting you after all. Read that last as you will."

By then Strayer had proposed a professorship at $10,000. Link was genuinely torn. On the one hand, he had been supremely happy at Northwestern, as had Margaret and the children. There he had received generous support for his research, enjoyed congenial colleagues, and attained a major voice in a department with a growing national reputation. On the other hand, Princeton was a more prestigious institution. It offered a much better library, a much larger department (twenty-six as against eleven), proximity to the publisher of his biography, and the possibility of association with the Institute for Advanced Study. Link had never bargained over salary, and he did not wish to start now. On February 5, 1955, he telephoned me to explain why he was going to say yes to Princeton. I managed to persuade him, not on grounds of friendship but on what was best for his career, to come to Evanston before giving an answer. When he arrived on the 9th, Northwestern was ready with a counteroffer of $12,500, which later became $13,000. Touched by this mark of confidence, Link was moved even more by the sentiments of his colleagues. Yet, although he stayed with me and ate every meal with me, I was still uncertain when he left on the tenth as to how he would decide. Perhaps he was too.

The balance may have been tipped by Harold W. Dodds. In talking with Link about the Princeton offer, its president seemed aloof, detached, and even indifferent, lacking the warmth and enthusiasm displayed in Evanston by Leland and Dean of Faculties Payson S. Wild. Persuaded that he could best pursue his career at Northwestern, Link made up his mind on February 17, 1955. "It was a hard decision to make," he wrote Wild that day, "for I was strongly attracted by the opportunities here. But we are certain we made the right choice." The same day he thanked me for "the way in which you helped me to see that this is the best decision," even without taking into account personal considerations. Margaret put it pithily when she wrote on the twenty-third: "How glad I am that Arthur made the trip to Evanston and talked with you."

This agonizing decision did not disrupt a productive year at the Institute. Besides completing a draft of the Wilson biography, Link read proof of *American Epoch*, wrote an essay for a volume to honor one of his North Carolina teachers, gave several lectures on Wilson, made suggestions to institutions planning to celebrate in 1956 the centennial of Wilson's birth, and dealt with the publisher's desire for a new edition of *Problems in American History*. He left Princeton in mid-June 1955 and, after some research in Philadelphia and Washington, settled in Montreat, North Carolina, to revise the manuscript. He was half done by late July when a reaction to a penicillin injection made him seriously ill and delirious. "I've never seen Arthur drunk" Margaret wrote me on August 2, "but now I know what he'd be like. He asked me last night where his deceased wife was!" A week's hospitalization followed, but he was back at work on the thirteenth, determined to finish the rewriting before he returned to Evanston. "I know it is perfectly foolish," he wrote me on the seventeenth, "but my inner compulsion drives me to try to do what I cut out for myself this summer." Happily, his brother-in-law, a doctor, intervened and restricted work to mornings. Rather dolefully Link reported to me on the twenty-second: "I think I can finish it with another ten days' work in Evanston." And he did.

The return to Evanston in September 1955 brought no respite to Link's crowded life. Although his new salary, the highest in the department, freed him from the need to teach summers or evenings on the Chicago campus, he carried the same load as his colleagues and directed a growing number of doctoral dissertations. He played a key role in planning for the future, seeking foundation support for new programs, and establishing with the Northwestern University Press a series to publish revised dissertations. During the autumn he made changes in the Wilson volume suggested by Jean McLachlan, Blum, Margaret, and myself; in December the manuscript went to the Princeton University Press. During those months he served his initial year on the Beveridge Award Committee of the American Historical Association and on the Board of Editors of the *Journal of Southern History*. In January 1956 he gave the first of over thirty lectures, at institutions as distant as Mississippi and New Mexico, to mark the centennial of Wilson's birth. The most important were the two Taft Lectures at the University of Cincinnati in March and the five Albert Shaw Lectures on Diplomatic History at Johns Hopkins in December. Also in 1956 he took on the ticklish task of coediting a revision of *Problems in American History*, and early in 1957 he participated in a seminar at the Institute for Advanced Study which discussed George F. Kennan's forthcoming *The Decision to Intervene*. Most important of all, however, was the release on December 28, 1956, of *Wilson: The New Freedom*.

That volume, in 471 pages of text, dealt mainly with domestic affairs during the first years of Wilson's presidency. It cast new light on the man and his cabinet, executive-legislative relations, party rivalries, and the battles over banking and the tariff. It showed Wilson moving slowly from championing laissez faire and a limited role of the government in economic matters to supporting the progressive social order envisaged by Herbert Croly. Four of the fourteen chapters covered events in Mexico and Central America to November 1914. The result was, in Link's words, "a considerable admixture of history and biography." The sixteen-page bibliography was restricted to sources cited in the footnotes. For a fuller analysis of the literature of the period the reader was referred to the thirty-one page essay in *Woodrow Wilson and the Progressive Era*. The book was praised, with varying enthusiasm, by such divergent reviewers as Commager and

Goldman, Freidel and Arthur Sears Henning, John D. Hicks and Gerald W. Johnson. In April 1957 it received one of the two Bancroft Prizes for distinguished studies in American history, diplomacy, and international relations. The other went to Kennan's *Russia Leaves the War*.

The second edition of *Problems in American History*, issued in March 1957, revealed anew Link's ability to deal with collaborators who were sometimes suspicious and often critical. The 1952 version had such defects as excessive length and little-used chapters. Most contributors were initially reluctant to cut their pieces by a third, and one actually withdrew. Many felt the royalties were too small to justify further work; a few believed the editors' share was unfairly large. After much correspondence to allay bruised egos, fifteen of the eighteen agreed to continue, while two cheerfully accepted, or so the editors stated, an obviously painful elimination. The number of pages was reduced from 929 to 706. The new roster substituted Edmund S. Morgan, Horace S. Merrill, and George E. Mowry for John W. Caughey, Oscar Handlin, and Henry F. May. Happily for Leopold and Link, this revision lasted nine years and made them even better known in small colleges and secondary schools. Happily, too, for the former, the coupling of the names Leopold and Loeb, which had plagued him since 1924, was now replaced by Leopold and Link.

The Shaw Lectures quickly found their way into print. Few changes in the spoken version were required, but Link asked Samuel Flagg Bemis, Scott, Margaret, and myself to read the manuscript. The finished product was ready by April 1957, and in November the Johns Hopkins Press published *Wilson the Diplomatist: A Look at His Major Policies*. In a text of 157 pages Link examined: Wilson and the conduct of diplomacy; Wilson and the problems of neutrality; Wilson and the decisions for war; Wilson and the liberal peace program; and Wilson and the debate over collective security. Keeping narrative and description to a minimum, he stressed analysis and interpretation, focusing on Wilson's policies toward Europe and world organization. He sought neither to praise nor to condemn, but concluded that Wilson's record was "an impressively favorable one," a tribute to his "steadfastness, idealism, courage, and ability to see things in their long-run perspective."

By late 1957 forces were at work which would reorient Link's career and end his fruitful years at Northwestern. The Woodrow Wilson Centennial Celebration Commission, created by Congress, had already explored the possibility of having some more permanent body prepare a scholarly edition of Wilson's letters and public papers. At the Pittsburgh meeting of the Mississippi Valley Historical Association in April 1956, its secretary asked Link and me about the wisdom and feasibility of such a project. In a joint letter of the twenty-third, written by Link, we endorsed the idea, analyzed the problems, and estimated that the correspondence and papers would require at least thirty volumes. Link believed that the Woodrow Wilson Foundation, the Rockefeller Foundation, and other groups might finance the enterprise. He favored a preliminary survey of available Wilson manuscripts and agreed to serve on a committee to advise the search. One of his doctoral students, David W. Hirst of the University of Maryland, with experience in the Manuscript Division of the Library of Congress, began the survey in mid-February 1957 and completed it in June. On May 16, 1957, the Woodrow Wilson Foundation took up the challenge from the expiring Centennial Commission. The Board of Directors voted to sponsor the publication of Wilson's letters and papers and to seek financial support "at the proper time." The first step, however, was to select an editor, and that task was entrusted to a committee of directors headed by Raymond B. Fosdick.

It is difficult to date when Link first considered becoming the editor. During 1956 and 1957 he followed with interest the Commission's activity and the Foundation's decision. He had an obvious stake in the selection and every reason to believe he was the person best qualified. But since we were both in Evanston, I have no letters to reveal his thinking. The earliest conversation that I can document occurred on November 2, 1957, when he drove Margaret and me to a dinner at the University of Chicago. Since Fosdick had just sought my ideas on possible editors, the subject was on our minds. Margaret and I warned against taking any step that might delay or supersede the biography. He was already immersed in the third volume, which would take Wilson to October 1915, and he had reason to believe he would be the Harmsworth Professor in 1958–59 and thus be able to complete his research in British manuscript sources. While not eager for the task, Link was convinced, as I wrote Blum on January 8, 1958, "that he could undertake the editing job without endangering the progress of the biography." Margaret recalls that by that date, in our discussions, Arthur declared that editing the papers would be a greater contribution to scholarship than finishing the biography.

Replying to Fosdick on November 13, 1957, I said that Link and Blum were the only logical candidates. Link's knowledge of Wilson was fuller and his interest deeper; Blum had more editorial experience. I suspected that neither man would actively seek the post; I could not be certain either would accept it. I emphasized the need for an associate editor, a support system, and an institutional affiliation. I was careful not to predict how Northwestern would respond if Link became editor. Fosdick's acknowledgement was noncommittal.

Further discussion ensued at the New York meeting of the American Historical Association in late 1957. A last-minute sore throat prevented Link from being present to read his paper on progressivism in the 1920s, and I enjoyed speaking his words without fearing criticism by the commentators. On the twenty-eighth, Arthur M. Schlesinger, Jr., a member of Fosdick's committee, asked whether I would allow my name to be considered as editor. In declining on January 6, 1958, I wrote that Link and Blum were much better qualified, although Blum would not take the job. "Arthur is, I firmly believe, available." I went on to say that I had originally thought he would not be interested for fear of jeopardizing the biography. "On talking with Arthur about this matter some weeks ago and after going over the same ground since my return from New York, I now think Arthur would be willing to accept the assignment if the proper arrangements can be made." Link recognized that editing could initially slow down his writing, but he was convinced that as he moved the biography past 1917, one project would supplement the other. I added: "I think that he is right." I ruled out serving as coeditor as both unnecessary for the enterprise and unfair to the department at Northwestern. As to what the university might do, I was confident that "this institution, which has done so much to obtain and keep the foremost Wilson scholar in the United States, would regard it as a privilege and an honor to play a part in the publication of the Wilson Letters and Papers."

More bluntly I wrote to Blum on January 16, 1958, that my sole concern was "(1) to make sure that Arthur Link has, as you well put it, the first refusal; (2) to do what I can to make sure that the project is in respectable hands if, again as you say, 'Fosdick won't have Arthur, or if Arthur won't have Fosdick'; (3) to prevent such an illogical solution of an admittedly difficult problem by simply deciding to assign the project to Princeton because of sentiment, or because the headquarters may be placed in 1879 Hall, or because Joe Strayer tells off some Assistant Professor, unacquainted with the Wilson era, to do the job and thus be assured of a permanent position at Old Nassau." Replying on the twenty-first, Blum, who had just gone to Yale, wrote that former president Charles Seymour agreed that Link should become editor only if he could "manage the job without abandoning the indispensable biography" and was given a talented associate editor. Blum added: "Seymour let slip that a year ago he urged Yale to go after Arthur instead of me. So you and I both profit from his lapse of influence here."

On February 20, 1958, Fosdick's committee unanimously chose Link to be editor, and he accepted. He was told that Princeton wanted him to make his headquarters there, and Fosdick intimated that the Woodrow Wilson Foundation would find it easier to raise the requisite funds if the project were so located. The next day Chairman Boyce telegraphed Fosdick that Northwestern would do everything possible to hold Link. A similar message went to other committee members. The same day Fosdick wired back to say that his group believed that "from every point of view Princeton offers advantages for the prosecution of the work which no other place affords." Writing on the twenty-fifth, Schlesinger sympathized with Northwestern's desire to retain Link and said that the university would be given ample opportunity to discuss alternative arrangements. He concluded: "There are, as you can imagine, strong reasons for housing the project at Princeton, but I do not know whether these are insuperable."

In a long letter to Fosdick on February 24, 1958, Dean of Faculties Wild reiterated Northwestern's determination to keep Link. He stated correctly that, on personal grounds, Link preferred to stay in Evanston "where his roots are deep and where he has found congenial surroundings." Wild recognized Wilson's ties to Princeton, but "we do not feel that, in the circumstances, Professor Link should have to move to Princeton if he genuinely wishes to stay at Northwestern and if the proper working arrangements are made with Northwestern, as we definitely hope." Wild concluded: "You suggested to Professor Link, I think, that the Foundation might find it easier to raise the necessary funds if the project were located at Princeton. I hope I am not lacking in objectivity when I suggest that Woodrow Wilson is a national and international figure and those interested in Wilson are not confined to Princeton alumni and the eastern seaboard. . . . It might even assist the development of the ideals of Woodrow Wilson were the project located in the Middle West which traditionally has not had the reputation for possessing an international point of view."

Wild talked with Fosdick in New York on March 14, 1958. Before he left, I wrote "If anyone can overcome the long odds that confront us, you can." It is doubtful whether Wild moved Fosdick and his committee, several of whom were Princeton alumni; but on the twentieth Fosdick telephoned Link to say that the committee had agreed to leave the decision as to where the editing would be done until after Link had filled the chair at Oxford and had returned to Northwestern for the academic year 1959–1960. The Board of Directors apparently approved this solution at its meeting on May 5, for the initial news release about the project did not mention Princeton University or where Link would work. I welcomed this respite but feared time was not on our side, especially after the Rockefeller Foundation granted Link $5,500 to assist his research in England.

In his annual report to Leland in July 1958 Boyce mentioned an air of uncertainty. "When the issue first developed," he wrote, "it seemed that Mr. Link felt he must go to Princeton to do the work required; then the strange silence of Princeton seemed to push Mr. Link back into the Evanston orbit. Later he visited Princeton . . . and was finally told . . . of the Department's wish to appoint him to a professorship and to have him do the work at Princeton." Boyce thought that Link's failure to specify his needs for 1959–60 was out of character, and he was puzzled by Link's insistence "that the decision was not his to make. It was, in so far as the writer could understand, to result from the will of higher power given articulation by the Woodrow Wilson Foundation. Several of us, his colleagues, impressed upon him that only Link could make the ultimate decision and that he could not continue to remain aloof and be unwilling to commit himself."

Link's acting "out of character" suggests that he was sorely troubled and wanted to delay as long as possible a decision that would profoundly affect his career and his family. While he was at Oxford, we exchanged more and longer letters than during any previous separation. From June 27, 1958, to June 8, 1959, he wrote twenty-four times, averaging about three single-spaced typed pages. As if by mutual agreement, we referred only occasionally, and then briefly, to the painful decision that lay ahead. Mostly he wrote about Oxford, travels, and progress on volume three. He manifested intense concern with departmental affairs and the unsuccessful attempts of Texas to lure Billington and of Michigan to steal Ver Steeg. He kept his eyes on the sales of *Problems in American History*, insisted on reserving his regular football tickets for the 1959 season, and took a proprietary interest in the book I was writing for Alfred A. Knopf.

Most of all he reported on what would become *Wilson: The Struggle for Neutrality*. By November 24, 1958, he completed the first draft, written in pencil, of 300,000 words. On January 12, 1959, after typing four chapters, he felt the total would not exceed 1,000 manuscript pages. By March 30 he had typed thirteen chapters in 815 pages with six more to go. In late April he hoped to finish in mid-June; actually he did so on June 5. But "seven months of uninterrupted outpouring and concentration," he wrote me on March 30, had left him "near, if not at the point of mental and nervous exhaustion." When I warned on April 19 against driving himself too hard and reminded him of the price he had paid in the past, he replied on the twenty-ninth, in words reminiscent of what he had written on August 17, 1955, "It is all very well for Margaret and you to be telling me all the time that I should go slower, but I remember the fact that there is an enormous amount yet to be done, and I will never get it done if I permit myself to slow down."

And what of the future? "I wish I could follow my impulse and say,"

Link wrote on March 6, 1959, "we will of course stay in Evanston. . . . But it would be the height of folly for me even to make a prediction at this time." But a decision could not long be delayed. On April 3 President Robert Goheen invited the project to affiliate with Princeton University and be housed in the Firestone Library. On June 23 the Rockefeller Foundation granted $150,000 toward collecting and filming the papers over a three-year period. On July 8 the Ford Foundation gave $175,000 for partial support of the editing over the subsequent seven years. The Woodrow Wilson Foundation allocated $500,000 from capital and income to underwrite the project for fifteen years and guaranteed to see it to completion. Finally, Goheen talked of, but had not yet offered, an appointment as professor. It was now up to Northwestern to respond before the Publications Committee met on September 18. Although arrangements had been made for 1959–60, no full discussion about later years could take place until Link reached Evanston on September 6, 1959.

When we talked the next evening, I sensed that he was leaning toward Princeton. Meetings on the following days with President J. Roscoe Miller and Wild seemed to effect a change. Northwestern offered to provide all facilities and services necessary to conduct the project until it was completed, be it for fifteen years or twenty-five. It would pay that part of Link's salary not covered by other funds, even if those outside sources were reduced in the future. Link could determine his own teaching load. For 1959–60 he would have two rooms adjacent to the history department. Beginning in 1960–61 the project would occupy a ten-room house close to the library, with office equipment and janitorial help included. Because Evanston was distant from repositories holding Wilson manuscripts, Northwestern would supplement, as Link deemed appropriate, the travel money included in foundation grants. Where needed, special purchases would be made for Deering Library. Members of the project staff, then in Washington, would receive faculty status and be assured of temporary residences when they moved to Evanston.

Such was the offer Link took east on September 13, 1959. An hour before he departed he assured me that he would not be rushed into a decision but would do what he believed to be best for the project. He thought Northwestern then had the edge, for he doubted, perhaps remembering 1955, that Princeton would come through. But in Princeton a few days later Goheen did come through, manifesting the warmth and eagerness that Dodds had earlier failed to show. At New York on the eighteenth, Link and his associate editor, John W. Davidson, surveyed the situation with the Publications Committee. All agreed to accept the Princeton option.

What prompted Link's decision? Since it is impossible to read the mind of even one's closest friend, only two things can be said with certainty. First, Link left Northwestern with the greatest reluctance. Margaret was loath to move as were, understandably, the children now aged thirteen, nine, eight, and five. Repeatedly in later years Link admitted that the happiest period of his academic life had been in Evanston. Second, Link decided, as he often insisted that he would, on the basis of what he thought best for *The Papers of Woodrow Wilson*. Princeton had the advantage of geography and a great library. Commuting to Washington would be much easier from there than from Evanston. The future publisher of the *Papers*, the Princeton University Press, would be just down the street. Firestone, with its many Wilson manuscripts, larger book collections, and rooms to house the project, provided something that Northwestern could not match.

These factors could be easily explained, but other unspoken considerations surely were at work. Princeton University carried more prestige than Northwestern. Its history department of twenty-nine outnumbered Northwestern's eleven, though it could be reasonably argued that the latter was superior in United States history. Although Link denied being subjected to pressure, the known wishes of the Woodrow Wilson Foundation must have played a part, since additional funds had to be raised. Then there was a possible role for Link at the Institute for Advanced Study, as he hinted in a letter to Kennan on October 9, 1959, written before his formal acceptance to Goheen. Finally, Link would have been less than human if he did not feel some vindication in being eagerly sought by a university that had let him be lured away in 1949 and had handled badly the attempt to bring him back in 1955.

The decision was not publicized at once. Not until October 8, 1959, were the Northwestern deans and the history department officially informed. Not until December 1 was the Evanston campus told. Not until December 5 did the Woodrow Wilson Foundation and Princeton University announce the full details. Everything was handled in the best taste. Tendering his resignation on October 8, Link wrote Leland: "I would not leave Northwestern University unless there were what I felt to be overpowering reasons for doing so. Even at this point it is difficult for me to contemplate breaking the very strong personal and professional ties that bind us to this institution and community." Having made his decision "only upon the grounds of the welfare of The Papers of Woodrow Wilson," he expressed gratitude to Northwestern for the support, understanding, and friendship "during a critical period in my career." He concluded: "If I have come to some maturity as a scholar and teacher, then much of the credit for this miracle must go to Northwestern University. I shall always feel that I am an integral part of this institution, and I will leave a part of myself here when we go to Princeton."

Even more eloquent was his public tribute to the Northwestern years. After the Board of Trustees on November 30, 1959, had accepted his resignation with very deep regret, Link issued a statement which the campus newspaper printed in full. After noting that the university officers had done "everything within their power to persuade me to remain" and after repeating the reasons why he thought he could better edit the Wilson papers in Princeton, he said: "I should feel deeply grieved if anyone drew the wrong conclusions from my decision to resign. I have . . . not only admiration but also deep affection for this university—its students, faculty, and administrative leaders. . . . They have made it possible in many ways to carry on scholarly research and writing. It is literally true that I could not have carried on the writing of my Wilson biography without the university's continuing generous assistance. One does not break easily such ties. . . . We will move next summer, but when we go we will leave much of ourselves behind, and we rejoice in the thought that we will never be strangers in this place."

My own feelings, somewhat bitter and not wholly accurate, were best expressed in a letter of December 13, 1959, to John M. Blum, who shared my fears that editing the papers would come to supersede writing the biography. "Arthur's impending departure," I wrote:

is a cruel blow to the university, to the department, and to me personally. And it came about in an ironical way that few outsiders can appreciate. You will recall how it all began soon after the New York meeting in 1957. The task was then to persuade Fosdick and Company that they should choose Arthur. And that task had to be faced only when Margaret and I, fortified by your advice, were unable to persuade Arthur that God was not calling him to the task. Making a virtue of necessity, we then strove to bring the Wilson project to Northwestern in order to anchor Arthur in Evanston. Then at the last minute the Princeton boys got in the game. Why shouldn't they? It would cost the department there not a cent, and they would draw upon Arthur's prestige. I was pretty certain in June 1958, when Arthur left for Oxford, that we were beaten. There was no reason to change my mind after our first conversations when he returned in September. Then a breath of hope appeared as he was genuinely flattered by the efforts made by Payson Wild and others to make it possible for him to stay here. He was still undecided when the Wilson people jumped the gun with a statement that he was moving. In mid-September he went to Princeton where Goheen played it just as skillfully as Dodds had bungled a comparable situation in 1955. At that point we lost to the facts of geography and distance. You know, and Arthur will tell anyone who talks with him, that he prefers to stay with this department and to live in Evanston; but he believes, and he is probably right, that the job can be done more efficiently along the Atlantic seaboard.

After he resigned, Link remained at Northwestern for almost an entire academic year. Although understandably, he kept aloof from the discussions regarding his successor, he taught full time, supervised the first steps in the Wilson project, and prepared for the printer the third volume of the biography. In June 1960 Sidney I. Roberts became the fourth person to complete a dissertation under Link; the first three were George S. McGovern, William H. Harbaugh, and Gerald N. Grob. Six more doctoral candidates, who would finish after June 1960, were working under his direction. They were James F. Findlay, Daniel R. Beaver, David W. Hirst, John E. Semonche, Justin L. Kestenbaum, and Claude E. Barfield. Link made important contributions to dissertations written under his colleagues, notably those by Benedict K. Zobrist, Warren F. Kuehl, Edward Lurie, and Fred H. Winkler. In April 1959 Link's election to the Executive Committee of the Mississippi Valley Historical Association brought further prestige to the department, for it marked the second consecutive year that Northwestern held two of the eleven elected seats on that body.

From Evanston Link oversaw the labors in Washington of his associate and assistant editors, John W. Davidson and David W. Hirst. Their mission was to obtain photocopies of all Wilson letters in public repositories and private hands. When a study room in the Library of Congress Annex was outgrown, space was rented during the winter in a nearby office building. In October 1959 Link engaged the services of Clifford F. Gehman, whose unique mastery of the obsolete Graham shorthand system would enable the editors to transcribe Wilson's hitherto undecipherable notes and comments. By March 1960 Link had assembled an Editorial Advisory Committee consisting of Samuel Flagg Bemis, Julian P. Boyd, Katharine R. Brand, Henry Steele Commager, Richard W. Leopold, and Arthur M. Schlesinger, Jr. In agreeing on January 29 to serve, I wrote: "Perhaps, too, this duty will tend to make me feel a little more kindly disposed toward a project which, without ever intending to do so, has intruded upon a personal and professional collaboration that has enriched my life and my scholarship."

Link brought back from England a semifinal draft of the third volume. It totalled 1,500 typed pages and carried Wilson to October 21, 1915. More than his previous writings, it drew upon hitherto unexploited British sources, especially the papers of James Bryce and Herbert Asquith. The latter was particularly valuable in containing copies of documents still under seal in the Public Record Office. Fifteen of the twenty chapters dealt with problems of neutrality; the other five broke new ground on Mexico, the Caribbean, and the Far Eastern crisis of 1915. As readers, Link enlisted new names: Herbert Nicholas, Sir Patrick Devlin, Ernest R. May, and Chihiro Hosoya. Bemis came to his aid for a second time, as did Hackett at Northwestern and Jean McLachlan of the Princeton University Press. She had edited this volume and its predecessor. The author thanked Davidson and Hirst and referred to Margaret and me as his most helpful critics and readers. The preface, dated December 26, 1959, barely hinted at the new findings; Link would wait until the preface of the fifth volume, published in 1965, to summarize his conclusions for the entire period from August 1914 to April 1917. *Wilson: The Struggle for Neutrality*, with its 693 pages of text, did not appear until the autumn of 1960, after Link had reached Princeton, but it was the product of and a fitting climax to his Northwestern years.

With its dedication to Raymond B. Fosdick, *The Struggle for Neutrality* also marked a transition to the Princeton years during which *The Papers of Woodrow Wilson* eventually superseded the biography. It is ironical that up to 1960 Link had not thanked in prefaces to his books any member of the Princeton history department, while before that date he had acknowledged the assistance of Billington, Scott, Cline, Hackett, and myself. Nor had he dedicated a book to any of his future colleagues. *The Road to the White House* was dedicated to Margaret Douglas Link. *Woodrow Wilson and the Progressive Era* was dedicated to his mother and father. Then followed *American Epoch*, to the late Edward Mead Earle; *The New Freedom*, to Richard W. Leopold; and *Wilson the Diplomatist*, to three "great teachers"—Howard K. Beale, Henry Steele Commager, and Fletcher M. Green.

Quite apart from scholarship, Northwestern was fortunate in having Link for eleven years. I need not tell you, I wrote Earle on May 21, 1953, "how enjoyable a companion Arthur is, how considerate and understanding a colleague he has been, how sound is his judgment in academic matters, and how discreet he has proven himself in personal relationships." Within the department he was closest to Scott, Boyce, Billington, and myself. None disliked him, although occasionally his prodigious publication and, after 1955, his high salary excited envy. The four Americanists worked in harmony despite differences in background, personality, and style. Each in his own way excelled in the classroom; each was eminent in his special field. All were thorough professionals and attended regularly the annual meetings of the American Historical Association and of the Mississippi Valley Historical Association, even when there was no subsidy from the university. Budgets were sometimes tight, as in May 1953 when Link, Ver Steeg, and I drove to Lexington. My junior colleagues wanted to take the cheapest motel room we could find in North Madison, Indiana, and I yielded only after they agreed to occupy the one double bed while I slept in the one single bed. Link's relations with graduate students were informal but not intimate; he never gossiped with them about their peers or departmental affairs. One recalls being examined orally at the Link home on some independent reading while perched on the toilet seat as Arthur painted the bathroom window.

I, too, was fortunate in having Link as a colleague from 1949 to 1960. We shared the survey course in American history, coedited the *Problems* volumes, agreed on almost every departmental issue or graduate student, and read each other's manuscripts, though obviously I read more than he did. We sat together at football games, and his vocal prowess there contrasted sharply with his restraint on the lecture platform. Indeed, after learning while at Oxford that Northwestern had defeated Michigan 55–24 and Ohio State 21–0, he wrote on November 10, 1958, that those victories almost made him regret having accepted in that year the Harmsworth chair. With Margaret we made an automobile tour of the Rockies in September 1953 and of the TVA country three years later. Sometimes togetherness threatened to go too far. In November 1951 we drove to the University of Chicago in a cold rain. I had to lean in front of him repeatedly to wipe the windshield. A few days later he came down with the mumps, a malady I was happy not to share.

The 206 letters we exchanged from 1949 to 1960 recall the fun we had and reveal the nature of our friendship. On September 29, 1954, he reported dining with a senior member of the Princeton department and hearing for the forty-third time about a European trip made a quarter century earlier. When Margaret asked me on August 2, 1953, whether I had ever seen Arthur drunk, I said no but added that someone else had. In mock seriousness Link wrote me on the seventeenth: "Since you will be my official biographer, I think it is essential that you have a true account of that celebrated episode. . . . What happened on that memorable occasion was this: Ray sneaked one of his powerful drinks on me without my knowing it. I felt myself getting high, told Margaret that I had had too much to drink, and asked your informant to drive me home. That is the long and short of it. . . . You may, therefore, write that I was high; please do not violate the historical canon by saying that I was drunk."

To be sure, we had disagreements, especially over the emphasis in the survey course in United States history. After one sharp exchange he wrote me on July 27, 1952: "Please don't think you ever have to apologize for anything you say to me. I think you know me pretty well by now and you know that I often speak my mind without any personal irritation. Of course, it is hard to do that by *letter* without giving the impression of irritation. Ours is, after all, a masculine friendship, and I am no Woodrow Wilson who has to be constantly soothed."

My feelings were best expressed in a letter of February 6, 1955, written right after a long telephone conversation about the offer he had received from Princeton. After hanging up last evening [I said while recalling events in 1954 when I was acting chairman],

> I realized that you might have been struck by my ostensibly unemotional and matter-of-fact attitude. I want to assure you that such was not my true feeling, that it took the very greatest will power to discuss your problem objectively and without the intrusion of personal feelings and appeals. I have always acted upon the assumption that between such close friends as you and I, certain things do not have to be said. On the other hand, that policy can be carried too far. And thus I want to say once and for all that your leaving Northwestern University will be for me a personal and professional loss, the extent of which I shudder to contemplate. It has been my fondest hope that we could keep the American quartet together. I knew it would be difficult, and you constituted the greatest difficulty. You know, as only Gray and Sim know, how hard I fought for Ray last year. I did everything I could to keep Clarence. And yet neither mattered as much to me as you. These things you and Margaret must have sensed; I hope you will forgive me for saying so now. For I say them for the record and for the record only. Your decision must be reached on other grounds. You must do what is best for your family and your career. Loyalty and affection for friends and other institutions must be a secondary consideration. I deplore these facts, but I recognize them. So there will be no appeal to you on the grounds of friendship and emotion.

When the second crisis erupted four years later, we both eschewed arguments based on friendship and emotion. Link's decision to leave was made, properly, on what he deemed best for *The Papers of Woodrow Wilson*. With his departure Northwestern suffered an irreplaceable loss, but it had been enriched by his presence during an extraordinarily productive period in his long and distinguished career.

Notes

This essay is based primarily on the more than 200 letters that I exchanged with Arthur S. and Margaret D. Link between March 1949 and June 1960, as well as on several written while this essay was in progress. All are in the Richard W. Leopold papers in the Northwestern University Archives. Other useful letters in that collection are those with Ray A. Billington, John M. Blum, Gray C. Boyce, Oscar Handlin, Frederick Merk, Thomas J. Pressly, Arthur M. Schlesinger, Arthur M. Schlesinger, Jr., Charles G. Sellers, Clarence L. Ver Steeg, and Raymond B. Fosdick. The Leopold papers contain minutes of the meetings of the Northwestern history department, interoffice memoranda, and a desk diary for each year from 1949 to 1960. The annual reports on the history department are in Dean Simeon E. Leland's papers in the University Archives, as are several of Leland's reports to President J. Roscoe Miller. Also of value in the University Archives are the papers of Payson S. Wild, Vice President and Dean of Faculties. Professor Link made available from his own papers in the Firestone Library at Princeton photocopies of the correspondence leading to his appointment at Northwestern in 1949. He also supplied photocopies of the Princeton University catalogs showing the membership of its history department for the years 1948–49, 1954–55, and 1958–59. David W. Hirst provided photocopies of items relating to the work of the Woodrow Wilson Centennial Celebration Commission. Richard A. Matré, Provost of the Loyola University Medical Center, recalled being examined while Link painted a bathroom window. Patrick M. Quinn, Northwestern's University Archivist, criticized constructively an earlier version of this essay. Most useful of all were the comments and suggestions by Margaret D. Link when she read that earlier version.

PART II
NEW PERSPECTIVES ON THE PROGRESSIVE YEARS

William A. Link

THE SOCIAL CONTEXT
OF SOUTHERN PROGRESSIVISM
1880–1930

In 1946, a young scholar of southern history barely out of graduate school advanced a reinterpretation of the Progressive Era South. The stereotype of the region as so "unbelievably backward, economically, politically, and socially" as to be incapable of sustaining any liberal reform movement needed exploding, wrote Arthur S. Link. A common objective of "greater economic, political, and social justice" united southern social reformers as diverse as Grangers, Greenbackers, Alliancemen, and Populists; along with early twentieth-century progressives, they sought to restructure the political system, stabilize the social structure, and extend popular control over the economy through the extension of the role of government. Link's reformers were governors, congressmen, legislators, and newspaper editors, whose primary objectives included state regulation and restrictions on the power of party machines; southern progressivism's culmination came during the presidency of Woodrow Wilson.

Although an admiring portrait, Link's assessment acknowledged "serious deficiencies." Committed to political reform, progressives were concerned neither with such deeply rooted social problems as the increase in farm tenancy nor with, implicitly, meaningful economic change for the mass of southerners. Similarly, they ignored the plight of blacks; while they condemned lynching, they opposed black political rights. "As far as progressive democracy went in the South," he concluded, "it was progressive democracy for the white man." Still, the reformers came out well; according to Link, they articulated the attitudes and political aspirations of most white southerners and led the fight against "conservatives and reactionaries."[1]

Four and a half decades after the publication of this seminal article, scholars continue to debate the origins, motivations, and consequences of reform along the lines just described. By including the category of social alongside political reform, subsequent historians of the Progressive Era South filled in the details of southern progressivism which Link initially sketched out. Still, by focusing on the narrow issue of whether reformers' stated motivations were genuine, the scholarly debate remains limited. Some historians, generally optimistic about the causes and consequences of progressivism, have stressed that reformers were motivated by humanitarian impulses and wanted, as Hugh C. Bailey enthusiastically writes, to "restore the mythical equality of opportunity which supposedly existed in the society of the past." Most of these optimists, like Link, have qualified their praise, but they agree that the reformers, impelled by humanitarianism and their view of regional progress, acted in accord with their announced objectives.[2] Other historians paint a more pessimistic portrait. In his classic *Origins of the New South, 1877–1913*, C. Vann Woodward characterized southern reform as a "paradoxical combination of white supremacy and progressivism" which had little relevance for the "political aspirations and deeper needs of the mass of the people"; despite the heralding of a new era of "washed, wormed, and weeviled Southerners," the condition of the rural masses probably worsened during the Progressive Era.[3]

Recently historians have grown even more critical. David L. Carlton contends that South Carolina child-labor reformers actually sought to extend middle-class control over mill families; their main objective was class stabilization. James L. Leloudis II asserts that while women school reformers in North Carolina espoused a humanitarian rhetoric, their goal was the molding of children into a manageable labor force. Extending this argument to the role of northern philanthropists in southern black education, James D. Anderson argues that their primary motivation in promoting "industrial" education was to develop an "economically efficient and politically stable" southern social system. Taken together, these pessimist historians have turned the optimist orthodoxy about progressivism on its head. Whereas optimist historians take reformers at their word and portray them as well-intentioned, democratic, and responding to documented social problems, pessimists assert that a mask of liberal rhetoric hid darker purposes and intentions. As J. Morgan Kousser writes, reality "differed . . . from the 'progressive' myth," for progressivism was for middle-class whites only.[4]

This essay suggests another model for understanding southern progressivism. Most scholars have examined only one part of southern progressivism—the reformers themselves—while they have neglected the social contexts that reformers encountered. They have assumed, incorrectly, that reform was primarily a personal, political process which can best be comprehended in the setting of elections, legislatures, and governors. Whereas scholars' emphases have been political and biographical, reform had its most important impact outside of politics: on processes, institutions, and communities. Although the traditional approach makes most rural southerners passive participants in reform, they in fact played a dynamic role.

In order to understand the full consequences of reform, we need to know less about the problematic category of motivation and more about reform's social context. In particular, we need to comprehend how social policy functioned in pre-bureaucratic culture; why reformers came to see traditional social policy as inadequate; with what consequences they began to transform it in the early decades of the twentieth century; and, perhaps most important, how rural southerners responded to these policy changes.

Pre-bureaucratic Social Policy and the Emergence of Reform

Despite variation over time and space, the pattern of governance remained similar for much of the nineteenth-century South. Government played a minor role in everyday life. The legal system complemented and buttressed other, more important, means of expressing power and hierarchy: racial, social, or geographical conflicts between groups ordinarily could be resolved without resort to government. In a society where personal and familial honor helped to shape interpersonal and group relations, the intervention of outsiders, especially government, met strong hostility. Where governmental power existed, it performed barebones functions. Few features of social policy were compulsory or coercive; except during grave emergencies, governmental policies deferred to the traditional sanctity of the individual and of personal liberty. This was a system of government in which bureaucracy played no role at all. Social policy and governance reflected social and political conditions, with factors such as class, locality, kinship, denomination, and political party determinative.[5]

Southerners shared a common political culture with other Americans, but distinctive conditions rendered southern social policy different. The absence of efficient overland transportation made centralized administration virtually impossible. Rather than settling in the compact villages typical of Europe and New England, most southerners peopled their communities in dispersed settlements; as late as 1910, historian Albert Bushnell Hart observed that most of them retained their frontier habits and lived "in the woods." Pretentious-sounding villages on maps often proved to refer to but two or three houses; nearly all of the rural churches were, according to Hart, "simply set down at crossroads," as were the schools and "mournful little cemeteries."[6]

In the rural South, centuries of isolation helped to form a restrictive definition of community. Localism fused with a rural republican ideology that articulated autonomy and self-reliance, stressed the dangers of concentrated power, and provided a political language for suspicion of outsiders. Southerners were the "historical partisans of personal liberty," explained one observer, and they were "naturally opposed to sumptuary laws of any kind."[7]

Two disparate instances of social policy, public health and liquor licensing, supply examples of the decentralized but also democratic style of pre-bureaucratic governance. Into the early years of the twentieth century, poor sanitary conditions produced major outbreaks of cholera, yellow fever, and smallpox. Mosquitoes, one of many menaces, made nights in Texas "memorable," a nineteenth century visitor remembered; there was no escape from them "except to hang yourself or run away." A Republican governor in Reconstruction Mississippi found his room "full of the hungriest, blood thirstiest crew of mosquitoes that ever presented a bill to me." Going from room to room to escape, he finally slept in his boots to protect his ankles and feet.[8]

Southern public health bureaucracies, despite efforts after Reconstruction to strengthen them, proved nearly powerless in practice. Health officials had scant knowledge about the etiology of disease and an even more incomplete comprehension of prevention. An observer was not far from the truth during the 1930s, when he claimed that a school boy then knew more about yellow fever than the entire Mississippi State Board of Health when it was created in 1877. In the case of yellow fever, physicians in Mississippi often skinned a calf and hung the meat to ward off contact with supposedly airborne infections. Others fired cannons, burned pitch, and prescribed limewater, garlic, and onions to deflect yellow fever-bearing miasmas. Treatment upon infection was hardly more effective.[9]

Even after the discovery of microscopic origins of disease revolutionized public health in the late decades of the nineteenth century, southern state health officials received necessary funds and political support only after epidemic disease had begun its periodic sweep. Few late nineteenth- and early twentieth-century state health officers could do more than gather scattered, inaccurate statistics and make pronouncements about the general condition of health. Even if localities did request help, state health officials were effectively limited to advice. When physicians in a western North Carolina county requested that the state test local dairies, the state health officer replied with undisguised sarcasm that, with an annual budget of only $2,000, he could ill afford "to indulge in 'luxuries.'"[10]

An even more serious problem was the lack of effective local health organization. Although most states provided for some form of local health organizations, in practice these were informal and almost completely powerless. In most states, local health officials performed few duties: periodically visiting the jail, fumigating the courthouse, and examining lunatics—for a minimal salary. They exercised supervisory powers over disease only in times of epidemic. Although local officials operated with near total autonomy, even conscientious health officials were dependent on their local medical practices. They thus exercised coercive power over their own patients with understandable reluctance. Whooping cough covered one eastern North Carolina community "like the dew," reported the county superintendent of health, but it would take "the Militia to undertake to carry out a quarantine." Because vigorous enforcement of quarantine would "rub the hair the wrong way" in an Appalachian community, local officials proceeded "slowly." Even if a local health officer tried to enforce regulations, communities often chose to ignore them.[11]

Local health officials also knew that little support would be forthcoming from state officials. Florida's health bureaucracy came into existence after a devastating outbreak of yellow fever in 1888, when the state legislature provided a State Board of Health with an assured revenue and with authority to restrict the inflow of yellow fever and smallpox from the Caribbean. Even so, the Board's actual power to aid local health officials—and to engage in any form of preventive public health—remained sharply curtailed. "We should like very much to hear from you occasionally," wrote Florida state health officer Joseph Y. Porter to a local health official. "I always appreciate the efforts of my medical brethren," he explained, "but I do not wish to impose upon them in forcing upon them a position which they do not care to fill and the requirements of which office they are indifferent to."[12]

Government's power over alcohol consumption provides another example of the limited scope of pre-bureaucratic southern social policy. The spread of the market economy during the nineteenth century spurred the commercialization of alcohol production, especially of corn whiskey; rising consumption, and excessive drinking, were commonplace in nineteenth-century southern life. In antebellum Mississippi, not only was it common to see "one who reeled as he walked," but only if Mississippians "lay and wallowed" were they regarded as drunk. Despite overdrinking, state and local governments before about 1905 avoided assuming a regulatory function over the distribution, sale, or consumption of alcohol. Although local option spread across the rural South in the post-Reconstruction period, illegal saloons, or "blind tigers," and bootleggers violated the law almost routinely, while federal internal revenue agents regularly collected taxes from dry counties in the South.[13]

The dispensary system of South Carolina, the boldest experiment in a state alcohol policy during the post-Reconstruction period, exposed the limits of state involvement. Under the leadership of Governor Benjamin R. Tillman, South Carolina adopted a dispensary law in 1892 that sought a middle ground between prohibition and the traditional "high license" system. Under the law, a State Commissioner purchased all liquors legally sold in the state. South Carolinians could then purchase alcoholic beverages in sealed packages of between one-half pint and five gallons upon a written application at local dispensaries; no alcohol could be consumed on the premises.

Although the results of this system were the closing of six hundred existing saloons in South Carolina and the opening of fifty-one dispensaries, Tillman's system adhered to familiar forms of governance. Rather than directly expropriating alcohol manufacturing and distribution—or abolishing it altogether, as prohibitionists preferred—the dispensary encouraged centralization of the liquor trade. Distillers remained unaffected, except that they now sold their alcohol to state dispensaries, and local distributorships followed a new system in which private individuals, awarded government franchises, worked as county dispensers on a profit basis. The dispensary system was, in fact, an excellent example of what Richard L. McCormick describes as "distributive" governance, which was typical of state-level administration during the pre-bureaucratic era.[14]

Defenders of dispensaries portrayed them as a compromise between the license system and absolute prohibition, but even this limited state regulation encountered popular opposition. Between July and mid-November 1893 alone there were eighty-eight tried cases of violations. Tillman responded with a hard-fisted policy of enforcement. He withdrew dispensary funds, which financed public schools, from those communities delinquent in enforcing the law, and established a force of special constables with wide-ranging powers.[15]

After reports that the upcountry town of Darlington was openly violating the law, Tillman dispatched a special force of four constables, who began raiding suspected violators. The use of special constables aroused popular indignation—fanned by the anti-Tillman press—and coalesced opposition to his program.

Opposition to the constables in Darlington and the dispensary system was expressed in a language of republicanism; the constables, composed entirely of outsiders, represented a military force with the power to violate personal liberty. Fear of outside intervention became a rallying issue, as rumors spread among the townspeople of spies arbitrarily searching the belongings of innocent women. Groups of armed men soon appeared, prepared to shoot the constables if they violated the sanctity of Darlington's homes.[16]

When Tillman threatened to send militia reinforcements, what became known as the Darlington Riot erupted. A mob, including "some of the best men in the State," convened at the Darlington courthouse and endorsed an anticonstable resolution and resistance to the execution of the law. Meanwhile the citizenry of nearby towns poured into Darlington, armed and spoiling for a fight. In early April 1894, a shootout occurred between eighteen constables and a local mob that left six dead and others wounded. When Tillman summoned the state militia to suppress what he called the "Whiskey Rebellion," all the state's militia units refused to serve. Facing civil war, Tillman issued a "peace proclamation" that eventually restored order. But the lesson was clear: heavy-handed, coercive government violated traditional sensibilities about the role of government in South Carolina.[17]

The Darlington Riot suggests that southern state and local officials walked a tightrope in enforcing aggressive social policy.[18] Tillman's dispensary—and coercive governmental intervention—was, in the experience of most southerners, the exception rather than the rule. Lacking any tradition of state intervention, southern state and local administrators were uniformly unsuccessful in constructing an effective bureaucracy. Instead, local communities held the upper hand. Sometimes operating in the spectacular fashion of the Darlington rioters, sometimes in less noticeable ways, southerners, white and black, were far from passive on the subject of governance. Because of the strength of community power, social policy in the nineteenth century remained decentralized and always required the approval of local communities.

Set in this social context, the emergence of southern progressivism takes on new significance. What reformers often portrayed as problems were actually social and political conditions long taken for granted. What reformers lamented as a decline in "community" was a contentious, intensely localistic, rural participatory democracy. Their prescription for social improvement and the means of enforcing it ran squarely into strong southern traditions of personal liberty and fear of and hostility toward outside intrusions.

If southern social reformers possessed a common characteristic, it was the belief that their region had undergone a serious crisis in the

late decades of the nineteenth century and that it faced renewed crises in the near future. To many, the problems were primarily moral rather than political or social, and southern progressivism drew from a grass-roots swell of moral reformers. Beginning in the 1880s, evangelical churchmen began to mobilize against what they perceived as increasing secularization and moral decline in southern society. Post-Reconstruction churchmen witnessed rapid social change that seemed to erode social, racial, and gender order. Assertive children and adolescents, the rising incidence of divorce, and urban-centered evils like dancing, card-playing, theater, and, above all, prostitution, all indicated a moral order in decline.[19]

The menace of alcohol, which embodied both individual and community corruption, became the central issue for moral reformers. To reformers, the connections between the saloon and moral decline were obvious, but they went a step further by linking corruption and moral decline to a passive social policy. Through the licensing system, government had allied with evil; through a permissive attitude toward prostitution and a policy of nonenforcement of Sabbath laws, government had become a willing participant in public corruption. By the 1890s, Christians were mobilized politically. "The time has come for *action*," declared one evangelical newspaper. "Every law that legalizes crime must be repealed; and every form of lawlessness must be punished by the strong arm of the law."[20] The erosion of moral values and traditional social organization was partly the reflection of rapid social and economic change, they acknowledged, but it was also the product of a corrupted political system. Prohibitionists thus became ardent advocates of restructuring governance by making state and local governments moral referees and by arming them with new coercive powers.

Near the turn of the twentieth century, reformers began to criticize and publicize what they considered evils in existing southern social and political institutions. The national popular press portrayed the South as a problem in need of solution.[21] Focusing on the South's unique social problems, these critics urged that the region abandon its traditions of localism and individualism in favor of a new ethos of civic-mindedness and cooperation. Other native southern social critics, agreeing with this analysis, drew from, even duplicated, the programs of social reformers elsewhere. But they were also self-consciously different, aware that their region possessed distinctive social conditions and problems. In the late nineteenth century, the South underwent a period of significant economic growth and discovered wholly new means of generating wealth in new sectors of industry, finance, and transportation. Yet the South remained a poor cousin, an underdeveloped society within the borders of a moderniz-

ing nation. The differences between southerners and Americans had become more, not less, obvious. The South retained a large, mobile, and ever-increasing rural population that would remain its majority well into the twentieth century. Social reformers in the North and Midwest addressed problems of rapid industrialization and the social and economic change that came with it. Not so with southern social critics. They believed that their social crisis came from underdevelopment and poverty, and their solutions were aimed at modernizing an entire people and an entire society. In the South, explained rural sociologist Eugene Cunningham Branson in 1902, isolation and poverty caused "social degeneracy and decay."[22] To avoid stagnation and eventual social and political instability, reformers believed that the South's entrenched patterns of individual and community conduct needed to change. They favored not only expanding railroad and hard-surfaced transportation to the hinterlands, but also extending the values of the outside world: an outward-directed standard of conduct and adherence to a modernized, cohesive "community." In advocating these changes, reformers clashed with rural precepts of personal honor, individualism, and community control that were cardinal principles of the nineteenth-century South. Thus establishing a refashioned notion of community with reinvigorated institutions ultimately meant wrenching those institutions from their social context.

Social reformers inaugurated their assault on traditional social policy with evangelical-style crusades. The first such crusade began in 1901, when reformers established the Southern Education Board (SEB) to coordinate a regional public-school campaign. Other crusades followed: a long campaign, beginning about 1902, to institute prohibition, first by state legislation, then by state constitutional amendment, and finally by federal constitutional amendment; a campaign, organized in 1904, to limit or eliminate child labor in factories; a campaign, inaugurated in 1909, to eradicate hookworm disease; and a campaign, which began in the South in the same year, to grant women the right to vote.

These crusades were closely connected. Educational reform attracted a variety of reformers who saw the schools as vehicles of wider societal changes and who later applied the methods of the educational crusade to other reform campaigns. Edgar Gardner Murphy, executive secretary of the SEB, spearheaded the child-labor crusade; Madeline McDowell Breckinridge, a veteran of Kentucky school reform, became a leading regional and national suffragist; and Wickliffe Rose, a Tennessee university professor and educational reformer, later headed the hookworm crusade and the Rockefeller Foundation's International Health Board.

Studies of southern progressivism have said little about the organizational bases of these crusades and how they mobilized public opinion and translated a crusade into long-term social policies. As several historians have suggested recently, trends in American Protestantism strongly influenced progressive reform, and, in the South, this was nowhere more apparent than in the crusades' style, organization, and objectives. Reformers, themselves suffused with evangelical values, adopted the technique and approach of the religious revival. Like the revival, the reform crusades sought to move public opinion toward a dramatic conviction of social sin. In the case of the educational crusade, the objective was public support for schools and higher local taxes. In the case of the hookworm crusade, the reformers sought to alter public attitudes about public health so as to make parasitic infection impossible.[23]

Careful advance preparations, including consultation with local leaders, assured success and public approval for the crusades. An example of thorough preparation modeled on evangelical methods comes from the Rockefeller Sanitary Commission, which was created in 1909 with a million-dollar endowment and led a five-year crusade to eradicate hookworm in the South. The commission's Administrative Secretary, Wickliffe Rose, endorsed a program of county dispensaries, traveling clinics that treated hookworm sufferers and preached the virtues of sanitation.

Rockefeller operatives laid a solid groundwork for each county crusade. They persuaded prominent citizens to endorse the dispensary and then organized a large delegation to meet with local officials to urge them to appropriate money for the dispensary. Success also depended on a massive publicity campaign, with printed placards and handbills announcing the dispensary and warning of the dangers of hookworms. "Parents who do not use this opportunity to rid their children of this dreaded-disease," read one placard in Alamance County, North Carolina, stood "squarely across their offspring's future, condemning them of times to an early death or a life of misery." These methods enabled the crusaders to reap a harvest of heavy turnout and public approbation.[24]

Among the most sophisticated employers of these evangelical-style methods were the prohibitionists, who conducted their campaign under the auspices of the Anti-Saloon League (ASL). Organized nationally in 1895, the ASL began to penetrate the South after the turn of the century. The league organized state chapters which conducted local campaigns and lobbied state legislatures. Like hookworm campaigners, ASL prohibitionists emphasized advance preparation and publicity. Relying on donations from local churches, the Virginia

league—like all the ASL state chapters, an interdenominational coalition—had an operating budget of $16,000 by 1906, only five years after its founding. As did other southern prohibitionists, the Virginia reformers used these funds to develop a sophisticated system of publicity.[25]

Examples abound of the staged preparation of early twentieth-century reform crusades. The patron saint of southern educational reform, northern department-store magnate Robert Curtis Ogden, led and financed a succession of railway expeditions transporting sympathetic northerners to Conferences for Education in the South. Ogden financed these extravaganzas as a way to coordinate the opinion of the "best men" of North and South and as a staging ground to organize the educational crusade. In 1902, the reformers launched a well prepared and well publicized crusade to improve southern schools. The child-labor crusade and the woman suffrage movement made similar use of staging and advance preparation.[26]

The centerpiece of all these crusades, as for nineteenth-century revivalists, was a public event designed to reverse popular attitudes. Crusaders spread the word through familiar means: a courthouse meeting, often held under a tent, before throngs streaming in from adjoining rural areas. During the early years of the crusade, educational rallies coincided with the visit of outside speakers; during the later years, local school improvement leagues, led and run by women, orchestrated the rallies. The results were often dramatic. Wickliffe Rose described a typical scene at a hookworm dispensary held in Sampson County, North Carolina. "As we neared the place," he wrote, "we met a line of buggies and wagons with whole families coming away; . . . a hundred or more people of both sexes and of all ages [were] waiting for attention."[27]

By the time southern suffragists emerged after 1910, these crusading techniques were well established. Like the other reformers, suffragists employed public events to rally public opinion behind the cause. The suffrage crusaders often organized parades which became, in the setting of southern towns, a startling dramatization of feminine assertiveness. The early suffrage parades occurred more or less spontaneously. Elisabeth Perry Collins remembered that suffragists in Greenville, South Carolina, attempted to join a community parade but were greeted by jeers and taunts. Lila Meade Valentine similarly remembered that it was "considered indecent for women to speak in public" and "to march in processions with their brothers." Yet parades, and other public suffrage demonstrations, soon became commonplace across the South.[28]

Like other crusaders, suffragists sent out visiting speakers, who

usually made their addresses at county seats. In some localities, suffragists organized "suffrage schools," which invited speakers and distributed suffragist literature. "Suffrage speakers have been present at the State Fair, most of the County Fairs, Farmers' meetings, and many picnics and other public gatherings and have aided greatly in extending the suffrage 'gospel,'" reported a Virginia suffragist in 1915. The most successful of these meetings featured speeches by suffragists of noted oratorical ability and statewide reputation, such as Lila Meade Valentine of Virginia or Madeline McDowell Breckinridge of Kentucky.[29]

Reformers focused the crusades almost entirely on public opinion. The primary purpose of the SEB's campaign in the Gulf Coast states, according to its field agent in 1903, was "to arouse an irresistible public opinion" for better schools. Although this was "a slow business," reformers would "hammer on" until educational enthusiasm became "a contagion with the people." The belief that a rallying crusade altered attitudes and shaped public opinion was pervasive among early twentieth-century social reformers. "Back of all progress, civic and educational," declared one of them, was "informed public opinion and quickened public conscience."[30]

The chief object of the reform revival became a kind of conversion experience through which collective public opinion radically recast its attitudes. The reformers' confidence in revival-based reform was not just based on its organizational style; they were convinced that reform would come suddenly. As in a revival, popular enthusiasm was carefully managed, staged, and manipulated. The Virginia novelist and feminist, Mary Johnston, explained that suffragists served as "a lighthouse in the middle of a lonely ocean" and "nuclei for . . . organized societies" out of which would come a "steady stream of converts." Another Virginian described educational reform in similar terms. Describing a commonwealth community that had become "turned upside down about the schools," the observer noted a stark contrast before and after the educational revival, and he predicted that "the broad and rapid sweep of its progress" would surely bring an "awakened spirit of the Va. people." A hookworm campaigner reported an equally startling effect on public opinion in northern Piedmont North Carolina. Although, at the outset of the campaign, the county superintendent of schools had been indifferent and "rather inclined to sneer at it," after the success of a local dispensary he worked "night and day for the cause and became the most enthusiastic man in the county."[31]

By reaching out to public opinion in terms which rural southerners easily comprehended, the crusades reaped a full harvest. Their suc-

cess provides additional evidence that the mass of southerners, far from passive objects of reform, performed an active role. Without the popular enthusiasm generated by the campaigns, it seems unlikely that political support for reform-oriented legislation would have materialized. And with what appeared to be a public consensus, reformers were able to convince legislators in state capitals to endorse sweeping new legislation that redefined governance and social policy in the South. Yet in redefining social policy, reformers clearly overstepped the mandate of the crusades. For if southern public opinion became aroused at the exposure of social conditions, it remained strongly committed to a pre-bureaucratic conception of governance.

A New Social Policy: Implementation and Resistance

Even as the reform crusades enjoyed early successes, a process had begun that would redefine the role of government in southern society. Early social reformers had criticized governance and endorsed a new degree of activism, but probably not all of them envisioned a full-blown bureaucratic, interventionist state. With the secular revival-crusades, reformers expressed common cultural attitudes and embraced traditional views of local autonomy and the solution of social problems. They believed that by altering public opinion, changed social conditions would follow.

In reality, the experience of implementing southern social reform would prove far more complex. At the root of social change, reformers came eventually to believe, lay the alteration of firmly rooted and popular folkways; democratically executed social policy would mean leaving the status quo unchanged. In taking the process of reform a step beyond the crusade model, then, reformers confronted a thorny dilemma. They discovered that implementing what they believed was a needed social change ran against local traditions and would necessitate the abandonment of community control. Operating within a restricted, disfranchised state made easier the rationalization of anti-democratic methods, as did cultural and attitudinal differences separating reformers and reformed. Yet continued problems in enforcing innovations in governance forced its practitioners to adapt and even to alter the new social policy.

The success of the reform crusades resulted in a host of new legislation. Southern state legislatures responded to the educational revival with new laws increasing state funds for schools and granting stronger powers to state school superintendents. Child-labor reformers persuaded most southern states to enact laws banning the employ-

ment of children in factories. Prohibitionists enjoyed a string of victories after 1905 in which statewide prohibition came into force by popular referendum or legislative enactment. Other reformers, operating in urban communities, obtained new laws or pressured municipal governments into enforcing existing ones to limit organized prostitution and ban business transactions on Sunday. In the wake of the hookworm campaign, state health departments experienced a dramatic growth in their coercive and regulatory powers. An offshoot of the general crusade for social betterment was the introduction of responsibility for social work and social welfare as part of state and local governments.

Increasingly, the agencies which these laws revitalized or created exercised centralized, bureaucratic governance. In some instances, as in the case of social efficiency modernizers, the transition from revival to bureaucracy was quick and almost unthinking. These reformers sought to change southern folkways by eliminating rural individualism and localism and substituting urbanized, dynamic values that would make social development along progressive lines possible. Social efficiency policy manifested itself primarily in a revamped approach to public schools and public health. With larger budgets and greater powers, educational and health bureaucracies expanded staff and exerted a supervisory role over local communities. State school superintendents expanded control earliest over teacher certification; they then focused on the curriculum. State departments of education also used new state funds to solidify their power. In order to receive money to build a new elementary school, for example, local communities had to accept centrally approved architectural designs. State officials also required that county and local school officials alter their approach to educational administration to fit that endorsed at the state level.[32]

The pattern in state health bureaucracies was similar. Most of the new power went to the executive officers of the state boards of health, and from their offices grew new supervisory staffs. Their powers were probably the most coercive of any agency of the new social policy. With new authority to establish quarantine—powers that had before only theoretically existed—state health officials expanded their role in preventive health care. They acquired increased control over public sanitation and, beginning in urban areas, enforced new standards with new rigor. Health officials also began to examine and treat schoolchildren. They introduced new programs of child and maternal welfare, of disease prevention through inoculation and basic sanitation, and participated in energetic programs to combat venereal disease and tuberculosis.[33]

Expansion of the state's welfare role constituted another category of the redefined social policy. The crusade to limit child labor was only one part of a broad effort to transform conceptions of the causes and solutions of poverty, social dislocation, and family disarray.[34] The crusade for woman suffrage could also be lumped, not inappropriately, into this category. Suffragists frequently contended that extending the franchise to women would make government more nurturing and maternal toward its citizens. Suffragists assumed—incorrectly as it turned out—that the vote for women would create a constituency for new legislation to uproot vice, wife-beating, child labor, and bad working conditions for women and to establish an equal role for women within the family.[35]

Another category of revised social policy involved the most ambitious effort to shape moral behavior in American history, state and national prohibition. In the South and elsewhere prohibitionists sought to redefine the relationship between government and the individual through a transformed social policy. Prohibitionists were the first to admit that there was never any time in which either statewide or later national prohibition was completely effective. Continued violations of prohibition, however, did not render it a failure, they argued. All civilized societies banned murder, but there would always be murder; larceny was illegal, yet it would always occur. Similarly, reformers reasoned, continued drinking was hardly an argument for prohibition's failure.

In a different category of social policy, race relations, most white social reformers welcomed disfranchisement and legally enforced racial segregation as necessary. Combined with a paternalism that dominated the thinking of social reformers, their belief in racial hierarchy exposed a dark, almost sinister side to southern progressives. But they also viewed political exclusion and *de jure* segregation as reforms that would stabilize white-black relations—which experienced a crisis of disturbing proportions during the 1890s—and, at least as they saw it, pave the way for black progress. To reformers, the disfranchised, one-party state provided opportunities for moderate, paternalistic racial policies. They believed that unlimited democracy and control by the mass of whites meant complete exclusion; the new administrative state, ironically, offered some benefits and services to blacks, those southerners most disinherited by progressive reform.

On the eve of World War I, then, a new approach to race relations was beginning to gain wider currency. Black education became a vehicle through which white reformers could seek black progress under the Jim Crow system. Programs, such as those which the General Education Board and the Rosenwald Fund sponsored, provided financial

resources for the improvement of black schools under the vague ru-
bric of "industrial education." Black educational reform also provided
a model for future white southern reformers who accepted segregation while endorsing a program of black progress. By the 1920s, however, white race reformers discovered an erosion of white and black
support for industrial education. In the pre–World War I period,
white moderates defined the "Negro Problem" primarily in terms of
black inadequacy; they believed that industrial education would transform black folkways with an infusion of Victorian standards of thrift
and hard work. By the 1920s, moderates allied with the Commission
on Interracial Cooperation (CIC), founded in 1919, espoused a different view: the primary problem was "discrimination" and "prejudice," not black inadequacy. Rejecting Victorian racial attitudes, CIC
reformers—despite rampant racism and generally bleak prospects
for blacks—sought improvements for blacks through the bureaucratic structures erected during the Progressive Era. Increasingly attracted to empirical definitions of racial problems, the CIC turned
toward the new social scientists of the South for answers. Will Winton
Alexander, the director of the CIC, thus established a close relationship with the Chapel Hill social scientist Howard W. Odum, who relied in turn on Alexander for advice, contacts with northern
philanthropic foundations, and a supply of some of the earliest southern students of race relations.[36]

Working closely with other practitioners of a new southern social
policy, CIC reformers enjoyed access to the educational and health
bureaucracies, and with them, they participated in state interracial
groups and conferences. Black public education and public health assumed a greater priority during the 1920s. A new network of social
scientists, typified by Odum and Wilson Gee of the University of Virginia, sponsored the incorporation of black welfare work into state
social welfare systems. By the end of the 1920s, what Alexander called
the "integration of the interracial movement with the official and volunteer social welfare agencies of many communities and states" had
already occurred in Alabama, Georgia, the Carolinas, Louisiana, Virginia, and Tennessee. In the remaining states interracialists claimed
"close and sympathetic relations" with social welfare agencies.[37]

In attempting to alter some fundamental characteristics of southern life, reformers had traveled a long road during the first three decades of the twentieth century. From the educational revival in 1901 to
the triumph of the woman suffrage movement in 1919, a series of
regional crusades popularized new ways of identifying and attempting to solve social problems. These crusades enjoyed widespread support from public opinion—a major objective—yet they also betrayed
a leadership style whose attitudes and intentions were far removed

from those of most rural southerners. It should come as little surprise that reformers—who were infused with the cultural and social values of the new industrial order, who came from self-confident and assertive town classes, and who regarded the traditional village and rural culture with disdain—would favor a new form of interventionism.

That the attempt to implement these changes met frequent opposition supplies still more evidence that rural southerners were more active than passive regarding both reform and its implementation. Although reformers and rural communities converged in the crusades because of their familiarity with rural evangelical traditions, the attempt to introduce bureaucratic governance was another matter. Indeed the introduction of policy innovations began a long struggle between reformers and local communities. Still, the nature of this opposition must be placed in context, for the great majority of those who opposed reform possessed no unifying ideology or group consciousness. Although social distinctions and conflicts affected almost every aspect of southern life, few country folk reacted to social reform and accompanying policy changes exclusively or even primarily in terms of class. Rather, usually viewing the issue as a contest between their community and outsiders, they resisted reforms because they and their parents had always opposed interference in local matters. Significantly, in almost every instance of resistance to southern social reform, the resisters refused to link arms with one another for one very clear reason: they were as suspicious, perhaps even more suspicious, of other rural southerners as they were of outside centralizers.

Nonetheless, the intensity of even this scattered opposition forced reformers to make concessions. Reformers discovered that the passage of a law, even with its new administrative baggage, rarely ensured its enforcement. Without state intervention, reformers depended on local support and cooperation. Often communities openly defied centralization. In many instances cooperation was entirely absent, and behind noncooperation lay the potent force of localism. Southerners had "jealously guarded" local autonomy for generations "at the cost of blood and treasure," observed a social reformer in 1905. It was therefore only natural that they would express a "traditional antipathy" toward "everything that savors of paternalism."[38]

Resistance was thus strongest wherever communities, especially rural communities, faced the deprivation of traditional autonomy. Benjamin Earle Washburn, who worked with the Rockefeller hookworm campaign and early county health programs in North Carolina, expressed his frustration with local resistance in a fable that he wrote about 1918. Public health conditions in his fictitious Miasma County, North Carolina, like the rest of the rural South, were atrocious. Open surface privies, which sanitarians regarded as public health threats,

prevailed; hookworms were of a "ferocious type"; and "everybody took Quinine except the Lady Principal of the County High School and she took Quin-een." Because of the "Rule and Fashion" that governed Miasma County, everyone existed in a "Run Down Condition from these causes" and was "Predisposed to Typhoid and Diarrhea—and these diseases did their part."

Local physicians only abetted Miasma's problems. "Old Doc Richards," who dispensed what was "Technically Known as Hot Air," opposed public health measures because, he claimed, they meant sacrificing personal liberty. As he reminded the locals, he "knew the county Much better than an Outsider could ever know it," and public health meant a tax increase to pay a "Rank outsider,—maybe some Yankee who wouldn't understand Miasma and her ways." The county commissioners appointed Richards as full-time county health officer.

Not surprisingly, Miasma's experiment with public health was brief. Hookworms and mosquitoes "didn't keep their contract with Doc; and Typhoid Fever was about as Gay As Ever and Infant Diarrhea acted like it had never heard of a Health Officer." The county commissioners abolished the failed local health structure, and Washburn's story reached its unhappy conclusion: Miasma County returned to the "Good Old Times when each family took care of itself without having the County or State Meddle with Its Personal Affairs."[39]

Washburn's fable was overdrawn, and it reflected the imperiousness of early twentieth-century health reformers. But it portrayed the frustration of reformers accurately. Countless other southern rural communities were as suspicious as Miasma County of the costly innovation of health reform and of the centralization and coercion that came with it. Rural southerners drew on a deep tradition of fear and anger toward the medical profession and public health measures such as vaccination. Recipients of nineteenth-century medical treatment often fared worse than they would have with no treatment at all, and rural southerners feared that modern public health would bring even more life-threatening ministrations. In fact, it is undeniable that public health measures were sometimes just that. Treatment for hookworm, which involved highly toxic substances such as thymol, carbolic acid, or oil of chenopodium, could result in violent, often fatal reactions, if taken improperly.

Reformers reported widespread indifference or hostility to public health throughout the rural South. Rural Kentuckians, wrote a health official in 1913, possessed no faith in preventive medicine or personal hygiene. Audiences refused to admit "the existence of Hookworm or other parasites; they do not believe that they are infected with these parasites even if they do exist." The Louisiana state health officer in

1916 made a similar observation. It would take a "world of education," he concluded, to persuade rural Louisianans to endorse the "most necessary sanitary reforms."[40] Although post–World War I reformers concluded that rural health depended upon the bureaucratization of county health systems, rural opposition often translated into the unwillingness of local government to finance public health work. In 1915, the Tennessee state health officer observed that funds were "tight, . . . especially in the cotton counties and in mining counties," and the county courts were "not disposed to open the strongbox." Throughout the 1920s, state officials faced local resistance to pay for reforms.[41]

In exchange for local cooperation, health officials had to acknowledge the importance of community control. Confronted with the problem of a man who refused to "observe any precautions at all" and who was "feared by the entire community" a Florida public health official appealed to the state health officer, Joseph Y. Porter, for help in 1916. Porter's response made a larger point about the limitations of state power. The State Board of Health, rather than a "judiciary body" with any "power to imprison or exert policy authority," could only influence local communities "by persuasive methods and persistent effort."[42]

Localism thus forced modernizers to modify their policies. Rather than extending the blessings of modern sanitation all at once, reformers had to introduce it incrementally, and they had their greatest successes where alliances were struck with local communities. Often the price of cooperation was the participation of local physicians. "I have not worked in a state where the citizens . . . were more annoying in their insistence" that local candidates be employed in public health positions, complained an International Health Board official about Louisiana in 1921. Most of these candidates had "some ax to grind," and thus public health work easily became mired in local politics.[43]

The necessity of compromise with localism became just as evident to modernizing school officials. In the cases of school consolidation and compulsory education, southern educators faced hostility and noncooperation. Because they depended even more than health officials upon local participation—through the support of tax revenues and attendance—school officials bowed to local opinion. School consolidation, which involved the closing of community schools and their centralization at some other location, carried a genuine potential for rebellion. When a Fayette County, Tennessee, community lost its school in 1929 to a consolidation, school patrons complained that educational officials "absolutely pay us no mind" and that "we have asked them a number of times for our school back but they will not do

us this favor." In fact, school officials usually compromised. Consolidation was an ideal solution for rural schools, observed the Florida state superintendent in 1919, "but it is a matter that always creates . . . dissatisfaction, and one that has to be handled very wisely."[44]

The dilemma of implementing centralization while retaining community cooperation was even more obvious in the instance of compulsory education. Enforcement introduced a strong degree of coercion to local school administration. Although every southern state had enacted effective compulsory education legislation by the end of the 1920s, enforcement still depended on the voluntary participation of local communities. In North Carolina, which enacted what was perhaps the strongest compulsory education law in the South after 1919, enforcement was sporadic and uneven. In rural communities, consistent enforcement would require farm families to give up the labor of children, and few were willing to make that sacrifice, and the best that school officials could do was to schedule schools so as to avoid mass desertion during peak labor demand.[45]

The introduction of new welfare policies met similar obstacles. Restrictions on child labor never enjoyed substantial support from rural parents. To be sure, few reformers attempted to restrict child labor on the farm, which they regarded as healthy and normal. But even in those areas of the South where reformers concentrated—the textile belt and the canneries of the Gulf Coast—enforcement lagged well into the 1920s. The preeminent southern child-labor advocate of his generation, Alexander Jeffrey McKelway, acknowledged widespread resistance in 1914. Although "hopeful and sanguine" about the effectiveness of legislation against child labor when he began the crusade, "with infinite sadness" McKelway admitted "how grievously I was mistaken."[46]

The primary problem for child-labor reformers, as for health and educational reformers, was to secure local cooperation. A reformer in Alabama wrote in 1913 that local officials exhibited "great laxity" in enforcement of the state's laws against child labor, especially in mill communities. The North Carolina reformer Charles Lee Coon reached a similar conclusion. Close investigation of working conditions, he wrote, revealed that the laws were "flagrantly violated in all sections of the State." In 1914, a National Child Labor Committee field agent discovered that nonenforcement was the rule in the South. When the investigator, Herschel H. Jones, asked a Columbus, Mississippi, sheriff—who was, by law, responsible for enforcement of the child-labor law—what the age limit for mill work was, he professed ignorance and admitted that he had in fact never visited the town's factory.[47]

Resistance to child-labor restrictions came not just from mill owners

concerned about lower labor costs but also from parents determined to use the labor of their children. Recent studies have shown that child labor was a central part of worker culture and, where given the chance to express their opinions, workers strongly opposed the reform. In 1909, a Macon, Georgia, labor leader, described child-labor reform as "a great joke" because "mill-workers themselves" opposed it. Although reformers usually dismissed worker opposition as indicative of pervasive "feudalism" in the mill village or of the degeneracy of workers' family structure, the noncooperation of workers figured prominently in the failure of child-labor legislation. Nor is there much evidence that children preferred the school to the mill, where most of their friends and family worked. One mother of mill workers told an investigator that it was "difficult to get children to school" because "she could not get them to go."[48] This pattern of reform and resistance also appeared in the case of woman suffrage. What we know about the woman suffrage movement in the South suggests that its base was overwhelmingly urban. The profile of its leaders and supporters resembled the profile of the leaders and supporters of other social reforms—that is to say, it was dominated by an upper middle-class, white, urban Protestant elite. When urban suffragists attempted to extend their base to the rural South, they often encountered indifference or hostility. Rural women in Kentucky treated suffrage "lightly," if at all, as a suffragist complained in 1910.[49]

Suffragists, facing the same quandary as other social reformers, defined an existing social condition as evil but ignored the condition's firm roots in rural society. Their attitudes toward reform, and the mass of southerners affected by it, was clearly paternalistic. What one suffragist declared about Lynchburg, Virginia, could easily be the complaint of any southern reformer. "We have organized a *club*," she reported in 1911, "but there is such a dense mist of 'chivalry' (!) obscuring the minds of our men, and enveloping their womenkind in its malarial haziness that we *need* illumination." Suffragists often expressed their impatience with the traditional ways of the rural South. After a visit to what she called a "little and *cliquey*" village which showed little interest in woman suffrage, a Virginia organizer pronounced country people "backward" and lacking in proper "leadership." A Kentucky suffragist came to a similar conclusion when she described rural people there as "hopeless . . . wooden heads" when it came to woman suffrage.[50]

A comparable problem of inaugurating an unpopular reform confronted prohibitionists. Whether enforced by local option, state law, or federal constitutional amendment, prohibition usually engendered popular resistance, but that did not necessarily doom the Noble Experiment to failure. Moderate prohibitionists did accomplish their

central objective: the abolition of the "open" saloon, from which, they maintained, sprang vice, crime, and social disorder. In 1919, radical prohibitionists, with the passage of the Volstead Act, transformed this moderate policy into an aggressive program of moral regulation. Their new departure, especially during the early years of implementation, did enjoy significant successes. Nationwide, consumption declined dramatically—by close to one-half—and the alcoholism endemic to working-class and frontier life disappeared. Alcohol was available but overpriced, reported a Virginia observer about state prohibition in 1917, and there was "not enough 'violation' here to disturb a prayer meeting."[51]

Regardless of reduced consumption, drinking persisted and an illicit trade developed. In North Carolina, Josiah W. Bailey, then Collector of Internal Revenue for the state's Eastern District, asserted in 1917 that moonshining rose in direct proportion to the reduction in bottled liquor from other states. Moonshining expanded from the mountain South into the rest of the region, providing irresistible opportunities for cash-poor farmers. Between 1920 and 1927, southern stills—most of them in Virginia, the Carolinas, Georgia, and Alabama—composed over half of those seized by federal agents across the nation, a proportion that grew to 90 percent by 1948.[52]

Southern state governments, as in the rest of the United States, made only a half-hearted effort at enforcement of federal prohibition. State prohibition, where it existed before 1920, relied on local enforcement; national prohibition brought little change. Typically, state legislators made no special appropriation and established no special enforcement machinery, instead throwing the problem entirely upon local government. The exception was Virginia, which established a Prohibition Commission in 1916, the only state in the Union to do so. The Commission had power not only to interdict illegal liquor trading but also to dismiss, through an "ouster" law, local officials who were derelict in enforcing prohibition. Nonetheless, the Virginia Prohibition Commission found effective enforcement not a simple task. Commissioner Peters complained of insufficient funds and staff and, despite support from the Anti-Saloon League, encountered stiff resistance from local officials. The ouster law proved ineffective and became a dead letter. When the state reduced the Commission's budget in 1920, vigorous enforcement of prohibition in Virginia came to an end.[53]

As with other forms of social policy, officials frequently faced indifference and passive noncooperation. Many southerners, even some prohibitionists, had reservations about the degree of coercion necessary to make the laws effective. "I am a PROHIBITIONIST," one Virginian wrote in 1919, "but not a fool on the subject." He voted to make

the Commonwealth dry "for the benefit of the fellow who can not use whiskey without getting drunk." Would it be possible, he wondered, for state officials to make some confiscated "very fine OLD MELLOW whiskey" available to him?[54]

Other southerners had more serious reservations. Josiah W. Bailey, North Carolina Baptist editor and staunch prohibitionist, predicted in 1907 that national prohibition was unworkable and would require "not only a China-like centralization, but a China-like power to behead." Advocates of prohibition found themselves in a dilemma: they faced the unpleasant choice of acknowledging widespread violations or of instituting an enforcement policy sure to provoke even greater opposition.[55]

Probably more than other advocates of a new social policy, prohibitionists experienced the persisting strength of individualism and localism in the rural South. In the Appalachian South, moonshiners engaged in a generation of violent struggle against "revenuers," the federal agents who sought payment of the federal excise tax; subsequently, they continued to do battle against prohibition agents. In many communities, moonshiners enjoyed public approval and support, and enforcement of the law provoked violence. "The moonshine work is get[t]ing to be so [dangerous] you will have to furnish me with a high power rifel [sic] or a repe[a]ting shot gun," reported an agent in mountainous Virginia.[56]

This essay has argued that a clearer assessment of early twentieth-century reform requires a reexamination of its social context and consequences. Most historians of southern progressivism have neglected the social environment that reformers sought to change and the impact on it of their policy innovations. By focusing on reformers and their motivations, scholars have placed responsibility for major intergenerational social and political changes on their shoulders.

The real significance of Progressive Era social reform is to be found in the society which reformers confronted: a dispersed, rural population with strong traditions of individualism and localism. What the reformers sought amounted to revolutionary changes in governance and the administration of social policy, and they succeeded in introducing a new measure of interventionism in state and local government, designed to reorient fundamental qualities of southern culture. Popular antagonism to these changes, although not always fully or effectively articulated, frequently imperiled programs of modernization and administrative centralization. The implementation of the reformers' new social policy brought about not only centralized governance, but also localized community resistance. Historians of Progressive Era reform in the South must include both in their analyses.

Notes

[1] Arthur S. Link, "The Progressive Movement in the South, 1870–1914," *North Carolina Historical Review* 23 (1946):172, 179–92, 194–95. For their careful readings of and useful suggestions about this essay, I am grateful to Edward L. Ayers, Lewis Bateman, O. Vernon Burton, Robert M. Calhoon, John T. Kneebone, Susannah J. Link, and Bruce A. Ragsdale. For their financial assistance, I must also acknowledge the Rockefeller Archive Center and the UNCG Research Council.

[2] Hugh C. Bailey, *Liberalism in the New South: Southern Social Reformers and the Progressive Movement* (Coral Gables, Florida, 1969), pp. 11–13; Dewey W. Grantham, *Southern Progressivism: The Reconciliation of Progress and Tradition* (Knoxville, Tennessee, 1983). For another view, see Joseph F. Kett, "Women and the Progressive Impulse in Southern Education," in Walter J. Fraser, Jr., R. Frank Saunders, Jr., and Jon L. Wakelyn, eds., *The Web of Southern Social Relations* (Athens, Georgia, 1985), pp. 166–80.

[3] C. Vann Woodward, *Origins of the New South, 1877–1913* (Baton Rouge, Louisiana, 1951), pp. 371, 395, 427–28.

[4] David L. Carlton, *Mill and Town in South Carolina, 1880–1920* (Baton Rouge, Louisiana, 1982); James L. Leloudis II, "School Reform in the New South: The Woman's Association for the Betterment of Public School Houses in North Carolina, 1902–1919," *Journal of American History* 69 (March 1983):887–88, 890; James D. Anderson, "Northern Foundations and the Shaping of Southern Black Rural Education, 1902–1935," *History of Education Quarterly* 18 (1978):392; Anderson, *The Education of Blacks in the South, 1860–1935* (Chapel Hill, North Carolina, 1988), p. 80; J. Morgan Kousser, "Progressivism—For Middle-Class Whites Only: North Carolina Education, 1880–1910," *Journal of Southern History* 46 (May 1980):191.

[5] On honor, see Bertram Wyatt-Brown, *Southern Honor: Ethics and Behavior in the Old South* (New York, 1982). For a different view of honor, see Edward L. Ayers, *Vengeance & Justice: Crime and Punishment in the 19th-Century American South* (New York, 1983), pp. 9–33. For a fuller discussion of the operation of governance in the instance of public education, consult William A. Link, *A Hard Country and a Lonely Place: Schooling, Society, and Reform in Rural Virginia, 1870–1920* (Chapel Hill, North Carolina, 1986), pp. 24–44.

[6] Albert Bushnell Hart, *The Southern South* (New York and London, 1910), p. 23.

[7] John E. White, "Prohibition: The New Task and Opportunity of the South," *South Atlantic Quarterly* 7 (April 1908):135.

[8] James Brooks Speer, "Contagion and the Constitution: Public Health in the Texas Coastal Region, 1836–1909" (Ph.D. dissertation, Rice University, 1974), p. 29; Marshall Scott Legan, "The Evolution of Public Health Services in Mississippi, 1865–1910" (Ph.D. dissertation, University of Mississippi, 1968), pp. 36–7.

[9] Margaret Warner, "Local Control Versus National Interest: The Debate Over Southern Public Health, 1878–1884," *Journal of Southern History* 50 (1984):407–28; Speer, "Contagion and the Constitution," p. 14; Legan, "The Evolution of Public Health Services in Mississippi," pp. 24–5, 35–8.

[10] Chase P. Ambler to Richard H. Lewis, September 7, 1905; Lewis to Ambler, September 9, 1905, Records of the North Carolina Division of Health Services, North Carolina Division of Archives and History, Raleigh; hereinafter cited as NCDHS.

[11] George M. Cooper to Watson S. Rankin, January 19, 1912; C. W. Hunt to Rankin, January 12, March 4, 1912, *ibid.*

[12] Joseph Y. Porter to B. P. Matheson, February 19, 1907, Records of the Florida State Board of Health, Series 46: Correspondence of the State Board of Health, 1899–1926, Box 13, Folder 3, Florida State Archives, Tallahassee; hereinafter cited as FSBH, followed by series, box, and folder numbers.

[13] Sellers, *The Prohibition Movement in Alabama*, pp. 26–7, 68; Jessie Mary Branch, speech before the Columbiana Temperance Union, *Clinton (Miss.) Argus*, March 1, 1884; Whitener, *Prohibition in North Carolina*, p. 12; William Graham Davis, "Attacking the 'Matchless Evil': Temperance and Prohibition in Mississippi, 1817–1908" (Ph.D. dissertation, Mississippi State University, 1975), pp. 214–19.

[14] On dispensaries, see Niels Christensen, Jr., "The State Dispensaries of South Carolina," *Annals of the American Academy of Political and Social Science* 32 (November 1908):75–85; John Evans Eubanks, *Ben Tillman's Baby: The Dispensary System of South Carolina, 1892–1915* (Augusta, Ga., n.p., 1950), pp. 66–83; Ellen Alexander Hendricks, "The South Carolina Dispensary System," *North Carolina Historical Review* 22 (April 1945):188–89. On "distributive" governance, see Richard L. McCormick, "The Party Period and Public Policy: An Exploratory Hypothesis," *Journal of American History* 66 (1979):279–98.

[15] Hendricks, "The South Carolina Dispensary System," pp. 188–89.

[16] W. F. Dargan, "A Last Word in the South Carolina Liquor Law," *North American Review* 159 (1894):52–60; Eubanks, *Ben Tillman's Baby*, pp. 87–104, provides the most complete account of the Darlington Riot, but see also Hendricks, "The South Carolina Dispensary System," pp. 193–97.

[17] For contrasting views of the Darlington Riot, see Benjamin Tillman, "History of the South Carolina Liquor Law," *North American Review* 158 (1894): 140–49, 513–19; Dargan, "A Last Word," pp. 52–60.

[18] Whitener, *Prohibition in North Carolina*, pp. 61–80; William F. Holmes, "Moonshining and Collective Violence, 1890–1895," *Journal of American History* 67 (1980):589–611, and "Moonshining and Whitecaps in Alabama, 1893," *Alabama Review* 34 (1981):31–49; Davis, "Attacking the 'Matchless Evil,'" pp. 157–69.

[19] For general accounts, see Hunter Parish, *The Circuit Rider Dismounts: A Social History of Southern Methodism, 1865–1900* (Richmond: The Dietz Press, 1938), pp. 305–61; John Lee Eighmy, *Churches in Cultural Captivity: A History of the Social Attitudes of Southern Baptists* (Knoxville: University of Tennessee Press, 1972), pp. 48–54.

[20] Philo, "Sabbath Desecration," *Alabama Christian Advocate*, March 15, 1888.

[21] For example, see M. L. Avary, "Old and the New Regime in the South," *Gunton's Review* 25 (October 1903):322–29; William Garrott Brown, "Of the North's Part in Southern Betterment," *Outlook* 78 (October 15, 1904):415–18; Albert Bushnell Hart, "Conditions of the Southern Problem," *Independent* 58 (March 23, 1905):644–49; "Light Breaking in the South," *Nation* 77 (Novem-

ber 5, 1903):356; Walter Hines Page, "The Real Southern Problem," *World's Work* 7 (December 1903):4167; "Southern (Not the Negro) Question," *Nation* 77 (October 22, 1903):315–16; "Southern Question," *Outlook* 76 (January 16, 1904):189–90.

22 Eugene Cunningham Branson, "The Real 'Southern Question,'" *World's Work* (1902):1889.

23 Robert M. Crunden, *Ministers of Reform: The Progressives' Achievement in American Civilization, 1889–1920* (New York: Basic Books, 1982); David B. Danbom, *"The World of Hope": Progressivism and the Struggle for an Ethical Public Life* (Philadelphia: Temple University Press, 1987); Ettling, *The Germ of Laziness*, pp. viii–ix, 162–64.

24 Benjamin Earle Washburn, *The Hookworm Campaign in Alamance County, North Carolina* (Raleigh: E. M. Uzzell & Co., 1914), p. 16. On the hookworm campaign, see William A. Link, "'The Harvest is Ripe, But the Laborers are Few': The Hookworm Crusade in North Carolina, 1909–1915," *North Carolina Historical Review* (forthcoming).

25 K. Austin Kerr, *Organized for Prohibition: A New History of the Anti-Saloon League* (New Haven: Yale University Press, 1985); Pearson and Hendricks, *Liquor and Anti-Liquor in Virginia*, pp. 222–45.

26 Link, *A Hard Country and a Lonely Place*, pp. 98–108; Davidson, *Child Labor Legislation in the Southern Textile States*, pp. 52–69, on the child labor crusade. There is no good single history of southern suffragists. But see Josephine Bone Floyd, "Rebecca Latimer Felton: Champion of Women's Rights," *Georgia Historical Quarterly* 30 (June 1946):81–104; Grace Elizabeth Prescott, "The Woman Suffrage Movement in Memphis: Its Place in the State, Sectional and National Movements," *West Tennessee Historical Society Papers* 18 (1964):87–94; A. Elizabeth Taylor, "The Origin of the Woman Suffrage Movement in Georgia," *Georgia Historical Quarterly* 28 (June 1944):63–79, "The Last Phase of the Woman Suffrage Movement in Georgia," *Georgia Historical Quarterly* 43 (March 1959):16–21; "The Woman Suffrage Movement in Texas," *Journal of Southern History* 17 (May 1951):194–209.

27 Wickliffe Rose to Frederick T. Gates, August 14, 1911, Series 2, Box 6, Folder 117, the Records of the Rockefeller Sanitary Commission, Rockefeller Archive Center, North Tarrytown, N.Y.; hereinafter cited as RSC, followed by series, box, and folder numbers.

28 Constance Ashton Myers, notes on an interview with Elisabeth Perry Collins (b. 1892), April 6, 1974, the Papers of Constance Ashton Myers, South Caroliniana Library, University of South Carolina; Lila Meade Valentine, address at the annual meeting of the Richmond Equal Suffrage League, January 7, 1919, Virginia Woman Suffrage Papers, 1910–1925, Virginia State Library and Archives, Richmond.

29 Elizabeth H. Lewis to Jessie Townshend, March 6, 1915; "Report of the State Secretary to the Fifth Annual Convention of the Equal Suffrage League of Virginia, Richmond, December 9–10–11, 1915," Virginia Woman Suffrage Papers.

30 Edwin A. Alderman, "The Southwestern Field," *Annals of the American Academy of Political and Social Science* 22 (June–December 1903):287, 291;

James Yadkin Joyner, "How the Southern Education Board Has Helped and Can Help the South," October 12, 1908, Southern Education Board Papers, Joyner Series, Box 32, Folder 19, Southern Historical Collection, University of North Carolina, Chapel Hill, Library.

[31] Mary Johnston, speech at a suffrage rally, May 26, 1910, the Papers of Mary Johnston (#3588), Box 27, Manuscripts Department, University of Virginia Library; "Report of Robert Frazer, Field Agent for Virginia of the Southern Education Board, Dec. 15, 1904," the Papers of Hollis Burke Frissell, University Archives, Hampton University Library; Benjamin Earle Washburn to C. L. Pridgen, July 6, 1913, RSC, Series 2, Box 7, Folder 129.

[32] Link, *A Hard Country and a Lonely Place*, pp. 124–48.

[33] William A. Link, "Privies, Progressivism, and Public Schools: Health Reform and Education in the Rural South, 1909–1920," *Journal of Southern History* 54 (November 1988):623–642.

[34] On the dialogue between supporters and opponents of child labor, see LeeAnn Whites, "The De Graffenried Controversy: Class, Race, and Gender in the New South," *Journal of Southern History* 54 (August 1988):449–78.

[35] Clipping in unidentified newspaper, June 24, 1914, the Records of the South Carolina League of Women Voters, South Caroliniana Library.

[36] Through the Alexander-Odum pipeline, for example, travelled Thomas Jackson Woofter, Jr., whose research on race relations was first sponsored by the Commission in Atlanta and who transferred his research base to Chapel Hill and Odum's Institute for Research in the Social Sciences. A similar path was followed, in reverse, by Arthur Raper, who collaborated with Odum and then became part of the CIC's research staff in 1927. For the definitive account of the origins of the CIC, see Charles Kirk Pilkington, "The Trials of Brotherhood: The Founding of the Commission on Interracial Cooperation," *Georgia Historical Quarterly* 64 (Spring 1985):55–80. Also see Wilma Dykeman and James Stokely, *Seeds of Southern Change: The Life of Will Alexander* (Chicago: University of Chicago Press, 1962), pp. 58–76, and Jacquelyn Dowd Hall, *Revolt Against Chivalry: Jesse Daniel Ames and the Women's Campaign Against Lynching* (New York: Columbia University Press, 1979), pp. 60–65.

[37] "Commission on Interracial Cooperation, Summary of Work 1925–26," Records of the Laura Spelman Rockefeller Memorial, Series 3.8. Box 96, Folder 975, Rockefeller Archive Center.

[38] Neal L. Anderson, "Child Labor Legislation in the South," *Annals of the American Academy of Social and Political Science* 25 (May 1905):503.

[39] Benjamin Earle Washburn, "The Dog in the Manger: Not a Fable," ca. 1917–1918, NCDHS.

[40] "Report of the Educational work for 1913. By the State Board of Health of Kentucky," RSC/S2/B3/F90; Oscar Dowling to John A. Ferrell, December 14, 1916, the Records of the International Health Board, Rockefeller Foundation Archives, Rockefeller Archive Center, Series 1.2, Box 24, Folder 373; hereinafter cited as IHB, followed by series, box, and folder numbers.

[41] Olin West to Ferrell, March 16, 1915, IHB/B4/F70; P. E. Blackerby to Ferrell, January 2, 1925, *ibid.*, Box 212, Folder 2709.

[42] Elise Louise Forrest to Porter, October 2, 1916; Porter to Forrest, October 4, 1916, FSBH/S46/B31/F2.

[43] Platt W. Covington to Ferrell, May 24, 1921, IHB/S1.2/B107/F1468.

[44] J. E. Gatley *et al.* to Perry L. Harned, January 24, 1929, the Records of the Tennessee Commissioner of Education, Series 1, Box 27, Folder 10, Tennessee State Library and Archives; W. N. Sheats to E. B. Currie, May 8, 1919, Record Group 400: Department of Education Records, Series 249B: General Correspondence of the State Superintendent, Box 3, Florida State Archives.

[45] See E. T. Atkinson to James Y. Joyner, February 26, 1918; A. T. Allen to R. E. Price, September 3, 1927, North Carolina Superintendent of Public Instruction Records, Series 5, Boxes 63, 103.

[46] McKelway, "Law Without Enforcement," *Child Labor Bulletin* 3 (May 1914):34–5.

[47] Mrs. W. L. Murdock, "Conditions of the Child Employing Industries in the South," *Child Labor Bulletin* 2 (May 1913):125–26; Charles Lee Coon, untitled MS., March 16, 1912, the Papers of Charles Lee Coon, Southern Historical Collection, Box 3, Folder 38; Herschel H. Jones, "Mississippi Reports and Interviews," December 1913–January 1914, entry dated January 2, 1914, the Papers of the National Child Labor Committee, Manuscripts Division, Library of Congress; hereinafter cited as NCLC Papers.

[48] Lewis W. Hine, "A Photographic Investigation of Child Labor Conditions in the Cotton Mills of Georgia," January 31, 1910; Harvey P. Vaughn, "Child Labor in Georgia," April 1913, NCLC Papers. On worker culture and child-labor reform, see Carlton, *Mill and Town in South Carolina, 1880–1920*; Hall *et al.*, *Like a Family*.

[49] Pearl L. Lockridge to Madeline McDowell Breckinridge, September 28, 1910, Breckinridge Family Papers.

[50] Elizabeth H. Lewis to Mary Johnston, March 23, 1911, Johnston Papers (#3588), Box 8; Lewis to Lila Meade Valentine, October 11, 1918, Virginia Woman Suffrage Papers; Dow Husbands to Madeline McDowell Breckinridge, October 9, 1914, Breckinridge Family Papers.

[51] Clark, *Deliver Us From Evil*, pp. 130–33; E. C. Payne to J. Sidney Peters, October 30, 1917, Virginia Prohibition Commission Records.

[52] Josiah William Bailey to R. L. Davis, January 16, 1917, the Papers of Josiah William Bailey, Manuscript Department, Duke University Library; Jack Temple Kirby, *Rural Worlds Lost: The American South, 1920–1960* (Baton Rouge: LSU Press, 1987), pp. 210–11.

[53] J. Sidney Peters to Westmoreland Davis, April 25, 1918; Charles T. Beall to Peters, March 11, 1919; "Law Enforcement Department," *The American Issue* (Richmond), October 1, 1921, clipping in Virginia Prohibition Commission Records.

[54] W. T. Berry to Peters, February 6, 1919, *ibid.*

[55] Josiah William Bailey, "The Political Treatment of the Drink Evil," *South Atlantic Quarterly* 6 (1907):113.

[56] *Richmond Virginian*, October 21, 22, 24, 1910; H. B. Smith to B. D. White, May 6, 1922, Virginia Prohibition Commission Records.

Steven J. Ross

CINEMA AND CLASS CONFLICT
LABOR, CAPITAL, THE STATE, AND
AMERICAN SILENT FILM

IN the years before the first World War, the United States was shocked by two horrifying labor tragedies. On March 25, 1911, 146 female garment workers, mostly young girls, were killed in a devastating fire that swept through the Triangle Shirt Waist Company in New York City. Three years later, National Guardsmen and company gunmen massacred sixteen men, women, and children by machine-gunning and setting fire to the tents of striking coal miners in Ludlow, Colorado. Within a few months of each event, the forces of labor, capital, and the state clashed once again. This time, however, their battles were fought not in the nation's workplaces, but on its movie screens.

The three films that closely followed these events presented markedly different views of the conditions in the nation's garment factories and coal mines. *The Crime of Carelessness*, produced in 1912 by the National Association of Manufacturers, turned attention away from employer neglect of safety laws and focused on worker responsibility for hazardous conditions in garment factories. *The Miner's Lesson*, produced in 1914 by the United States Bureau of Mines in cooperation with the Anthracite Coal Operators, attributed mine deaths and accidents, which played an important role in Ludlow and other coal strikes, to worker stupidity and not state or mine-owner cupidity. In contrast, *What Is to Be Done?*, produced in 1914 by socialist Joseph Weiss, showed audiences how capitalist exploitation prompted the strike at Ludlow and graphically portrayed the forces of the state and capital conspiring to murder innocent men, women, and children.[1]

As these and hundreds of similar films demonstrate, the struggles between labor, capital, and the state were waged in a wide range of arenas. Between 1900 and 1930, workers were locked in battle on several fronts: with individual employers in the workplace; with employ-

ers' associations that launched open shop drives; with courts that overturned prolabor legislation and enjoined union pickets; with police, militias, and federal troops used to break strikes; and, though less well known, with capitalists and state agencies over the political uses of mass culture. Attacks and defenses of unionization, workers' control of production, syndicalism, socialism, worker cooperatives, Americanization drives, corporate benevolence, and state power were waged not just in workplaces, courthouses, and legislatures, but in movie theaters and auditoriums throughout the nation. Although workplace conflicts often involved thousands of workers, their film counterparts reached millions of ordinary and not so ordinary Americans. By 1910, 26 million people, 28 percent of the population, attended movies each week. A decade later, 50 million Americans, nearly half the population, attended films in the 15,000 movie theaters and 22,000 churches, halls, and schools that screened them.[2] Never before had so many people been presented with such graphic depictions of the nation's labor struggles.

If we understand politics and power in the broadest sense, as the ability to influence or gain control over others—family, friends, coworkers, community or nation—then mass culture, and movies in particular, certainly constituted an important realm of politics and power in the Progressive and Post-war eras. Yet, mass culture was not a monolithic entity imposed from above to keep the masses quiet, but an arena of struggle between different groups and classes who used different media to win greater public support for their cause. Film scholars have examined how middle-class Progressive reformers made films espousing a broad range of causes including women's suffrage, child-labor laws, sexual education, aid for widows, and political and prison reform.[3] Less well known, however, is how various labor and radical organizations, capitalists, and government agencies made and used theatrical and nontheatrical (documentaries, educational, and industrial) films to promote their interests and attack their enemies.

Films emerged as class weapons right from the start and not, as some have argued, in the late 1920s and 1930s.[4] Labor, capital, and the state quickly recognized the popularity and power of this new instrument and used it to present visual representations of their ideologies to a mass public. For millions of Americans, movies and newsreels provided an important visual language that allowed them to see what was happening in the nation—or at least what producers wanted them to see. Workers used the screen to show a mass public that their cries of injustice were real; that class conflict *did* exist within our borders. Capitalists and federal agencies parried these visual

claims and advanced their own ideological positions by making films showing the extraordinary efforts they had undertaken on behalf of employees and citizens.

Despite the importance of these struggles, they have not been chronicled by modern scholars. Although film studies has moved away from the pure textual criticism that characterized the post-structuralist phase of the 1970s, its practitioners have still not fully grasped the methodological possibilities of using nonfilm sources, such as labor newspapers and archives, to explore how capitalist and state power shaped the products of the movie industry. Similarly, working-class and political historians have slighted the important role movies played in class struggles. To understand the politics and complexities of mass culture we need to develop new approaches that integrate text and context. This essay attempts to bridge the chasm separating working-class, political, and film histories by examining how labor, capital, and the state relied upon one medium of mass culture, the movies, as a vital weapon in their ongoing struggles for greater power and legitimacy. It focuses on the films made during the silent era, their purposes, and their messages. It also endeavors to raise, though not fully answer, critical questions that might guide future research: How does a "ruling" class establish and maintain hegemonic control over mass culture? What is the relation between ideology and film as practiced by labor, capital, and the state? What internal contradictions beset each of these actors? How were their films received and what effect did they have upon audiences?[5]

By 1910, political skirmishes over film were well under way. Although the bastions of the old middle class decried the movies' assaults against traditional Victorian values, others rushed to the defense of this new medium. "Moving picture theaters which are just now being condemned by a great number of people," Francis Oliver, chief of the Bureau of Sciences, explained in 1910 to a gathering of business leaders in New York, "were a potent factor in the education of the foreign element and were therefore a benefit to the city." Jane Elliot, a columnist for the *Moving Picture World*, insisted the movies were the "Working Man's College," because they provided him with a broad and liberal education. Yet, the key issue for concerned parties was the kind of education these "students" would receive. Would movies be used to enlighten and educate, or, as the Washington (D.C.) Central Labor Union warned, "to prejudice the public's mind against organized labor?"[6] Over the next two decades, business, labor, and state leaders offered their own distinct answers.

It would be a mistake to reduce any of these groups and classes to a

single homogenous entity. Different needs produced different kinds of films and different ideological messages within as well as between classes. Capitalist involvement with silent films, for example, took two main forms: movie industry firms that handled production, distribution, and exhibition operations, and, businesses outside the industry that commissioned others to make their films. Since much has already been written about the former, we will look only briefly at the ways they entered labor-capital struggles.

Between 1905 and the outbreak of World War I, films focusing on what *Moving Picture World, Film Index,* and *Variety* reviewers called "Labor-Capital" stories generally fell into one of three categories: anti-union films, pro-union films, and a group I call progressive films. The anti-union open shop drive inaugurated by employers' associations at the turn of the century was accompanied by scores of films that reinforced this strand of capitalist ideology by portraying unionists as lazy and greedy individuals or as radical troublemakers and anarchists who resorted to unnecessary violence against essentially kind bosses. These politicized messages were conveyed through story lines, intertitles, and visual imagery. Films such as *The Blacksmith's Strike* (1907), *The Strikers* (1909), *The Right to Labor,* (1910), *The Strike* (1912), and *The Strike at the Centipede Mine* (1915) depicted strikes and mass movements as savage affairs led by corrupt union leaders or foreign-born "outside agitators"—unmistakable on the screen with their long wild hair and foreign-looking pointy beards—who played upon the violent tendencies of their disciples. Viewers were rarely offered any insights into the reasons why men and women joined unions or launched strikes. Instead, complained one group of trade unionists in 1910, strikers were simply shown "blowing-up bridges, and committing other depredations."[7]

Movies condemning unions and strikes were also accompanied by a small number of films offering positive depictions of workers and their struggles. Union movie-goers and their families flocked to films, such as *The Blood of the Poor* (1911), *The Struggle* (1913), *The Better Man* (1914), and *The Blacklist* (1916), that exposed the evils of absentee ownership and employer exploitation, and defended the rights of workers and their organizations to fight for a better life. Yet, while these films were critical of individual capitalists, few challenged the capitalist system itself. Only *The Jungle* (1914), adapted from Upton Sinclair's novel and directed by socialist August Thomas, and *Why?* (1913), presented viewers with a staunch defense of socialism.[8]

Most "Labor-Capital" films neither praised nor vilified labor unions but simply explored the problems confronting wage earners and offered some possible solutions. Taken collectively, these films constitute

what I call the progressive approach. Reflecting the progressive ideology of the times and its condemnation of what Theodore Roosevelt termed the "malefactors of great wealth," these films deplored extremes in class condition, denouncing both great wealth and great poverty. They were scathing in their attacks on trusts, monopolists, rapacious landlords, money lenders, and the idle rich, while sympathetic to the plight of the honest and often unemployed working poor. They called for reform but decried radicalism. *The Power of Labor* (1908), *A Corner in Wheat* (1909), *Capital vs. Labor* (1910), *How the Cause Was Won* (1912), and *A Poor Relation* (1914) condemned the exploitation of workers at the hands of greedy employers, but rarely endorsed collective action by the exploited as a means of solving those ills. Instead, these and other progressive films counseled workers to await patiently outside intervention by middle-class reform groups, clergy, government, or repentant capitalists.[9]

Unlike movie production firms whose primary goal was profit, businessmen outside this industry were freer to make films for a variety of political purposes and not just for short-term economic gain. Large manufacturers, railroad companies, bankers, and other major capitalists recognized the popularity and power of movies at an early date and hired film companies to make two types of films: nontheatrical "industrial" films (as they were popularly known) for improving sales, efficiency and productivity; and, more commercially oriented theatrical films for swaying public opinion in favor of business and against workers and their unions.

Within a few years of their arrival on the business scene, industrial films were widely hailed by manufacturers and trade journals as invaluable tools for the farsighted corporation. By 1913, companies such as Bethlehem Steel, National Cash Register, International Harvester, Jaspar Machine, and various producers of iron goods, oils, fountain pens, milk, soap, and dynamite made films of company operations and products which they used to bolster sales. Trade periodicals such as *American Industries, Automobile, Iron Age, Iron Trade Review, American Machinist, Machinery, Engineering Record,* and *Variety* counseled manufacturers on the ways in which firms utilized "industrials" to promote products, train sales personnel, improve production, and raise investment capital. As demand for this new service grew, entrepreneurs organized film companies that specialized in producing and distributing industrials, and studios created separate departments to handle these films.[10]

Although most industrials dealt with traditional business concerns, some ventured into more hotly contested terrains. Labor-capital battles for control of production, which historian David Montgomery

has so masterfully described, entered a new phase after 1913, as manufacturers made films that undermined traditional apprenticeship and promoted the industrial efficiency programs so bitterly opposed by workers. The *Cleveland Citizen* warned its union readers in May 1913 about a manufacturing firm that recently hired a movie company to help them implement the "ill-famed 'Taylor' system of scientific management."

> Every detail of the work performed by a first-class worker, who has been put on to a certain job, is reproduced on the film, while at the same time a stopwatch records the time employed for every move. The best films are afterwards shown to the other workers of the same shop, enabling them to imitate the time-saving performance of their best mate who, by the way, had been especially taught his task beforehand.[11]

These micro-motion studies, insisted movie producers and journalists, were especially effective in eliminating "soldiering"—the worker practice of slowing down on the job—and transferring greater control over training apprentices to management. Movies could teach young workers in days and weeks what unions wanted to teach them over months and years.[12]

These brief industrial films, which usually ran ten to twenty minutes, were shown to customers, employees, chambers of commerce, and employer associations. Yet, in many instances, more ambitious companies produced theatrical films that played before mass audiences in movie houses throughout the nation. As big business came under scathing attack from muckraking journalists and labor organizations, the National Association of Manufacturers (NAM), the American Bankers' Association, the New York Central Railroad, and several other business organizations made feature films aimed at improving their public image, disparaging the claims of their critics, and generally projecting capitalist ideology in a more favorable light.

Of all these organizations, NAM was by far the most aggressive in using film for corporate propaganda. Whereas the Ludlow tragedy prompted John D. Rockefeller to hire public relations mogul Ivy Lee, the tremendous outcry generated by the Triangle fire led NAM to produce two films in 1912 which portrayed employers' heightened concern for workplace safety. *The Workman's Lesson* and *The Crime of Carelessness* are excellent examples of the subtle ways capitalists used movies to promote their interests—and of the complexities of modern textual criticism. Film reviewers accepted both works at face value and praised their producers for attributing equal blame for unsafe working conditions to employers and employees and calling upon

both sides to work together to insure future safety.[13] However, a close "reading" of the latter movie reveals a different set of political messages.

The film opens with a textile mill owner promising a fire inspector to clear all materials blocking his fire exits. The narrative quickly shifts to a love story between two affianced mill workers, Tom and Hilda. When Hilda catches Tom smoking a cigarette near highly inflammable materials, she makes him put it out. However, several days later, Tom, reprobate that he is, commits the "crime of carelessness" by casually tossing a match into a trashbin. The factory is quickly consumed by fire. When the workers try to escape they find the fire exits blocked or locked. Certain death is avoided when Tom grabs an ax and chops through a wooden wall. Yet, Tom's moment of heroism is quickly forgotten when he confesses his role in starting the blaze. Instead of upbraiding the mill owner for locking the fire exits, the workers all turn on Tom. When the mill owner refuses Hilda's plea to rehire Tom, she blames him for the near deaths caused by unsafe conditions in the mills. The boss is dumbstruck! It is clearly the first time he has considered the possibility that he might share in the blame. Instantly realizing the wrongs of his ways, he rehires Tom and insists, "We are both to blame; I for not making the factory safe, you for smoking."[14]

It is important to bear in mind that the film was made in the aftermath of the Triangle fire and the trial of the factory owners, for it clearly attempts to shift responsibility away from bosses and onto the shoulders of workers. The employer's failure to provide fire escapes, his callous locking of all fire exits, and his broken promise to the fire inspector are never seriously questioned. The viewer clearly sees that the fire was Tom's fault and raises the possibility that the Triangle fire was really caused by some careless seamstress. Even when the boss benevolently admits his mistakes, they are portrayed as mistakes of carelessness not greed, of neglect not exploitation. The fact that real mill and garment factory owners had persistently ignored union demands for improved safety conditions is totally ignored. In the movie, it is the mill owner, not the workers who eventually leads the movement to make the factory safe.[15]

Paternalistic messages of concerned capitalists and reckless workers provide the central themes of *The Workman's Lesson* (1912) and *Steve Hill's Awakening* (1914). In the former, viewers learn it is better for employees to trust management than their fellow workers. As in NAM's previous picture, the story line seemingly calls for labor-capital cooperation in installing and using safety devices. However, what we actually see is a young foreign-born worker who almost loses

an arm after foolishly listening to an older worker, probably a union man, who refuses to use safety equipment. Workers are shown as stubborn and just plain stupid in contrast to their enlightened and concerned employers. *Steve Hill's Awakening*, made by the New York Central Railroad Line after several train wrecks in 1914, shows how a railway yardman's carelessness causes his death and leaves his family destitute. When his son, Steve, takes a job in the same yard many years later, he is soon dismissed for carelessness. Obviously, carelessness was a genetic flaw found only in blue collar workers. Steve finally "awakens" to the importance of "Safety First" after a nightmare in which he dreams of accidents and maimings caused by worker neglect.[16]

The most ambitious industrial entrant into the cinematic world was the Ford Motor Company. Instead of hiring an outside producer to make its films, Ford opened its own motion picture department. By 1916, it was releasing over four million feet of film a year. The *Ford Educational Weeklies* featured short reels of assembly-line production, management improvement techniques, English classes for foreign employees, and scenes of happy workers frolicking at company-sponsored outings. Like NAM and the New York Central, Ford parried union attacks against poor working conditions, by producing longer films, such as *Safety First* (1916), which showed "in actual operation all the mechanical safeguards that have been installed in the Ford shops where 29,000 workers are employed."[17]

How many people saw these films? Where did they see them? What did they think of them? Unfortunately, there is little information about audience size or reception of nontheatricals. However, we do know that Ford, NAM, the New York Central, the American Bankers' Association, and other corporations took great efforts to ensure that their films would be widely distributed. Films promoting corporate paternalism, notes film scholar Kay Sloan, "circulated through the nation's movie houses as if they were no different from slapstick comedies, westerns, and historical dramas."[18] To ensure that its films would reach areas without movie theaters, the New York Central built a special traveling movie car and brought its film to small towns along their line—a practice soon adopted by other railroad firms. Feature films and nontheatrical releases were also widely distributed to churches, schools, businesses, and voluntary organizations.[19]

The power and appeal of movies among the working class was apparently so great that many capitalists used films, as Diane Waldman argues, "as part of an overall strategy to diffuse worker discontent, to discourage union activity and to exert corporate influence over areas of employees' lives outside the workplace itself."[20] H. J. Heinz, hoping that carefully chosen, wholesome entertainment might help reduce

drunkenness and increase efficiency among his workers, built a movie theater on the grounds of his Pittsburgh factory in 1915. The following year, John Rockefeller built a 1,240 seat luxury theater at his Pueblo, Colorado, steel works. Apparently these ventures proved successful, for movies became an increasingly important part of the growing number of employer-sponsored industrial recreational programs around the nation.[21]

Federal and state agencies joined capitalists in using films for propaganda purposes. Beginning in 1908, the Departments of Agriculture and Interior began producing nontheatrical films to publicize their activities and serve the needs of their particular constituencies. During the next decade, various government bureaus and departments made films demonstrating large-scale farming practices, the flight of the Wright Brothers, public works projects, national park activities, coal-mining techniques, venereal disease prevention, and the workings of the civil service merit system. City and state officials throughout the country were also active in producing or exhibiting films. Though not engaged in mass culture on the same scale as commercial films, government movies nevertheless reached masses of Americans. Federal officials took their films into some "communities where motion pictures had never been seen before."[22]

The ideological messages of government films were as complex and varied as the government itself. Most early films focused on seemingly apolitical areas of public service. And yet, those touching on labor-capital-state relations revealed a more class-biased orientation. The state was no more neutral in its filmmaking activities than it was in its frequent use of troops to settle strikes. Films produced by the Bureau of Mines (Department of Interior), often in cooperation with major corporations, advanced anti-union, procapitalist themes. *The Miner's Lesson* (1914) and *Sanitation in Mining Villages* (ca. 1915) showed how industry and state officials sought to ensure the safety and health of ordinary workers. Yet, both films repeatedly depicted workers as either too stubborn or too stupid to follow the rules and guidelines set by paternalistic government officials and bosses. The fact that miners' unions had forced coal operators and state officials to adopt health and safety reforms played no role in any of these productions.[23]

State visions of its partnership with capital in promoting workplace safety and Americanization programs are dramatically illustrated in the film *An American in the Making* (1913). Produced by the Bureau of Mines under the direction of U.S. Steel's Committee of Safety, this well-made melodrama follows the adventures of Bela Tokaji as he leaves his poor Eastern European home to join his steel-worker brother in Gary, Indiana. Passing through immigration at Ellis Island

faster than any immigrant in American history, Bela travels to Gary, "the Workingman's Model City," where he meets his prosperous and very American-looking brother. Bela wants to celebrate his arrival in a saloon, but his brother refuses any libation and takes him to "a better place than the saloons for his leisure hours," the Y.M.C.A. When Bela shows up for work the next day, he, and the viewer, are shown how the company safeguards the lives of its employees. In each of the dozen scenes of steel-making activities, workers are never seen using safety equipment until foremen demand that they do. The film cuts to six years later, and Bela has been transformed into a real American. He marries the teacher at the company-run English school that he faithfully attends, starts a family, and moves into a beautiful home.[24]

The film's message is clear: the company protects those who cannot protect themselves and offers prosperity to those who follow its guidelines. Employers and state authorities are constantly concerned with the welfare of the workers, both inside and outside the workplace. Workers, on the other hand, are depicted as childlike and dependent and show no initiative. Only through faithful obedience to external authority rather than internally generated organizations like unions can success—shown here as a good job, pretty wife, large home, and happy family—be achieved. These themes were reemphasized in a U.S. Steel publication that described the film as the story of an "ignorant Hungarian peasant . . . stupid and uneducated," who ultimately thrives because of the company's safety and welfare programs.[25]

The movie-making endeavors of capitalists and government agencies did not go unheeded by labor organizations. The mushrooming of anti-union films led delegates to the AFL convention in December 1910 to call for a boycott of movie theaters showing films that "prejudice the minds of the general public against our movement by falsely and maliciously misrepresenting it." Moviegoing workers were urged to avoid spending hard-earned leisure dollars on actors "whose mediocre ability and craving for a laugh at any cost, are always attested by such expressions as "I can't do it, I'm a union man," or "Impossible; I belong to the union." These appeals were heeded. In a Brooklyn theater "mostly patronized by workingmen and women," spectators walked out when the manager ran an anti-union film "showing alleged outrages by miners during a strike."[26] During the next several years, AFL officials, local trade unionists, and labor newspapers wrote letters to studios, producers, and anticensorship officials calling for more honest depiction of the struggles fought by union men and women.[27]

Labor and radical organizations entered the realm of mass culture as producers as well as consumers. As early as 1907, workers, unions,

and radicals began making and using movies as a means of reaching millions of Americans with *their* political visions of past, present, and future struggles. "We are going to make the projecting lens a weapon for labor," pledged one working-class filmmaker. These films were used for publicizing union battles, raising funds, attracting greater turnouts of meetings and rallies, promoting the candidacy of radical politicians, and educating an undifferentiated mass public about the reasons why unions were a necessary part of American life and justice.[28] The possibility of producing a simple one- or two-reel film for between $500 and $2,500 enabled many labor organizations to enter the cinematic world. By 1914, the proliferation of films "that tend to excite class feelings," led progressive reformer Frederic Howe to warn of the day "when the movie begins to portray the labor struggle conditions in mine and factory, and when it becomes the daily press of industrial groups, of classes, of Socialism, syndicalism, and radical opinion."[29]

The move into this new arena of class struggle occurred at a critical moment in the history of labor and radical organizations. The AFL was in the midst of a concerted drive to recruit new members and defeat the open shop campaign. The Socialist party appeared on the verge of becoming a major third party. Local candidates were capturing city council, mayoral, and legislative seats around the nation, and its presidential standard bearer, Eugene V. Debs, garnered nearly one million votes in the 1912 election. Militant labor organizations such as the Western Federation of Miners and the Industrial Workers of the World were gaining support and winning battles on the western frontier. Yet each realized the necessity of developing new methods of propaganda to counter the tremendous economic, political, and military power available to employers. With newspapers and magazines either misrepresenting or failing to report their cause to the public, movies seemed one way of reaching millions of potential new members and allies who, though reluctant to listen to labor's messages, might come to see films.[30]

To attract a mass public, worker filmmakers concentrated their greatest energies on producing feature films that would entertain, as well as educate, movie-going audiences. These early "worker-made" films—that is, films made or produced by labor or radical organizations—adopted the Progressive Era's tone of condemning exploitative monopolists and nonproductive capitalists. But they also offered viewers solutions that went far beyond simple cries for patience and outside intervention. Despite the frequent ideological divisions among and between unionists and radicals, their films all recommend collective action, in the form of trade unionism, socialism, strikes, and in-

dependent politics, as the best response to capitalist exploitation. The three most prominent worker-made features of the period, *A Martyr to His Cause* (1911), *From Dusk to Dawn* (1913), and *What Is to Be Done?* (1914) advocate collective activity over individualism and offer positive screen images of workers, unions, radicals, and mass action. Yet, their specific emphases reflect the politics of their makers. "Labor" was no more a single entity, in the workplace or on the screen, than was "capital."

The AFL was the first labor organization to produce feature films. Its battle with open shop advocates intensified in April 1911 when International Association of Bridge and Structural Iron Workers' secretary-treasurer John McNamara and his trade unionist brother James were kidnapped and transported to Los Angeles where they were arrested for the June 1910 bombing of the *Los Angeles Times*, the nation's most anti-union newspaper. The "Crime of the Century," as it was dubbed by the press, provided new opportunities for labor's enemies to associate trade unionism with anarchism. The AFL quickly responded to the incident by producing *A Martyr to His Cause*, made in 1911 at the W. H. Seeley studio in Ohio. The film offers a strident defense of the McNamaras and trade unionism in the form of a melodrama that traces the life and career of John, who is portrayed as the innocent victim of open shop crusaders. Reversing the dominant screen images of the times, *Martyr* depicts unionists as peaceful, law-abiding men who love their parents and their country, and who risk their lives in defense of justice and democracy. Employers and their private police are shown brazenly breaking the law to serve their own selfish interests. In an emotional closing scene, John calls upon the public "to suspend judgments in these matters until opportunity for a fair and full defense has been afforded."[31]

In *From Dusk to Dawn*, filmmaker Frank E. Wolfe drew upon his experiences as a trade unionist and socialist and offered viewers a broad course of action that followed worker struggles from the shop floor into the political arena. Determined to "take Socialism before the people of the world on the rising tide of movie popularity," Wolfe conveyed his messages through the story of a young iron molder, Dan Grayson, and his laundress girlfriend, Carla Wayne, who battle against the exploitation of employers and indifference of politicians. The images of worker carelessness and of employer and state benevolence seen in capitalist and government films are challenged by scenes showing Dan and Carla futilely preaching workplace safety to their bosses. When Dan's pleas are ignored and an explosion kills Carla's brother and several others, the couple embark upon a quest for justice that begins with unionizing their shops and ends with Dan's

election as governor on the Socialist ticket. The film's closing scene has Dan signing a bill guaranteeing all wage earners the right to work. [32]

What Is to Be Done?, made in New York by Socialist actor and unionist Leon Weiss, uses the specter of the employer-instigated violence at Ludlow to legitimize worker demands for union recognition and greater power. As in *From Dusk to Dawn*, the film's politics are delivered in the palatable form of a love story between a capitalist's "liberal son" and a radical stenographer who organizes workers at his father's factory. Weiss used scenes of workplace struggles replete with strike-breakers, gangsters, stool pigeons, and corrupt police to show audiences that the repression at Ludlow was a regular occurrence and not simply an isolated affair. Our heroine wins the day after recounting the story of Ludlow at an arbitration hearing and warning employers to settle with the union or face similar violence and public censure.[33]

Weiss, Wolfe, and the AFL concentrated on turning out entertaining films that promoted their cause before heterogeneous mass audiences and not just the already converted. They succeeded, for all three films played in commercial movie houses across the country. *Martyr* was seen by over 50,000 people during its opening run in Cincinnati and attracted similarly large crowds in other cities. *From Dusk to Dawn* played in Marcus Loew's theaters throughout the Northeast and in the Midwest and on the Pacific Coast.[34] While some organizations turned out theatrical releases for the masses, others produced films and newsreels for more select audiences. The Label Council of New York and the Western Federation of Mines bypassed commercial theaters in favor of showing their films at union halls and auditoriums.[35] Others screened worker-made and progressive feature films to raise funds for strikers, stir up support for antimilitia bills, heighten opposition to militarism, and attract larger crowds to meetings and rallies.[36]

The growth of this independent working-class film movement was hindered by the frequent opposition of state authorities. Local and state censorship boards often thwarted worker and studio efforts to portray wage earner self-activity in more positive ways. Most of the scholarship on censorship focuses on local fears about sex and crime. But radicalism and class conflict were of equal concern to many boards. Films perceived as threatening class harmony were often suppressed in their entirety and not, as was the case in films dealing with controversial sexual or criminal themes, simply cut in a number of places. This was especially so in such cities as Chicago, Detroit, and Springfield, Massachusetts, where censorship was controlled by the police, or in Ohio, where it was controlled by the Industrial Relations

Commission. Worker-made and progressive commercial films portraying working-class struggles, such as *From Dusk to Dawn*, *The Mirror of Death* (1914), which features a scene of Mexican workers attacking a mine owner, and *The Strike at Coaldale* (1914), in which miners are shown winning a strike, were all prohibited by local authorities.[37]

Far from being the "Democratic Art," as film historian Garth Jowett has described it, movies were subject to the class dictates and prejudices of government officials. Audiences could not freely choose the films they would see. State censorship, socialist film critic Louis Gardy warned in 1914, was a dangerous "weapon of reaction" used to "uphold all the viciousness of the present system and stifle any movement which may bring a better day." Gardy's fears were confirmed several years later when National Board of Review of Motion Pictures (NBRPM) chairman W. D. McGuire informed Gompers of the "way censorship was used to oppose the legitimate activities of the labor union men" and pointed to several instances in which films were "condemned by state censorship boards because they presented arguments favorable to labor."[38]

State intrusions into mass culture and its ties with movie industry personnel reached unprecedented dimensions during World War I. On April 17, 1917, just eight days after declaring war, President Wilson created the Committee on Public Information (CPI) and charged it with using the mass media to "sell the war to the American public." CPI chairman George Creel, a former newspaperman, organized a special Division of Films which quickly cranked out feature films and newsreels for theaters and patriotic societies across the nation. Creel and his aides understood that mass culture could be used to appeal to specific, as well as general, parts of the "masses." Some features were intended to rouse the patriotism of the general population, such as *Pershing's Crusaders* (1918) and *America's Answer* (1918); others were aimed at particular groups, such as *Labor's Part in Democracy's War* (1917), *Our Colored Fighters* (1918), and *Women's Part in the War* (1917).[39]

The motion picture industry was the immediate benefactor of the government's increased reliance upon film. Film companies produced, distributed, and exhibited CPI's films, and assisted other federal departments in making films to promote their war work. Wilson formalized these relations in July 1917 by creating the War Cooperation Board, which attached representatives from the National Association of the Motion Picture Industry to virtually every government agency. Universal, Mutual, Gaumont, Hearst-Pathe, Paramount, Bray, Hodkinson, and other producers answered the call of duty and turned patriotism into profits. Indeed, the movie industry played

such an important role in the war effort that it was declared an "essential industry" and its key personnel exempted from military service.[40]

Movie industry magnates soon learned that the government expected a *quid pro quo* in return for its "favors." As the war drew to a close, state involvement with the film industry grew more overtly political as federal agencies endeavored to promote their vision of postwar class harmony by reshaping the content and ideology of theatrical and nontheatrical films. The agencies pressured studios to produce certain kinds of "labor-capital" films, they tactfully called for movie industry cooperation in their Americanization campaign, and they made their own films, often in cooperation with large manufacturers.

While the Justice Department relied upon the courts and "red squads" to suppress the threats posed by Bolshevism and other radical organizations such as the Industrial Workers of the World (IWW), other agencies believed that film provided an equally effective way of accomplishing the same results. David Niles, head of the Labor Department's Motion Picture Section, insisted that movies could suppress the rising tide of labor strife and "do more to stabilize labor and help bring about normal conditions than any other agency." Niles used his position as chairman of the Joint Committee on Motion Picture Activities of the United States Government and Allied Organizations (created in November 1918 to prepare the nation for post-war readjustments), to pressure studios and production companies into making certain kinds of films. Movies dealing with labor themes, he instructed them, should offer "constructive education" by portraying the hero "as a strong, virile American, a believer of American institutions and ideals." Niles asked all directors and producers to confer with him before starting productions dealing with socialism or labor problems and threatened federal censorship for those who failed to comply.[41]

Federal censorship of films that portrayed undesirable aspects of class conflict was a real and costly threat to commercial filmmakers. During the war, CPI censors withheld lucrative export licenses from films dealing with political corruption, adultery, and mistreatment of Indians. But they were especially critical of those depicting negative aspects of class relations in America. Films showing strikes and labor riots, hunger and poverty, or ghetto slum conditions were rejected because they were a "bad testimonial to American democracy." Filmmakers could not risk losing even more profitable domestic markets during peacetime.[42] Thus, fears that foreign markets might be lost combined with a sense of patriotism and the realization that government agents were indeed monitoring productions with labor themes,

led several companies to send scenarios and completed films to Niles and his colleagues for their approval.[43]

The unprecedented explosion of strikes and labor militancy after the armistice gave new urgency to Niles's work. By 1919, 4.1 million workers belonged to unions, a 49 percent increase since 1916. Employers' determination to roll back war-time concessions and their unwillingness to negotiate with union representatives prompted a series of massive strikes. In Seattle, a general strike by 60,000 workers paralyzed the city for several days. In Boston, the police walked off their jobs demanding higher pay and union recognition. In the nation's steel mills and coal mines, wage earners launched strikes for better pay and better working conditions. By the end of 1919, over 4 million men and women had participated in 3,500 strikes.[44]

Federal officials quickly moved to thwart labor militancy and sustain their notions of proper class relations by recruiting movie personnel into the government's Americanization campaign. Begun well before the war, the campaign aimed at turning immigrants, especially immigrant laborers, into fully assimilated, "100 percent Americans." The frequent arrest, deportation, and imprisonment of radicals under the Espionage Act of 1918 helped set federal standards for loyal Americanism. Several states followed suit by passing criminal syndicalism laws aimed at silencing the IWW. However, the tremendous outburst of militant labor and radical activity in 1919 led government officials to consider other means of deterring the perceived "Bolshevik" influence on immigrant workers and organized labor.[45]

In December 1919, Secretary of the Interior Franklin K. Lane, acting with the approval of Congress, met with movie industry magnates in New York and secured their pledge to assist the government in using film "to carry on a nation-wide campaign to combat Bolshevism and radicalism" that would "crush the Red Movement in America."[46] Sounding the "keynote of the government's campaign against radicalism, syndicalism, and sovietism, and for one hundred percent Americanism," Lane asked for films that would dissuade the immigrant laborer from listening to the voices of "violent discontent" and turn him into "a cheerful fellow-worker in the making of America."[47] Within several weeks, the newly constituted Americanism Committee of the Motion Picture Industry of the United States, comprised of the nation's leading production, distribution, and exhibition firms, began circulating suggested scenarios to producers aimed at combating the "revolutionary sentiment so assiduously and insidiously being fomented in this country."[48]

The Americanism Committee ultimately fell short of its ambitious goal of releasing 52 one- and two-reel nontheatricals. Nevertheless,

the few films it did turn out received widespread attention and distribution.[49] The Committee's first and most prominent release, *The Land of Opportunity* (1920), boldly reveals its class biases and, like earlier capitalist films, portrays industrialists as the true friends of workers. The villain, Merton Walpole, is a sleazy looking, idle "Bolshevik" millionaire who carries around a copy of *Classes Versus Masses* by Yakem Zubko and spouts what fellow Civic Club members clearly regard as ridiculous radical cant. When he tells them, "The Courts—the government—faugh! You rich men buy them and then blind the eyes of the poor by your big gifts to flashy charities"—a sentiment many unionists would certainly endorse, they simply jump up and tell him he is "a Bolshevist." Walpole is eventually cured of his radicalism when the club's butler, a "real" worker, reveals how honest Abe Lincoln saved him from sure death. Moved by the story, Walpole tears up his radical tract, throws it in the fire, and decides to become a true American—one who accepts rather than tries to change the world.[50]

The visual campaign against labor radicalism intensified in the first-run films that played before the nearly 50 million Americans who faithfully flocked to the movies each week. As control and ownership in the film industry changed, so too did the products that appeared on the screen. The once artisanal industry was supplanted in the teens and early twenties by an oligarchic "studio system," whose investors included the nation's leading corporations and whose executives faced increasingly militant efforts to unionize all aspects of production.[51] Films sympathizing with the exploitation of poor workers by monopolists, or calling for greater mutual understanding between labor and capital, were greatly outnumbered by features offering hostile representations of workers, unions, and radical organizations. *The Red Dawn* (1919), *The Right to Happiness* (1919), *The Face at Your Window* (1920), *You Find It Everywhere* (1921), *The Stranger's Banquet* (1922), *Little Church around the Corner* (1923), and dozens of similar films portrayed workers as the honest but simple-minded dupes of corrupt union leaders, outside agitators (generally IWW members), or Bolshevik agents. "When radicals are pictured in the films," observed one socialist film critic, "they are not shown as champions of the people, but as traitors of the deepest dye." These films, most of which were produced or released by companies that had encountered the greatest problems with studio unions, did not merely reflect "society," they reflected everyday life on the studio lots.[52]

Hollywood also offered viewers more topical films that presented somewhat embellished versions of recent labor conflicts. *The World Aflame* (1919) dramatizes Mayor Ole Hanson's smashing of the Seattle general strike, and *Virtuous Men* (1919) and *The Great Shadow* (1920)

explore shipyard strikes similar to the one that ignited the Seattle conflict. These films echoed the claims of many employers by portraying strikes as the work of nefarious Bolshevik agents acting under orders from Moscow. The underlying causes of industrial unrest, such as post-war inflation and low wages, were simply ignored. The IWW also came in for comic attack in *Biff! Bang! Bomb!* (1920) and more serious vilification in *Riders of the Dawn* (1920), in which IWW "agitators" in the western wheat country are wiped out by patriotic vigilantes. The kinds of state-sponsored repression denounced by workers and radicals are heralded as state heroism in *Bolshevism on Trial* (1919), where slimy Bolshevik agents are defeated by government surveillance and military action. If force was needed "to knock the weak-kneed props from under red radicalism and IWWism in America," said one sympathetic film reviewer, "then force should be used."[53] The AFL, however, denounced these films as instruments of "misrepresentation in the American-wide campaign against labor and labor organizations" and called for "truth and a fair deal for all."[54]

Leading industrial corporations across the nation also enlisted in the film war against Bolshevism and labor militancy. The goals of the Americanism Committee and the Americanization movement meshed well with the post-war needs and strategies of big business. Led by the National Association of Manufacturers and Chambers of Commerce, employers responded to the labor upheavals of 1919 with a renewed open shop drive aptly called the "American Plan." For many companies, movies seemed an effective means of combatting labor radicalism and portraying welfare capitalism, the carrot on the end of the anti-union stick, as part of their commitment to American ideals. "Industrial films which sell American industries and American industrial democracy to our alien workers and, too, to our unassimilated hyphens," insisted the editors of *Educational Film Magazine* in February 1920, were especially "valuable, particularly as an offset to soviet propaganda with its wild utopias of workman-ownership, workman-management, and a workman-classless republic which only a dreamer like Lenin sees as a reality at the present day."[55]

The companies most aggressive in crushing unions and implementing the American Plan during the 1920s were also the most aggressive in making films to teach the worker, especially the immigrant, "to conduct himself as a thinking individual," and not as part of a class.[56] The railroad companies, in particular, relied on film to spread their gospel of Americanism. *The Americanization of Tony* (ca. 1919), made by the Pennsylvania Railroad, showed immigrant rail hands how the "privileges of citizenship must be paid for in sobriety, work well-done, and love for his fellow man." The Northern Pacific Railway Company set up its own motion picture division in the early 1920s to make films

dealing with the "present phase of industrial unrest; The menace of what is popularly referred to as 'Bolshevism'; . . . [and] Americanization."[57] The Ford Motor Company, whose infamous Sociological Department sent agents into workers' homes to investigate their moral behavior, used the *Ford Educational Weekly* to discourage ethnic loyalties and promote the ideology of classless Americanism.[58]

Corporate imposition of company unions in the early 1920s was accompanied, and perhaps fostered, by industrial films that promoted the advantages of "Employee Representation" plans over trade unionism. Pioneered by the Colorado Fuel and Iron Company after the Ludlow massacre, these "works councils," as they were sometimes called, brought together representatives from management and labor to discuss their problems in a supposedly democratic manner.[59] The Virginia-based Riverside and Dan River Mills Company, one of the largest textile firms in the South, made a film in the early 1920s publicizing its great experiment in "Industrial Democracy." The movie showed how factory government was patterned after the federal system, with a cabinet composed of the company president, executives and superintendents, a senate composed of mill foremen, and a house of representatives composed of workers. "The picture is made to make it appear that company unions are to be desired above bona fide trade unions," complained Samuel Gompers, "and while the picture shows the meetings of the house, the senate and the cabinet nothing can be found on the screen that will tell of the heartaches in the minds of the employees." Indeed, when the workers' house refused to approve a wage cut ordered by the cabinet several years later, it was simply dissolved and the cut enacted.[60]

Post-war businesses also continued making industrial films for less overtly ideological, though no less important, purposes. Industrial film companies like Innovation Films, Charles Raymond Thomas, Bray Studios, and Rothacker Film Manufacturing Company urged employers to stop "treating industrial motion pictures as a plaything" and use them "for general educational purposes, direct sales promotions, and for the development of the good will of the public and the employees."[61] National Cash Register, Burroughs Adding Machine, General Electric, Metropolitan Life, and dozens of other companies responded by hiring filmmakers to make movies aimed at training apprentices and other personnel, teaching efficiency techniques, advertising products, increasing productivity, promoting employee education, and harmonizing industrial relations. Corporate demand for these films mushroomed so dramatically that by 1927 the U.S. Bureau of Foreign and Domestic Commerce created a special Motion Picture Section solely to represent industrial film companies.[62]

Industrial corporations who were making their own films also

gladly assisted government agencies engaged in movie-making activities. The Bureau of Mines continued churning out dozens of films made in cooperation with such prominent open shop advocates as U.S. Steel, General Motors, Peabody Coal Company, and Westinghouse Electric and Manufacturing Company. Movies like *The Story of Steel* (1924) and *When a Man's a Miner: The Story of Safety in the Coal Mines* (1924) merged government messages of "Safety-First" with sympathetic portrayals of welfare capitalism. *The Story of Steel* demonstrates how U.S. Steel, which brutally crushed the great steel strike of 1919, pays careful attention to the "safety and welfare of its employees." Bolshevism and unionism are clearly unnecessary in such a benevolent environment. Scenes of steel making alternate with scenes of the lovely homes "purchased under the provisions of the [company's] home-owning plan" and of the educational, recreational, and medical opportunities extended to employees and their families.[63]

Not all government films took such a conservative or condescending view of workers. The state was no more monolithic than labor or capital. Between 1920 and 1931, the Women's Bureau of the Department of Labor produced four films that offer sympathetic depictions of the conditions, contributions, and needs of women wage earners. *When Women Work* (1930) portrays the "tremendous struggle for existence . . . [which] woman has shared with man" since the beginning of time and ends with an appeal for "Equal Opportunity; Equal Pay; [and] Reasonable Hours" for the nation's 8.5 million working women.[64] Nevertheless, the production and distribution activities of the Bureau of Mines, which maintained the largest collection of industrial films in the world by the end of the decade, greatly overshadowed all other agencies. Demand for their movies was extraordinarily high; over 665,000 people viewed their products during a three-month period in 1929.[65]

Manufacturing companies drew on this vast array of government and industrial films to educate and entertain their employees. The Carnegie Steel Company employed films such as *The Workman's Lesson, How a Workman Became a Cashier* (ca. 1917), and *The House that Jack Built* (1917) to show new employees how through hard work "men of one economic and social level quickly rise to higher social strata and achieve new positions of opportunity and responsibility." Movies also augmented many of the management-sponsored industrial recreation programs whose "primary purpose," observes one scholar, "was to avert labor discontent."[66] The Simonds Manufacturing Company, the Emerson-Brantingham Company, Ford, and scores like them built special screening rooms and ran a mix of industrials, newsreels, and comedies for employees during lunch time or evenings. Companies

like Western Electric occasionally rented movie theaters to show films to employees, while others, like Rockefeller's Colorado Fuel and Iron Company, sponsored regular programs of free films for their workers. Employee pacification was often the implicit, if not the explicit, goal of these film programs. "In industrial plants where films were shown," concluded one English observer, "the men have remained more contented than they otherwise would be. Besides the films took them away from Socialist and extreme radical meetings."[67]

For capitalists to extract the greatest propaganda value from these films, they needed to reach a larger audience than just the employees of several hundred scattered factories. They needed to reach the audiences who watched movies in commercial theaters and in the thousands of churches, halls, schools, and voluntary associations also equipped with motion picture projectors and screens.[68] As in the prewar years, NAM took the lead in carrying the message to a diverse movie-hungry public. In the fall of 1922, they opened the Motion Picture Bureau and launched a vigorous drive to provide, at no charge, carefully selected nontheatrical films to churches, factories, community groups, and the like. Distribution networks were set up in twelve areas around the nation and offered a regular monthly mix of popular short subjects, such as *Making American League Baseball*, and more politically pointed films, such as *The Workman's Lesson*, *The Crime of Carelessness*, *An American in the Making*, and *The Menace*.[69]

Inspired by their initial success, NAM went a step further the next year and, much to the consternation of trade unionists and socialists, organized the American Motion Picture Company (AMPC). Capitalized at $3 million, the AMPC's executive board was headed by NAM president John Edgerton (who served as its chairman), National Founders' Association president William Barr (its president), and a "number of lesser capitalists and employers and a sprinkling of clergymen and educators." A letter sent to potential investors in the summer of 1923 promised that the company would use movies "to combat the radical and revolutionary forces that are invading our country, and which, if left unchallenged will undermine our present system of industrial, religious and social life." By purchasing the assets of the Church Motion Picture Corporation, the AMPC obtained a large number of films, and a well-established distribution and exhibition network that supplied movies to over 5,000 customers each week.[70]

The AMPC's quest to reach a wider public was aided by the rapid growth of companies specializing in the distribution of industrials and nontheatricals. "If the regular theater program is loaded with anti-labor propaganda," lamented communist filmmaker and distributor William Kruse, "the non-theatrical program is saturated with it."[71]

The Civic Film Service, Bureau of Commercial Economics, the Community Motion Picture Bureau, and dozens of similar firms made sure that these films reached chambers of commerce, boards of trade, factories, schools, churches, Y.M.C.A.s, and civic organizations around the nation. The Instructive Film Service, formed for the sole "purpose of spreading the gospel of Americanization" and aiding the "task of overcoming strife, strikes, and unrests of all sorts," reached millions of additional viewers by distributing industrial films to the nation's commercial movie theaters. These ventures, warned Chicago trade unionists, comprised "nothing less than a plan to use the stupendous power of the movies . . . to lull the people into contentment with social and industrial conditions as they are, and to position their minds with propaganda against workers' organizations." [72]

The increased ties between business, the film industry, and the state and the antilabor emphasis of their movies created such marked concern among labor and Left leaders because they understood the tremendous power the screen exerted on shaping public consciousness about workers and their organizations. "The picture houses are used for propaganda," socialist critic Louis Gardy observed in May 1920, "the producers sensing that it is here that the proletariat gathers in the evening, and thus it is the richest field for agitation, be it for anti-union, anti-social or for charitable purposes." Capitalist fantasy might become public reality if presented often enough. Such films, warned the Communist *Daily Worker*, were especially harmful in "moulding the minds of the millions of boys and girls who go to the showhouse every chance they get and filling them with an illusion world always friendly to the present capitalist system and hostile to the organized labor movement." [73]

If capital and state agencies could use film to attack workers and their organizations, then workers could use it to "mould public opinion for the benefit of Organized labor." Far from pacifying wage earners, movies, argued one labor daily, could "inspire men and women to want a less imperfect society." [74] In the months after the armistice, nearly a dozen labor and radical groups organized commercial movie companies that promised to present their visions of social, economic, and political progress to a mass public. At the same time David Niles was sending his heavy-handed letter to producers, the Brotherhood of Railroad Trainmen bought their own Hollywood studio and hired Upton Sinclair to make films depicting struggles of railway laborers. A year later, militant trade unionists and socialists organized the Labor Film Service (LFS) in New York and the Federation Film Corporation (FFC) in Seattle and financed and distributed worker-made features and newsreels "to counteract the vicious propaganda of

which labor and other advanced movements are the victims." In Chicago, the Communist-led International Workers' Aid (IWA) produced newsreels and distributed radical and Russian-made films throughout the United States. In Washington, the AFL produced and distributed *Labor's Reward* (1925), a film extolling the advantage of union shops.[75]

Like the AMPC and similar capitalist ventures, these worker-owned film companies used the screen to promote their political agenda for the 1920s: government control of industry, opposition to open shop and Americanization drives, support for ongoing strikes, calls for industrial unionism, and worker ownership of production. Their movies differed markedly from those produced by business and state. Concerned about the negative impact of antilabor "Hollywood" films on the public consciousness, they ignored less costly industrial nontheatricals in favor of producing commercial feature films that would play in first-run and neighborhood theaters throughout the country. "We have an opportunity," explained FFC director John A. Nelson, "of reaching and educating the non-union man of today who can be made the loyal union man of tomorrow."[76] To that end, they made entertaining melodramas whose esthetics were similar to those produced by the studios; whole plot lines often revolved around love stories between sympathetic men and women. But unlike the heroes and heroines of studio features, the heroes and heroines of these films were unionists or socialists, while the villains were manufacturers and state authorities.

The contemporary struggles of workers were never lost amid the tears and heartaches of the melodramatic framework. Each film brought workplace concerns and depictions of collective action directly to the screen. Yet the different political perspectives of their makers meant that each film advocated a different cause or method of activism. Seattle workers answered Hollywood's misrepresentations of their strike and their unions by organizing the Federation Film Corporation in November 1919. Their first film, *The New Disciple* (1921), uses a love story between a factory worker and the owner's daughter to show how employees overcome the joint oppression of employers and trusts by organizing, with the help of local farmers, worker-cooperatives.[77] *Labor's Reward* (1925), produced by the AFL, focuses on the romance between a union man and a nonunion woman and shows how the closed (union) shop and the steadfast purchase of the union label brings about the greater prosperity and personal freedoms enjoyed by organized labor.[78] *The Passaic Textile Strike* (1926), a docudrama produced by the Communist activist Alfred Wagenknecht and distributed by the Chicago-based IWA, uses the heart-rending story of an exploited eastern European family to show how militant

collective action by a wide-range of rank-and-file native- and foreign-born workers, including blacks, Hispanics, and women, were powerful enough to defeat the combined opposition of textile mill owners, police, and the courts.[79]

Worker-made features visualized labor's opposition to the open shop and the American Plan and exposed the lies of their enemies. These films reversed the dominant images of perfidious union organizers and radicals seen in theatrical releases and of munificent welfare capitalism and state benevolence seen in nontheatricals. Workers are consistently portrayed as the seekers of justice, while capitalists and state authorities are shown as the perpetrators of violence and lawlessness. *The New Disciple*, based in part on Woodrow Wilson's "New Freedom," demonstrates how employers use scabs, hired thugs, lock-outs, and red squads "to destroy the principles and power of the union" and impose "the so-called 'American plan.'"[80] *The Contrast* (1921), blames the virtual civil war in the West Virginia coal fields on the greed and violence of mine owners and their private armies. Funded by contributions from embattled coal miners in West Virginia, Ohio, and Pennsylvania and distributed by the LFS, the movie exposes viewers to the "conditions of the struggle producing unionization of the miners, the contrast between the 'consumption' standards of the owners and the workers." Scenes of lockouts, blacklisting of union leaders, impoverished miner tent colonies, and cave-ins caused by owner negligence show the harsh conditions of everyday life and stand as powerful rebuttals to the halcyon images presented by the Bureau of Mines. Similarly, scenes of a hungry child rummaging through the mine owner's garbage and stealing the remains of his pampered dog's dinner show how little employers cared about the welfare of workers' families. Only after a victorious coal workers' strike *forced* owners to accede to their demands did miners secure decent wages, and improved living conditions for their families, and more humane working conditions.[81]

Worker-film companies complemented their feature films with newsreels made to counter the anti-union, antiradical pronouncements of capitalist-controlled newspapers and commercial newsreels. In August 1920, the LFS, run by former union organizer and frequent Socialist candidate Joseph D. Cannon, inaugurated a regular newsreel series that covered "every phase of the workers' life in the shop, in the factory, in his union during strikes, and on the picket lines."[82] The FFC's *Labor News Weekly* and *Economic Digest* promoted the cause of worker-cooperatives by featuring stories of "well-conducted labor enterprises from all parts of the United States and the world."[83] The railway brotherhoods' Motive Motion Picture Corporation, though unable to raise sufficient capital to make feature

films, produced newsreels of worker parades calling for government control of the railroads.[84] Pictures of militant strikes, mass protests, demonstrations, and radical rallies were also seen in the newsreels produced by Chicago communists.[85]

Smaller unions around the country made more modest efforts to use movies and movie theaters to counter employer assaults and bring labor's message to the public. The International Typographical Union produced a three-reel film, *His Brother's Keeper* (1925), which showed the social and economic benefits enjoyed by its members: apprenticeship training programs, health care, pension and mortuary plans, and a luxurious retirement home for elderly printers.[86] Striking Kansas coal miners, though lacking the funds of larger worker-film cooperatives, produced and distributed newsreels in 1921 of the harsh conditions in the state's mines. Taking a slightly different and cheaper path, Brooklyn laundry workers, New England cigarmakers, and eastern shoemakers defended strikes and resisted open shop drives by producing slides which they showed in local movie houses.[87] Movies were also screened by unions and radicals in New York, Los Angeles, Chicago, St. Louis, Philadelphia, Seattle, and other cities to attract people to meetings, rallies, and fundraisers, as alternatives to employer-sponsored recreation programs, and as a means of promoting greater sociability among members.[88]

For worker-filmmakers, as well as for capitalists, the success of their endeavors depended upon getting their products shown before a mass public. In this area, they fell short of their movie industry and business-world counterparts. "Pictures that are favorable to the working class," lamented the editors of the Butte *Bulletin*, "have difficulty in getting a place to have them shown, as the picture palaces are owned and controlled by the capitalist class."[89] Free markets no longer prevailed in this oligarchic industry. With the major distribution and exhibition facilities controlled by the studios and with large chains unwilling to handle their products, the LFS, FFC, AFL, and IWA set up independent networks that placed their films in neighborhood theaters, some first-run houses, union halls, auditoriums, and mining camps throughout the country. Although their runs typically lasted only several days, *The Contrast*, *The New Disciple*, *The Passaic Textile Strike*, and other worker-made films were widely viewed and praised by workers and some movie critics. Popular demand was often so great that several films were brought back to local theaters for return engagements. "Hundreds of thousands of workers have seen these films," boasted one IWA supporter, "and the financial surplus of $25.000 [for two IWA releases] can be cited as an added favorable result."[90]

Despite their modest initial success, these worker-film companies

never managed to reach a mass public on the sustained basis they had envisioned. By the end of the 1920s, virtually all of them had disappeared. The refusal of wealthy labor organizations like the AFL to fund or endorse these financially strapped companies, which Gompers perceived as too radical, played a large role in the demise of several firms. Without the official approval of the AFL and its 3 million potential customers, distributors and exhibitors were simply unwilling to risk handling these films. Yet, the ultimate failure of these firms had more to do with the protracted opposition of capitalists and state authorities than with their internal shortcomings. The mounting costs of producing well-made, entertaining feature films—a minimum of $40,000 to $80,000 in the early 1920s and several hundred thousand dollars by the late 1920s—made it imperative that these companies, which were self-sustaining operations, plug into established distribution and exhibition networks. However, as a few powerful corporations and studios assumed greater control of these operations, worker-film companies, as well as many other independent film producers, were squeezed out of the marketplace. "Motion picture theaters all over the country which are controlled by the movie trust," grumbled one labor paper, "have been forbidden" to show their products. Voicing similar complaints, independent filmmaker Murray Garsson noted in 1925 how the "unfair methods of the big companies are more throttling to competition today than ever before." Moreover, when "block-booking" practices forced even the local neighborhood theater owner to fill his yearly bill with studio releases, labor and independent filmmakers lost their last industry ally.[91]

The combined actions of state censors, federal authorities, and capitalists proved equally damaging to the workers' struggle for the screen. The appearance of worker-made films in the 1920s led local censorship boards to exercise the kind of class power that federal officials only threatened. Maryland law empowered authorities to censor all films and newsreels with "inflammatory scenes and titles calculated to stir up antagonistic relations between capital and labor." The New York Motion Picture Commission, and its counterparts across the nation, denounced films that "seek to undermine and revolutionize our form of government through insidious propaganda," and severely cut or completely censored movies, such as *The Contrast*, *The Jungle* (reissued by the LFS in 1922), *The Passaic Textile Strike*, and the IWA's *Breaking Chains* (1927) and *The Miners' Strike* (1928), which offered positive images of domestic strikes or the revolutionary activities of foreign workers.[92]

State censorship was most severe where class conflict was most pronounced. In Kansas, where striking coal miners battled owners, mili-

tia, and the courts, censors banned *The Contrast* on the grounds that it "lays too much stress upon the power of the strike and is chiefly labor union propaganda." In Ohio, New York, and Pennsylvania censors prohibited newsreels of local and regional strikes on the grounds that they "tend to incite to riot and disorder." [93] Employers, fearing the power such movies and newsreels might have upon their workers, often pressured politicians and local boards to censor films harmful to their interests. The establishment of a censorship board in strife-plagued West Virginia, NBRMP head W. D. McGuire reported in 1921, was "traced directly to capitalistic interests and originated from the fact that several pictures were shown indicating the success of trade unionism as opposed to capitalism." That same year, the governor of Pennsylvania ordered his board to eliminate from newsreels "scenes showing the strikers in the coal regions . . . struggling to secure their rights." [94]

Federal officials also feared the impact worker-made films might have upon public sympathies and labor militancy. Shortly after the establishment of the Labor Film Service in 1920, the young J. Edgar Hoover assigned agents form the Bureau of Investigation to provide him with extensive reports of the organization and its films. Agents were also assigned to report on the activities of Federation Film Corporation head John Arthur Nelson. Indeed, some of the most complete reviews of worker films can be found in the Bureau's records. [95] Officials at the Department of Agriculture, fearing that the planned rerelease of *The Jungle* would reflect poorly on their inspection service, pressured the LFS to cut several scenes that raised disturbing questions about the relation between the department and meat packers. Perhaps it was simply coincidence, but after Cannon refused this request he found it impossible of find an uptown New York theater owner to exhibit the film. [96]

With the arrival of "talkies" in the late 1920s, the initial struggle for control of the movies came to an end. Studios, theater chains, industrialists, and federal agencies, all of which were able to afford the exorbitant costs of making these films and wiring theaters in which to show them, continued presenting their antilabor messages to theatrical and nontheatrical audiences. Worker-owned film companies, strapped for funds and unable to overcome the opposition of the movie industry and government censors, soon collapsed. Labor and radical organizations did not, however, concede control of mass culture to capital and the state. By the late 1920s, they turned their attention and energies toward its newest medium: the radio. In Chicago and New York, audiences heard messages broadcast over stations owned, respectively, by the Chicago Federation of Labor and the So-

cialist party. In other cities, workers and radicals broadcast regular shows over local stations that regaled listeners with music, songs, variety acts, and news of strikes, mass demonstrations, and critical political events.[97]

These early battles over film offer some important lessons, especially for theorists studying how hegemony is established and for historians still debating the relative importance of culture, the workplace, and the state. Mass culture is not simply imposed from above upon a passive and unconscious public. From the early 1900s to the late 1920s, it was actively used by some among those masses to further their own class needs. Movies should be seen not as independent or isolated cultural products, but as powerful instruments that link the broader worlds of work, culture, and politics. Indeed, film has a *context* as well as a *text*, and the two are interdependent in determining the film's meaning. The silent films discussed here cannot be fully understood apart from the context of the era's bitter class struggles. During the first three decades of the twentieth century, labor and radical organizations repeatedly clashed with movie industry personnel, manufacturers and employer associations, local and state censors, and federal agencies, all of whom made or supported films depicting worker self-activity, unionism, and radicalism in the worst possible light. Each used film as part of larger efforts to promote their goals and thwart their enemies. If workers and radicals ultimately failed in their quest, it was because they were beaten by opponents who exercised considerable power to do so. This was cultural politics in its broadest sense.

The outcome of these contests has shaped the politics of contemporary film. Contrary to the claims of movie industry executives, audiences have little voice in deciding what kinds of films will be made. But the range of films available today—from the more liberal *Norma Rae* (1979) and *Reds* (1981) to the more conservative *F.I.S.T.* (1978)— and the types of political messages they convey have been profoundly affected by the struggles of the past. By forcing worker-film companies out of the mainstream of mass culture, capital and the state ensured that their depiction of past and present would dominate the screen. Labor and radical organizations continue to make documentaries and nontheatricals for small, select audiences. But they have never reached the screen again in such concerted fashion. Feature films advocating the causes of worker-cooperatives, socialism, industrial unionism, and militant collective action now seem as distant as the organizations that espoused them.[98]

Notes

[1] *The Crime of Carelessness*, produced in 1912 by the Thomas A. Edison Company for the National Association of Manufacturers; *The Miner's Lesson*, produced in 1914 by the Bureau of Mines (Department of Interior) in cooperation with the Anthracite Coal Operators. These films were viewed by the author at the Film Studies Center, Museum of Modern Art, New York City (henceforth cited as MOMA), and the Motion Picture Room, National Archives, Washington, D.C. (henceforth cited as NA). Information concerning *What Is To Be Done?* is taken from a copy of the shooting script in the Copyright Records (file LU3228), Motion Pictures, Broadcasting and Recorded Sound Division, Library of Congress (henceforth cited as Motion Pictures, LC), and the *New York Call*, Nov. 22, 1914. The research for this article was made possible by a grant from the John Randolph Haynes and Dora Haynes Foundation. I would also like to thank Charlie Musser, Ed Perkins, Robert Sklar, and the members of the Los Angeles Social History Study Group for their helpful comments and criticisms.

[2] For early attendance figures see Russell Merritt, "Nickelodeon Theaters 1905–1914: Building an Audience for the Movies," in Tino Balio, ed., *The American Film Industry* (Madison, 1976), p. 63. For later figures see New York *Daily Worker*, April 14, 1924.

[3] Kay Sloan, *The Loud Silents: Origins of the Social Problem Film* (Urbana, 1988); Louis Jacobs, *The Rise of American Film: A Critical History* (New York, 1968); Robert Sklar, *Movie-Made America: A Cultural History of the Movies* (New York, 1975); Myron Loundsbury, "'Flashes of Lightning': The Moving Picture in the Progressive Era," *Journal of Popular Culture*, 3 (Spring 1970), 769–97; Thomas Brandon, "Populist Film," unpublished manuscript, Thomas Brandon Collection, MOMA; Steven J. Ross, "The Unknown Hollywood: Political Filmmaking in the Progressive Era," *History Today*, 40 (April 1990), 40–46

[4] For works that locate and explore class battles over film during this later period see Russell Campbell, *The Cinema Strikes Back: Radical Filmmaking in the United States, 1930–42* (Ann Arbor, 1982); William Alexander, *Film On the Left: American Documentary Film From 1931 to 1942* (Princeton, 1981). Bert Hogenkamp, "Worker's Newsreels in the 1920's and 1930's," *Our History*, 68 (1977); and the special issue devoted to "American Labor Films" in *Film Library Quarterly*, 12 (1979).

[5] My analysis of these movies is partially based on my viewing of 114 silent films made by the movie industry, capitalists, labor organizations, and government agencies. A number of these films and their locations are cited in the texts and notes. Movie reviews and articles about film in labor newspapers are an invaluable and underutilized source of information. I have relied most heavily upon runs of the following newspapers for 1900–1930: *New York Call*, Los Angeles *Citizen*, (Chicago) *New Majority* (later the *Federation News*); Seattle *Union Record*; and the *Daily Worker* (published in Chicago and later New York).

[6] *Moving Picture World* (hereafter cited as *MPW*), July 2, Aug. 27, 1910; Los Angeles *Citizen*, Sept. 2, 1910. For early concerns and attacks on motion pictures see "Pictures and Politics," *MPW*, Dec. 5, 1909; Lary May, *Screening Out*

the Past: The Birth of Mass Culture and the Motion Picture Industry (New York, 1980); Garth Jowett, Film the Democratic Art: A Social History of American Film (Boston, 1976); Sklar, Movie-Made America.

[7] Los Angeles Citizen, Sept. 2, 1910. For movie industry reactions to labor complaints see Moving Picture News, Oct. 8, 1910.

[8] By 1911 working-class and radical newspapers were reviewing films and telling readers which to avoid and which to see. For reviews of The Jungle see Variety, June 26, 1914; MPW, June 20, 1914. Worker reactions to the film are described in New York Call, May 31, June 28, 1914. For reviews of Why? see MPW, May 3, June 14, 1913; Moving Picture News, June 13, 1913.

[9] A more detailed analysis of "Labor-Capital" films is presented in Steven J. Ross, "Struggles For the Screen: Workers, Radicals, and the Political Uses of Silent Film," American Historical Review (forthcoming). For a general discussion of the images of workers in silent films see Brandon, "Populist Film," passim; Sloan, Loud Silents, pp. 53–77; Jacobs, Rise of American Film, pp. 147–52; Philip Foner, History of the Labor Movement in the United States: Vol. III (1900–1909) (New York, 1964), pp. 49–60.

[10] Watterson Rothacker, "Industrial Uses of the Moving Pictures," Scientific American, 106 (June 15, 1912), p. 536; "Growing Use of Commercial Motion Pictures," Iron Age, April 10, 1913; "Motion Pictures in Industry," Iron Trade Review, Feb. 6, 1913; New York Call, March 7, 1914. The Industrial Film Company, organized in Chicago in December 1909, was apparently the first company to specialize in this particular line of endeavor. Anthony Slide, The American Film Industry: An Historical Dictionary (New York and Westport, Conn., 1986), pp. 169–70.

[11] Cleveland Citizen, May 10, 1913. Struggles over control of production and the imposition of scientific management are described in David Montgomery, Workers' Control in America (New York, 1979) and The Fall of the House of Labor: The Workplace, The State, and American Labor Activism, 1865–1925 (New York, 1987).

[12] "Many Inventions; the Movie and Shop Efficiency," Outlook, 103 (March 29, 1913), 736–37; L. A. Nelson, "Movies and Efficiency," Illustrated World, 24 (Feb. 1916), 775–78; Ernest A. Dench, "Industrial Applications of Motion Pictures," Machinery 23 (Oct. 1916), 133–38; Ernest A. Dench, "Training Your Employees by Motion Pictures," American Gas Engineering Journal, 107 (Dec. 22, 1917), 575–76.

[13] Moving Picture World, June 29, Dec. 28, 1912. It is not surprising that NAM hired the Edison Company, famous for its early monopolistic control over the movie industry, to make the film. Two years earlier, a Cleveland labor newspaper accused NAM of being behind the spate of anti-union films flooding the screen. Cleveland Citizen, Dec. 10, 1910.

[14] Quotations are from the film's intertitles. The movie was scripted by Progressive writer James Oppenheim and is available at MOMA.

[15] The events surrounding the Triangle fire and union struggles within the garment industry are examined in Leon Stein, The Triangle Fire, (Philadelphia, 1962).

[16] MPW, June 29, 1912; Oct. 17, 1914; Variety, Dec. 19, 1914. Two other

railroad company films, *The House That Jack Built* (1917) and *The Rule of Reason* (1917), also ascribed workplace accidents to worker carelessness. Jacobs, *Rise of American Film*, p. 281.

[17] *New York Call*, July 2, 1916. Ford's early film activities are also discussed in *Ibid.*, Jan. 23, 1916; A. B. Jewett to W. D. McGuire, May 24, 1916, National Board of Review of Motion Pictures Collection, Box 4, Special Collections, New York Public Library (henceforth cited as NBRMP). Many of these films and newsreels are at the National Archives; see Mayfield Bray, *Guide to the Ford Film Collection in the National Archives* (Washington, D.C., 1970).

[18] Sloan, *Loud Silents*, p. 4.

[19] *Moving Picture World*, Oct. 17, 1914. The distribution of these types of films is described in "The Y and the Movie in the Industrial Community," *Educational Film Magazine*, 1 (April 1919), 26–27.

[20] Diane Waldman, "'Toward a Harmony of Interests': Rockefeller, the YMCA and the Company Movie Theater," *Wide Angle*, 8 (ca. May 1986), 42.

[21] *Ibid.*, p. 44; Jacobs, *Rise of American Film*, p. 281; Jackson M. Anderson, *Industrial Recreation: A Guide to Its Organization and Administration* (New York, 1955), pp. 55; Leonard J. Diehl and Floyd R. Eastwood, *Industrial Recreation, Its Development and Present Status* (Lafayette, Indiana, 1940), pp. 7–14; Bureau of Labor Statistics, "Welfare Work for Employees in Industrial Establishments in the United States," *Bulletin of the United States Bureau of Labor Statistics*, #250 (Washington, 1919), pp. 82–85 (henceforth cited as *Bulletin of the BLS*); Stuart D. Brandes, *American Welfare Capitalism* (Chicago, 1976). For a general over-view of welfare work in Milwaukee factories before the war see Gerd Korman, *Industrialization, Immigrants, and Americanizers: The View From Milwaukee, 1866–1921* (Madison, 1967), pp. 87–109.

[22] Richard Dyer MacCann, *The People's Films: A Political History of U.S. Government Motion Pictures* (New York, 1973), p. 54. By 1916, the Bureau of Mines, Reclamation, Public Health, Indian Affairs, Signal Corps, Civil Service Commission, and others were making films. For descriptions of early federal film activity see *Ibid.*, pp. 43–55; Raymond Evans, "The U.S.D.A. Motion Picture Service, 1908–1943," *Business Screen Magazine*, 5 (1943), 19–231, 32–33; "Films By American Governments," *Films*, 1 (Summer 1940), 5–33; and Records of the Departments of Interior (RG 48) and Labor (RG 174), National Archives. For an overview of the scope of federal filmmaking and a list of surviving films see "Motion Pictures in the National Archives," unpublished typescript finding aid (45 pages) in the Motion Picture Room, NA. In the summer of 1913, over 100,000 people attended outdoor screenings of antituberculosis films in New York City. Local and state film activities are described in *New York Call*, July 1, 1912; June 16, July 14, 1913; *MPW*, June 14, 1913.

[23] *The Miner's Lesson* was produced in cooperation with the Anthracite Coal Operators and *Sanitation in Mining Villages* with the New Jersey Zinc Company. Both films can be viewed at the National Archives.

[24] Quotations are from the film's intertitles. A copy of the film can be found in the NA.

[25] Committee of Safety [U.S. Steel], *Bulletin*, Dec. 1918, pp. 5–6, quoted in Korman, *Industrialization, Immigrants, and Americanizers*, p. 159. Korman's

work provides an excellent summary of state and corporate attitudes toward Americanization. Government views on the subject can also be found in the Bureau of Immigration film, *The Americanization of Stefan Skoles* (1916). *New York Call*, July 20, Aug. 27, 1916.

²⁶ *Report of the Proceedings of the 30th Annual Convention of the American Federation of Labor . . . for 1910*, p. 338 (henceforth cited as *AFL Proceedings*); *New York Call*, May 15, 1911.

²⁷ *New York Call*, July 10, 13, 1911; *AFL Proceedings . . . 1916*, pp. 114, 278, 302; Samuel Gompers to James L. Pauley, Feb. 4, 1917, Fred J. Doward to Gompers, Jan. 21, 1917, Box 15 NBRMP.

²⁸ *The Western Comrade*, July 1913. Details of the Cripple Creek film can be found in *Cleveland Citizen*, Sept. 14, Oct. 26, 1907. For a more detailed analysis of the rise and fall of labor and radical filmmaking during the Silent era, as well as an analysis of specific films, their images, politics and reception, see Ross, "Struggles For the Screen."

²⁹ Frederic C. Howe, "What To Do With The Motion Picture Show: Shall It Be Censored," *The Outlook*, 107 (June 20, 1914), 412–16, quoted in Sloan, *Loud Silents*, p. 6.

³⁰ For an overview of union and radical activity during this era see Montgomery, *House of Labor*; James R. Green, *The World of the Worker: Labor In Twentieth Century America* (New York, 1980); Melvyn Dubofsky, *We Shall Be All: A History of the IWW* (New York, 1969); James Weinstein, *The Decline of Socialism in America: 1912–1925* (New Brunswick, 1984).

³¹ The quotation is from the movie's intertitles. The film cost $2,577 to make and distribute. For a copy of the scenario see Philip S. Foner, "A Martyr To His Cause: The Scenario of the First Labor Film in the United States," *Labor History*, 24 (Winter 1983), 103–111. Correspondence concerning the film can be found in the "Executive Council Minutes," Oct. 16, 1911–Jan. 13, 1912, reel 4, American Federation of Labor Records: The Samuel Gompers Era (henceforth cited as AFL Records).

³² *The Western Comrade*, July 1913. For reviews of the film see *Ibid.*, Oct. 1913, Los Angeles *Citizen*, Sept. 19, 1913, *New York Call*, Oct. 5, 1913.

³³ *New York Call*, Nov. 22, 1914; shooting script in LC copyright section.

³⁴ The lack of booking statistics prevent any exact attendance figures. Booking information concerning the exhibition of these films see Foner, *Martyr*, p. 106; Milwaukee *Social-Democratic Herald*, Oct. 14, Nov. 4, 1911; *AFL Weekly News Letter*, Sept. and Oct. 1911; *New York Call*, Sept. 28, Oct. 12, 1913, Nov. 22, 1914, Jan. 5, 1915; *California Social Democrat*, Oct. 18, 25, 1913.

³⁵ "Executive Council Minutes," Jan. 21, 1913, reel 4, AFL Records; *New York Call*, Feb. 26, April 5, 1916.

³⁶ The varied uses of films are described in Ross, "Struggles For the Screen."

³⁷ *New York Call*, Sept. 28, 1913; *Variety*, March 3, 1914; William D. McGuire to Samuel Gompers, Feb. 3, 1917, Box 15, NBRMP. *The Mirror of Death* and *The Strike at Coaldale* were theatrical films produced by Lubin and Eclair studios, respectively.

³⁸ *New York Call*, July 2, 1914; William D. McGuire to Samuel Gompers, Feb. 5, 1917, Box 5 and McGuire to Thomas Ince, Jan. 3, 1917, Box 4 NBRMP. Gardy was the film critic for the *New York Call*. The initial reference is to Jow-

ett, *Film, the Democratic Art*. Repeated calls by labor and radical organizations for an end to censorship fell upon deaf ears. See *Ibid.*, July 12, 1914; Feb. 4, 1916; *AFL Proceedings . . . 1916*. For discussions of early censorship see *Ibid.*; May, *Screening Out the Past*; Sklar, *Movie-Made America*; Robert Fischer, "Film Censorship and Progressive Reform: The National Board of Censorship of Motion Pictures, 1909–1922," *Journal of Popular Film*, 4 (1975), 143–50; Kathleen D. McCarthy, "Nickel Vice and Virtue: Movie Censorship in Chicago, 1907–1915," *Journal of Popular Film*, 5 (1976), 37–55; Francis G. Couvares and Kathy Peiss, "Censoring the Movies: The Problem of Youth in the 1920s, unpublished paper, presented at the convention of the Organization of American Historians, Reno, April 1988.

[39] *Pershing's Crusaders* and *America's Answer* had over 4,000 screenings. The CPI planned to distribute films to "2280 colored theaters for colored people in the United States." C. S. Hart Memorandum, March 28, 1918, Records of the Committee on Public Information, RG 63, Box 130 NA. The work of the CPI and its Division of Films is discussed in "Progress Report of the Department of Scenarios and Outside Production," August 10, 1918, Records of the CPI, RG 63, Box 41; [George Creel]. *Complete Report of the Chairman of the Committee on Public Information* (Washington, D.C., 1920); James R. Mock and Cedric Larson, *Words That Won the War: The Story of the Committee on Public Information, 1917–1919* (Princeton, 1939); Stephen Vaughn, *Holding Fast the Inner Lines: Democracy, Nationalism, and the Committee on Public Information* (Chapel Hill, 1980).

[40] For movie companies and federal agencies participating in the War Co-operation Board see *New York Times*, July 29, 1917. For movie industry relations with the CPI and federal agencies see sources in previous note; Records of the Committee on Public Information, RG 63, NA; *Variety* Aug. 31, 1917; *New York Times* July 7, Aug. 26, 1918; Craig Campbell, *Reel America and World War I* (Jefferson, N.C., 1985); Michael T. Isenberg, *War On Film: The American Cinema and World War, 1914–1941* (Rutherford, N.J., 1981).

[41] Niles's Letter of November, 1918 is quoted in *Variety*, Nov. 29, 1918. The Joint Committee on Motion Pictures, comprised of movie industry and government personnel, operated in the post-war era as the Joint Conference for Government and Allied Departments Engaged in Motion Picture Activities.

[42] For a list of these films and the reasons for their rejection see comments in "Films Rejected for Export," Records of CPI, 30-B3, RG 63; also see [Creel], *Complete Report*, pp. 103–105.

[43] Among the movies Niles and his colleagues dealt with were the anti-Bolshevik films *The Boomerang, Virtuous Men*, and *The Red Viper*. David K. Niles to Hugh L. Kerwin, March 12, 1919, Matthias Radin to Department of Labor, Oct. 16, 1919, Box 25; Tom Moore to W. E. Allen, April 1, 1919, Box 137, Records of the Department of Labor, RG 174. Niles also monitored and "censored" government and nontheatrical films dealing with labor themes. Niles to Roger Babson, Dec. 13, 1918, and, Babson to the Secretary of Labor, Dec. 14, 1918, RG 174, Box 137; Robert Starr to Samuel Gompers, July 18, 1919, RG 174, Box 25; W. D. McGuire to Gompers, Feb. 14, 1919, Box 15, NBRMP; *Variety*, Nov. 19, 1919.

[44] For a general overview of labor activity during this period, see Foster

Rhea Dulles and Melvyn Dubofsky, *Labor in America* (Arlington Heights, 1984), pp. 215–32; Montgomery, House of Labor; Green, *World of the Worker*; Dubofsky, *We Shall Be All.*

[45] The Americanism campaign and crackdown against radicalism are described in John Higham, *Strangers in the Land: Patterns of American Nativism, 1860–1925* (New York, 1965), p. 237; Korman, *Industrialization*, pp. 136–94; Robert H. Ferrell, *Woodrow Wilson and World War I, 1917–1921* (New York, 1985), pp. 200–18; David M. Kennedy, *Over Here: The First World War and American Society* (New York, 1980); Paul L. Murphy, *World War I and the Origin of Civil Liberties in the United States* (New York, 1979); and sources mentioned in previous note.

[46] *Los Angeles Times*, Jan. 3, 1920. Lane's efforts were endorsed by the Joint Congressional Committee on Education, which called upon the movie industry "to upbuild and strengthen the spirit of Americanism within our people." *New York Times*, Dec. 18, 1919. Also see *Ibid.*, Jan. 12, 1920; *Wid's Yearbook, 1920–1921* (nd) p. 383.

[47] *Educational Film Magazine*, 3 (Feb. 1920), 8; "The Immigrant and the 'Movies': A New Kind of Education," *Touchstone*, 7 (July 1920), 327–28.

[48] "Look Through Lincoln's Eyes," letter circulated by the Americanism Committee, ca. Jan. 1920, Box 164, NBRMP. For examples of suggested scenarios see W. A. Ryan to David Horsley, June 15, 1920, David Horsley papers, folder 28, Margaret Herrick Library, American Academy of Motion Picture Arts and Sciences, Beverly Hills, Cal. (hereafter cited as AMPAS); also see W. A. Ryan to George Kleine, May 19, 1920, Box 1, George Kleine Collection, Library of Congress, Washingon, D.C.

[49] Distribution was handled by the National Association of the Motion Picture Industry, whose members made up 95 percent of the nation's producers and distributors, as well as firms, such as the Community Motion Picture Bureau, which focused on nontheatricals. Jack Connolly [NAMPI] to Chief Clerk, Department of Labor, Jan. 3, 1921, Dept. of Labor records, RG 174, Box 25; Leslie Sprague [Community Motion Picture Bureau], *Americanization Through the Motion Pictures* (n.p., ca. 1919–1920), pamphlet in NBRMP, Box 2. The Americanization campaign even reached into state governments as Connecticut's Department of Americanization produced *The Making of an American* (1920). *Educational Film Magazine* 3 (Feb. 1920), 22.

[50] Quotations are from intertitles. The copy of the film in the LC. Other Americanism Committee releases included *The Land of Mystery* (1920), *Democracy, The Vision Restored* (1920), *One Law For All* (1920), and *Strangers Beware* (1920). Reviews and labor reactions to these films can be found in *Educational Film Magazine*, 3 (Feb. 1920), 9; 3 (March 1920), 20; *New York Call*, Nov. 4, 1920; March 5, 1921; Campbell, *Reel America*, p. 135; Samuel Gompers to W. D. McGuire, Oct. 18, 1920, Box 15, NBRMP.

[51] Labor conflicts reached a bitter peak in July 1921, when the International Alliance of Stage and Theatrical Employees launched a year-long boycott of films produced by the eleven leading studios. The relationship between the film industry and its unions is discussed in *Los Angeles Times, The Forty-Year War For A Free City: A History of the Open Shop in Los Angeles, October 1, 1929* (L.A.,

1929), pp. 23–26; Louis B. and Richard Perry, *History of the Los Angeles Labor Movement* (L.A., 1929); Murray Ross, *Stars and Strikes: Unionization of Hollywood* (N.Y., 1941); Ross, "Struggles For the Screen."

[52] *New York Call*, May 5, 1920. Goldwyn, Fox, Famous-Players Lasky, Metro, and Universal Studios were the focus of labor strife as well as the producers of anti-union films. Select Pictures, which distributed many of these films, was headed by Lewis J. Selznick, who also chaired the Americanism Committee. The relationship between changing film images and the changing structure of the film industry will be explored in my forthcoming manuscript, *Working Class Hollywood: Workers, Radicals, and the Movies.*

[53] Quotation is from review of *Bolshevism on Trial* in *Educational Film Magazine*, 1 (June 1919), 29. Copies of this film and *Dangerous Hours* are at the LC.

[54] For a copy of this resolution, passed at the AFL Convention in 1920, and a cover letter sent to the nation's leading producers see Frank Morrison to Universal Film Manufacturing Company, Nov. 15, 1920, Convention File 1920, reel 30, AFL Records.

[55] *Educational Film Magazine*, 3 (Feb. 1920), 8. For an excellent overview of the American Plan and welfare capitalism in the 1920s, see Irving Bernstein, *The Lean Years: A History of the American Worker, 1920–1933* (Boston, 1960); Sanford M. Jacoby, *Employing Bureaucracy* (N.Y., 1985).

[56] James E. Lough, "The Screen The Best Friend of Americanism," *Educational Film Magazine*, 4 (Oct. 1920), 9.

[57] A brief description of *The Americanization of Tony* can be found in "Selection of Films" file of the Community Motion Picture Bureau, Brandon Papers, T401, MOMA; Memorandum: Programs For Northern Pacific Railway Company," January 22, 1920, Brandon Papers, T401, MOMA; also see Eastern Film Corporation to W. D. McGuire, Feb. 11, 1922, Box 4, NBRMP. The Pennsylvania Railroad also made a number of "Safety-First" films such as *Shorty the Car Inspector, Good and Bad Firing,* and *Smoke Prevention. Moving Picture Age*, 4 (Jan. 1921), 12. Unfortunately, I have no evidence of how workers responded to these films.

[58] "Ford Educational Library Launched," *Educational Film Magazine*, 4 (Aug. 1920), 9; Bray, *Guide to the Ford Film Collection, passim*, The filmmaking activities of various corporations are surveyed in Jerome Lachenbruch, "Industrial Film As An Americanizer," *Educational Film Magazine*, 3 (Feb. 1920), 15.

[59] Some 490 firms established company unions during the turbulent years of 1919 to 1924; only 73 were established in the calmer period between 1924 and 1928. Over 200 firms adopted Employee Representation plans by the end of 1921, and 400 by 1928. Bernstein, *Lean Years*, pp. 170–88; Green, *World of the Worker*, 102–03.

[60] Samuel Gompers to Will Hays, July 20, 1923, *AFL Convention* 1922, reel 31, AFL Records. Bernstein, *Lean Years*, pp. 36–37.

[61] *American Industries*, 21 (Feb. 1921), 46; 23 (Sept. 1922), 43.

[62] The making and uses of post-war industrials are examined in "Industrial Film Notes," *Educational Film Magazine*, 1 (Feb. 1919), 31; Alfred Pittman, "How Movies Can Help You Train Workers," *Factory*, 25 (July 1, 1920), 29–32; "New Industrial Uses of the Movies," *Literary Digest*, 66 (Aug. 14, 1920),

91, 94–96; Dr. James Herbert Kelley, "Five Ways Every Factory Can Use Films," *Moving Picture Age*, 4 (Jan. 1921), 11–12; Arthur H. Loucks, "Industrial Pictures Coming Back," *American Industries*, 24 (Sept. 1923), 12, 28; "Industrial Films and Their Uses," *Journal of Industrial Welfare*, 10 (Oct. 1928), 317–19; E. I. Way, "Growth of Industrial Films," *Congressional Digest* (Nov. 7, 1928), pp. 299–301.

[63] Quotations are taken from intertitles. Copies of both films are in NA. For a synopses of these and other films made in cooperation with corporations see "List of Motion Pictures, U.S. Bureau of Mines, May 1921," Dept. of Interior Records, RG 48, Box 304; U.S. Employment Service, Dept. of Labor, *Industrial Films, A Source of Occupational Information* (Washington, 1946).

[64] Not surprisingly, these films were more warmly received by labor unions than their Bureau of Mines counterparts. A copy of this film, as well as *Behind the Scenes in the Machine Age* (1931), can be found in the Motion Picture Section, NA. The other two films were *When Women Work* (1920), and *The Woman Worker Past and Present* (1924). For a discussion of the Bureau's film endeavors and their reception see U.S. Department of Labor, Women's Bureau, *2nd Annual Report of the Director of the Women's Bureau for the Fiscal Year Ended June 30, 1920* (Washington, 1920), p. 12; *3rd Report . . . 1921*, p. 21; *4th Report . . . 1922*, pp. 16–17; *6th Report . . . 1924*, p. 15; *7th Report . . . 1925*, p. 17; *11th Report . . . 1929*, p. 23; *13th Annual . . . 1931*, p. 27; *14th Report . . . 1932*, p. 22.

[65] "Modern Industry 'On the Films': U.S. Government Production," *Discovery*, 10 (May 1929), 162–64. By 1922, the Department of Interior's Bureau of Education possessed over 8 million feet of film which it loaned for free to interested parties. [Bureau of Education], "Distribution of Motion Picture Films," April 25, 1922, Dept. of Interior Records, RG 48, Box 304. For a complete list of government films see the card catalogue in the Motion Picture Room, NA.

[66] Kelley, "Five Ways Every Factory Can Use Films," *Moving Picture Age*, 4 (Jan. 1921), 12; Anderson, *Industrial Recreation*, p. 56. A survey of 430 companies in 1926 found that 316 (73.5%) had instituted recreational programs by that year as opposed to 188 (43.7%) in 1916–1917; 61 (19.3%) companies showed films on a regular basis. For an analysis of post-war programs see *Ibid.*, pp. 53, 56–61; U.S. Dept. of Labor, Bureau of Labor Statistics, "Health and Recreation Activities in Industrial Establishments, 1926," *Bulletin of the BLS*, #458 (Washington, 1928), pp. 39.

[67] Sir Gilbert Parker article in *Vanity Fair*, quoted in New York *Call*, Nov. 18, 1928. Corporate film activities are discussed in *Moving Picture Age*, 4, (Jan. 1921), 12; 4 (Feb. 1921), 29; 4 (March 1921), 17–18; *Educational Film Magazine*, 1 (Feb. 1919), 31; 3 (Feb. 1920), 8; Waldman, Toward a "Harmony of Interests," 44–48; A. S. Young [International Harvester Co.] to G. P. Hutchins [Community Motion Picture Bureau], July 16, 1919, in Brandon Collection, T401, BLS, "Welfare Work For Employees," *Bulletin of the BLS*, #250, pp. 82–85; BLS, "Health and Recreation Activities," *Bulletin of the BLS*, #458, pp. 1, 31–41; Diehl and Eastwood, *Industrial Recreation*, pp. 13–15.

[68] New York *Daily Worker*, April 14, 1924.

[69] The first advertisement for the Motion Picture Bureau appeared in the

September 1922 issue of NAM's monthly periodical, *American Industries*. A list of the twelve circuits and the films they distributed first appeared in *Ibid.*, 23 (July 1923), 44.

[70] *New York Call*, Aug. 6, 1923. The AMPC's plans are discussed in William H. Barr, "To The Members of the National Founder's Association: *Weekly Newsletter* No. 272, April 10, 1923, Convention Records, 1922, reel 31, AFL Records; (Chicago) *New Majority*, May 5, 1923. The AMPC also purchased and put their logo on Americanization films like *The Land of Opportunity*. For the Church Motion Picture Corporation see "Memorandum. The Church Motion Picture Corporation," Paul Smith to W. D. McGuire, Jan. 5, 1922, Box 2, NBRMP.

[71] Chicago *Daily Worker*, Oct. 6, 1924.

[72] Julius Frankenberg to the Secretary of the Interior, Feb. 2, 1923, Dept. of Interior Records, RG 48, Box 304. In 1921, the Bureau of Commercial Economics was distributing over 21 million feet of nontheatrical film, free of charge to interested parties. Kelley, "Five Ways Every Factory Can Use Films," *Moving Picture* 4 (Jan. 1921), 11. For other organizations involved in the distribution of these films see Frances Holley to Albert B. Fall, May 7, 1921, Dept. of Interior Records, RG 48, Box 304; W. D. Heydecker to U.S. Department of Interior, Nov. 23, 1922, in *Ibid.*; George Zehrung, "Bettering The Industrial Film," *American Industries*, 23 (April 1923), 31; *Educational Film Magazine*, 4 (Aug. 1920), 9; Ford Motor Company to People's Institute, March 16, 1922, Box 4 NBRMP; Leslie Sprague [Community Motion Picture Bureau], *Motion Pictures in Community Service* (n.p., ca. 1919–1920), and Leslie Sprague, *Motion Pictures in the Mill* (n.p., ca. 1919–1920), pamphlets in Box 2, NBRMP.

[73] *New York Call*, May 2, 1920; Chicago *Daily Worker*, Sept. 1, 1925.

[74] David Horsley, "The Power of Public Opinion," Feb. 18, 1919, in Horsley Papers, Upton Sinclair file, AMPAS; (Chicago) *New Majority*, Jan. 8, 1921.

[75] Quotation is from a circular letter written by LFS director Joseph D. Cannon to potential investors, ca. June 1920, Investigative Case Files, reel 941, Records of the Bureau of Investigation, National Archives. The MMPC, LFS, and FFC were joint-stock ventures capitalized at $200,000, $50,000, and $100,000, respectively. The history, activity, and reception of these ventures are analyzed in Ross, "Struggles For the Screen."

[76] Seattle *Union Record*, March 25, 1920.

[77] For a description of the film, its images of workers and employers, and its political messages see Seattle *Union Record*, May 9, 11, 12, 1921; *New York Call*, Dec. 19, 1921; *Wid's Daily*, Dec. 12, 1921; *MPW*, Dec. 31, 1921; Chicago *Daily Worker*, March 18, 1923.

[78] A summary of the movie's images and plot line see John J. Manning, "Labor's Reward," *American Federationist*, 32 (Nov. 1925), 1056–58; L.A. *Citizen*, Aug. 14, 1925; (Chicago) *Federation News*, Dec. 26, 1925. I have just discovered a partial nitrate copy of the film and am in the process of working on its restoration with the U.C.L.A. Film and Television Archives staff.

[79] A copy of this film is housed at MOMA. For reviews see (Chicago) *Daily Worker*, Sept. 23, Oct. 18, 1926, May 10, 1927; Brandon, "Populist Film," Chapter on 1920s, file D43, MOMA.

[80]*New York Call*, Dec. 17, 1921.

[81]*New York Call*, Sept. 25, 1921. For reviews of the film and its images see *Ibid.*, June 4, 1921; Los Angeles *Citizen*, Sept. 23, 1921; (Chicago) *New Majority*, April 4, 1922.

[82]*New York Call*, Aug. 10, 1920. For descriptions of newsreels see *ibid.*, Aug. 13, 23, Sept. 3, 1920, Dec. 28, 1921.

[83]*New York Call*, June 13, 1920; also see "Minutes of the Seattle Central Labor Council," Sept. 20, Oct. 25, 1922, Records of the Seattle Central Labor Council, Box 8, Special Collections, University of Washington; (Chicago) *New Majority*, Aug. 19, 1922.

[84]The activities of the MMPC are described in Los Angeles *Citizen*, March 7, 1919; Seymour Hastings to David Horsley, July 2, 1920, Horsley papers, folder 17, AMPAS; Sloan, *Loud Silents*, pp. 52–53, 76–77.

[85]The *Daily Worker* produced a sporadic newsreel series entitled *The Film Extra*. For examples of these and other Chicago-based newsreels and documentaries see *New York Call*, Dec. 29, 1922; New York, *The Worker*, Oct. 20, 1923; Chicago *Daily Worker*, Nov. 17, 1924; New York *Daily Worker*, April 26, 1927; Aug. 7, 1928; March 14, 1929.

[86]Seattle *Union Record*, Sept. 28, 1925.

[87]*New York Call*, July 29, 1921; *Ibid.*, July 1, 1920; *Ibid.*, Oct. 11, 1921; "Union Label and Organizing Campaign Meeting, Washington, D.C.," May 6, 1925, Convention File 1924, reel 32, AFL Records.

[88]For examples see *New York Call*, April 4, 1922; Los Angeles *Citizen*, April 14, 1922, May 13, 1927; (Chicago) *New Majority*, March 24, Dec. 1, 1923; (Chicago) *Daily Worker*, July 18, 1925; (New York) *Daily Worker*, June 2, 1927, Feb. 18, 1929; Seattle *Union Record*, Nov. 5, 1927; Anderson, *Industrial Recreation*, p. 53.

[89]Butte *Bulletin*, quoted in New York *Call*, Oct. 27, 1922.

[90]Chicago *Daily Worker*, Sept. 26, 1925. Each of the major worker-film companies set up distribution offices in a number of cities, and hired agents to arrange showings in neighborhood theaters, auditoriums and union halls. When theater owners proved reluctant to screen these films, the film companies often rented their own theaters. The efforts to reach the screen, as well as worker reception of these films, are discussed in Ross, "Struggles For the Screen."

[91]Los Angeles *Citizen*, Jan. 12, 1923; (Chicago) *Daily Worker*, Nov. 11, 1925. The increased monopolization of production, distribution, and exhibition are analyzed in Benjamin B. Hampton, *A History of the Movies* (New York 1931); May Huettig, *Economic Control of the Motion Picture Industry* (Philadelphia, 1944); Jacobs, *Rise of American Film*, pp. 289–92; Douglas Gomery, "The Growth of Movie Monopolies: the Case of Balaban and Katz," *Wide Angle*, 3 (1979), 54–63; Douglas Gomery, "The Movies Become Big Business: Publix Theaters and the American Chain Store Strategy," *Cinema Journal*, 18 (Spring 1979), 26–40.

[92](Chicago) *Daily Worker*, April 14, 1924; *Annual Report of the Moving Picture Commission For the Year 1922* (Albany, 1922), p. 10. Among the foreign films distributed by the IWA and censored by state officials were *Russia Through The*

Shadows (1921), *The Fifth Year* (1924), *Russia and Germany: A Tale of Two Republics* (1924), *Beauty and the Bolshevik* (1924), *Potemkin* (1926), *The End of St. Petersburg* (1928).

[93] W. D. McGuire to American Federation of Labor, Sept. 24, 1921, Box 15, NBRMP. Chicago *Daily Worker*, March 18, 1925. For other examples of censorship see *Ibid.*, April 14, 1924, Feb. 26, 1919; W. D. McGuire to R. Murray, April 21, 1921, Box 43; McGuire to Samuel Gompers, July 12, 1922, Box 15, NBRMP.

[94] W. D. McGuire to R. Murray, April 21, 1921; Charles Stelze to Dr. Herbert Gates, March 17, 1921, Box 43 NBRMP.

[95] For reports on the LFS, see J. E. Hoover to Brigadier General A. E. Nolan, Dec. 8, 1920, Hoover to Nolan, Jan. 10, 1921, Agent H. J. Lennon "Report on 'The Contrast' Moving Picture Propaganda," March 17, 1921, Investigative Case Files, Bureau of Investigation, Reel 941, NA, For Nelson, see Agent E. Kosterlitzky, "Reports," April 9, 15, 1918, in *Ibid.*, reel 512.

[96] The correspondence between the U.S. Department of Agriculture and the LFS is reprinted in *New York Call*, Jan. 26, 1922.

[97] The Chicago Federation of Labor opened WCFL in July 1926. The next year, socialists in New York opened WEVD. The AFL also investigated the possibilities of opening a national radio station. For detailed descriptions of union forays into radio during this period see "Radio Broadcasting" section in Convention Records 1925, reel 33, AFL Records; Nathan Godfried, "The Origins of Labor Radio: WCFL, the 'Voice of Labor,' 1925–1928," *Historical Journal of Film, Radio, and Television*, 7 (1987), 143–59.

[98] Although an occasional radical film, such as *Matewan*, reaches the screen, it rarely gets the kind of publicity, distribution, or exhibition play accorded to more conservative films.

It is a pernicious notion that a man may do what he will with his own. . . . A man may not breed diseased cattle. No more should he be allowed wantonly to waste forests or to make lands impotent.

—Liberty Hyde Bailey
1910

The farmer's attitude and interested cooperation had to be considered. An autocratic, overhead program of compulsion, no matter how right it may be, is not possible in individualistic America.

—William A. Lloyd
1926

William H. Harbaugh

THE LIMITS OF VOLUNTARISM
FARMERS, COUNTY AGENTS, AND THE CONSERVATION MOVEMENT

THE concept of voluntarism has long been a celebrated tenet of the American commitment to political and economic freedom. Although often equated with laissez faire, voluntarism neither precluded planning nor discountenanced intervention in the marketplace. On the contrary, it assumed that coordinated, but noncoercive, action was essential to the ordering of a free society. Much of the nation's social infrastructure originated in the voluntary activities of citizen groups, and notwithstanding the dramatic expansion of government in the twentieth century, citizen action remains a striking feature of the modern polity. Yet, as the collapse of corporate welfarism during the Great Depression suggests, voluntarism was ill-equipped to resolve many important economic issues.[1]

Even before the Great Depression shattered illusions, the emergence early in the twentieth century of a public awareness[2] of the maltreatment of the land by farmers and ranchers put one kind of voluntarism to the test. Stimulated by the adjurations of Theodore Roosevelt, the findings of federal commissions, and the teachings of county agents, progressive activists strove from the turn of the century to convert farmers and ranchers to scientifically acceptable ecological practices. This, the agricultural phase of the first great conservation movement, challenged a wide array of rural values. Some were endemic to country people everywhere, others reflected distinctively American patterns of land use and land holding. All, including the belief that a man's property was his own to use or abuse, were deeply rooted.

In time, the abler and usually more prosperous farmers adopted those soil-nurturing practices which demonstrably served their short-term interests. But only a small minority of them and hardly any marginal farmers whatever faced up to such critical long-term problems

as the loss of soil through washing or blowing. This disregard by all classes of even their own posterity's interests prompted New Dealers, the heirs of the progressive tradition so powerfully set forth by Arthur Link in his *American Epoch*, to search for a political strategy that would promote conservation and yet maintain the form of voluntarism. The cultural and economic aspects of the developments which led to that quest are the central concern of the pages that follow.

I

For three centuries after the founding of Jamestown, American farmers lived by the Biblical injunction to "subdue" the earth, but only rarely did they honor the corollary injunction to "replenish" it. Blessed with an abundance of land and favored by a political ethos that sanctified small, individual holdings, they conceived it their interest to "mine" the soil, sell out at a profit, and take up cheaper land elsewhere. As an Illinoisan confessed before the Civil War, "us western farmers have been skinning God's heritage, taking the cream off, and leaving for parts unknown, until humanity has a heavy bill against us for wasting the vital energies of mother earth." Fifty years later, fewer than one-half of the nation's more than six million farmers had been working the same soil longer than five years. "I sold my land in Iowa for twice what I paid in Montana," a transplanted Midwesterner explained.[3]

By the coming of the New Deal, according to the more extreme estimates, erosion had destroyed or rendered useless one hundred million acres—an area equal to Illinois, Ohio, North Carolina, and Maryland combined. Another two hundred million acres had lost between one- and three-fourths of their topsoil, and a like amount was beginning to erode.[4] Within a generation, lamented the dean of the college of agriculture at the University of Illinois, "lands that had been thousands of years in the making were ruined." Each year 3.6 billion metric tons of soil, three-fourths of it cropland, washed away. "Probably in no country in the world," concludes a recent text, "had such a short period of farming caused such tremendous soil wastage."[5]

Some of the damage was natural. Members of the de Soto expedition found the lower Mississippi River flooded in 1543, and travellers on the Great Plains reported dust storms years before permanent settlers plowed up the sod.[6] Nevertheless, much of the loss was induced by man: by lumbermen whose clear-cutting damaged watersheds; by ranchers whose overgrazing depleted the range; by farmers whose

destruction of grassland intensified soil washing and blowing. In many sections of most agricultural states, noted the United States Industrial Commission in 1902, "modern methods . . . are hardly to be regarded as factors in the conditions of farming." Even rotation of crops, a principle known and in general practice in England over two hundred years ago, was just beginning to be adopted widely in Ohio and Illinois. Farther west, from the semi-arid regions of the Dakotas down to the Panhandle of Texas, the planting of crop after crop of wheat on the same fields was almost universal.[7] The Easterner who views western Iowa, Kansas, and Nebraska, wrote the Iowa farm editor, Henry Wallace, in 1898, "can scarcely believe his eyes when he sees thousands of . . . intelligent men deliberately pursuing a policy which has been condemned . . . for at least 150 years, and which in the end has brought poverty to the men who have practiced it."[8]

Actually, some eastern husbandry was considerably less advanced than Wallace implied. Old timers in New York were said to laugh at the idea of plowing under leguminous crops, even though continuous planting of rye had "completely worn out" their land,[9] and numbers of their counterparts in the remote reaches of Upper New England were reported to be no more enlightened. The "inactivity, disinterestedness, and thriftlessness" of the large majority in New Hampshire, complained a special agent of the United States Department of Agriculture in 1910, made possibilities there even less "hopeful" than in Vermont.[10]

All the worst features of northern agriculture were compounded with a vengeance in the South. "[T]hese people seem to be shamed to farm," a newcomer to Georgia wrote near the end of the century, ". . . plowing around stumps for forty years . . . and many other things of the kind." Land, observed an Alabaman, was becoming too poor even to support negroes. "Our sothern [sic] people as a rule must be driven into adopting a different system."[11] By every measure save the number of farms and farmers, the region lagged far behind all others. Soil depletion was more extensive, output per farm worker much lower, the one-crop system more insidious. "If we had a single acre of clovers, alfalfa, or vetch in the county when the Demonstration Work started, I do not know it," a Georgia county agent remarked in 1915.[12] The soil of his county, a Texas agent reported in 1918, had lost 25 percent of its fertility "by farming the same" year after year.[13] The South used more commercial fertilizer than any other region, yet the per-acre yield of virtually every food crop it produced fell well below the national norm—40 percent below it for corn and wheat and about 25 percent for vegetables. Moreover, the output of tobacco per acre declined from 1900 to 1920; and though that of cotton held steady, it

did so mainly because yields from new land, especially in Texas, offset the decline in the Southeast.[14]

Assuredly, not all the nation's farming was so deficient. Secretary of Agriculture David M. Houston estimated in 1913 that about 40 percent of the land was "reasonably well cultivated,"[15] and two years later Cooperative Extension Service leaders concluded that perhaps 20 percent of the more than two thousand farmers in many Corn Belt counties were growing "as good corn" as any government functionary could grow.[16] Concurrently, mortgage agents of the Connecticut General Life Insurance Company found considerable praiseworthy husbandry in Iowa, Missouri, South Dakota, and Mississippi as well.[17] Much of the limestone soil in Pennsylvania and the Shenandoah Valley was more fertile in 1900 than it had been in 1800, and much of the land still under cultivation in New England was not greatly poorer in plant food than when the Pilgrims landed.[18]

Contemporary commentators tended to blame the despoliation of southern and midwestern lands on the nation's two million tenants, 40 percent of whom had worked the same farm two years or less. They were constrained to "mine" the soil, *Wallaces' Farmer* explained, because their short tenure obliged them "to get every dollar they can out of [it]"; they act on the motto, "'after me the deluge.'"[19] On average, tenants put fewer acres into soil-restoring grasses and raised less livestock than did owners. The more progressive landlords tried to preserve their property by putting conservation provisions into leases. Iowa contracts frequently required that slopes be seeded, crops rotated, and manure spread, while Wisconsin leases usually specified which parts of the farms were to be kept in permanent pasture.[20] But tenants often balked. "If you want manure on [the land] . . . ," a North Dakotan wrote his absentee landlord, "you can put it on yourself."[21] One-year leases encouraged the neglect. The solution, concluded *Wallaces' Farmer*, was to extend them and give tenants a vested legal interest in improvements:

> The landlord can confiscate any increased fertility the tenant may have put into the soil. . . . So long as the tenant is liable to the confiscation of soil improvement, he naturally does not want to do any more improving than is absolutely necessary; and having no security that he will remain on the farm more than a year, he does not try.[22]

These patterns were hardly universal. By the early 1920s tenants in New York were operating larger farms, growing more crops, keeping more cows, and producing more per worker than owner-operators.[23] In thickly settled parts of the Midwest, moreover, perhaps half of all tenants were young men working land owned by close relatives.

"[H]ustling and wide-awake" in the view of numerous observers, they were said to have greater "breadth of vision" than their elders, especially if they stood to acquire the land.[24] They inclined, consequently, to be more soil-conscious than unrelated tenants or workers on corporate farms.[25] An indeterminate portion of the remainder—the "thriftless 'hand-to-mouth' fellows whom no landlord wants if he can help it," according to a Wisconsin economist—were crowded onto the poorest land.[26] Many landlords shared responsibility for the maltreatment of the land. Retired farmers in most cases and "a good sort on the whole," they often encouraged tenants to farm exploitatively because they needed all they could get from their half-share to pay expenses in town. "The able-bodied Illinois farmer who 'retires' and simply 'puts in his time' about town," complained a civic-minded banker, "is a detriment to the country, the town, himself and his farm." The tenant who can meet the exactions of the landlord and still make a living, declared a large, and progressive Illinois operator, "has got to be an . . . accomplished soil robber."[27] Yet the landowners themselves averaged less than 3 percent on their investment across the Middle West.

Through much of the South, tenancy was as unrelieved a curse on the land as on the physical and psychic well-being of the tenants. Erosive land use was more severe on tenant farms than on owner-operated ones, despite the correlation of tenancy and clear-till crops.[28] One reason for this, concludes a probing study of Georgia, the most tenant-ridden state in the nation, was that owners themselves were too impoverished to take the long view. Land was a resource to be exploited until it was exhausted, if it could not be sold quickly at a profit, and more than "occasional" attention to tenants and croppers was therefore unnecessary.[29] Graphically, a North Carolinian described the consequences. The tenant on a two-horse farm in Wilson County, "a good man, as he seemed to be," had promised to keep up the terraces:

> The land-owner did not see the land in some years. . . . After a while [he] . . . went and looked over the land and found that this tenant had plowed down the terraces (because the land was better there) . . . and had run his rows straight up and down the hill. He utterly ruined the farm, and left it.[30]

By 1920 tenants numbered almost one-half of the South's more than three million operators. Of these, perhaps 50 percent were croppers who supplied only their labor and made about $150 a year in the cotton regions. Burdened by debt, debilitated by disease, and disinclined even to grow their own vegetables, they gave the land only such

care as they were forced to give it.[31] Meanwhile almost everyone but the most progressive farmers ignored the warnings of federal and experiment station scientists that even bottomland was being rendered "worthless" by sand washed down from steep hills planted in corn or cotton. Short of "moving on" or recultivating abandoned land, the solution for owner and tenant alike was to ply the soil with more and more commercial fertilizer.[32]

Nationally, the million or so first and second generation immigrant farmers probably raised the quality of land care somewhat. Wherever Germans or Swedes settled, a Grange leader noted, land prices rose.[33] "Unlike the restless American, with his ears ever pricked to the hail of distant opportunity," wrote the acerbic Wisconsin sociologist, E. A. Ross, "the phlegmatic German identifies himself with his farm, and feels a pride in keeping it in the family generation after generation." The tenancy rate of all immigrants ran substantially below that of native-born whites, and by 1920 the average value of immigrant-owned farms was $15,464 as compared to $11,601 for native-born whites.[34] Regrettably, this extraordinary success owed more to immigrants' willingness to forego immediate pleasure—to work women and children in the fields and to live meanly for some years—than to soil-conserving techniques.[35]

Most immigrants to the grain regions of the Middle West adapted readily to prevailing mono-cultures, and in some areas Russian-Germans put even more land into grain than did Old Stock farmers. One result, writes a recent student of Norwegian immigrants, was that "poor farming" in the Old Country became "good farming" in the New Country—at least until the land ran down, as it invariably did.[36] Still, by comparative standards, immigrants treated their soil with considerable care, especially after they entered the period of "cultural rebound."[37]

Concurrently, small colonies of Bohemians in Virginia, Germans in Alabama, Italians in Arkansas, Swiss-Germans in Tennessee, and larger groups of Germans and Bohemians in Texas were proving that the southern social and economic structure was not all-inhibiting for those not born into it. And though it would be extreme to say, as one scholar did, that immigrant farmers were "largely if not mainly" responsible for such change as occurred in the South, European immigrants in the South did do better economically and did treat the land more sensitively than their black or white counterparts.[38]

II

By 1910 study of accelerated wind and water erosion, as scientists term man-induced erosion, was well under way. In 1894 F. H. King of

the Wisconsin Experiment Station devised a plan to reduce soil blowing and that same year Chief Chemist Harvey W. Wiley of the USDA
posited a program for the recovery of washed soils.[39] Soon afterward
federal scientists began to make county soil surveys and, in 1899, to
publish reports. Six years later a pathfinding survey of Louisa County,
Virginia, by Hugh Hammond Bennett probed sheet erosion—the loss
of soil from the runoff of rain water. The following year it was estimated that American rivers carried a billion tons of soil into the sea
every year.[40]

  These and similar developments became at once cause and effect of
the emergent conservation "crusade."[41] President Theodore Roosevelt declared in his first annual message in 1901 that forest and water
problems were perhaps "the most vital internal questions" facing the
nation, and in numerous communications thereafter he spoke
learnedly and presciently on ecological concerns. He reminded Congress and the nation that storage of water, not production of lumber,
was the forest's most important use. He pronounced the "enormous
loss of fertility" through soil washing the "most dangerous of all
wastes now in progress." He deplored the loss of carrying power
wrought by "uncontrolled grazing" on the public range. He dilated
on the consequences of deforestation:

> Denudation leaves naked soil. When the soil is gone, men must go; and
> the process does not take long. . . . What has thus happened in northern
> China, what has happened in central Asia, in Palestine, in North Africa,
> in parts of the Mediterranean countries of Europe, will surely happen in
> our country if we do not exercise . . . wise forethought.[42]

Roosevelt's preferred solution was direct government intervention.
"The forest can only be protected by the State, by the nation," he asserted, "and the liberty of action of individuals must be conditioned
upon what the State or nation determines to be necessary for the common safety." He supported Chief Forester Gifford Pinchot's imposition of grazing controls on the ranges within the National Forests, and
he tried, in vain, to win authorization to regulate grazing on the three
hundred million acres of public grassland outside the Forests.[43] He
also opposed indiscriminate settlement by homesteaders. The people,
he complained, "refuse to face squarely the proposition that much of
these lands ought to be leased and fenced as pastures, and that they
cannot possibly be taken up with profit as small homesteads." De-
fiantly, in 1907, he created twenty-one new National Forests embrac-
ing sixteen million acres just hours before a law prohibiting the
Executive from taking such action went into effect.[44]

  Thereafter, Roosevelt resorted increasingly to moral suasion. He

denounced those who destroy the forests, who "reap what they have not sown," and who "exhaust the land for their own immediate profit." He commended the Department of Agriculture's demonstration work in the South. And he underlined the interdependence of water, forestry, and agriculture. Declaring "that every stream is a unit from its source to its mouth," he appointed the Inland Waterways Commission in 1907. The year following he urged the first national conference of governors to accept a comprehensive plan for development of natural resources. "No wise use of farm exhausts its fertility," he averred. "So with forests." Soon afterward he appointed the Federal Commission on the Conservation of Natural Resources. He also called a private conservation conference of representatives of the United States, Canada, and Mexico. Finally, he appointed Liberty Hyde Bailey, the eminent Cornell agriculturist, head of a national commission on rural life.[45]

Moved partly by neo-Malthusian fears that population would exceed the food supply by the end of the century, the Country Life Commission hoped to hold the most efficient producers to the farm by improving the quality of rural life.[46] Inclusion of Henry Wallace and Gifford Pinchot in its membership assured the Commission a conservation component, and its report of 1909 decried the "exploitational" nature of much farming, deplored the failure of tenants to maintain the land, and pronounced soil wash " 'the heaviest impost borne by the American farmer.' " In words that bore Pinchot's imprimatur, it called for development of woodlots and communal purchase of forests in poor or hilly areas; and in words that just as surely bore that of Wallace, it warned that the single crop syndrome was beginning to appear in the wheat regions, "where the yields are constantly growing less and where the social life is usually monotonous and barren." Pointing to demonstration work in the South as a "marked example" of how people could be taught to diversify, the report urged that the system be extended to the North.[47]

By then the stewardship concept which infused Roosevelt's and Pinchot's public philosophy was being related increasingly to farmers. "No man really owns his acres," Bailey told the Second National Conservation Congress in 1910; society would have to act against those who refused to become "voluntary" conservationists.[48] "In a higher sense," declared the president of the National Soil Fertility League two years later, "the man in whose name the title stands is not the real owner of the land. . . . The fertile fields were placed here by God Almighty for the use of humanity for all time."[49] William Jennings Bryan had already said as much. All men were transients, the Great Commoner averred in 1911. "What rights has the tenant of today to

impoverish the estate upon which generations to come must live?" [50]

Indubitably, such rhetoric raised the public consciousness and stimulated a measure of action; all through the period, the inclusion of soil conservation clauses in farm leases and loan agreements seems to have grown.[51] Fundamentally, however, the traditional conception of property "rights" prevailed: no Progressive Era state legislature made a serious effort to outlaw soil-depleting or watershed-destroying practices; nor did Congress even consider making care of the land a condition of entitlement under the Homestead laws.[52]

III

Increasingly, in these circumstances, interest turned to direct education. A decade earlier the Industrial Commission had concluded that neither the agricultural colleges nor the experiment stations were "effecting anything like the mutually helpful service [they] . . . were intended to bring to the practical development of farming." And understandably so.[53] As Secretary Houston remarked of the stations' proliferating publications, "many farmers do not get these bulletins, do not read them if they get them, do not understand them if they read them, and do not apply them if they understand them."[54] More frustrating still, many who did understand them disregarded them. "I used to raise and feed cattle at a small profit, and often at a loss," a Midwesterner explained:

> Now I am older, I am mining the soil; for I have learned that renters and land buyers are not willing to pay for stored-up fertility. . . . This soil is three feet deep. . . . [A]t its present rate of decrease in fertility, it will be raising good corn long after the fertility has leeched out of my bones. . . . I am with those Dakota farmers who prefer to put in their wheat and then go fishing rather than raise fodder corn and cattle after the advice of reformers.[55]

By then the demonstration work begun by Dr. Seaman Knapp in Texas in 1902 had raised the output of cooperating farmers markedly, and on that and other accounts Knapp's system was widely acclaimed. "[N]ext to the Farmers' Union," a Georgia farm leader asserted, demonstration work was "the greatest force through the South today to influence the common farmer for the upbuilding of the country."[56] Northern railroad and agri-business interests soon espoused the demonstration concept, and between 1910 and 1914 they installed 227

agents across the North. Meanwhile the colleges and experiment stations grudgingly endorsed creation of a national county agent system.[57] The colleges, declared a committee of their association in 1912, should try to reach *all* farmers, though not so much because of "sentimental regard for that last unfortunate man" as because of the need to foster soil conservation at every intellectual level.[58]

President Woodrow Wilson duly pronounced demonstrations the only kind of work "which generates real education," and early in 1914 he signed into law the Smith-Lever bill to create a national county agent system. Drafted partly by the National Soil Fertility League and the Association of Agricultural Colleges and Experiment Stations, the measure had been gestating since 1909.[59] It aimed to raise the quality of farm life by education; and though its proponents put greatest emphasis on increasing productivity, they proposed to realize the increase by nourishing the land. "This country is destroying the fertility of its soil," Albert B. Cummins of Iowa warned in the Senate debate. "Presently our land will be as barren as any that can be seen elsewhere."[60]

Declaring themselves unalterably opposed to "centralization of power and domination" by the federal government, Smith-Lever's framers fostered what they termed the "vital and to some extent . . . new principle" of close cooperation between the states and the federal government. To this end, the act authorized matching grants to states and vested control of demonstration work in the colleges under reasonably flexible federal guidance. Full responsibility for joining the program and partial responsibility for funding it devolved to the counties. Individual farmers could choose whether or not to cooperate.[61] Never, declared one of the system's administrators, had there been a more determined effort to leave to the people served a larger "amount of both initiative and performance."[62]

The deference to localism had profoundly undemocratic consequences in practice. Not only did it tend to lock agents into a quasi-dependent relationship with county elites,[63] it virtually assured that appropriations for work among blacks, most of whose land needed more rehabilitation than that of whites, would be inequitable. As the director of extension work in Virginia explained to USDA officials, "The reason we spent more money for white agents and less for negro work was because it is easier to get the Counties to appropriate for white work."[64] White agents were supposed to fill the void, and many tried conscientiously to do so. But most commonly their involvement with blacks was nominal. "I have not done any special work with them," a Virginian candidly wrote. "I send them circular letters at times."[65]

IV

The Cooperative Extension Service, as the system was named, won acceptance but slowly. Unwilling to believe that business and agriculture had reciprocal interests, many North Central farmers regarded county agents as illegitimate children fathered by unscrupulous merchants and bankers; for several years, they refused to authorize their counties to join the system. "RESOLVED," declared the Farmers' Society of Equity at St. Paul in 1915, "That the propaganda miscalled Better Farming, originally financed by Big Business but whose County Agents are now maintained at the expense of the farmers, is not to the best interest of the farmers of the North West."[66] Fearful that agents would encourage homesteaders to plow up and fence in the range, High Plains sheep and cattle ranchers also kept them out of leading livestock counties.[67] The more isolated the area, the less likely it was to affiliate. Two-thirds of the two hundred midwestern counties that had no agents in 1921 were in the Missouri Ozarks or the western plains of Kansas and Nebraska.[68] Some farmers could ill-contain their hostility. "I could see a look of contempt come over his face," a Texas agent recalled, "and very often he would tell me that he did not believe in *book learning* and that he was already paying too much taxes and he did not want any man sticking his nose in his business."[69] Others received their new advisers "with about the same sham courtesy" their fathers had shown college and experiment station personnel.[70] More often, they simply ignored the agents' counsel. One could not find a "better, more friendly, set of people" than the farmers in his county, an early Iowa agent observed, but in spite of the presence of a "good many live ones," they were "pretty well contented with things as they are."[71]

The need to serve as many as three thousand farmers in some counties heightened the importance of the demonstration principle. Unable to work directly with all farmers, agents had little recourse but to seek out the more responsive and, almost by definition, better-educated and more successful farmers. Within limits, this worked. A Michigan farmer reflected:

> I do not think that the county agent gets credit for nearly all the good he does ... He may get one man out of a dozen to put in tile drainage, fertilize a field scientifically. ... A good share of the other eleven men will follow ... when they see him raising better crops and stock. They have not attended the agent's schools or demonstrations and in all probability have made fun of them, yet they are profiting by his teachings.[72]

Soil conservation *per se* was only incidental to extension work in the North. "We seek first," a Wisconsin agent explained with simple elo-

quence, "to help the farmer in a financial way with the hope that in the end it will mean better farm conditions, a better home, and better educational facilities for the family. . . . The ultimate object of this work is to make Oneida County a more desirable place to live."[73] Nonetheless, rotation, legumes, and natural fertilizers all served short-term conservation objectives, and within a few years sensitivity to soil depletion, as distinguished from sheet and wind erosion, had risen all across the North. The letters of hundreds of farmers bear on this point: from Connecticut came an assertion that the agent's suggestions on rye and soy beans "were winning back the fields"; from Illinois that "we feel to maintain the production of our soil is one great thing that the county and Nation needs"; from Nebraska that the agent had improved the region's "drainage"; from Idaho that he had introduced "better ways of tilling"; from Oregon that there had been a "remarkable increase" in crop rotation since he was hired. "[T]here is no question," concluded a corporate farm director in Minnesota, "but that the general average of farming done here is better than it would be if the agent had never come."[74]

Most gross statistics were just as compelling. From 1914 to 1924, when the number of participating counties reached 2,084—three-quarters of the agricultural counties in the country—agents conducted almost three million demonstrations, made more than ten million visits, and participated in almost a million meetings. In the South, the yield of lint cotton on the million and one-half acres worked by demonstrators more than doubled that of nondemonstrators. In the nation at large, almost a million and one-half corn growers improved their practices. Across the West a four-fold increase in corn acreage stimulated the growth of dairying and, especially, ranch farming. "You see all those silos," a Colorado agent remarked as he and a high Extension Service official looked down from a hilltop during a horseback inspection in the mid-1920s. "Ten years ago there was not a silo in the county and not a cornfield in the valley."[75]

Agents also brought experiment station findings on soil-conserving legumes to tens of thousands of once skeptical farmers. Before Smith-Lever, a Minnesotan reported in 1917, alfalfa "was unknown" in his county; now three hundred farmers were growing it.[76] By 1924 the nation had ten and one-half million acres in alfalfa, much of it planted by the 56,297 farmers whom agents had advised in a single year. Acting under protest at times, for they feared the farmers' ridicule, agents also carried out instructions from Extension officials to promote sweet clover as a forage crop. Plantings in Ohio grew from less than 100 acres to 150,000 in ten years, and comparable progress occurred in Kansas, Nebraska, and other midwestern states. But the

most sensational advance occurred in soybeans: from less than two thousand acres to more than two million.[77]

Other developments were less encouraging. Many farmers remained disengaged from the entire system. "There is everywhere a big group of farmers who are not well read and who are doing very little thinking," an Iowa agent typically reported. Soil improvement, complained a Wisconsin agent years after demonstration work had begun, was simply not well understood by the average farmer. Hardly less demoralizing was the reaction of rich and poor owners alike to price fluctuations. Whenever corn or wheat rose, agent after agent reported, much "falling back" ensued.[78] Impressed, nonetheless, by the palpable progress, Extension leaders held to the faith that "grass roots" education would persuade farmers to reshape their universe. Emphatically in 1926, William A. Lloyd, head of county agent work in the western states, reaffirmed the system's aversion to coercion: "An autocratic, overhead program of compulsion, no matter how right it may be, is not possible in individualistic America."[79]

V

Meanwhile South Central agents worked indefatigably to halt sheet erosion. Most of the world's worn-out lands were worn out because the surface soil had washed away; and though rotation and contour planning could reduce washing considerably, they were not nearly as effective as terracing.[80] For years, however, ignorance and contrariness deterred acceptance of terraces. In Oklahoma, where some fields had lost their topsoil from rain runoff in less than fifteen years, farmers often failed to notice the loss until clay appeared. They would agree to dig drainage ditches, for they could perceive their function readily enough. But even some who conceded that their fields were being destroyed insisted that terraces wasted too much land or that the government should construct them.[81] Many of those who did put them in had to be led by hand. "It took two or three hours to convince a man that terracing his land would benefit it," one agent recalled, "and I had not only to run the lines but help him build a drag and then stay with him until the terrace was built."[82] As the rueful observation of a Texas agent suggests, design and upkeep came even harder: "A lot of broken terraces all over the country after each fair sized rain is poor advertising for the program."[83]

Although terracing had first flowered in the Southeast in the nineteenth century, its progress under the county agent system was most notable in Texas. Farmers in the subhumid regions of the state took

to terraces more readily than elsewhere because they preserved moisture even as they contained soil washing. The Federal Land Bank of Houston also spurred construction in the 1920s by conditioning loans on protection of vulnerable fields. Agents located demonstrations on hillsides in almost every appropriate county, and in one six and one-half year period a single agent, C. W. Lehmberg of Runnels County, directed the terracing of a quarter million acres. Custom-built terraces cost between $2 and $3.50 an acre, home-built ones $1 to $1.75. On average, each raised land values $8.54 an acre by increasing productivity from a third to a half. County supervisors assigned highway crews to the work at cost for tenants and landowners alike, and by the early 1930s a quarter of the land which could benefit from the procedure had been terraced.[84] All told, southern agents conducted 166,577 terracing demonstrations on more than four million acres during the first ten years of Smith-Lever. Proudly, William A. Lloyd pronounced these lands "a new national asset, as much so as if it were added to the country's territory by purchase or conquest."[85]

In the Southeast, terraces and soil-saving dams covered fewer than three-quarters of a million acres by 1930. "[I]t is a sad commentary . . . ," a sympathetic observer wrote, "that the section that developed terracing is today one of the major problem areas of soil erosion. . . . [F]aulty construction and maintenance, and above all, the continuance of clear tillage have nullified the good results . . . expected."[86] Oblivious to it all, West Virginia mountaineers meanwhile persisted in clearing land which washed down to bedrock within three or four years.[87]

In the North, Extension leaders continued to emphasize soil depletion rather than erosion despite the Missouri Experiment Station's finding in 1924 that rain wash removed twenty times more plant food than did crops. Hugh Bennett, the primal force of the nascent soil conservation movement, doubtless exaggerated when he said in 1928 that most farmers north of Oklahoma and Tennessee had never seen a terrace. But he was probably correct in asserting that those who had seen them had heard "so much about plant food stolen by crops and so little about soil stolen bodily by erosion" that they had no interest.[88]

VI

The drive for diversification, and with it much of the hope that erosion could be stayed, meanwhile faltered in the Southeast.[89] By the 1920s, to be sure, agents, specialists, bankers, and editors had persuaded farmers to put more than two million acres into summer leg-

umes; the same forces had also stimulated modest progress in peanuts, soybeans, and livestock.[90] But cotton and tobacco continued to bring in more cash than any other crops could have done, and for a generation more the one remained King and the other Queen.

Bradford Knapp, who succeeded his father as head of demonstration work in the South in 1911, believed that creditors fixed the type of farming by insisting on maximum production of cotton, and in 1912 he launched a campaign to persuade bankers to push diversification. Permanent reduction of the soil's productive power by the single-crop syndrome, he admonished an audience of bankers and businessmen in 1915, was reason enough to lead "any thinking man" to worry about "ultimate disaster." Bankers should withhold credit from farmers who refused to diversify. But they should also reduce their rates, for no business could stand up under the charges that some southern farmers had to pay for goods advanced to them. "Can you blame the . . . little, or tenant farmer, if . . . he does not diversify, when he well knows that . . . the small banker or supply merchant . . . [bases his credit] on the number of acres of the one cash crop that he is going to produce?"[91] Yet Knapp quite understood the economic importance of cotton, and in 1915 he changed his slogan, though not his theme, from "diversification" to "safe farming." By this he meant production of enough grain, vegetables, and livestock for food and expenses; continued cultivation of cotton for cash; and use of winter legumes to reduce soil blowing and build up fertility.[92]

Progress was considerable. In Georgia the state leader claimed that cowpea demonstrations "had returned many times" the agents' salaries and that agents were refusing to take on cooperators unless they agreed to "some definite plan" of soil building.[93] There and elsewhere bankers began to insist that agents' instructions be followed and that insurance companies write mortgages only on farms of superior soil, slope, and cultivation.[94] All through the South the acreage in corn, peanuts, soybeans, cowpeas, velvet beans, and crimson clover increased, and in Alabama alone the use of winter legumes jumped from 6,970 pounds in 1918 to 530,000 in 1924.[95]

The force of traditionalism and the scarcity of money continued, nevertheless, to thwart many programs. The farmers are "very superstitious," a Missouri agent remarked in reporting their refusal to replace commercial fertilizer with legumes and stable manure. "[T]hey say they have always used this kind of fertilizer and their fathers before them used it."[96] Deeper in the South, where almost everyone wallowed in short-term debt, the impulse to plant more cotton in good years proved irrepressible. As Knapp wrote when prices rose in 1915, the Service would have to make "a harder fight than ever" to hold

such slight gains as had been made.[97] The need for cash similarly wed farmers to tobacco in parts of Virginia. "The farmers tell me," reported a sympathetic agent, "'we're poor, and our land is poor, and how are we going to improve it and make a living at the same time.'" All that he could do, he added, was urge them "to grow enough on their farms not to have to buy every thing."[98]

In 1938, following a third of a century of voluntarism, moral suasion, and buffeting by market forces, the state of southern agriculture was appraised by the National Emergency Council of the New Deal. Thousands of farmers, the Council noted, had learned the importance of terracing and contour plowing. But thousands of others were still following the "destructive practices of the past," including the plowing of furrows up and down hillsides. The Council further noted that the South contained 61 percent of the nation's badly eroded land; that 27,500,000 tons of nitrogen and phosphorous compounds leached out of its soil each year; and that it spent more for fertilizer annually than for agricultural training in its land-grant colleges, experiment stations, and extension services combined.[99]

Nor was that all. In Pittsylvania County, Virginia, for example, only 8 percent of the fields were being contour plowed and only 10 percent were in crop rotation.[100] Some sections of the Southern Piedmont had lost all their topsoil—ten inches of loam and clay—since the turn of the century. Many Kentuckians still deemed it a mark of industry to "wear out a farm." And parts of the Tennessee River basin—the "'bad lands'" of the East, in Bennett's apt characterization—had been ruined almost beyond redemption.[101]

VII

The filling out of the semi-arid West between 1900 and 1930 further dramatized the difficulty of bringing public and private interest into rough balance under a voluntaristic order. Soil blowing was even more destructive than sheet erosion on some parts of the Great Plains, and after the Dust Bowl of the 1930s, it became a commonplace that the break-up of the sod by wheat farmers had served no national economic purpose. "If this plowing of new land had been necessary in order to meet an urgent human need for breadstuffs," acidly commented the Committee on the Future of the Great Plains, "the injury to the land would at least have been the better of two evils. But the result was actually to produce an unsaleable surplus."[102] Yet through the 1920s, only an occasional voice protested the relentless advance of the farming frontier. Dispassionately, agents on the Southern Plains

reported the sod-busting that followed the plummeting of livestock prices after World War I. "Three good seasons for wheat and the acreage has been more than doubled," wrote one. "The plow is gradually pushing the cattle out," remarked another. Wheat was the major crop in his county, explained a third, and he was therefore giving it "first attention." The state extension services set the agendas, and few agents moved beyond them: diversification to maintain fertility and foster self-sufficiency; terracing and summer fallowing to preserve moisture. To be sure, many agents did criticize the levelling of terraces to free extra land for wheat, but even they seem to have had no presentiment of disaster.[103]

In Montana, meanwhile, the social and ecological disruptions that accompanied a spectacular influx of homesteaders beginning early in the century was painfully demonstrating that much of the unreserved public domain was better suited to grazing than to small-scale farming. Stockmen, forest rangers, and agents agreed that grazing should be regulated and that farming should be confined to viable areas, but Congress remained wedded to the homestead ideal. Partly to stimulate settlement, it even raised the allotment in 1909 from 160 to 320 acres—somewhat more than an irrigated homestead needed and considerably less than a dry farm required.[104]

The increase in acreage, the shameless propaganda of the railroads and civic boosters, several years of above average rainfall, and war-inflated wheat prices proved irresistible; from 1910 to 1922 prospective homesteaders filed claims on 42 percent of Montana's land. Many claimants were workmen, tradesmen, and professional men from the humid regions who had never farmed before. "They came to this state to get free land and started farming," an agent reported in astonishment. "The government," wrote county agent leader M. L. Wilson, "literally invited the butcher, baker, and candlestick maker to 'get a free home' on the public domain."[105] Some were petty speculators, intent on selling out as soon as they had "proved up." But perhaps a full half were experienced farmers who planned to settle permanently. "I thought by coming out West . . . ," a Midwesterner explained, "there would be a better chance for the boys."[106]

The weather soon shattered their dreams. Drought reduced pockets of settlers to poverty in 1916, even before the wave of newcomers crested, and by 1919 it had driven down wheat yields to 2.4 bushels per acre in much of the state. By the end of six or seven more years, twenty thousand mortgages had been foreclosed, one of two farmers had lost his land, and more than one-half of the states' commercial banks had failed. "We . . . were so goddam poor," recalled one who stuck it out, "we couldn't afford to leave."[107]

From the conservationists' standpoint, of course, many of these same people were exploiters before they became victims. Determined, in the biting words of the director of the Montana Experiment Station, "to get the longest possible present return with the least regard to what the future may bring," they put in crop after crop of wheat in the expectation that rising land values would allow them to sell out at a profit after the soil ran down. Some refused to keep livestock because they preferred to live in town or needed to work there during the winter, others sold off such few cows as they owned when wheat prices rose. No appeal, not to future interest and surely not to conscience, could move them. "They say," fulminated the editor of the *Rocky Mountain News*, "when they wear the land out they will do something else." [108] The harsh truth, as the historians of the Wyoming extension service remark, was that pioneering "was a system that emphasized personal rights and ignored public interests and responsibilities." [109] Two or three other developments in the twenties confirm that judgment.

In north central Montana, light wheat soils had begun to blow soon after settlement, and as early as 1916 one agent was prophesying that someday the area would "again be marked as a desert in the geographies." By 1920 drifting soil had destroyed or damaged 15 percent of the crop. [110] Two years later, when M. L. Wilson began his much remarked survey of "The Triangle," a north central region half the size of Iowa, winds had shifted the topsoil so badly that five of seven thousand settlers in one section had given up. [111] Wilson urged those who remained to alternate strips of row crops with legumes. But only 108 operators were following the procedure a decade later, and a half century after that many were still shunning it because of its minor inconveniences. The trouble, grumbled Henry L. Lantz, one of several perspicacious agents brought into the service by Wilson, was that occasional years of heavy rainfall had encouraged "gambling." [112]

Meanwhile the persistence of drought and the continued ravaging of the grasslands spurred the Montana Extension Service to create two programs with national implications. Both embodied land use planning and modest subsidies, and both served as prototypes for larger programs under the New Deal. They also involved considerable voluntary coordination. The first, the Malta Plan, resettled submarginal grain farmers on units which combined dry and irrigated lands in proportions sufficient to form a viable ranch farm. This meant, as Lantz remarked after the New Deal expanded the program, that instead of "trying to make wheat grow where a little grass grew," the land would be finally used for what it was "best adapted." [113]

The second program reflected conflicts endemic to ranchers and

homesteaders throughout the West. But it also reflected the failure of sheep and cattlemen to control grazing voluntarily because, in Lantz's angry charge, of the resolve of some "to get all the feed possible [from the range] and to get it at the lowest expense."[114] In 1926 ranchers in southeastern Montana sought help in regulating and rehabilitating 108,000 acres on which 6,000 cattle and sheep had grazed a decade earlier. By then drought, gophers, sod-busting, and fences left by homesteaders had reduced the area's carrying capacity by almost two-thirds. In due course agent Paul Lewis worked out an arrangement with the ranchers' association, the federal government, the Northern Pacific Railway, and other landowners which gave the stockmen's organization a ten-year lease under terms well calculated to upgrade the range. So successfully did this work out that Congress wrote a number of the arrangement's most constructive features into the Taylor Grazing Act of 1934.[115]

Conditions in Utah were even worse than in Montana. To the familiar litany of soil blowing, declining productivity, and abandoned homesteads were added alkaline soil and irrigation-induced erosion. Overgrazing was rampant, except in the National Forests, and by 1934, 60 percent of the rangeland was severely eroded. As elsewhere, ignorance figured importantly. Inexperienced homesteaders sank their savings in unproductive tracts, and some irrigated land that could never produce a living until well into the 1930s. Eventually, a great many gave up, though a surprisingly large number of marginal farmers held on, "beaten and broken victims of a false hope that could not be realized."[116] Successive plantings of the same crop was also the pattern in many other parts of the West. In Arizona, where even potatoes showed the effects of soil depletion, agents reported little interest in educational work despite severe reductions in cotton yields. Resignedly, the director of the state extension service acknowledged that his state was no exception to the rule that "[l]ittle thought is usually given to a permanent type of agriculture in a new country"; a certain percentage of farmers had to learn the old lesson yet another time "in the same expensive manner."[117]

In the Northwest, agents in the Big Bend country of Oregon made no inroads whatever against soil blowing. A disillusioned homesteader reported that he had repeatedly planted alfalfa, and repeatedly blowing sand had destroyed it.[118] In Washington the fine dust mulch formed by summer fallowing increased the susceptibility of fields to blowing. Marked increases in water erosion also followed the path of settlement, though agents did persuade some farmers to dam gullies and plant sweet clover. By the early 1960s, 15 or more percent of the Palouse in Whitman County had lost *all* its original topsoil. As

a recent analysis concludes, deficiencies in scientific and technical knowledge were partly responsible: at the time, agents and farmers "had neither proven conservation practices nor the expertise and equipment to implement them."[119]

VIII

The concurrent failure of the Forest and Extension Services to convert Easterners to woodlot management and Westerners to shelterbelts casts yet another light on the limits of voluntarism. Late in the 1890s, with considerable fanfare, Gifford Pinchot had offered to have federal foresters prepare tree-planting plans for small farmers at no charge. Only 262 of the 2 million owners of farm woodland applied for assistance, and few of them were dirt farmers. (Among the applicants was Sarah Delano Roosevelt, mother of Franklin.)[120] The program soon petered out, and for some years the Forest Service preoccupied itself with one of its signal accomplishments: restoration of the carrying capacity of the hundred million acres of grasslands within the National Forests.[121]

Passage of the Smith-Lever bill in 1914 revived hope that farmers could be induced to manage their woodlots. Projects were begun in Indiana and Tennessee, and the Forest Service's chief of state cooperation announced that the new legislation had given the work "a tremendous impetus."[122] But in truth, the program gathered hardly any momentum at all. Few agents had the slightest training in forestry, and most states were slow to appoint specialists to guide them. In the South, only Virginia, Georgia, and Texas even had forestry departments. Not surprisingly in these circumstances, the lone mention of trees in William A. Lloyd's 59-page review of the county agents' accomplishments to 1924 is a passage on stump removal in the cut-over lands.

In 1919 Pinchot joined the voluntarism-coercion issue in a statement directed mainly at commercial lumber interests. "Forest devastation will not be stopped through persuasion," he asserted. "[It] has been thoroughly tried out for the past twenty years and has failed utterly."[123] Neither Congress nor the new Chief Forester, William B. Greeley, supported Pinchot's call for mandatory controls. "I could not visualize practical results in growing trees on the 75-odd per cent of forest land in private ownership by abandoning co-operate methods and trying to force the change down the throats of the landowners," Greeley explained.[124] When, accordingly, Congress passed the Clarke-McNary forestry bill in 1924, it implicitly reaffirmed the voluntarist

philosophy of Smith-Lever. Although the measure sought principally to strengthen the state-federal fire protection program, it also aimed to foster reforestation of cut-over timberland and submarginal farmland. Two matching-aid provisions authorized modest appropriations to states—one hundred thousand dollars in each instance—to support nurseries and help farmers plant or improve woodlots, windbreaks, and shelterbelts.[125]

Greeley hoped that forestry in America, as in France, would become almost instinctive—"a part of our farm lore, on the same footing as the growing of corn or potatoes or wheat."[126] But partly because five heavily timbered states—Kentucky, Colorado, Montana, Washington and Oregon—lacked forestry specialists as late as 1932, extension work languished.[127] Even in northeastern states with sophisticated programs, agents found it difficult to sensitize farmers.[128] In New York, where Governor Franklin D. Roosevelt won authority to reforest a million acres of submarginal farmland, many localities pursued tree planting programs aggressively under the direction of agents.[129] But just as in Pennsylvania, where Pinchot, who was now governor, brought all the lawful power of the state to bear on forestry matters, most programs were community- rather than farmer-generated.[130] "The average farmer does not raise a crop of weeds in his potato patch . . . ," grumbled the Massachusetts specialist, "but he seems to be willing that such case may occur in his woodland."[131] Rarely did demonstrations draw many observers, and rarely did farmers agree to become cooperators. For too long, concludes a historian of rural Maine, the forest had been the enemy—a resource "to be mined like a gravel pit rather than cultivated like a crop."[132]

Short-term economic considerations often weighed even more heavily than cultural factors in some regions. Standing timber was usually taxed annually, and many operators had no recourse but to sell it off. Thus, timber sales accounted for almost a quarter of farm income in a tier of northern Minnesota counties, and though Federal Land Banks began in the 1920s to advance loans on properly managed woodlots, this hardly satisfied the immediate needs of marginal farmers.[133] In Georgia, where portable sawmill operators wrought incalculable devastation, the sale of timber was all that prevented many boll weevil-ridden farmers from going under. And in Texas, where the Extension Service specialist complained that the farmer "rarely ever" received half the real value of his stumpage, farmers were "glad" to sell at any price.[134]

Agents on the prairies and western plains were only slightly more successful in persuading farmers to plant shelterbelts. Designed to reduce soil blowing by lining vulnerable fields with rows of trees, shel-

terbelts went back to the late nineteenth century. Federal scientists had viewed them skeptically at first, for they idled considerable land and were costly to establish, but in 1916 the Northern Great Plains Field Station at Mandan, North Dakota, began a demonstration project which encompassed 200,000 square miles in four states and involved 4,670 separate plantings.[135] Clarke-McNary stimulated further interest,[136] and by 1934 more than two hundred million trees had been distributed, many at cost and some at no charge, although farmers usually paid shipping costs. About 30 percent survived.[137]

Yet the hope that Clark-McNary would inspire a mammoth shelterbelt program proved illusory. Some farmers were unable to pay freight charges, and most of those who could pay them soon lost enthusiasm. By 1931 only 4,676 farms from North Dakota to Texas had shelterbelts, and only one in a hundred in the entire country had improved its forestry practices in any way.[138]

A measure of fault lay with the agents. Borne down by their regular duties and lacking confidence in their own expertise, they put less than 1 percent of their time into forestry or woodlot programs.[139] More critical, however, was the farmers' indifference.[140] In 1933, in a nation of six million farms, 150 million acres of woodlots, and millions upon millions of acres of fragile cropland, only ninety-five hundred farmers cooperated with county agents in woodland management, seven thousand in forest plantings, and forty-five hundred in windbreaks.[141]

Epilogue

Not even the dust storms of the 1930s persuaded New Deal policy makers that mandatory conservation controls were politically feasible, much less philosophically acceptable. M. L. Wilson, by then Assistant Secretary of Agriculture, believed that Hugh Bennett exaggerated the crisis and that matters would work themselves out through gradual changes fostered by the Extension Service. Farmers, he said, in commenting on a draft of a model soil conservation district contract in 1935, must be "educated to cooperate voluntarily"; there should be no "attempt to impose regulation from above."[142] President Roosevelt acquiesced, though he was hardly convinced. The nub of the question, he later wrote to Henry Wallace, was whether

> a farmer in up-State New York or Georgia or Nebraska or Oregon [who], through bad use of his land, allows his land to erode, . . . [has] the inalienable right as owner to do this, or has the community, i.e., some form of governmental agency, . . . the right to stop him?[143]

Opportunity costs combined with complacency or contrariness to thwart conservation goals to the end of the New Deal and beyond. When the rains returned to the Dust Bowl, many farmers uprooted their shelterbelts or let them die of neglect. Then, during the postwar Green Revolution, fertilizer-induced increases in productivity weakened the "punch" of the old argument that soil losses would eventually reduce yields. Plainly, a half century of moral suasion by county agents and others had failed to induce marginal farmers to subordinate their economic needs, or prosperous farmers their economic desires, to ecological imperatives.[144]

Beginning, finally, to face the limits of voluntarism, the USDA and the newly created Soil Conservation Service groped for a formula that would serve the public interest in conservation and yet honor the polity's commitment to choice. Increasingly, they fastened on cost-sharing. Thus the government remunerated farmers for putting land into the soil bank and paid rent to them for the land on which the Forest Service planted trees in the expanded Shelterbelt Project. Subsequently, analysts concluded that farmers would have to be compensated for at least two-thirds of the costs before they would pursue long-term conservation objectives voluntarily. In some cases, however, the costs were prohibitive. To reduce erosion to tolerable levels on parts of the Rolling Plains of Texas, for example, wheat and cotton production would have had to be reduced by 56 percent and net returns by 63 percent. Nor did independent state action offer any recourse. In Iowa, which had lost as much as one-half of its topsoil in 150 years, the legislature enacted a model subsidization law in 1971. But partly because the act put Iowa farmers at a comparative cost disadvantage to farmers in states with no conservation laws, it was never fully enforced. Fourteen years later, Congress wrote powerful economic incentives into the 'sod-busting' provisions of the farm bill of 1985. Meanwhile, in spite of many unheralded achievements by the SCS and the Extension Service, the continued movement of a half billion tons of sediment down the Mississippi each year and the recording of higher levels of soil blowing in Montana and Wyoming in 1989 than at any time since record keeping began in 1955 testified graphically to the functional limits of voluntarism.[145]

Notes

[1] I am grateful to the University of Virginia and the Woodrow Wilson Center for support in the research and writing of this paper. I appreciate, also, the thoughtful critique of Robert C. McMath, Jr., the commentator at the Princeton Symposium, and for the further suggestions of Edward Ayers, Da-

vid B. Danbom, Michael H. Ebner, H. R. Harbaugh, Douglas Helms, William A. Link, Richard Lowitt, Alan Marcus, and Olivier Zunz.

[2] The emphasis here is on "public." Scientists, of course, had long been aware of the abuse of the land. See, among other works, Margaret Rossiter, *The Emergence of Agricultural Science* (New Haven, 1975) and Alan I. Marcus, *Agricultural Science and the Quest for Legitimacy* (Ames, Iowa, 1985).

[3] Fred A. Shannon, *The Farmer's Last Frontier: Agriculture, 1860–1897* (New York, 1945), p. 169; quoted in *Montana* (1909): 1. (This was a state development brochure.)

[4] Eugene Davenport, "Scientific Farming," *Annals of the American Academy* XL (March 1912): 46; generally, Hugh Hammond Bennett, *Soil Conservation* (New York, 1939) and *Soils & Men: Yearbook of Agriculture 1938* (Washington, D.C., 1938).

[5] Frederick R. Troeh, J. Arthur Hobbs, and Roy L. Donahue, *Soil and Water Conservation for Productivity and Environmental Protection* (Englewood Cliffs, N.J., 1980), p. 45.

[6] Bennett, *Soil Conservation*, pp. 80–81; R. Douglas Hurt, *The Dust Bowl: An Agricultural and Social History* (Chicago, 1981), pp. 4–12.

[7] *Final Report of the United States Industrial Commission*, XIX (Washington, D.C., 1902), 45.

[8] *Wallace's Farmer and Dairyman*, February 11, 1898; George Headly, "Rotation of Crops," *Annual Report*, Iowa Department of Agriculture, 1901, 60.

[9] Willard Davis, Letter-to-the-Editor, *Country Gentleman*, June 11, 1908.

[10] "Reports of F. E. Robertson, November 1, 10, and December 2, 1910," *Extension Service Annual Reports: New York*, National Archives, Reel 1, hereinafter cited as ESAR.

[11] Major Demarest to W. F. Massey, April 15, 1895, and Clarendon Davis to W. F. Massey, undated but post-1900, Massey Papers [photoduplicate], Virginia Polytechnical Institute and State University.

[12] "Annual Report of the Agent for Decatur County, 1915," ESAR: Georgia, Reel 1.

[13] John P. Jenkins, "AR for Clay County, 1918," ESAR: Texas, Reel 5.

[14] Unless otherwise indicated, all gross statistics are taken from Census Reports.

[15] Quoted in David B. Danbom, *The Resisted Revolution* (Ames, Iowa, 1978), p. 41.

[16] C. B. Smith, "County Agent Work in the North and West," address at a Conference of State Leaders, St. Louis, November 16–19, 1915, copy in Record Group 16, National Archives, Correspondence, Office of the Secretary of Agriculture, Acc. 274, Drawer 81.

[17] [Charles G. Woodward and Sam G. Huntington], "Our Farm Loans. A Late Inspection From the Home Office," *Connecticut General Bulletin* IX (November 1912), Archives of the Cigna Insurance Company, Bloomfield, Connecticut.

[18] Generally, see Richard H. Shryock, "British vs. Germans in Colonial Agriculture," *Mississippi Valley Historical Review*, XXVI (June 1939): 39–54; John Donald Black, *The Rural Economy of New England* (Cambridge, Mass., 1950);

Paul Glenn Munyon, *A Reassessment of New England Agriculture in the Last Thirty Years of the Nineteenth Century* (New York, 1938).

[19] *Wallaces' Farmer*, January 1, 1909. This was a lively and frequently discussed issue in the agricultural press. See, for example, *The Progressive Farmer*, January 9, 1908.

[20] Donald L. Winters, "Tenant Farming in Iowa, 1860–1900: A Study of the Terms of Rental Leases," *Agricultural History*, XLVII (January 1974): 131–50; H. C. Taylor, *Methods of Renting Farm Lands in Wisconsin*, Wisconsin AESB, 198 (Madison, July 1910).

[21] Allan G. Bogue, "Foreclosure Tenancy on the Northern Plains," *Agricultural History*, 39 (January 1965): 3–16.

[22] *Wallaces' Farmer*, April 18, 1914.

[23] John Frederick Harriott, "Farm Tenure In New York" (Ph.D. Diss. Cornell University, 1926).

[24] George H. Von Tungeln, *et al.* "The Social Aspects of Rural Life and Farm Tenantry in Cedar County, Iowa," 445–46; B. H. Hibbard and J. D. Black, *Farm Leasing Systems in Wisconsin*, Wisconsin Res. AESB 47, (Madison, October 1920), 60. Writing in 1927, Gustave W. Kuhlman, "A Study of Tenancy in Central Illinois," *Journal of Land and Public Utility Economics*, 3 (August 1927): 290–97, reported that a majority of operators, but not so many absentee landlords, appreciated the use of legumes in the rotation.

[25] As the incidence of corporate farming increased during the early 1920s, farm managers began to give more attention to soil maintenance and improvement. See the account of the University of Illinois' Third Annual Conference of Landlords and Managers in F. A. Buechel, "Relationships of Landlords to Farm Tenants," *Journal of Land and Public Utility Economics*, 1 (July 1925): 336–42.

[26] A. J. Englehorn, *Farm Tenure in Iowa, VI. Landlord-Tenant Relationships in Southern Iowa*, Iowa AESB 372 (Ames, August 1938); Hibbard and Black, *Farm Leasing Systems*. Tobacco share tenants in Wisconsin seem to have had many of the characteristics of some of their southern counterparts. They had little means, were frequently in debt for a year's living by the time the crop was ready to market, and had a reputation, in some instances, for abandoning the land when the crop did not promise to turn out well. Taylor, *Methods of Renting Farm Lands*, 14.

[27] B. F. Harris, "1913 and What It Stands for in Illinois Agriculture," *Wallaces' Farmer*, January 16, 1914. Harris, who was chairman of the Agricultural Commission of the American Bankers Association, deplored Illinois's extreme emphasis on corn, "the grip of corporations" on its dairy business, and the state's high incidence of tenancy. A. P. Grout, "The Rape of the Soil," *Proceedings*, Third National Conservation Congress, (1911), 210.

[28] Stanley W. Trimble, "Perspectives on the History of Soil Erosion Control in the Eastern United States," *Agricultural History*, 59 (April 1985): 162–80.

[29] W. A. Hartman and H. H. Wooten, "Georgia Land Use Problems," Georgia AESB 191 (1935), 69–70, 91. Georgia's tenancy rate in 1920 was 66.6 percent. Discounting croppers, it was 51.3 percent.

[30] H. F. Freeman to Editor, *Progressive Farmer*, February 21, 1905.

[31] *Report of the Country Life Commission*, Senate Doc. 705, 60th Cong., 2d Sess., 1909, 39–40.

[32] See, for example, the report in Thomas D. Clark, *The Greening of the South: The Recovery of Land and Forest* (Lexington, Kentucky, 1984), p. 33, of a federal survey of Fairfield County, S.C., in 1911.

[33] *Report of the United States Industrial Commission on Immigration and on Education*, XV (Washington, D.C., 1901), 529.

[34] Edward Alsworth Ross, *The Old World and the New*, (New York, 1914), p. 53; Alexander E. Cance, "Immigrants and American Agriculture," *Journal of Farm Economics*, 7 (January 1925): 102–14. For a summary commentary on the continuing controversy over persistence rates see D. Aidan McQuillan, "The Mobility of Immigrants and Americans: A Comparison of Farmers on the Kansas Frontier," *Agricultural History*, 53 (July 1979): 576–96. But also see Russel L. Gerlach, *Immigrants in the Ozarks* (Columbia, Missouri, 1976), Terry G. Jordan, *German Seed In Texas Soil* (Austin, Texas, 1966), and several of the essays in Frederick C. Luebke, ed., *Ethnicity on the Great Plains* (Lincoln, Nebraska, 1980).

[35] Virtually all contemporary commentators stress the greater industry of immigrant farmers and the severity of their wives' and children's lives in the first generation. The sources on this are too numerous to list, but see Alexander E. Cance, "Immigrants and American Agriculture," *Journal of Farm Economics*, 7 (January 1925): 102–14.

[36] Jon Gjerde, *From Peasants to Farmers: The Migration from Balestrand, Norway, to the Upper Middle West* (Cambridge, Eng., 1985), p. 184; Bradley H. Baltensperger, "Agricultural Change among Nebraska Immigrants, 1880–1900," in Luebke, *Ethnicity on the Great Plains*.

[37] *Reports of the Immigration Commission*, Sen. Doc. 633, 61st Cong., 2d Sess., (Washington, D.C., 1910), Part 24, *Recent Immigrants in Agriculture*, Vols. I and II. The concept of cultural rebound, which involved a return to some of the more desirable European practices, is set forth in Jordan, *German Seed*.

[38] Walter M. Kollmorgen, "Immigrant Settlements in Southern Agriculture," *Agricultural History*, 19 (April 1945): 69–78 is a strong brief for the superiority of immigrant husbandry in the South. Jordan, *German Seed in Texas Soil*, pp. 93–94, finds Texas Germans to have been no more diversified in 1880 than Old Stock farmers. *Abstracts of Reports of the Immigration Commission*, Vol. I, 589, is the source of the statement about Texas Bohemians.

[39] F. H. King, *Destructive Effects of Winds on Sandy Soils and Light Sandy Loam With Methods of Protection*, Wisconsin AESB 42 (Madison, 1894); *Washed Soils: How to Prevent and Reclaim Them*, USDA Farmers' Bulletin 20 (Washington, D.C., 1894).

[40] T. Swann Harding, *Two Blades of Grass: A History of Scientific Development in the United States Department of Agriculture* (Norman, Oklahoma, 1947), p. 196.

[41] Although Samuel P. Hays's *Conservation and the Gospel of Efficiency* (Cambridge, Mass., 1959) splendidly fulfills the author's purpose of analyzing decision-making and aspects of the political structure in the Progressive Era, it is also the best book on the first conservation movement as a whole.

[42] Roosevelt's Annual Messages are reprinted in Hermann Hagedorn (ed.),

The Works of Theodore Roosevelt (20 vols., National Edition, New York, 1926), Vol. 15.

[43] Hays, *Conservation and the Gospel of Efficiency*, Chaps. IV and V; *Report of the Public Lands Commission*, Sen. Doc. 189, 58th Cong., 2d Sess. (Washington, D.C., 1905).

[44] William H. Harbaugh, *Power and Responsibility: The Life and Times of Theodore Roosevelt*, (New York, 1961), pp. 327–29.

[45] Theodore Roosevelt to Liberty Hyde Bailey, August 10, 1908, Elting E. Morison (ed.), *The Letters of Theodore Roosevelt*, (Cambridge, Mass., 8 vols., 1951–54), VI, 1167–70.

[46] See, in particular, William L. Bowers, *The Country Life Movement in America 1900–1920* (Port Washington, N.Y., 1974) and Danbom, *The Resisted Revolution*.

[47] *Report of the Country Life Commission*, U. S. Congress, Senate, S. Doc. 705, 1909.

[48] Second National Conservation Congress, *Proceedings* (St. Paul, Minn., 1910), 208.

[49] Fourth National Conservation Congress, *Proceedings* (Indianapolis, Ind., 1912), 292.

[50] Third National Conservation Congress, *Proceedings* (Kansas City, Mo., 1911), 225.

[51] Generally, Taylor, *Methods of Renting Farm Lands*.

[52] See the fascinating account in Bogue, "Foreclosure Tenancy," of a futile effort to win enactment of a land-care bill in North Dakota. An exception to the generalization about Progressive Era state legislatures is Kansas, which empowered county commissioners in 1913 to order soil conservation work on the land of negligent farmers.

[53] *Report of the Industrial Commission*. Generally, Roy Scott, *The Reluctant Farmer* (Urbana, Ill., 1970).

[54] *Hearings Before the Committee on Agriculture*, HR, 63rd Cong. 1st Sess. on DH. R. 7951, September 23, 1933, 33. Twenty percent of midwestern farmers did not speak English at the time. No one knew the functional illiteracy rate of them or any other group.

[55] Unsigned Letter-to-Editor, *Wallace's Farmer*, January 31, 1913.

[56] See generally, Gladys Baker, *The County Agent* (Chicago, 1939); E. Gentry, "AR of the State Agent, 1909–10," ESAR: Georgia, Reel 1.

[57] For the situation in North Dakota, including farmer opposition, see David B. Danbom, "Politics, Science and the Changing Nature of Research at the North Dakota Agricultural Experiment Station, 1900–1930," *North Dakota History* 56 (Summer 1989): 17–29.

[58] *Proceedings of the Annual Convention of the Association of American Agricultural Colleges and Experiment Stations Held at Atlanta, Georgia, November 14, 1914.*

[59] Wilson's statement is in U.S., Congress, House Report No. 110, *Cooperative Agricultural Extension Work*, Dec. 8, 1913, 63d Cong., 2d Sess., 4. Generally, see Dewey W. Grantham, Jr., *Hoke Smith and the Politics of the New South*, (Baton Rouge, 1958) and, for earlier background, Roy Scott, *The Reluctant Farmer* (Urbana, 1970).

[60] *Congressional Record*, 63d Cong., 1st sess., 1827.

[61] In addition to Grantham and Scott, see Edward H. Beardsley, *Harry L. Russell and Agricultural Science in Wisconsin* (Madison, Wis., 1968) and W. A. Lloyd, Untitled Paper read at Amherst, Massachusetts, in January, 1915. Copy in the W. A. Lloyd Papers, National Agricultural Library.

[62] W. A. Lloyd, "County Agent Work," unpublished paper delivered at Chicago, Illinois, November 12, 1919, copy in the Lloyd Papers.

[63] This point, which is documented by Gladys Baker, *The County Agent*, Grant McConnell, *The Decline of Agrarian Democracy* (Berkeley, Cal., 1953) and others, can be and has been misread. Successful demonstration work depended on emulation. See below, p. 29.

[64] John Hutcheson to C. B. Smith, November 13, 1922, Correspondence of Albert C. True, RG 33, National Archives.

[65] Joel Schor, "The Black Presence in the U. S. Cooperative Extension Service to 1983: A Profile," Unpublished manuscript, (May 1983).

[66] Quoted in Merrill G. Burlingame and Edward J. Bell, Jr., *The Montana Cooperative Extension Service* (Bozeman, Montana, 1984) p. 40. The Society had 2,700 members in Montana at the time.

[67] George W. Boyd and Burton W. Marston, *The Wyoming Agricultural Extension Service* (Laramie, Wyo., 1965), p. 13; Burlingame and Bell, *The Montana Cooperative Extension Service*, p. 40; "The County Agent in the Saddle," *Extension Review* 2 (November, 1931): 166.

[68] W. A. Lloyd, "Status Of County Agent Work in The Northern and Western States," unpublished paper given at the Extension Conference of the Twelve Central States, Chicago, March 22–23, 1921. Copy in the Lloyd Papers.

[69] A. R. Tisdale, "AR for Walker County, 1915," ESAR: Texas, Reel 2.

[70] W. A. Lloyd, Untitled Paper read at Amherst, Mass., January 1915, Lloyd Papers.

[71] "AR for Madison County 1914," Extension Service Papers, Iowa State University.

[72] Statement of George H. Wallis, Nov. 17, 1917, in "WHAT THE FARMERS THINK OF THE WORK," a file of hundreds of excerpts of letters from farmers who had been cooperators two or more years, in RG 16, Secretary's Office, 1918, Acc. 234, Dr. 111, National Archives.

[73] W. D. Juday, "AR for Oneida County, 1915." ESAR: Wisconsin, Reel 1. Extension officials estimated that there was a pressing need to raise the incomes of at least half of all farmers.

[74] Statement of H. C. Miller, Northford, Conn., March 6, 1919, in a scrapbook in the records of Connecticut Cooperative Extension Service, University of Connecticut. Statements by Peter E. Unzicker, Washburn, Ill., November 27, 1917; T. F. McGlashan, town unknown, Neb., December 7, 1917; name unknown, Hibbard, Idaho, December 12, 1917; J. Carl Nelson, McMinville, Ore., December 6, 1917; C. R. Wright, Fergus Falls, Minn., December 7, 1917, all in "WHAT FARMERS THINK OF THE WORK." Wright, the corporate farm director, added that he had a farm manager "of considerable ability" and therefore did not use the agent as much as other farmers.

[75] William A. Lloyd, *County Agricultural Agent Work Under The Smith-Lever Act, 1914 to 1924*, USDA, Misc. Circ. 59 (Washington, D.C., May, 1926). The acreage in corn rose from 793,000 to 2,637,000.

[76] F. E. Lammers, Lakeville, Minn., December 4, 1917, in "WHAT FARMERS THINK OF THE WORK."

[77] Lloyd, *County Agricultural Agent Work.*

[78] "AR of the Agent for Cherokee County, 1920," Cooperative Extension Service Records, Iowa State University; E. V. Royal, "AR for Adams County, 1926," ESAR: Wisconsin, Reel 9.

[79] Lloyd, *County Agricultural Agent Work*, p. 20.

[80] F. L. Duley, *Controlling Surface Erosion of Farm Lands*, Missouri AESB 211 (1924), quoted in H. H. Bennett and W. R. Chapline, *Soil Erosion A National Menace* USDA Circ. 33 (Washington, D.C. April 1928), Part I. "Some Aspects of the Wastage Caused by Soil Erosion," by H. H. Bennett, 6.

[81] Testimony of Hugh H. Bennett, *Hearings*, Agriculture Department Appropriations Bill for 1930. 70th Cong., 2d Sess. November 21, 1928, 314.

[82] Davis, "Economic Waste from Soil Erosion," 217–18; M. R. Bentley, "AR of the State Engineer for 1910," ESAR: Texas, Reel 11; Memoir of Tom M. Marks, Harmon County, Oklahoma, printed as "In the Early Days," *Extension Review*, 4 (July 1933): 53.

[83] Fred S. Reynolds, "AR for Stonewall County, 1930," ESAR: Texas, Reel 68. Most commonly, farmers failed to fill in gullies properly. Reports further indicate that specifications in bulletins were not always applicable to local conditions.

[84] S. P. Lyle, "A Terracing Record," *ibid.*, 3 (June 1932), 90; "Terracing Texas," *ibid.*, 4 (March 1933), 23; [C. W. Lehmberg of Runnels Country was the agent who made the record]; "Terracing Texas," *ibid.*, 4 (March 1933), 23; Adam C. Magee, "AR for Shackleford County, 1929," ESAR: Texas, Reel 64. "Moisture Conservation in New Mexico," *Extension Service Review*, 2 (May 1931): 69.

[85] Lloyd, *County Agent Agricultural Agent Work*, 30. Lloyd's reference included the 669,696 acres of stump land cleared in the South, as well as the 5,846,837 acres newly drained and 4,365,380 acres brought under irrigation throughout the nation.

[86] *Ibid.*, 38; Arthur R. Hall, *The Story of Soil Conservation in the South Carolina Piedmont*, USDA, Misc. Pub. 407 (November 1940), and the same author's "Terracing in the Southern Piedmont," *Agricultural History* 73 (April 1949): 107–109. Hall reports that 83 percent of 524 terraced fields in a sample were not maintained correctly.

[87] Bennett, *Hearings*, 325.

[88] Donald C. Swain, *Federal Conservation Policy: 1921–1933* (Berkeley, Cal., 1963), pp. 156–57; Bennett, *Soil Conservation*, 19.

[89] Trimble, *Man-Induced Soil Erosion*, 106, reports that cotton grown under rotation on a 7 percent slope in Georgia lost only 12 percent as much soil per acre as cotton grown with no winter cover. The loss was no greater than the rate of new soil formation.

[90] O. S. Fisher, *Ten Years of Agronomy Extension: 1915 to 1924*, USDA Circ. 22 (Washington D.C., February, 1928).

[91] See the eight-page review by Knapp of his work on the occasion of his resignation, Bradford Knapp, Memorandum for the Secretary [of Agriculture] and Dr. [Albert] True, January 12, 1920, Correspondence of the Office of Secretary, RG 11, Acc 234, Dr. 498, National Archives. Also see Bradford A. Knapp, "My Hopes and Ideals for the Co-Operative Demonstration Work," *Progressive Farmers*, May 13, 1911, in which he listed soil maintenance and building as the second of four objectives. His speech to the bankers was published as "Diversified Agriculture and the Relation of the Banker to the Farmers," USDA, Circ. 50, July 2, 1915, 4.

[92] Knapp, Memorandum.

[93] J. Phil Campbell, "AR of the State Agent, 1915," ESAR: Georgia, Reel 1.

[94] W. G. Middlebrook, "AR for Bibb County, 1915," ESAR: Georgia, Reel 1; Knapp, "My Hopes and Ideals"; Charles G. Woodward and Samuel G. Huntington, "Our Farm Loans: A Late Inspection From the Home Office," *Connecticut General Bulletin* IX (November 1912): 115–17.

[95] Fisher, *Ten Years of Agronomy Extension*, 19.

[96] William L. Flauery, "AR, 1915," Extension Service Records, Missouri, Joint Collection—University of Missouri and the Missouri State Historical Society.

[97] Bradford Knapp, "Memorandum for the Secretary," October 6, 1915, True Papers, Box 14.

[98] S. F. Coffman, Nottoway County, statement at the Virginia Annual Extension Meeting, January 24, 1914, Blacksburg, The Papers of John D. Eggleston, Virginia Polytechnic Institute and State University. E. W. Grubs, "AR for Galveston County, 1915," ESAR: Texas, Reel 1, reports that he had failed to induce a single farmer to handle his manure properly because most of them could not afford a shed or pit. (Why money was needed to dig a pit he did not say.)

[99] National Emergency Council, *Report to the President on The Economic Conditions of the South* (Washington, D. C., July 1938). See Section 2, "Soil."

[100] Trimble, *Man-Induced Soil Erosion*, p. 107.

[101] *Hearings*, Ag. Dept. App. Bill, 1930, 70th Cong., 2d Sess, Nov. 21, 1928, 310; Clark, *The Greening of the South*, p. 77; Dicken and Brown, *Soil Erosion in Kentucky*, p. 58.

[102] President's Committee on the Great Plains, *The Future of the Great Plains* (Washington, D.C., 1936), excerpted in George McGovern, ed., *Agricultural Thought in the Twentieth Century* (Indianapolis, Ind., 1967), p. 221.

[103] Charles T. Sherman, "AR for Sherman County, 1929," ESAR: Texas, Reel 64.

[104] George Frederic Stratton, "Million-Acre Pastures Go Begging," *The Country Gentleman*, (January 12, 1918), 8–9, 43.

[105] Wilson found that in one typical township in the North only 23 of 58 homesteaders had been previously identified with farming. M. L. Wilson, *Dry Farming in the North Central Montana "Triangle*," Montana AESB 66 (June 1923), 28. He further found that most had come from humid states. Contemporaneous comments by agents tend to confirm Wilson's report that many homesteaders were inexperienced. George W. Boyd and Burton W. Marston,

The Wyoming Agricultural Extension Service and The People Who Made It: 1914–1964 (Laramie, 1965), p. 3, reports that many Wyoming homesteaders also knew little or nothing about farming. Also see Garry L. Null, "Specialization and Expansion: Panhandle Farming in the 1920s," *Panhandle-Plains Historical Review*, 47 (1974): 130.

[106] John P. Fabrick, "MIA History Group Interview on the North American Mortgage Co.," Montana State University; quoted in *Montana* (1909); Daniel N. Vichorek, *Montana's Homestead Era* (Helena, Montana, 1987), pp. 56, 101. M. L. Wilson concluded that the average dry land farmer in 1916 had a working capital of about $2500 and that the more successful ones had a larger amount. Wilson to Charles E. Grossman, November 20, 1916, The Papers of M. L. Wilson, Montana State University.

[107] Vichorek, *Montana's Homestead Era*, pp. 56, 101. The banking crisis in Wyoming was comparably severe. See Peter W. Huntoon, "The National Bank Failures in Wyoming, 1924," *Annals of Wyoming*, 54 (Fall, 1982): 34.

[108] Murray E. Stebbins, "AR for Valley County, 1918," ESAR: Montana, Reel 3; Peter R. McGorry, "The Montana Agriculture Station," (M.A. Thesis, Montana State University, 1975), 44; Frank R. Grant, Man of Vision, Voice of Conviction: Robert N. Sutherlin and the *Rocky Mountain Husbandman* (Ph.D. Diss., University of Montana, 1984), p. 280.

[109] Boyd and Marston, *The Wyoming Agricultural Extension Service*, p. 4.

[110] Paul P. Banker, Annual Reports, 1916, 1920, Reels 1, 5.

[111] Burligame and Bell, *Montana Cooperative Service*, 214. The reference was to Philips County, which is larger than the State of Connecticut. John T. Schlebecker, *Cattle Raising on the Plains 1900–1961* (Lincoln, Neb., 1963), pp. 91–95.

[112] Burlingame and Bell, *Montana Cooperative Service*, 115; Leon Lyles, "Predicting and Controlling Wind Erosion," *Agricultural History*, 59 (April 1985), 207; Henry L. Lantz, "AR for Philips County, 1928," ESAR: Montana, Reel 17; Vichorek, *Montana's Homestead Era*, 36.

[113] Burlingame and Bell, *Montana Cooperative Service*, p. 215, notes that Wilson had been thinking along the same lines as Lantz. Henry Lantz, "AR for Phillips County, 1928," ESAR: Montana, Reel 17 gives his early views.

[114] Burlingame and Bell, *Montana Cooperative Service*, p. 97, drawing on Wilson's "'Triangle'" study; Henry Lantz, "AR for Philips County, 1928," ESAR: Montana, Reel 17.

[115] Burlingame and Bell, *Montana Cooperative Service*, pp. 216–17. Also see Schlebecker, *Cattle Raising on the Plains*, pp. 92–93, for the stockmen's changing attitude toward regulation of the public range.

[116] Brian Q. Cannon, "Struggle against Great Odds: Challenges in Utah's Marginal Agricultural Areas, 1925–39," *Utah Historical Quarterly*, 54 (1986): 310. The quotation is from Marion Clawson et al., *Types of Farming in Utah*, AESB 275 (Logan, Utah, 1936): 66, as printed in Cannon: 313.

[117] M. M. Winslow, "AR for Yuma County, 1920," Cooperative Extension Service Records, University of Arizona; C. B. Brow, "AR for Pima and Santa Cruz Counties, 1920," *ibid.*; "Fifth AR of the State Director, 1919," *ibid.*; "Sixth AR of the State Director, 1920," *ibid.*

[118] George Macinko, "The Ebb and Flow of Wheat Farming in the Big Bend, Washington," *Agricultural History* 59 (April 1985): 215–28. State Report, 1915, "UMATILLA Project," ESAR: Oregon, Reel 1.

[119] James F. Shepherd, "Soil Conservation in the Pacific Northwest Wheat-Producing Areas: Conservation in a Hilly Terrain," *Agricultural History* 59 (April 1985): 234.

[120] Harold T. Pinkett, *Gifford Pinchot: Private and Public Forester* (Urbana, 1970), pp. 47–51; Samuel Trask Dana, *Forest and Range Policy: Its Development in the United States* (New York, 1950), pp. 120–21.

[121] See U. S. Congress, Senate, *Report of the Public Lands Commission*, Sen. Doc. 189, 58 Cong. 3, 1905, for analysis of the five-to-one vote in favor of government regulation of the range in a poll of 1400 stockmen by the Forest Service. Also see Richard Goff and Robert H. McCaffree, *Century In The Saddle* (Denver, Colorado, 1967) for glimpses of stockmen's changing attitudes.

[122] J. Girven Peters, *Forest Conservation for States in the Southern Pine Region*, USDA Bull. 364 (Washington, D.C., April 15, 1916), 12.

[123] Dana, *Forest and Range Policy*, p. 212.

[124] William B. Greeley, *Forests and Men* (Garden City, N.Y. 1951), p. 106.

[125] Harold K. Steen, *The U.S. Forest Service, A History* (Seattle, 1976), pp. 173–195, and William G. Robbins, *American Forestry: A History of National, State, & Private Cooperation* (Lincoln, Neb., 1985), pp. 96–103, offer dispassionate analyses of the Clarke-McNary bill and its origins.

[126] USDA, "Report of the Forester," *Yearbook 1922*, 249.

[127] See, for example, Thomas B. Burleigh, "AR of State Leader in Forestry for Georgia, 1929," ESAR: Georgia, Reel 35.

[128] R. Y. Stuart, "Forest Service Aids For Extension Workers," *Extension Service Review* 3 (June 1932): 81.

[129] "County Forestry Program," *Extension Service Review*, 1 (November, 1930): 98. Chaquauqua County formed a forestry council in 1927 and employed a county extension forester, the only one in the nation. See "Report of the Forestry Specialist for 1914," ESAR: New York, Reel 16 for a statement on cooperation in 429 plantings in 47 counties.

[130] Pinkett, *Gifford Pinchot*, pp. 138–50.

[131] R. B. Parmenter, "AR of the Forestry Specialist, 1927," ESAR: Massachusetts: Reel 13.

[132] Clarence Albert Day, *Farming in Maine 1860–1940* (Orono, 1963), p. 267.

[133] Raphael Zon, "Forestry and Land Development in the Lake States," *Journal of Land and Public Utility Economics* 1 (January 1925): 36–43.

[134] Duppre Barrett, "AR of Extension Specialist in Forestry, 1929," ESAR: Georgia, Reel 35; Hartman and Wooten, *Georgia Land Use Problems*, p. 126; C. W. Simmons, "AR of the Forestry Specialist, 1932," ESAR: Texas, Reel 78.

[135] Davis, "Economic Waste from Soil Erosion," 207–20. Davis concluded that shelterbelts were limited practically to valuable crops such as fruits and garden vegetables. Thomas R. Wessel, "Prologue to the Shelterbelt, 1870 and 1943," *Journal of the West* VI (January 1967): 119–34.

[136] Forty counties in Wisconsin held schools in 1933, and 2,600 farm families set out windbreaks; earlier, in Iowa, some thirty thousand people watched

4-H Club boys and girls demonstrate them. J. F. Wotja, "Director's Annual Report, 1926," ESAR: Wisconsin, Reel 9; F. B. Trenk, Forestry Specialist, quoted in "Director's Annual Report, 1933," ESAR: Wisconsin, Reel 20; *Extension Service Review* 2 (February 1931): 22.

[137] Wessel, "Prologue to the Shelterbelt"; William H. Droze, *Trees, Prairies, and People: A History of Tree Planting in the Plains States* (Denton, Texas, 1977).

[138] Droze, *Trees, Prairies, and People*, p. 45.

[139] Eric Wing, "AR for Windham County, 1932," Cooperative Extension Service Records, Connecticut, University of Connecticut.

[140] Joseph A. Gibbs, "AR of Extension Forester, 1928," Cooperative Extension Service Records, University of Connecticut, reports that only five tree-planting demonstrations were staged in 1928 and that the four planned thinning demonstrations were cancelled because "the owners failed to find time or possessed insufficient interest."

[141] *Yearbook*, 1933, p. 74.

[142] M. L. Wilson to Charles W. Eliot II, October 2, 1935, quoted in Robert J. Morgan, *Governing Soil Conservation: Thirty Years of The New Decentralization* (Baltimore, 1965), p. 40. "Typescript of Interview with M. L. Wilson," Columbia University Oral History Office," pp. 1622, 1830, 1858.

[143] Arthur M. Schlesinger, Jr., *The Age of Roosevelt: The Coming of the New Deal* (Boston, 1959), p. 343.

[144] Hurt, *The Dust Bowl*, 135–36. Hurt notes that tenants were remiss in upkeep from the beginning. Hurt also reports that the Soil Conservation Service did not regard shelterbelts as an effective form of erosion control and therefore let the program languish, partly by requiring farmers to purchase the trees.

[145] Gove Hambidge, "Soils and Men—A Summary," *The Yearbook of Agriculture 1938* (Washington, D.C., 1938), 17. For the USDA's continuing effort to find an effective formula, see Douglas Helms, "New Authorities and New Roles: SCS and the 1985 Farm Bill," forthcoming, Soil and Water Conservation Society. Rosenberry and Moldenhauer, "Economic Implications of Soil Conservation," cite a 1967 study which found that only two groups of farmers could justify terracing when forced to contribute more than 50 percent of its cost: high income farmers who stood to realize a substantial tax saving, and low income farmers who felt that terracing would allow more intensive row cropping. See also Melvin G. Blase and John F. Timmons, *Soil Erosion Control in Western Iowa: Progress and Problems*, Iowa ESB 498 (Ames, Iowa, 1961). In March, 1989, according to *USA Today*, March 24, the SCS reported greater levels of soil blowing in Montana and Wyoming than at any time since records began to be kept in 1955.

PART III
THE STRUGGLE OVER THE LEAGUE OF NATIONS

Ralph B. Levering

PUBLIC CULTURE
AND PUBLIC OPINION
THE LEAGUE OF NATIONS CONTROVERSY
IN NEW JERSEY AND NORTH CAROLINA

THE issue of whether the United States should join the League of Nations, and whether it should do so by ratifying the Treaty of Versailles as negotiated by President Woodrow Wilson or by including reservations or amendments, led to one of the great debates in the history of American foreign relations. The debate boiled down to whether America should seize the opportunity to provide world leadership for peace through wholehearted participation in the League of Nations; or whether it should set limits upon its commitment or even, as some Americans believed, remain entirely outside the League and its "entanglements." Many Americans at the time considered the issue to be extremely important, and so did numerous political leaders and scholars of later generations.[1]

One key component of this debate—the events in Washington between 1918 and 1920 involving conflicts between President Wilson and the Senate and divisions within that body—has been analyzed repeatedly and in detail by historians and political scientists.[2] In comparison, another important factor, public opinion on the issue, has received scant attention.[3] This imbalance in the scholarly literature may have resulted partly from the inherent difficulty of analyzing public opinion prior to the arrival of modern polling techniques in the mid-1930s; it also may have stemmed from the challenge of establishing convincing links between public opinion and the specific actions of elected officials.[4]

Public opinion was important in the League debate for two main reasons. First, almost everyone involved in public life at that time considered it highly significant. President Wilson, Senator Henry Cabot Lodge, other officials, newspaper and magazine editors, business and religious leaders—to all of these, public thinking on the League mat-

tered. To most leaders, America should not take such a portentous step toward permanent international involvement without broad public support; conversely, hesitant senators should not block League membership if the overwhelming majority of the American people favored it.[5] Second, especially at the height of the League debate in 1919, it was widely believed that the outcome could play a large role in the 1920 election. Because public opinion is expressed most effectively in elections, leaders of both parties had to be concerned about the potential political impact of the League fight. Anxious to regain the presidency after eight years and apparently out of step with majority opinion on the League, Republicans had to be especially concerned about how the issue might affect their prospects in 1920.

Granting the importance of public opinion on the League issue, the question remains of how best to study it. One approach, used in most previous studies, has been to examine opinions in various groups in American society—for example, Protestant churches, liberals, and the Irish.[6] This approach has increased knowledge of opinions within these groups; but because each of them had members in many states, it has not aided in understanding the pressures and crosscurrents of opinion within states that affected the thinking of particular senators as they prepared to vote on American membership in the League. Because senators were products of the political cultures of the states which they represented, and because the voters of those states would decide whether they would be permitted to continue in office, the best way to assess politically relevant opinion on the League is to study it at the state level.

This essay examines public opinion on the League issue in two states, New Jersey and North Carolina. No two states—perhaps not even ten—could be representative of the entire nation; the United States in that era was characterized by diverse cultures, economies, and politics across state and regional lines, as well as within particular states. Selecting two states along the East Coast is not necessarily unrepresentative, for the nation's population at that time still lived largely east of the Mississippi. Indeed, only 26 percent (28 million) of the nation's 106 million inhabitants in 1920 lived west of the Mississippi, whereas 40 percent (42 million) resided in the East Coast states between Maine and Florida.[7] As long as at least one state was chosen from the northern side of the Civil War and at least one from the southern, the choices would reflect continuing divisions in the nation.

What these states offer above all else is the opportunity for comparison and contrast: New Jersey was heavily urban, industrial, recent immigrant, and Republican, whereas North Carolina was largely rural, agrarian, old-stock (white and black), and Democratic. In the key

votes on the League in November 1919 and March 1920, New Jersey's two Republican senators—Joseph S. Frelinghuysen and Walter Edge—voted with Senator Lodge, while North Carolina's two Democratic senators—Furnifold W. Simmons and Lee S. Overman—supported President Wilson. Thus, the two states were representative in the sense that they contributed to the stalemate that resulted in neither Lodge's nor Wilson's forces being able to muster a two-thirds vote in the Senate to pass the treaty. They also were representative in that neither produced a strong leader in the League fight (e.g., a Lodge or a William E. Borah for the Republicans, or a Gilbert Hitchcock for the Democrats) whose influence in national politics might have skewed opinion at the state level. Before proceeding to analyze the debate over the League in these two states between November 1918 and March 1920—the period in which the issue was in the spotlight—it is necessary to describe the political cultures[8] of the two states, including the outlooks of their major leaders at the time. These political cultures provided the soil from which general public opinion and the senators' positions on the League issue developed and took definite shape.

I. Contrasting Political Cultures

Viewed as a whole, the citizens of New Jersey and North Carolina at the close of World War I shared five overarching attitudes: an expectation of continuing economic and social progress; a belief in the importance of religion in the lives of individuals and of society; a strong sense of patriotic pride in America; a pronounced tendency toward partisanship in politics; and a desire for an enduring peace. With partisanship subdued in wartime, the remaining attitudes, widely shared throughout America, had helped the nation to unite sufficiently to make a major contribution to victory in the war, and held the promise that the United States could take the lead thereafter in bringing about international peace and prosperity.

Although shared attitudes made it possible for the people and leaders of the two states to unite in common cause, the contrasts between their political cultures were at least as pronounced. Three differences in particular make it relatively easy to understand how the senators from New Jersey and North Carolina—like most senators from the Northeast and Midwest on the one hand, and from the South on the other—could end up voting against each other on the League.

First, the people of each state were very different in background. The majority (58 percent) of New Jersey's 3.2 million residents either were born abroad or had at least one foreign-born parent. This ma-

jority included roughly 1 million persons of German, Irish, and Italian extraction, plus large numbers of recent immigrants from Eastern Europe and Russia and smaller contingents from Canada, England, Western Europe, the Middle East, and East Asia. Except for the Irish, these relative newcomers generally were not leaders in either political party; but their large numbers made them a force to be reckoned with in elections. Whites with deeper roots in America made up 38 percent of the population, and provided the leadership—and many of the votes—for the Republican party. Old-stock whites also held most of the positions of leadership in the economy, in the media, in education, and in the Protestant churches. Blacks comprised less than 4 percent of the population, and tended to be ignored by the political parties and the media. In short, Jerseyians were a highly heterogeneous people, many of whom had strong and recent ties with European peoples whose fate was being decided (or, in the case of the Irish, not being decided) at the Versailles Conference.[9]

Except for a desire for lasting peace and continuing trade with Europe, most of North Carolina's 2.6 million residents had less direct interest in the decisions at Paris. Old-stock whites (69 percent), largely of English and Scotch-Irish descent, dominated every aspect of the state's economic and political life. Blacks, who made up nearly 30 percent of the population, generally were not permitted to vote and in most other ways were relegated to second-class status; immigrants and children of immigrants totaled less than 1 percent, and had no discernible impact on public affairs.[10]

A second significant difference involved contrasts in the two states' economies and cultures. Although industry was increasing, especially in sectors related to farming such as cotton and tobacco, North Carolina remained primarily a rural, agricultural state. In 1920, only 19 percent of the population lived in places with more than 2,500 residents, and not a single city had as many as 50,000 residents. While such growing Piedmont cities as Charlotte, Winston-Salem, Greensboro, and Raleigh provided considerable leadership, especially in journalism and industry, small-scale farming and courthouse politics still set the overall tone for the state. Compared with the Northeast, per capita income remained low and the pace of life, relaxed.[11]

In contrast, New Jersey was industrialized, urbanized, and relatively cosmopolitan. Located between the teeming cities of New York and Philadelphia and heavily influenced by both, the Garden State had eleven cities with populations above 50,000, including five with more than 100,000: Newark (415,000), Jersey City (298,000), Paterson (136,000), Trenton (119,000), and Camden (116,000). The state's population was 78 percent urban; many of these city residents worked

in the factories and offices that made New Jersey one of the nation's leaders in manufacturing and services. Newark, the nation's fifteenth largest city, boasted two newspapers with impressive circulations: the *Newark Evening News* (circulation, 92,000) and the *Star-Eagle* (circulation, 50,000). Even Newark's third-ranking paper, the *Ledger*, had a circulation (32,000) considerably greater than the leading North Carolina paper, the *News and Observer* (Raleigh), (circulation, 22,000). A further evidence of cosmopolitanism is the fact that New York and Philadelphia newspapers and magazines, published in many languages, circulated in New Jersey much more widely than out-of-state publications did in North Carolina.[12]

An issue that divided business and political leaders in the two states grew out of their contrasting economies. Manufacturers and Republican spokesmen in New Jersey traditionally had supported a high tariff; they disliked the downward revision of tariff rates passed by the Democratic Congress in 1913, and feared that the nation might be swamped with cheap imports once the war in Europe ended. When the G.O.P. regained control of Congress in the 1918 elections, the *Camden Post-Telegram*, a staunchly Republican paper, noted gleefully that "American manufactures will be protected . . ." Conversely, North Carolina's Democratic leaders had supported lower tariffs—a typical response in agricultural regions—and now feared that Republicans would seek higher tariffs.[13]

The third, most important difference between the two states was that most Jerseyians considered themselves Republicans and looked down on Democrats, whereas most North Carolinians were loyal Democrats who believed that Republicans represented dictation by the North (as during Reconstruction) and political rights for blacks (as during Reconstruction and the 1890s). Both states had significant progressive movements involving members of both parties that peaked in the decade after 1905; the one in New Jersey, in fact, ended up splitting the Republican party as many reformers joined Theodore Roosevelt's Progressive party in 1912 and others supported Wilson. By 1916, however, the Republicans were largely reunited, with moderates and conservatives in control of the party machinery. Former Progressives continued to be active in public affairs, however, and provided much of the state's vocal support for the League in 1919–20. In North Carolina, progressive Democrats likewise championed the League.[14]

New Jersey's Republican leanings were underscored by the fact that Jerseyians did not give Wilson, their governor between 1911 and 1913, anywhere near a majority of their votes for president in either 1912 or 1916. Nor did the state heed his appeal to elect a Democratic

governor and senator in 1916. The conservative winner in the 1916 senate race, Frelinghuysen, proclaimed two years later that the Republican party's "accomplishments have rendered luminous the history of the greatest of the peoples of the earth. No wonder we love the . . . designation, the 'Grand Old Party,' for there is not a page in its history of which we are ashamed." Although Democrats could win particular elections with a combination of an attractive candidate and timely issues, New Jersey normally was a Republican state in national politics until the Depression.[15]

After blacks were disfranchised in 1900, Democrats established solid control of North Carolina politics. The Republican party was not moribund—it normally won roughly 40 percent of the statewide vote—but Democrats won all races for governor and senator throughout the first half of the twentieth century, and lost only three races for Congress between 1900 and 1920. Republicans formed the majority in some western counties and could win races in parts of the industrializing Piedmont; but their influence was minimal in the eastern part of the state, where blacks had continued to be concentrated after the ending of slavery. In addition to controlling state government and the resulting patronage, Democrats owned every daily newspaper in the state, much to the despair of the hard-working but outmatched Republican leaders. According to a newspaper account, one party leader, assessing the situation in early 1919, "professed to abundant consolation in the fact that the Republican party still exists in spite of the fact that Democracy is taught in the schools, communicated by the press and preached from the pulpit."[16]

Like a Grand Canyon butte bathed in early morning sunlight, the contrasting political cultures of the two states became starkly visible during the last few weeks of the 1918 election campaign. As usual, even in midterm elections, the stakes were high: in addition to contests for all the seats in the House of Representatives, New Jersey was electing a new senator to replace a retiring Democrat, and Senator Simmons was running for reelection in North Carolina. Jersey Republicans wanted to help to end the era of Democratic majorities in the House and Senate that had begun in 1913, while North Carolina Democrats wanted to ensure their continued mastery of Tar Heel politics and their strong support in Congress for President Wilson. Nationally, selective efforts to keep partisanship out of this wartime campaign collapsed when, on consecutive days in late October, former President Theodore Roosevelt attacked Wilson's Fourteen Points as being too conciliatory to serve as the basis for peace with Germany, and Wilson appealed to the country to elect a Democratic Congress to assist him in bringing about a satisfactory peace.[17]

Many Jersey Republicans, believing that they had loyally supported the Democratic administration during the war, were incensed by Wilson's appeal. "The President has asked the people to sign blank checks, make Congress a rubber stamp and put the stamp in the President's hands," Senator Frelinghuysen asserted. "He impugns the patriotism of loyal Republicans," the *Camden Post-Telegram* complained. Warren King, president of the New Jersey Manufacturer's Council, stated that Wilson wanted a Congress "subservient to his will," but the American people were "not yet ready for a Dictator in any guise . . ." Governor Walter Edge, the Republican candidate for the Senate and a supporter of Wilson's foreign policy, expressed "regret" that the president had "made the struggle for world democracy a partisan political issue at home." But, judging by letters to Senator Frelinghuysen and other indicators of public sentiment, most reactions by Republicans in the state were not so restrained. William Starr Myers, a prominent Princeton professor and lecturer, summed up what many Jerseyians were thinking when he wrote in his diary on election day: "Voted a practically straight Republican ticket. *My* answer to Wilson's damnable partizanship."[18]

In North Carolina, Democratic politicians and newspapers voiced not one word of public criticism of Wilson's appeal and a similar one issued by Treasury Secretary William Gibbs McAdoo. Governor Thomas Bickett denounced Roosevelt's statement, and the *Charlotte Observer* dismissed him as "a politician of the baser sort" who, along with other northeastern Republicans, had injected partisanship into the campaign by "engendering suspicion in the minds of [the American] people against the greatest War Government the world ever saw." The *News and Observer*, the state's most influential paper, also stood squarely behind Wilson, praising his appeal and warning voters that "[u]nder Republican rule there was a privileged class in this country." For several days before the election, the paper ran a banner headline above the masthead on page one: "Vote Tuesday to Uphold President Wilson."[19]

Tar Heel voters obliged on November 5, reelecting Senator Simmons and retaining all ten congressional seats for the Democrats. But New Jersey, like most of the North and West, went Republican, thus giving the G.O.P. control of both houses of Congress. During the campaign, the dominant political assumptions and values in the two states had been contradictory and foreign to each other. In both, partisan loyalties—not immediate issues—had been decisive. The practical implications of this wide gulf for Wilson's peace plans, however, remained uncertain.

II. The First Phase of the League Debate,
Mid-November 1918–Late February 1919

In both states, but especially in North Carolina, the period between the armistice agreement ending World War I (11 November 1918) and Wilson's first return to America from the Paris Conference (23 February 1919) featured highly favorable news coverage of the president and his foreign policies, and generally positive public comments on the League of Nations. The president's trip to France, with side trips to Britain and Italy, was the big story in American newspapers in December and January, and the release of a draft of the League of Nations Covenant in mid-February kept the peace conference at the center of the nation's attention. The news coverage of these developments, and of the efforts of the assembled leaders to prevent the spread of Bolshevism in Europe, dwarfed the coverage given to the senators in Washington who opposed Wilson and the League. The eloquent president, who had led the nation to victory in war and now sought to achieve lasting peace, was winning praise from statesmen and cheers from large crowds in Europe. It was Wilson's and America's time of triumph, and it made such good copy that even Republican papers provided extensive front-page coverage.[20]

Except for some staunch Republicans, opinion-makers in both states—politicians, church leaders, editors, and others with the ability to disseminate their views—largely supported Wilson's efforts to achieve lasting peace, including the establishment of a League to prevent future wars. The attentive public—the roughly 10-20 percent of the adult population which followed foreign policy issues closely and was relatively knowledgeable about them, but which normally could not disseminate opinions widely except through letters to the editor—also appears to have supported the League idea, though the historical evidence concerning them is more sketchy than for the opinion-makers. The evidence is even sketchier for the remainder of the population, often called the mass public, though it is significant that most Jersey and Tar Heel politicians of both parties considered support for the League idea to be prudent in early 1919. Even at this time of widespread approval of Wilson's peace policies, however, substantial differences remained in the ways in which the two states reacted to the League.[21]

In North Carolina, support for Wilson and for the League were inextricably linked. From the speeches and statements of high Democratic officials down to ordinary citizen's letters to newspapers, praise of Wilson as virtually a world savior was a recurring theme. Governor Bickett took the lead. "We are grateful for Woodrow Wilson," the gov-

ernor's Thanksgiving Proclamation declared, "that God brought him 'to the kingdom for such a time as this,' and through him made America the hope of all peoples who seek blessings of liberty under laws of righteousness." In a speech in Charlotte on December 1, Bickett defended Wilson's controversial decision to attend the peace conference, asserting that this "son of a Presbyterian minister" was needed to assure a just settlement. And on January 9, the governor urged the General Assembly to pass a resolution supporting Wilson's efforts to "incorporate in the Treaty of Peace such a League of Nations as will in every practicable way make war between enlightened nations forever impossible." Both houses passed the resolution within a few days, making North Carolina the first state to endorse the League after the end of the War.[22]

Strong praise linking Wilson and the League came from other leading Tar Heel Democrats, including Senator Overman and Secretary of the Navy Josephus Daniels. Overman wrote in December that Wilson was America's "first great international leader and one of the renowned world figures of all time." Daniels, the progressive Raleigh newspaper editor whose prestige had risen during his service in Wilson's cabinet, told the General Assembly on February 13 that "it has thrilled every American with pride that all Europe gives primacy to our chosen spokesman of world liberty," and he promised that Wilson would return from France "with the foundations of the treaty that will insure us peace . . ."[23]

So far as can be determined, most Tar Heels shared Overman's and Daniels's sentiments. The state publications of the three leading denominations strongly supported Wilson and the League. The Baptist *Biblical Recorder* editorialized that Wilson "has led the world up to the highest plane it has ever occupied"; the Methodist *North Carolina Christian Advocate* called Wilson "our great ruler and servant"; the *Presbyterian Standard* asked its readers to pray for the success of the peace talks. A Methodist conference in November passed a resolution lauding the president's leadership in war and peace, and a state convention of Masons in January applauded loudly when the keynote speaker offered similar praise for the president. One letter writer called Wilson "the world's greatest statesman," and another said that he had "immortalized democracy."[24]

Although support for Wilson's work for peace was widespread and continuous in North Carolina during this period, editors and other opinion-makers in the state had only a vague idea of how the League would operate. Neither Daniels's paper, the *News and Observer*, nor the leading paper in the western part of the state, the *Charlotte Observer*, was able to offer anything more than generalities in its commentaries

on the League. In its first editorial focusing on the issue, on December 17, the *News and Observer* stated weakly that "a league of nations founded on the consideration of mutual helpfulness in a business way might settle peace now and for the future." In an editorial published three days earlier, the *Charlotte Observer* insisted that the League would be "an effective anti-war machine," but offered no specifics to support this assertion. Even after the draft of the constitution appeared in February, the pro-League editorialist remained mired in vague generalities. Using a rural metaphor, the *Charlotte Observer* noted that the "anti-war fence" established by the League "appears to be horse-high and pig-tight"; but it did not specify the materials from which the fence had been built nor how it would be maintained. Similarly, the *News and Observer* asserted in one editorial that the League "will be a powerful force for the prevention of war . . . ," and then seemingly contradicted itself two days later by acknowledging that the organization would be "just as big a success as the nations that are negotiating it are big enough to make it." The only thing the editorialist seemed sure about was that Republican opponents of Wilson and the League were base obstructionists motivated by partisanship and envy of the president's successes.[25]

The scattered Republican weekly newspapers around the state disagreed with this portrait of G.O.P. senators. They also criticized Wilson, as when the *Union Republican* (Winston-Salem) editorialized on January 2 that the president's "fourteen points are utterly inadequate as a working basis and principle for making peace." Unlike some Democratic newspapers, Republican journals also printed letters critical of Wilson and the League. G.O.P. leaders, still smarting from their defeat in the 1918 elections and perhaps recognizing Wilson's personal popularity in the state, generally refrained from commenting on issues relating to the peace during this period.[26]

Whereas Tar Heel opinion appears to have been overwhelmingly pro-Wilson and pro-League from November 1918 through February 1919, the situation in New Jersey was much more complex. Republicans (except for Wilson-haters) wanted the president to succeed in establishing a lasting peace in Paris, but they did not want him to do it alone or to get too much credit for it. Irish Americans considered themselves to be loyal Democrats, but they disliked Wilson's closeness to British leaders. Like the Irish, most other immigrants were proud to be Americans; yet the vocal members of these groups seemed more interested in having Wilson advance the claims of their former homelands than in having him focus on American concerns. There were consistent and fervent supporters of Wilson's peace plans, especially among strong progressives of both parties, many of whom were teach-

ers, ministers, journalists, and other professionals active in the mainstream Protestant churches. But progressives now were a minority in both parties, and their churches were alienating many Jerseyians by leading the movement in the state for prohibition. Given the diversity of the state's population and the divided loyalties within as well as between individuals and groups, public opinion on the League in New Jersey was always more volatile and uncertain than in North Carolina.

There were two other important contrasts with North Carolina. First, New Jersey experienced a genuine, multifaceted debate on the merits of the League and on whether America should participate in it. This debate began in the winter of 1918–19, peaked in the spring and early summer, and then gradually ebbed in the ensuing months. Second, although the Tar Heel senators were known to be loyal supporters of Wilson, how New Jersey's Republican senators would vote on the issue remained in doubt for many months after the debate began, thus making it appear that public opinion might well affect how the votes were cast. This uncertainty lent an element of drama to the Jersey debate that was largely missing in North Carolina.

Advocates of Wilson's peace policies took the initiative in the Garden State between November 1918 and February 1919. They did so through their control of the leading newspapers in the two largest counties, Essex (*Newark Evening News*) and Hudson (*Jersey Journal*), as well as the dominant daily in the state capital (*Trenton Times*). These papers highlighted the president's triumphs in Europe and gave favorable coverage to the efforts of the main pro-League lobbying group in the state, the League to Enforce Peace (LEP). Because of this support, and because no organization was working against Wilson's policies, the pro-League forces held the advantage in the early months.

The most powerful advocate of Wilson's policies was the *Newark Evening News*, the state's largest newspaper, which counted among its estimated 277,000 readers many of the more prosperous and well-educated residents of Newark and the surrounding region. A trumpet of progressivism in North Jersey, the *Evening News* had liked both Wilson and Roosevelt in the presidential campaign of 1912, and had favored Wilson over the more conservative Charles Evans Hughes in 1916. The paper was widely respected for its thorough news coverage, its earnest and well-informed editorials, and its independent, nonpartisan stands. Led by its founder, Wallace Scudder, and his son Edward, the *Evening News* was poised in late 1918 to lead the fight for a progressive peace that would justify the world's sacrifices during the war.[27]

During the period between the election and late February, the *Eve-*

ning News published hundreds of front-page stories and scores of editorials relating to the peace conference and Wilson's goals there; virtually all of these were favorable to the president and his policies. In editorial after editorial, the paper advocated a "democratic internationalism" that alone could build "a peace of justice that will not contain the seeds of future wars." It called the League the "indispensable framework" for a lasting peace, and urged the United States to undertake specific responsibilities under the League—for example, agreeing to become a mandatory power in areas taken from Turkey—in order to give the new organization a "physical foundation." Viewing the war as resulting from "anarchy" in world affairs, the *Evening News* argued that "[l]aw, organized by a society of nations, must be substituted for it." In addition to seeking a "moral peace," America's self-interest dictated such a course: "For our own protection we must have a voice in the political rearrangement of the world, helping to order it and to keep it so ordered that war will not be thrust upon us." Finally, the *Evening News* placed its preferred course in the middle of the political spectrum: safely between the Bolsheviks who demanded world revolution on the left, and the "Entente junkers" who were "recklessly selfish" and backward looking on the right. "The peoples of the world do not have to fear the Peace Conference," the paper editorialized on February 3. "Their enemies are the Lodges and Trotskys."[28]

The impact of the *Evening News* and other pro-League newspapers on public opinion cannot be determined precisely; but they definitely had some effect, especially on the attentive public, as evidenced by anti-League Senator Frelinghuysen's comment in correspondence with the editors of New York City's Republican newspapers that, for analysis critical of the League, "[p]opulous North Jersey depends entirely on the New York papers."[29]

The effort to translate pro-League sentiments into an irresistible political force was centered in the New Jersey branch of the League to Enforce Peace, which had succeeded during the war in building active support for a League among prominent Jerseyians of both parties. Headed by Henry Van Dyke of Princeton, a respected writer and lecturer who had served as ambassador to the Netherlands, the organization sought to broaden its base by establishing active groups in every county while remaining, as one leader put it, "entirely nonpartisan."[30]

The LEP suffered a setback in October 1918 when William Starr Myers, angered by Wilson's partisanship, resigned as secretary of the state organization. Thereafter the LEP had some positive accomplishments, such as getting Governor Edge to name roughly five hundred

prominent Jerseyians of both parties to attend a regional LEP meeting in New York City in early February. More negatively, and in contrast to North Carolina, in January Governor Edge declined a request from the LEP to endorse the League of Nations, and the largely Republican state legislature ignored pleas to pass a pro-League resolution. Like many peace groups before and since, the LEP also was unable to build strong local chapters or to include recent immigrants and other ordinary citizens in its activities. An inspiring speaker who spent much of his time on pro-League lecture tours outside the state, Van Dyke was not an effective organizer. Partly as a result, the LEP had only limited impact on public opinion, both in the winter of 1919 and thereafter.[31]

Meanwhile numerous immigrant groups—including Irish, Italians, Germans, Poles, Ukrainians, and Syrians—demonstrated active concern about the fates of their former homelands, but little interest in whether Wilson would succeed in establishing the League of Nations. Indeed, among the many gatherings of ethnic groups described in the state's major newspapers, only a Ukrainian meeting in Trenton on December 29 passed a resolution calling for a League. During this period most immigrants apparently were willing to let this issue be debated by the state's old-stock leadership, including its senator and senator-elect.[32]

Senator Frelinghuysen, whose correspondence with Jerseyians betrayed a strong political dislike of Wilson and a determination to assert senatorial prerogatives in regard to the peace treaty, took a cautious but largely negative position on the League in a speech in Trenton on January 14. He accused Wilson of failing to inform Congress of his specific thinking on the League, expressed concern about maintaining the Monroe Doctrine, and vowed that he never would "relax my efforts along the lines of national preparedness, irrespective of 'scraps of paper' in the guise of League of Nations treaty . . ." Seemingly responding to Frelinghuysen in a speech in New York the next day, Senator-elect Edge was more positive: "I want to see the plans and specifications, as you do. But I am not willing . . . to take any position that will prevent or delay peace on earth and good will toward men." Edge also praised Wilson's "contribution" to winning the war, and stated his wish that "this great country assume the position it ought to occupy, above partisanship, at the head of the council of nations."[33]

Although Wilson and the League clearly had many supporters, including the group of Newark ministers who on February 8 petitioned Senator Frelinghuysen to support the League, overall Jersey sentiment on the issue had not taken definite shape by the time Wilson

returned from Paris in late February—if indeed it ever would crystal-
lize sufficiently to have political force. Even Edge, a veteran politician
with a record of being able to gauge popular thinking, was reduced to
generalities in trying to describe public opinion on the issue in a February 15 speech: "If I read the spirit of the American people correctly
it does not resist a willingness at all times to do our full duty and assume our responsibilities abroad, as well as at home, but in my judgment . . . our first duty is to take care of our home affairs." Perhaps
the most accurate conclusion one can draw about the first stage of the
state's debate over the League is to say that it was inconclusive.[34]

III. The Debate at High Tide,
Late February–Early July 1919

The League controversy in the two states peaked during the four and
one half months beginning with Wilson's address at Boston on February 24, 1919, upon his first return from France and ending with his
speech in New York at the time of his second voyage to America on
July 8. The president's speech in February, which received banner
headlines in both states, was widely viewed as initiating the formal
debate over the League. Although Wilson began this phase of the controversy, his speeches and activities no longer dominated news and
editorial coverage; and, at least in New Jersey, critics as well as supporters received respectful hearings in lecture halls, in churches, and
in the press. Indeed, New Jersey experienced a vigorous, intense debate that must rank as one of the major public discussions of a foreign
policy issue in the state's history.

What is impressive is how seriously Jerseyians—at least among
opinion-makers and the attentive public—considered the issue, and
how much effort they put into debating it. Every indicator of public
opinion reflected this interest: the frequency of letters to the editor
and columns and editorials on the subject; the number of speeches
and debates on the league, and the large attendance at many of them;
the number of letters to the state's senators, and the importance the
writers attached to the issue; and, perhaps, most significant, the willingness of political leaders to speak out repeatedly, even at the risk of
alienating some of their constituents. As applied to New Jersey, Wilson's claim on March 4 that "the overwhelming majority of the American people is in favor of the League of Nations" was too sweeping.
Although the majority almost certainly was sympathetic to the League
idea, what seems clear from their actions is that many Jerseyians were
not yet ready to commit themselves totally to Wilson's specific pro-

posal, and that they wanted the issue to be discussed and debated as fully as possible.[35]

Public interest was most evident in the hundreds of meetings held in the state on the issue between March and June. Among the highlights were a pro-League speech by Henry Van Dyke in Trenton on March 21 that attracted an audience of 1,900; a debate on April 13 in East Orange between progressive Everett Colby and conservative Henry A. Wise Wood; a strongly anti-League speech in Camden on April 29 by Edward Stokes, chairman of the Republican State Committee; and pro-League speeches by several nationally prominent advocates (including Taft, Rabbi Stephen S. Wise, and Helen Varick Boswell, president of the Republican Women's Clubs) at the state convention of the League to enforce Peace in Trenton on June 6. In addition to one-day meetings, a group of churches in Montclair organized a series of well-attended lectures on the issue on five consecutive evenings in early April, and the Newark Board of Education sponsored a series featuring pro- and anti-League speakers that took place over several weeks.[36]

Public interest also is apparent in the relatively large number of letters to the editor that appeared in Jersey papers during this period. Whereas no letters on the League appeared in the *Newark Evening News* between January 1 and February 23, eight were published between February 24 and April 14. Of these, four supported the League, three opposed it, and one did not take a stand, urging instead that Americans "refuse to precipitate in a matter of such overmastering importance." Several of the others were equally thoughtful. One pro-League letter noted that America already had abandoned its traditional policy of isolation in regard to Europe by entering World War I; another commented that it was not possible to create a "flawless document," but that the Covenant could be amended as needed. An anti-League writer criticized an *Evening News* editorial implying that people who agreed with isolationist William Borah lacked intelligence; another, C. P. Connolly of East Orange, praised the nationalistic passages in George Washington's Farewell Address and accused the paper of "following the fast-waning light of an iridescent dream." Like many of the League's opponents in New Jersey, Connolly was quite conservative, as the following statement in the letter suggests: "This League of Nations in its present form has been the dream of international Socialists for years, and international socialism means international atheism." A pro-League writer, Isabelle Ross-King, offered an equally emotional argument. Implying that women suffered more than men from war, she urged that "the women of our country ... rally to the support of our President and all the other fine statesmen who are fighting so nobly for humanity."[37]

Amidst all the arguments offered by pro- and anti-League speakers and letter-writers, the public debate over the League took definite shape in the spring and early summer of 1919. The basic dividing line between supporters and opponents, at least among old-stock Republicans and independents, typically came down to one's overall political orientation; that is, to whether one considered oneself to be progressive or conservative. In the great debate that spring, the pro-League leaders were all progressives: Colby, Van Dyke, the Scudders, Frederick W. Kelsey, and Bishop Edwin S. Lines, among others. Conversely, the League's vocal opponents in the state—Frelinghuysen, Stokes, Republican National Committeeman Hamilton Kean, and State Comptroller Newton Bugbee—were all staunch conservatives. Located in the middle, where they tried to keep lines of communication open to both wings, were the state's moderate Republicans: most notably Edge, but also others such as Newark's City Commissioner Thomas L. Raymond, who along with Bugbee was seeking the Republican nomination to succeed Edge as governor. In contrast to the progressive supporters and the conservative opponents of the League, Edge and Raymond were inconsistent in their public statements, seemingly offering encouragement first to one side and then to the other.[38]

The two Jerseyians who spearheaded the League debate during this period were Colby and Frelinghuysen. Colby, a former state senator and Progressive party leader from East Orange, in late February announced his support for Wilson's peace program, stating that the League of Nations "is so full of promise for the future peace of the world that it rises far above all party issues." On March 5 he sent a telegram to Frelinghuysen, challenging him to joint debates on the League throughout the state. When the senator declined soon thereafter, the pro-League *Trenton Times* commented that there was a "suspicion" that he was afraid to debate the issue. As an alternative, Frelinghuysen sent Colby a list of ten questions to answer concerning the League, which offered him an opportunity for additional publicity. To question eight, which asked whether there was "any good reason why the proposed League should not be discussed, criticized and thoroughly understood," Colby responded:

> None whatever. It should be discussed, and of course, thoroughly understood. . . . yet I fail to find either in your question or the speeches made in the Senate, sufficient reason for the Senators' arrogant threat to the world that they would wreck the noblest ship ever placed upon the ways if it was not rigged and dressed in sail to their entire liking. And I say this in spite of the president's inexcusable attitude toward the Senate.[39]

Although Frelinghuysen lacked Colby's eloquence, he possessed two key assets: first, as a senator, he was assured ample publicity for

his views; and second, his close ties with other conservatives gave him substantial influence in the state G.O.P. He also was determined to fight Wilson and the League, he told a friend in June, even if it destroyed his political career. A fervent nationalist, Frelinghuysen felt most comfortable by spring with the position, trumpeted by Senator Borah and others, that America should have nothing to do with the League. But he also was a loyal Republican, and he tacitly agreed to follow Senator Lodge rather than joining the irreconcilable opponents.[40]

While Colby worked to build support for the League through speeches and through his jockeying with Frelinghuysen, the senator strove just as diligently to turn public opinion against it. In late February he attacked Wilson's peace policies in a Senate address; in March he issued several statements detailing his views on the League; and from April through June he made anti-League speeches throughout the state. A friend of the ultraconservative George Wharton Pepper of Philadelphia, head of the League for the Preservation of American Independence, Frelinghuysen helped to organize a meeting of prominent conservatives in Newark on May 1 at which a state branch was established. Although this group was never as active as the League to Enforce Peace, the state's pro-League forces now had well-funded competition.[41]

The climax of Frelinghuysen's campaign against the League came in an address to more than fifteen hundred gathered in Trenton on June 21 for a convention of the State League of Republican Clubs. The senator urged that the party adopt as its motto the phrase "America First," and denounced Wilson for violating this precept. He concluded with a statement that summed up the arguments he had been making for the past several months:

> From this viewpoint of 'American First' I am opposed to any scheme which commits to all sorts of 'entangling alliances' with foreign peoples; which is sure to embroil us in wars thousands of miles away, which do not concern us . . . ; which subjects us to a Council of Nine, in which we have only one vote; which, in effect, ignores Congress as the war-declaring power and the Senate as the peace-making power; which forms a super-government . . . ; which repudiates the principles laid down by Washington and the nearly century-old doctrine of Monroe, which has barred the shores of America to foreign spoilation.

Dominated by conservatives, the convention passed a resolution opposing the League. Frelinghuysen's anti-League, anti-Wilson efforts had borne fruit.[42]

While Jersey's old-stock leaders were waging a battle over the League on fairly even terms, immigrants—especially Irish, Italians,

and Germans—became more actively concerned about the fates of their former homelands. During the spring and early summer of 1919, this concern was not necessarily anti-League or even anti-Wilson; but the growing disillusionment about the terms of peace for particular countries harmed the president politically, removing the halo that had surrounded him when he first arrived in Europe in December and January.

Of the three major immigrant groups, the Irish, the backbone of the Democratic party in the state, had by far the greatest political influence. Their chief concern—the desire for an independent Ireland, free of British rule—had considerable public support outside the Irish community; and the leaders of the movement, both in Ireland and in America, knew how to achieve substantial press coverage for their cause. The fact that many important Irish-American meetings occurred in either Philadelphia or New York made them virtually local news for Jersey papers; but the press probably would have covered the story even if this had not been the case, for some of their editors and many of their readers were Irish Americans with a strong interest in the issue. In spring 1919 the state's Irish-American leaders faced a serious dilemma. Like virtually all Irish Americans, they strongly supported independence for Ireland and wanted Wilson to work hard to achieve it at the peace conference. Yet, as loyal Democrats, they knew that criticizing Wilson or the League might well hurt the party in the state at a time when they had a good chance to regain the governorship. Accordingly, Irish-American political leaders—notably Frank Hague and Edward Edwards of Jersey City, and James Nugent and Charles Gillen of Newark—either remained silent on the issue or praised Irish freedom while offering no criticism of Wilson. Eamon De Valera and other Irish leaders, in contrast, made frequent attacks on the League.[43]

Although Irish Americans avoided criticisms of Wilson, their insistence on freedom for Ireland was unmistakable. It came in the form of impassioned speeches at public meetings across the state, in resolutions adopted by acclamation and sent to the president in Paris, and in substantial fund-raising efforts for the Irish cause. There were widespread feelings of indignation that a more just order was being created on the continent but not in Ireland. "American boys of Irish extraction who went to France and bared their breasts to the foe did so with the understanding that they were fighting for the liberation of the world, and that includes Ireland," an Irish-American speaker told a cheering audience of more than two thousand in Newark on June 22. "Show me that England has any more right in Ireland than the Kaiser had in Belgium," a Jersey City resident commented, "and I will walk on my head from here to San Francisco."[44]

Many of the state's Italian Americans likewise had strong feelings about events in Europe in the late winter and spring of 1919. In a meeting on February 26, for example, Italian Americans in Trenton passed a resolution urging Wilson to support "the just aspirations of Italy" in her dispute with Yugoslavia over the port city of Fiume. Two months later, when Wilson dramatically asserted that the principle of self-determination required that Fiume belong to Yugoslavia, more than six hundred Italian Americans met in Trenton to denounce the president's stand. The state's leading newspapers, however, strongly supported Wilson. Using language that it never employed in referring to the more established Irish, the *Trenton Times* commented that "citizens of foreign birth or descent need to be taught that there can be no divided allegiance."[45]

With the traumatic war against their former compatriots so recent, the state's German Americans, centered in Newark, avoided the limelight throughout 1919. If the scant coverage of their activities in the English-language press is representative, they had virtually disappeared from the state's political culture—except, of course, on election day in November, when many of them helped to elect Edwards, a strong opponent of prohibition, as governor. Meanwhile their leading newspaper, the *New Jersey Freie Zeitung* (Newark), supported American membership in the League and sharply criticized Lodge's opposition in an editorial in early March. Like many other ethnic Americans, its editor hoped that Wilson would secure a just peace based on "mankind's noblest instincts." Even though the *Freie Zeitung* was dismayed by the harsh terms of the settlement when it became public in late spring and began to see some merit in Republican criticisms, the paper still hoped that America would join the League, partly in order to lower the reparations that Germany was required to pay. Overall, the *Freie Zeitung*'s editors—and many other Jerseyians—probably would have agreed with the sentiments expressed in a letter published in the *Newark Evening News* on June 25: "The treaty now to come before our Senate may not be just what we would like it to be, but it may be the best thing for the world. We have had enough of strife."[46]

While Jerseyians experienced a vigorous discussion of the League and of Wilson's peace policies generally throughout the spring and early summer, the evidence suggests that most North Carolinians remained strong in their support for Wilson and confident in the expectation that the peace treaty, including the League, would be ratified handily. With both senators and most of the public backing the president, there was no urgent need for a campaign to build support for it, and indeed there was none: the League to Enforce Peace did not establish chapters in the state, and no political leader focused on the issue. Not taking public opinion for granted, elected officials made

pro-League speeches and statements fairly frequently, and Democratic newspapers included a steady stream of favorable publicity. Overall, North Carolinians remained confident of Wilson's leadership, but the issues surrounding his peace policies continued to be more abstract and distant than in New Jersey.

Although there were fewer meetings, letters to the editor, and other indicators of public opinion than in New Jersey, the existing evidence suggests overwhelming support for the League in North Carolina during this period. Bipartisan, pro-League sentiment may well have peaked in March. On the 12th, a mass meeting in Morgantown, in the Republican-leaning western part of the state, unanimously "indorse[d] the aims and purposes of the League of Nations for the future peace and welfare of all people on earth . . ."; later that month, a crowd estimated at eight thousand in Wilson, in the Democratic east, adopted a pro-League resolution without a dissenting voice. Even the partisan *Union Republican* found "no objection to some League or agreement . . ." Perhaps the best gauge of public sentiment is the fact that all the Democrats and half of the Republicans in the General Assembly backed a resolution on March 15 supporting Wilson's peace policies. Although a few Republicans voted against the resolution out of loyalty to the national party, a reporter noted, all of them "appeared to be in favor of the League and to desire even more of it than the democrats had asked them." In short, Governor Bickett exaggerated only a little when he noted that "[in] North Carolina all classes of people, regardless of politics, religion, race, color or previous condition of servitude, believe that the League is the surest guarantee to the future peace . . ."[47]

Between February and July pro-League resolutions were passed unanimously by numerous groups, including the North Carolina Merchants Association, the state convention of Elks Clubs, the Women's Missionary Society of the Lutheran Church, and a large convention of Baptists. In these and other cases, there is no evidence that any debate took place before the resolutions were accepted. This lack of discussion, in turn, raises the issue of whether the League really mattered very much to North Carolinians, or whether many of them simply found it easy to voice approval (or alternatively, to remain silent) when pro-League statements were placed before them. Responding to an inquiry from a national magazine, a Raleigh journalist offered a telling insight into the level of public interest: "The people in this community trust Wilson. They have not, of course, analyzed the proposed constitution of the League, but they do not believe Wilson and his associates could be misled or that there is any purpose to mislead them at Paris."[48]

Congressman John H. Small, a fervent League supporter, repeatedly expressed concern about the lack of an organized campaign in the state, and questioned whether North Carolinians were as directly involved in the struggle as they needed to be. "I am sure that our two distinguished Senators will do all in their power for the ratification of the covenant," Small commented in early June, "but our people should give renewed strength to their senators in some tangible form." Except for passing resolutions, writing occasional letters to newspapers and senators, and organizing study groups in some churches and colleges, there is little evidence that North Carolinians cared deeply about the League.[49]

The fact that virtually no local Republican opponents of the League were quoted in the state's major newspapers meant that Democratic politicians and journalists did not have to take criticisms of the League seriously, as they did in New Jersey. The absence of a genuine two-party system contributed to a lack of debate. No national Republican leaders spoke in the state from March onward; Lodge, Borah, and other opponents of Wilson were ridiculed and equated with German and Russian villains in the major dailies. Dominated by Democrats, the Baptist convention in early July heard several pro-League speakers, but not a single anti-League one. In the absence of opponents to sharpen debate, political speeches and editorials remained laden with mellifluous generalities, such as the *News and Observer*'s claim on June 30 that Wilson "has set humanity on a new road" and "lock[ed] the door against further war by the League."[50]

Tar Heel leaders, confident in the correctness of the president's course and of public support for the League, never even hinted that Wilson might have to compromise with his Republican opponents before American participation in the League could become a reality. Instead, their mood was upbeat as Wilson returned from Paris for the second time in early July, with Senator Simmons predicting ratification of the treaty and a Democratic victory in 1920 and the *Greensboro Daily News* insisting that public opinion would "force the senate to act earlier than some . . . leaders had anticipated." The *News and Observer* expressed this hopeful feeling most concisely: "Peace has been signed. The people want the peace ratified."[51]

IV. Wilson's Position Deteriorates Amid Declining Public Interest, July 1919–March 1920

In retrospect, the third stage of public debate on the League, lasting from Wilson's return to Washington in July 1919 until the Senate

failed to consent to the Treaty of Versailles for the second time in March 1920, turned out to be an anticlimax. Although most of the public continued to support ratification, it is not certain that the majority (at least in the North) favored ratification without the significant reservations that Senator Lodge and other Republicans demanded. What is clear is that the president's popularity declined during these months as inflation, labor-management disputes, prohibition and other issues angered many Americans and heightened doubts about Wilson's leadership. Even his serious illness beginning in late September did not trigger widespread public support. "In the present temper of the country it is probably . . . popular" to attack Wilson, the *Newark Evening News* acknowledged in November. "Let us drop Wilson and talk about America." Although the president remained more popular in North Carolina, the overall trends were similar in the two states: the emergence of other issues that competed for public attention, a hardening of political opinion on the League, an increase in criticisms of Wilson, and a sense that the debate had become deadlocked well before the Senate ended its deliberations. As the president's popularity waned, even North Carolina's loyal Democratic senators admitted that compromise would be required to ratify the treaty.[52]

In New Jersey, public meetings on the League, letters to newspapers and to senators, and the activities of pro- and anti-League organizations all decreased in the summer and fall of 1919—and virtually stopped in the winter of 1920—as the Senate proceeded with its seemingly endless debate and as other issues come to the fore. Whereas the League was the focus of public discussion in the winter and spring of 1919, three other issues became equally prominent after June: which party would win control of state government; what, if anything, could be done to prevent prohibition from being imposed; and how Jerseyians could help to bring about Irish independence. Briefly, the Democrats won the governorship in November largely by taking an unequivocal stand against prohibition. Responding to pressure from Irish Americans within their party, they also undermined pro-League strength in the state by inserting in their platform a plank stating that the Senate should not agree to U.S. membership before Irish independence was achieved. Republicans, sensing the unpopularity of their support for prohibition, unsuccessfully sought to make the campaign a referendum on the Democratic administration in Washington; at least superficially, their platform united mild reservationists and strong reservationists behind ratification of the peace treaty with reservations. Thus, neither political party backed Wilson's position as the Senate debated the treaty throughout

the summer and fall and as Wilson embarked on his strenuous speaking tour across the Midwest and West in September. Moreover, the news stories and editorials devoted to the gubernatorial campaign and to the many meetings in the state for Irish freedom tended to shift media attention away from the League issue, notwithstanding the considerable coverage devoted to the Senate debate and to the president's trip.[53]

Meanwhile political opinion on the League issue hardened, with supporters becoming increasingly strident and uncompromising and with opponents of Wilson growing ever more confident in their position. With few public meetings after June, proponents largely stated their views through letters to the editor and editorials. One frequent correspondent, Frederick W. Kelsey, denounced Lodge and his allies as "reactionary obstructionists" and characterized some New Jersey opponents as "un-American, vindictive fault finders." One writer implied that a German-American critic was a traitor, and another asserted that Senator Frelinghuysen's opposition to the treaty was "giving aid and comfort to the enemy." One advocate dubbed Lodge "the ostrich-head peacock from Massachusetts." Pro-League editors also became bitter and vindictive. The *Newark Evening News* linked opponents with "Sinn Fein. . . . the near Bolsheviki and . . . the pro-enemies." Rejecting the Lodge reservations, the *Evening News* argued that it would be "better to have a belated America that has declared itself of noble spirit by the vote of its citizens than an America on time but with its moral standing smirched with compromise." After the treaty was defeated on November 19, the angry editors repeatedly castigated Lodge, expressing the hope on one occasion that "some-day—perhaps soon—the treaty may cut Mr. Lodge dead."[54]

Opponents of the League also wrote letters to the editor and published numerous editorials in papers like the *Camden Post-Telegram* and the *Atlantic City Daily Press*. Republicans pointed out specific failings of the treaty, such as the Shantung settlement, and decried Wilson's dealings with the Senate, "the co-ordinate treaty-making power." They also argued in November that it was Wilson and the Democrats, not Lodge and the Republicans, who were responsible for delaying ratification of the treaty. "Had the President been willing to accept the reservations formulated by a majority of the Senate," the *Post-Telegram* editorialized on November 20, "the Treaty would have been ratified."[55]

If the rhetoric of the League opponents generally was less harsh than that of the supporters, perhaps it was because they now were confident of victory; that is, they knew that Wilson lacked the votes to pass the treaty without reservations. As Wilson toured the country

making impassioned pleas for public support, New Jersey's senators felt assured of Republican success. "I doubt very much if the President will make much headway in his 'swing around the circle,'" Frelinghuysen wrote a correspondent on September 8. Two days later, Edge asserted in a speech in Jersey City that the G.O.P. appeared to have won the treaty fight. "I feel absolutely confident that any American reading the reservations attached to the treaty will give them their unqualified approval," Edge commented after the Senate vote of November 19. Having failed to get Wilson to move toward compromise in a lengthy discussion with him at the White House on July 22, Edge felt justified in supporting Lodge's position. And so did Frelinghuysen, who insisted that the Republicans were safeguarding "American rights and interests" by modifying Wilson's "unworkable and dangerous" proposal.[56]

There is considerable evidence that, after the deadlock in November, most politically aware Jerseyians wanted the Senate to compromise and ratify the treaty. Except for the Irish-American community, still angered by Wilson's lack of support for their cause, most Jerseyians probably would have agreed with William Howard Taft's comment on November 30 that he "would rather have the treaty with reservations than nothing at all." The Central Presbyterian Church of Montclair passed resolutions to that effect on December 7, and a large crowd turned out to hear Taft urge compromise in Watchung three weeks later. In a vote at Rutgers University on January 13 that included 585 students and 60 faculty members, 302 (47 percent) favored a compromise, 170 (26 percent) supported Wilson, 120 (19 percent) backed Lodge and 53 (8 percent) opposed ratification in any form. At Rutgers and among the 158,000 ballots that same day at colleges and universities across the country, faculty tended to be more favorable toward Wilson's position than students, and students more supportive than faculty of compromise. But compromise received the largest number of votes among both groups, nationally as well as locally.[57]

Although many Jerseyians supported compromise, there is little evidence of activity designed to try to achieve it. The Jerseyian who had worked the hardest as an organizer for the League to Enforce Peace, Anne MacIlvaine of Trenton, wrote Henry Van Dyke in December that she was "too exhausted to be any further help." Encouraging her plans for a vacation in the West Indies, the Princetonian responded that LEP had done all it could for the League, and that "there is nothing left to do except to let conscience work among the people, and remorse, if possible, bring the frivolous senators to repentance."[58]

Whether or not Van Dyke was correct in his judgment, LEP and other organizations in the state were quiescent as the Senate headed for its second vote. When Wilson refused to compromise, Jersey's senators again voted with Lodge to pass the treaty, and to oppose it without them. Putting the vote on the treaty with reservations in a positive, pro-Republican light, the editors used the following headline in the March 20 *Atlantic City Daily Press*: "Peace Treaty Defeated in Senate, Vote of 49 to 35; N.J. Senators Favor it." In contrast with November, pro-League editors did not blame Republicans for defeating the treaty. The *Trenton Times*, which had grown increasingly critical of Wilson's unyielding stance throughout the winter, reprinted a long editorial from the *Philadelphia Enquirer* that placed the entire blame on the president's "stubbornness" and "egotism." While believing that the Republican opposition was "ninety-nine one-hundredths sham and partisan bunk," the *Newark Evening News* admitted that it would be impossible to have a "'who killed cock robin' debate over the fate of the treaty." As in the Senate, the League debate in New Jersey ended in a frustrating, apparently pointless stalemate.[59]

The president's position also deteriorated in North Carolina between July 1919 and March 1920. From the end of the war though the early summer of 1919, Wilson's leadership for peace had triggered enthusiastic, broad-based support in the state. By fall 1919, however, the president's inability to deal effectively with pressing domestic issues had tarnished his image, and his leadership and policies were drawing guarded criticisms from Tar Heel Democrats and sharp attacks from the state's Republicans. Although most Democrats remained loyal to Wilson on the League and other issues, there were fewer references to the president's "greatness" and more hints that he should permit the Senate to work out its own compromise on the treaty. With Republican strength on the rise, there also was less emphasis on Wilson and more on the entire Democratic record since 1913 and on the need to remain loyal to the party to prevent G.O.P. inroads. Although the two senators and other leading Democrats sincerely wanted the treaty ratified, maintaining power in the state took precedence over any particular policy goal in Washington.[60]

Between Wilson's return from Paris in July and the first Senate vote on the treaty in November, there was a much more open and wide-ranging debate on the League in North Carolina than there had been earlier. Prominent Republicans, including Marion Butler and John Motley Morehead, publicly criticized the League; letters to the editor in the major papers were about evenly divided between pro- and anti-League positions; and even some pro-Wilson journals like the *Biblical Recorder* argued that "some reservations should be made" in order to

"make plain the meaning of certain clauses as we Americans under-stand them."

Precisely why both sides came to be represented in the public dis-cussion of the League among Tar Heels at this time is unclear. It may have resulted partly from what Roland F. Beasley, the editor of the *Winston-Salem Sentinel*, called "the general restlessness and unsettled state of public opinion . . ." It also may have stemmed from the blatant partisanship of pro-League Democrats such as former Governor Locke Craig, who was criticized for commenting in late July that North Carolinians were "with President Wilson right or wrong," but that of course he was "absolutely right" on the peace treaty.[61]

Two well-publicized developments in late July and early August sig-naled the arrival of relatively open debate on the League. The first was the visit of Senator James A. Reed, a Missouri Democrat strongly opposed to U.S. membership in the league, who addressed a large audience in Goldsboro on July 24. "Missouri Opponent of League of Nations Invades North Carolina Today," a headline in the *News and Observer* read; an editorial in the same paper assured Tar Heels that Reed "has nothing to offer." But the damage had been done: for the first time a nationally known opponent had spoken in the state, and his argument that the League would undermine U.S. sovereignty and the Constitution could not be dismissed entirely. On August 2, Parker Anderson, a Republican who owned newspapers in Wilmington and Greensboro, made an impassioned attack on Article X of the treaty at the annual meeting of the North Carolina Press Association. In case of another war in Europe, he argued, Article X meant that "my boy and your boy will have to go." Anderson also charged that his col-leagues, in seeking a unanimous endorsement of the League, were blindly following President Wilson and knew little about the details of the treaty. The resolution supporting the president passed thirty-one to three, but not before Anderson had made it clear that North Caro-linians had the right to oppose the treaty in public forums.[62]

The strong pro-League vote at this meeting, and equally over-whelming endorsements of the peace treaty at several other conven-tions in late summer and fall, suggest that most North Carolinians continued to back Wilson. Unlike the straw polls in New Jersey, votes at the University of North Carolina in November and again in January showed majority support for Wilson's position on the League. Most Tar Heel Democrats clearly were remaining loyal to the president. Yet there were dissenters, like the "good democrat" from Brevard who argued in November that "President Wilson should have kept his feet upon the earth while gazing at the stars in evolving a peace treaty, intertwined with a league of nations." Even supporters like the editors

of the *Greensboro Daily News* admitted that the treaty "is not perfect"; but, they continued, "it is so near perfect that by rejecting it we should commit enormously greater wrongs against humanity than we shall by accepting it with its admitted defects." [63]

The state's Democratic editors and politicians put aside all doubts and solidly supported Wilson and the League when the treaty was defeated for the first time on November 19. The *Charlotte Observer* accused Senator Lodge of "autocracy," and condemned the Senate for "dishonoring the President." Claiming that Wilson had exhibited "a spirit of compromise and conciliation," the *News and Observer* argued that "[t]he G.O.P. has badly overreached itself." The *Asheville Citizen* contended that the "hosts of radicalism and bolshevistic revolution everywhere are heartened . . . by the action of leader Lodge and his followers." In early December, a former mayor of Charlotte summed up a frequently expressed view of why the Senate defeated the treaty: "Lodge and his gang hate Wilson because he is a southerner and a democrat, and was President during the greatest war this country ever had." [64]

The defeat in the Senate was deeply disappointing to many Democrats, but at least it was a foreign policy issue distant from Tar Heels' immediate concerns. Closer to home was the contest for an open seat in Congress in the ninth district, which included the Charlotte area and several largely rural counties to the west and north, to be decided on December 16. Both the national and state G.O.P. saw this race as a good opportunity to establish a beachhead in the Democratic South, one that could be expanded in subsequent elections. Conversely, the Democrats, recognizing the growing unpopularity of the Wilson administration, were determined to keep the state's congressional delegation entirely Democratic, so that the Republicans would not have momentum going into the 1920 campaign. The G.O.P. nominated Morehead, a wealthy former congressman and state party leader; the Democrats countered with Clyde Hoey, a young attorney.

Given the dissatisfaction of many voters with Democratic leadership, Hoey's inexperience and relative lack of name recognition, and the Republican leanings of several western counties, Morehead probably should have won the election. Instead, he lost a tight race by roughly one thousand votes, partly because he did not campaign in his own behalf, and partly because the Democrats pulled out all the stops to win. Hoey ran hard on Wilson's record, including the League of Nations: "Every mother and father who gave a son . . . has a right to demand that this League shall be adopted . . ." Equally important, the Democrats brought in several big names from Washington, notably Secretary of the Navy Josephus Daniels and their Senate leader,

Gilbert Hitchcock. These speakers extolled the administration's accomplishments, including new banking laws, aid to farmers, and victory in the war. Imploring the voters to keep the Democrats in power,
Daniels scornfully recalled what Republicans had done during the reconstruction following the last major war. Hitchcock insisted that Senate Democrats stood ready to make a reasonable compromise on the
League, and warned that a Republican victory might doom the treaty
by sending the wrong message to Washington. Aided by these campaigners, by fervently pro-Democratic coverage in the major papers,
and perhaps by the anger resulting from the defeat of the treaty, the
Democrats maintained control of the ninth district and hence the
state's congressional delegation. The state's political culture remained
safely Democratic.[65]

With the election behind them, Tar Heel Democrats could disagree
among themselves again. At the Jackson Day dinner in Washington on
January 8, William Jennings Bryan criticized Wilson's call for a "great
and solemn referendum" on the league in the 1920 elections and
urged Senate Democrats to go ahead and ratify the treaty, obtaining
"such compromises as may be possible." Disagreeing sharply with
Bryan, the *Charlotte Observer* insisted that the people wanted "Wilson's
Treaty," whereas the *News and Observer* declined to choose between the
two positions. Senator Simmons, who worked hard throughout the
winter to effect a compromise that would not totally undermine Article X, commented that he likewise was "neither a supporter of the
president nor Mr. Bryan in this matter."[66] As in New Jersey, there is
little evidence of public involvement in the issue in the winter of 1920:
no public meetings occurred, and the number of letters to the editor
declined sharply. Meeting in Greensboro on March 3, the Republican
state convention passed a resolution supporting Lodge's stand on the
treaty, but otherwise little effort was made to influence events in Washington one way or another. The editors of the *Greensboro Daily News*
did become angry when Wilson refused to meet with Simmons in
March to discuss a possible compromise on Article X; the paper accused the president of "humiliating the men who are trying sincerely
. . . to help him . . ." When the treaty went down to defeat again on
March 19, the editors described Wilson as "one of the most prodigious
statesmen we have ever produced, but a most confoundedly uncom-
fortable person to live with." The more partisan *Charlotte Observer*
praised Senators Simmons and Overman for "standing by him [Wil-
son] to the last"; the *News and Observer*, also loyally Democratic, excor-
iated Lodge and urged the American people, in the upcoming
campaign, to demonstrate their desire to fulfill "their duties to the rest
of the world manfully and courageously." Deeply disappointed, North

Carolina's Democratic spokesmen at least could take comfort in reaching their own conclusions about why the Senate had failed to consent to the treaty.[67]

V. Conclusion: Were North Carolinians More Internationalist?

From the 1940s through the 1960s, a debate occurred among academics and journalists about whether the South historically had been more internationalist than other regions, and whether this alleged southern distinctiveness on foreign policy issues had ended during and after World War II. Among other things, proponents of the idea of greater internationalism in the South before 1941 repeatedly cited the region's approval of Wilson's stand on the League of Nations.[68]

Not surprisingly, this study found strong support in North Carolina for Wilson and the League; but it does not follow that Tar Heels generally were more ardent advocates of an active American role in world affairs than were Jerseyians. Indeed, the contrary view may well be more persuasive for several reasons. First, there appears to have been more public discussion and debate concerning the League in New Jersey, which is consistent with the findings of Gabriel A. Almond and other political scientists that largely rural populations tend to be "less attentive to problems of foreign affairs" and less likely to "belong to organizations in which foreign affairs are discussed."[69] Second, the overall quality of the debate on the League was superior in New Jersey. Jerseyians who made speeches or wrote letters on the issue tended to be better informed about the provisions of the treaty and the likely implications of U.S. membership in the League. Third, Jerseyians tended to be more closely linked to Europe, whether through education, travel, trade, or direct ties to former homelands. Lacking North Carolinians' partisan incentives for backing Wilson, many Jersey Republicans nevertheless gave vocal support to the League and pressed their senators to work to approve the treaty. As we have seen, this pro-League sentiment appears to have influenced Senator Frelinghuysen's decision to support Lodge rather than the irreconcilables, despite his strong antipathy toward both Wilson and the League. In short, Jerseyians of that era tended to be better educated, more urban, and in closer touch with Europe; and their senators, while opposing Wilson's position, twice helped to form majorities that voted to consent to the treaty.

To suggest that Jerseyians were at least as internationalist as North Carolinians is not to deny that conservative Republicans in the state

often were intensely nationalistic, or that some ethnic leaders single-mindedly championed European causes. Nor is it to doubt the commitment to internationalism of many North Carolinians, especially among middle-class progressives active in the state's mainline Protestant churches and in such professions as education and law. As a rule, support for the League was sincere and deeply felt; yet it had the added benefit of providing a weapon to keep the state's Republicans on the defensive. The votes in both states in the fall of 1919 strongly support the proposition that local factors and domestic concerns are more important than foreign policy issues in deciding most American elections.

Given their strong desire for ratification and growing weariness with Wilson's leadership, Democratic supports of the League in North Carolina can be faulted for not putting pressure on Senators Simmons and Overman to join most of their northern counterparts in both parties to consent to the treaty in March 1920, after it had become apparent that the U.S. would enter the League that year with the Lodge reservations or not at all. In the absence of such pressure, the senators' safest course politically was to stay with Wilson, which is what they did. Thus, the comparatively quiescent public opinion in North Carolina in the winter of 1919–1920 made it easy to support the president to the end; yet it is not clear that the senators would have been hurt politically if they had voted with Lodge the second time, especially if they both had done so and had explained their action as helping to formally end the war and achieve Wilson's goal of American membership in the League.[70]

Whether or not Tar Heel senators and their constituents merit censure on the League, Wilson certainly does. Having served as president for six years by early 1919, he had more than enough experience in Washington to know that the issue would not be decided by what he called "the overwhelming majority of the American people" who supported the League, but rather by the senators from the forty-eight states, each of whom would weigh his particular political circumstances and beliefs, as well as the pressures he was receiving from within his party and from the voters who elected him. Because partisanship was almost certain to influence voting on the treaty, especially in the wake of the bitter 1918 election, the president would need to bridge the gap between the largely Republican political cultures of the North and West, and their Democratic counterparts in the South. By the fall of 1919 it was apparent to many of his contemporaries that Wilson had only two realistic ways to get the treaty ratified: either offer substantial concessions to his northern opponents, or give the green light to loyal southern senators to vote with Lodge and pass the

treaty. By choosing to do neither, the ailing president made the biggest mistake of his political career.

Notes

[1] The influence of the debate over the League of Nations was greatest during World War II, when the United Nations was being created. See Robert A. Divine, *Second Chance: The Triumph of Internationalism in America during World War II* (New York, 1967). I appreciate the assistance of Sara Barton and Matthew Levering in researching this project, and financial support from Davidson College and the New Jersey Historical Commission.

[2] Useful studies emphasizing events in Washington include Denna F. Fleming, *The United States and the League of Nations, 1918–1920* (New York, 1932); Thomas A. Bailey, *Woodrow Wilson and the Great Betrayal* (New York, 1945); Kurt Wimer, "Executive-Legislative Tensions in the Making of the League of Nations" (Ph.D. diss., New York University, 1957); Leon Boothe, "Woodrow Wilson's Cold War: The President, the Public, and the League Fight, 1919–1920" (Ph.D. diss., University of Illinois, 1966); David Mervin, "The Senate Opposition to the League of Nations: A Study in Legislative Executive Conflict" (Ph.D. diss., Cornell University, 1968); and especially Lloyd E. Ambrosius, *Woodrow Wilson and the American Diplomatic Tradition: The Treaty Fight in Perspective* (New York, 1987).

[3] Studies of public opinion on the League issue include Wolfgang J. Helbich, "American Liberals in the League of Nations Controversy," *Public Opinion Quarterly* 31 (Winter 1967–68); James L. Lancaster, "The Protestant Churches and the Fight for Ratification of the Versailles Treaty," *Public Opinion Quarterly* 31 (Winter 1967–68): 597–619; Kenneth R. Maxwell, "Irish-Americans and the Fight for Treaty Ratification," *Public Opinion Quarterly* 31 (Winter 1967–68): 620–41; and John B. Duff, "The Versailles Treaty and the Irish-Americans," *Journal of American History* 55 (December 1968): 582–98. An interesting study of press opinion, albeit limited to early 1919, is Frank Abbott, "The Texas Press and the Covenant," *Red River Valley Historical Review* 4 (Spring 1979): 32–41.

[4] I consistently have found the study of past public opinion—both its formation and its relationship to policy-making—to be more art than science. A challenging view to the contrary, of value to all historians working in this field, is Lee Benson, "An Approach to the Scientific Study of Past Public Opinion," *Public Opinion Quarterly* 31 (Winter 1967–68): 522–67.

[5] An editorial in *News and Observer* (Raleigh) epitomized this view: "Peace has been signed. The people want peace ratified." "Ratification," *News and Observer*, 1 July 1919, p. 4.

[6] For references, see footnote 3 above.

[7] U.S. Department of Commerce, Bureau of the Census, *Abstract of the Fourteenth Census of the United States 1920* (Washington, 1923), 16, 18.

[8] For a discussion of political culture in relation to public opinion, see Bernard C. Hennessey, *Public Opinion*, 3d ed., (Belmont, Calif., 1975), 161–88.

⁹*Ibid.*, 18, 100, *passim*. For a more detailed discussion of New Jersey's population in the early twentieth century, see Joseph Francis Mahoney, "New Jersey Politics After Wilson; Progressivism in Decline" (Ph.D. diss., Columbia University, 1964), 5–10.

¹⁰*Ibid.*, 18, 100–1. For a general discussion of North Carolina during this period, see Hugh Talmage Lefler and Albert Ray Newsome, *North Carolina: The History of a Southern State*, 3d ed., (Chapel Hill, 1973), pp. 555–97, and J. G. de Roulhac Hamilton, *History of North Carolina*, III, (Chicago, 1919), pp. 316–94.

¹¹*Ibid.*, 55, 61, 75. On rural life in North Carolina at the time, see Sydney Nathans, ed., *The Quest for Progress: The Way We Lived in North Carolina, 1879–1920* (Chapel Hill, 1983), pp. 3–19.

¹²*Ibid.*, 50, 55; *American Newspaper Annual and Directory* (Philadelphia, 1919), 604; *News and Observer*, 17 October 1919, p. 10. Senator Joseph S. Frelinghuysen noted the influence of out of state newspapers in New Jersey in a letter written in July 1919: "The Camden people very largely form their opinions from the Philadelphia newspapers." Frelinghuysen to George Wharton Pepper, 22 July 1919, Box 6, J. S. Frelinghuysen Papers, Rutgers University Library.

¹³"A Republican Congress," *Camden Post-Telegram*, 6 November 1918, p. 6; "G.O.P. Plans to Rebuild Old Protection Wall, Says Simmons," *Charlotte Observer*, 2 March 1920, p. 7.

¹⁴For New Jersey politics, see Arthur S. Link, *Wilson: The Road to the White House* (Princeton, 1947), pp. 133–307, and Mahoney, "New Jersey Politics After Wilson," 13–317. For North Carolina politics, see Lefler and Newsome, pp. 563–75; Dewey W. Grantham, *Southern Progressivism: The Reconciliation of Progress and Tradition* (Knoxville, 1983), pp. 76–78; and Link, "The Wilson Movement in North Carolina," *North Carolina Historical Review* 23 (October 1946): 483–94. Staunch supporters of the League in New Jersey included Frederick W. Kelsey, Everett Colby, and Edward Scudder; *News and Observer*, owned by Josephus Daniels, a prominent Democrat who served as Secretary of the Navy under Wilson, was a leading advocate of the League and other progressive causes in North Carolina.

¹⁵Joseph S. Frelinghuysen, speech in Trenton, 1 October 1918, Frelinghuysen Papers, Rutgers University library. Joseph Francis Mahoney has written that the Republican victory in 1916 "stemmed primarily from the failure of Wilson and the state candidates to find an issue that would unsettle the normally Republican majority." Mahoney, "New Jersey Politics After Wilson," 312.

¹⁶Although brief, Grantham, *Southern Progressivism*, pp. 74–78, is the best account of Democrats in North Carolina politics in this era. For the Republican predicament, see Joseph S. Steelman, "Republicanism in North Carolina: John Motley Morehead's Campaign to Revive a Moribund Party, 1908–1910," *North Carolina Historical Review* 42 (Spring 1965): 153–68. See also Marion Butler's extensive correspondence with fellow Republicans in 1918–19 in the Marion Butler Papers, Box 36, Southern Historical Collection, University of North Carolina Library. The quotation is from Frank Smethurst, "Radicals After Warren's Scalp," *News and Observer*, 16 February 1919, p. 1.

[17] For examples of how Roosevelt's and Wilson's appeals were presented in news stories, see "Wilson's 14 Principles Thoroughly Mischievous Says Colonel Roosevelt," *Charlotte Observer*, 25 October 1918, p. 1, and "Wilson Appeals For a Congress to Support Him," *Charlotte Observer*, 26 October 1918, p. 1.

[18] "Says Wilson Wants Dynasty Government," *New York Times*, 27 October 1918. p. 10; "Mr. Wilson's Partisan Appeal," *Camden Post-Telegram*, 26 October 1918, p. 6; press release by Warren C. King, 30 October 1918, box 10, Frelinghuysen Papers; "Wilson's Appeal to Voters Stirs Hot Resentment," *Atlantic City Daily Press*, 28 October 1918, p. 2; William Starr Myers' diary, 5 November 1918, Myers Papers, Princeton University Library.

[19] Letter from Edwin Yates Webb to F. M. Williams, 25 October 1918, Webb Papers, Box 14, Southern Historical Collection; letter from Thomas A. Warren to Romulus A. Nunn, 28 October 1918, Nunn Papers, Box 7, Duke University Library; "Wants Taft to Flay Roosevelt," *Charlotte Observer*, 26 October 1918, p. 1; "Roosevelt," *Charlotte Observer*, 26 October 1918, p. 6; "The Judas Price," *News and Observer*, 28 October 1918, p. 4; "That This Government Shall Not Perish From the Earth," *News and Observer*, 2 November 1918, p. 4.

[20] For examples of page-one coverage in a Republican newspaper, see "Wilson to Greet People of Italy," *Camden Post-Telegram*, 2 January 1919, p. 1; and "President Warmly Welcomed in Rome," *Camden Post-Telegram*, 3 January 1919, p. 1. Democratic and independent newspapers often carried several page-one stories relating to the peace conference. See, for example, *News and Observer*, 29 December 1918, p. 1, and *Newark Evening News*, 8 January 1919, p. 1.

[21] The classic discussion of the stratification of the public into "opinion-makers" and "opinion-holders," with the latter divided into "attentive public" and "mass public," may be found in James N. Rosenau, *Public Opinion and Foreign Policy* (New York, 1961), pp. 27–41. The question of where to draw the line between the attentive and mass publics is always a difficult one, depending partly on public interest in a particular foreign policy issue. My own sense is that the League of Nations, like the debate over whether to enter World War II or the Iran hostage crisis, attracted substantial public interest, so that the attentive public in this case may well have been larger than normal.

[22] Governor T. W. Bickett, Thanksgiving Proclamation," *News and Observer*, 20 November 1918, p. 1; "Glad Wilson Is To Be Present," *Charlotte Observer*, 2 December 1918, p. 4; "Governor's Recommendations to General Assembly of 1919, *News and Observer*, 10 January 1919, p. 1.

[23] Lee Slater Overman, "President Wilson as World Leader," *The Forum* 60 (December 1918): 647; "Address of Secretary Daniels Before the General Assembly," *News and Observer*, 14 February 1919, p. 12.

[24] "The Idealist," *Biblical Recorder*, 5 February 1919, p. 1; "The Peace Conference," *North Carolina Christian Advocate*, 20 February 1919, p. 3; "Goodbye –Welcome," *Presbyterian Standard*, 25 December 1918, p. 4; "Favors Changes in Church Creed," *Charlotte Observer*, 15 December 1918, p. 1; "North Carolina Masons Hold Opening Session," *News and Observer*, 22 January 1919, p. 1; letter to editor from S. S. Harris, *News and Observer*, 16 December 1918, p. 16; letter to editor from S. F. Conrad, *Charlotte Observer*, 22 December 1918, p. 6.

[25] "Why League of Nations," *News and Observer*, 27 December 1918, p. 4;

"The Anti-War Machine," *Charlotte Observer*, 24 December 1918, p. 6; "The League," *Charlotte Observer*. 15 February 1919, p. 6; "The League's Constitution," *News and Observer*, 15 February 1919, p. 4; "Taft and White," *News and Observer*, 17 February 1919, p. 4. For examples of editorials criticizing Republicans, see "Anything to Disagree," *Charlotte Observer*, 22 December 1918, p. 6; "A Grand Advance for Mankind," *News and Observer*, 18 February 1919, p. 12; and untitled editorial, *News and Observer*, 24 February 1919, p. 4. The last of these editorials argued that the Republicans' protectionist leanings explained their anti-League stand.

26 Untitled editorial, *Union Republican* (Winston-Salem), 2 January 1919, p. 2; letter to editor from "one of the boys," *Union Republican*, 9 January 1919, p. 2. In addition to printing its own material, the *Union Republican* published stories and editorials from such sources as the Republican Publicity Association and the *National Republican*, both of which were located in Washington, D.C.

27 For the *Evening News*'s endorsement of Wilson in 1916, see "Issues Raised in Vain," *Newark Evening News*, 6 November 1916, p. 6. In another editorial that same day, the *Evening News* endorsed several Republican candidates for Congress.

28 The quotations, cited in order, are taken from the following *Newark Evening News* editorials: "Vital Things First," 9 January 1919, p. 8; "Clemenceau and Wilson," 6 January 1919, p. 8; U.S. as Mandatory Power in Turkey," 8 February 1919, p. 8; "Law or Anarchy?", 15 January 1919, p. 8; "A People's Mandate," 7 January 1919, p. 8; "Enmeshed," 31 January 1919, p. 8; "Lodge Serves Notice," 1 November 1918, p. 8; "Recklessly Selfish," 1 February 1919, p. 8; "Asquith Puts a Poser," 3 February 1919, p. 8.

29 Quoted in Ralph B. Levering, "The League of Nations Controversy in New Jersey" (seminar paper, 1969); copy in author's possession.

30 Letter from William H. Parry to members of the League to Enforce Peace in New Jersey, 14 January 1919, Henry Van Dyke papers, Firestone Library, Princeton University.

31 "Names Jersey Peace Delegates to League's Atlantic Congress," *Newark Evening News*, 23 January 1919, p. 17; "Wants Legislation to Endorse League," *Trenton Times*, 7 January 1919, p. 3. Evidence of administrative problems include lack of coordination between Van Dyke and Parry, who replaced Myers as secretary of the New Jersey branch in late fall; on this point see Henry Van Dyke to W. R. Boyd, Jr., 17 January 1919, Van Dyke papers.

32 For an example of immigrant activities on behalf of their former homelands, see "Friends of Irish Freedom Meet, Elect Officers for New Year," *Newark Evening News*, 20 January 1919, p. 10; for the pro-League resolution, see "Ukrainians Favor League of Nations," *Trenton Times*, 31 December 1918, p. 1.

33 "He happens to be a law unto himself, and does things in his own way, irrespective of laws and constitutions," Frelinghuysen wrote to a constituent in November 1918. Joseph S. Frelinghuysen to J. Albert Van Winkle, 23 November 1918, Box 10, Frelinghuysen Papers, Rutgers University Library. Frelinghuysen wrote another correspondent, who had complained about Wilson's appointment of Colonel Edward House as a peace commissioner, that "the Senate as the Treaty making power will undoubtedly have something to say

and I believe it will be in a forcible manner." Frelinghuysen to P. E. Alliot, 21 November 1918, *Ibid.* For Frelinghuysen's speech in Trenton, see "Frelinghuysen Attacks Policies of President," *Newark Evening News*, 15 January 1919, p. 7; for Edge's speech in New York, see "Edge and Smith Address Convention of Food Men," *Newark Evening News*, 16 January 1919, p. 6.

[34] "Ministers Ask Senators' Support Movement for League of Nations," *Newark Evening News*, 11 February 1919, p. 12; "Governor Edge Makes Plea for Americanism," *Newark Evening News*, 17 February 1919, p. 6.

[35] For examples of correspondence between constituents and senators, see Arthur O. Townsend to Joseph S. Frelinghuysen, 17 March 1919, Frelinghuysen Papers; and William Edge to William Starr Myers, 10 March 1919, Myers papers. The quote from Wilson is in Arthur S. Link, ed., *The Papers of Woodrow Wilson*, vol. 55 (Princeton, 1986), p. 413.

[36] "League Compact of Free Nations," *Trenton Times*, 22 March 1919, p. 3; "Colby and H. A. W. Wood Debate Nations League," *Newark Evening News*, 14 April 1919, p. 11; "Stokes Denounces League Covenant," *Trenton Times*, 30 April 1919, p. 4; "Brilliant Leaders Put Patriotism Above Party," *Trenton Times*, 7 June 1919, p. 1; "Fears, 'Gray Minds' May Dictate Peace," *Newark Evening News*, 2 April 1919, p. 11; "Thinks Nations' League Will Elevate Humanity," *Newark Evening News*, 23 April 1919, p. 26.

[37] Letters to the editor of *Newark Evening News* from M. S. Waters, 28 February 1919, p. 8; Borden D. Whiting, 24 February 1919, p. 8; E. R. Dodge, 28 March 1919, p. 8; C. P. Connolly, 31 March 1919, p. 8; and Isabelle Ross-King, 14 March 1919, p. 8.

[38] For Edge's views, see "Edge in Middle on League Plan," *Trenton Times*, 28 February 1919, p. 1, and "Edge Would Like Covenant Revised," *Trenton Times*, 27 March 1919, p. 1; for Raymond's views, see "Raymond Sees Danger in Wilson 'Treaty-Making,'" *Newark Evening News*, 10 April 1919, p. 17, and "Raymond, Giving Flag Day Talk, Favors League for Lasting Peace," *Newark Evening News*, 16 June 1919, p. 16.

[39] "Colby to Go Through State to Advocate Nations League," *Newark Evening News*, 26 February 1919, p. 5; "Major Colby Challenges Frelinghuysen to Debate," *Newark Evening News*, 5 March 1919, p. 12; "Frelinghuysen Won't Debate Colby," *Trenton Times*, 13 March 1919, p. 1; "Scared Off?", *Trenton Times*, 15 March 1919, p. 6; "Answers Frelinghuysen on League of Nations," *Newark Evening News*. 1 April 1919, p. 1.

[40] For Frelinghuysen's willingness to risk political ruin in fighting the League, see Myers' diary, 21 June 1919, Myers papers.

[41] "Senate Renews Its Attack on League Outline," *Newark Evening News*, 28 February 1919, p. 1; "Frelinghuysen Outlines His Position on the League," *Newark Evening News*, 10 March 1919, p. 1; "Frelinghuysen Defends His Position on League," *Newark Evening News*, 19 March 1919, p. 9; "Frelinghuysen on League He Favors," *Trenton Times*, 25 April 1919, p. 2; "Form Branch to Present Other Side of League," *Newark Evening News*, 2 May 1919, p. 14.

[42] "Republican Doctrines Before League of Clubs," *Newark Evening News*, 21 June 1919, p. 1; "Republican Clubs Line Up Against Nations League," *Newark Evening News*, 23 June 1919, p. 3.

[43] Mayor Gillen of Newark, for example, flew the Irish flag at city hall on St.

Patrick's Day, but limited his public comments to "[it's] a grand flag, boys." "Free Flag of Erin Flies at City Hall," *Newark Evening News*. 17 March 1919, p. 11. Mayor Hague's Jersey City was the last municipality in Hudson County to pass a resolution supporting Irish freedom. There also was no public criticism of the League in the speeches at the time by Hague, Edwards, and Director of Public Safety Charles F. X. O'Brien. See *Jersey Journal* (Jersey City), 2 July 1919, p. 1. In an interview in April, De Valera called the league "a new holy alliance" that gave dictatorship to a few countries. "De Valera Says Ireland Never Took German Gold, Assails the League of Nations," *Newark Evening News*, 10 April 1919, p. 17.

⁴⁴ For examples of pro-Irish meetings, see "Irish Call for an End to 'British Occupation,'" *Newark Evening News*, 17 March, 1919, p. 10, and "Friendly Sons of Orange Urge Claims of Ireland," *Newark Evening News*, 18 March 1919, p. 11. The quotation from the speaker is in "Audience at Krueger Hall in Applause for De Valera," *Newark Evening News*, 23 June 1919, p. 10. The Jersey City resident is quoted in *Jersey Journal*, 22 May 1919, p. 7.

⁴⁵ "Trenton Italians Ask Wilson's Aid," *Trenton Times*, 28 February 1919, p. 11; "Trenton Italians Denounce Wilson," *Trenton Times*, 28 April 1919, p. 4; "No Divided Allegiance," *Trenton Times*, 1 May 1919, p. 6.

⁴⁶ This paragraph is based largely on editorials that appeared in the *New Jersey Freie Zeitung* on 20 November 1918, 5 March 1919, and 12 July 1919. For more details on German-American thinking, see Levering, "The League of Nations Controversy . . .", pp. 11–12. The last quotation is from a letter to the editor by 'E.R.D.'," *Newark Evening News*, 25 June 1919, p. 8.

⁴⁷ "Burke County Citizens Favor League of Nations," *Charlotte Observer*, 13 March 1919, p. 7; "Alabama Congressman Liked Wilson Citizens," *Charlotte Observer*, 22 March 1919, p. 11; "The League of Nations," *Union Republican*, 20 March 1919, p. 2; "Tar Heel Republicans Favored Wilson Draft," 17 March 1919, p. 11; "The League Advances Rather Than Abandons the Monroe Doctrine," *Charlotte Observer*, 28 February 1919, p. 1.

⁴⁸ "Merchants O.K. Wilson Efforts," *Charlotte Observer*, 19 June 1919, p. 1; "Beard to Head State B.P.O.E.," *Charlotte Observer*, 26 June 1919, p. 1; "League Endorsed Widely in State," *News and Observer*, 4 July 1919, p. 3; "Baptist Seaside Assembly Endorses League of Nations," *Greensboro Daily News*, 2 July 1919, p. 12; "Nation-Wide Press-Poll on the League of Nations," *Literary Digest* 61 (April 5, 1919): 15.

⁴⁹ "Small Advocates Wider Publicity About the League," *News and Observer*, 12 June 1919, p. 2. See also "Small Would Speak for the League of Nations," *Charlotte Observer*, 1 March 1919, p. 2. For activities in churches and colleges, see "Sunday School to Talk of League of Nations," *Charlotte Observer*, 26 February 1919, p. 9; "Announcement of Debate Triangles," *News and Observer*, 4 March 1919, p. 3.

⁵⁰ For examples of editorials that ridicule Republicans, see "Is Borah Bluffing?", *News and Observer*, 13 May 1919, p. 4, and "Borah's New Idea," *Charlotte Observer*, 2 July 1919, p. 6. The quotation is from "The President Returns," *News and Observer*, 30 June 1919, p. 6.

⁵¹ "Visits of Republican Leader to the 3rd District Mean Strife," *Greensboro*

Daily News, 6 July 1919, p. 1; "May Expedite Action," *Greensboro Daily News*, 4 July 1919, p. 4; "Ratification," *News and Observer*, 1 July 1919, p. 4.

[52] "America, Not Wilson," *Newark Evening News*, 29 November 1919, p. 8.

[53] On the primacy of prohibition in the gubernatorial campaign, see "Campaign Issues," *Trenton Times*, 18 October 1919, p. 6, and Warren E. Stickle III, "The Applejack Campaign of 1919: As 'Wet' as the Atlantic Ocean," *New Jersey History* 89 (Spring 1971): 5–22. On the Democratic plank on Ireland, see "Stresses Jersey Democrats Call for Irish Recognition," *Newark Evening News*, 2 October 1919, p. 1. On the Republican efforts to inject national issues, see "Bugbee Defeat Means Democrats Win in 1920," *Newark Evening News*, 24 October 1919, p. 22, and "Result Here as Stokes Sees It," *Trenton Times*, 24 October 1919, p. 3.

[54] Letter to editor from Frederick W. Kelsey, *Newark Evening News*, 1 December 1919, p. 8; letter to editor from Frederick W. Kelsey, *Newark Evening News*, 3 February 1920, p. 8; letter to editor from Charles J. Ferris, *Newark Evening News*, 24 July 1919, p. 8; letter to editor from Raymond Brush, *Newark Evening News*, 12 December 1919, p. 8; "Against and for the League," *Newark Evening News*, 15 July 1919, p. 8; "Leave No Doubt," *Newark Evening News*, 7 October 1919, p. 8; untitled editorial, *Newark Evening News*, 16 December 1919, p. 8.

[55] Letter to editor from Benjamin F. Edsall, *Newark Evening News*, 9 August 1919, p. 8; "The Explanations about Shantung," *Camden Post-Telegram*, 19 July 1919, p. 6; "As the President Expounds the Treaty," *Camden Post-Telegram*, 9 September 1919, p. 6; "The Senate's Action on the Treaty," *Camden Post-Telegram*, 20 November 1919, p. 6; untitled editorial, *Atlantic City Daily Press*, 18 November 1919, p. 12.

[56] Frelinghuysen to F. B. Bard, 8 September 1919, Box 10 Frelinghuysen Papers; "Edge and Bugbee Speakers at Garven Faction Dinner," *Newark Evening News*, 11 September 1919, p. 15; "Jersey's Senators Tell Treaty Views," *Newark Evening News*, 20 November 1919, p. 1; William Hard interview with Walter Edge, undated, William Hard Papers, Princeton University Library.

[57] Taft Urges Ratification of Treaty in Some Form," *Newark Evening News*, 1 December 1919, p. 23; "Treaty Compromises Urged in Resolutions of Montclair Church," *Newark Evening News*, 10 December 1919, p. 19; "League Necessary to Clinch War, Says Taft," *Newark Evening News*, 29 December 1919, p. 13; "College Wants Compromise on League," *The Targum* (Rutgers University), 13 January 1920, p. 1; "League of Nations Referendum Favors Compromise on Treaty," *The Targum*, 20 January 1920, p. 1.

[58] Letter from Anne MacIlvaine to Henry Van Dyke, undated (December 1919?) and letter from Van Dyke to MacIlvaine, 23 December 1919, in Henry Van Dyke Papers.

[59] "Peace Treaty Defeated in Senate, Vote of 49 to 35; N.J. Senators Favor It," *Atlantic City Daily Press*, 20 March 1920, p. 1; "Peace Treaty Defeated," *Trenton Times*, 20 March 1920, p. 6; "A Horse of Another Color,"*Newark Evening News*, 24 March 1919, p. 8; "Co-operation or Isolation," *Newark Evening News*, 20 March 1919, p. 8.

[60] An example of the guarded criticism of Wilson is an editorial in the *News*

and Observer in regard to the president's speaking tour: "The fight in the Senate is close. Mr. Wilson is needed in Washington. His illness may be a blessing in disguise." "The President's Illness," *News and Observer*, 28 July 1919, p. 4.

[61]"Amendments Killed," *Biblical Recorder* 85 (22 October 1919): 7; "The Newspaper and the Task of Reconstruction," *News and Observer*, 28 July 1919, p. 1.

[62]"Senator Jim Reid with Republicans; Missouri Opponent of League of Nations Invades North Carolina Today," *News and Observer*, 22 July 1919, p. 1; "Senator Reed," *News and Observer*, 24 July 1919, p. 4; "Goldsboro People Hear Senator Reed," *News and Observer*, 25 July 1919, p. 2; "Anderson Starts Much Discussion," *News and Observer*, 3 August 1919, p. 1; "Editors of the State Endorse Peace Treaty," *Greensboro Daily News*, 3 August 1919, p. 12.

[63]"Phi Legislature Endorses the Adoption of the Paris Covenant of the League," *The Tar Heel* (UNC), 8 November 1919, p. 1; "College Students Uphold President on Peace Treaty," *News and Observer*, 11 January 1920, p. 1; letter to editor from J. E. Lathrop, *Asheville Citizen*, 26 November 1919, p. 4; "An Imperfect But Highly Valuable Instrument," *Greensboro Daily News*, 8 September 1919, p. 4.

[64]Untitled editorial, *Charlotte Observer*, 19 November 1919, p. 6; "Republican Success," *Charlotte Observer*, 21 November 1919, p. 6; "Treaty Will Be Ratified," *News and Observer*, 21 November 1919, p. 4; "Overplayed," *News and Observer*, 19 November 1919, p. 4; "The Senate Reactionaries Win," *Asheville Citizen*, 20 November 1919, p. 4; "One-Minute Interviews," *Charlotte Observer*, 4 December 1919, p. 10.

[65]"Rousing Rally for Hoey in Opening Speech," *News and Observer*, 6 December 1919, p. 1; "Daniels Calls on Ninth to Support Hoey in Election," *News and Observer*, 11 December 1919, p. 1; "Result of Election in Ninth District Might Determine Fate of Peace Pact, Says Hitchcock," *Charlotte Observer*, 16 December 1919, p. 1.

[66]"The Wilson Proposition," *Charlotte Observer*, 10 January 1920, p. 6; "A Militant Democracy," *News and Observer*, 10 January 1920, p. 4; "Treaty Outlook Brightest Yet Senators Think," *Charlotte Observer*, 12 January 1920, p. 1.

[67]"Marion Butler Remains a Power in State G.O.P.," *News and Observer*, 4 March 1920, p. 1; "The President's Letter to Senator Hitchcock," *Greensboro Daily News*, 10 March 1920, p. 4; "All That Is Left Is Regret," *Greensboro Daily News*, 21 March 1920, p. 4; "The Defeat and the Cause," *Charlotte Observer*, 21 March 1920, p. 6; "Treaty with the People," *News and Observer*, 20 March 1920, p. 4.

[68]A good summary of the debate up to 1957 is contained in Alexander DeConde, "The South and Isolationism," *Journal of Southern History* 24 (August 1958): 332–46. For an opposing view, arguing that the South historically was more internationalist, see Alfred O. Hero, Jr., *The Southerner and World Affairs* (Baton Rouge, 1965), pp. 3–7.

[69]Gabriel A. Almond, *The American People and Foreign Policy* (New York, 1950), p. 132. V. O. Key, Jr., noted that Southerners "have far lower levels of political participation than do other Americans." Key, *Public Opinion and American Democracy* (New York, 1961), p. 104.

[70] As Dewey W. Grantham has noted, most southern Democratic senators stayed with Wilson in the March voting, whereas only a few Democrats from outside the region sided with the president. See Grantham, "The Southern Senators and the League of Nations, 1918–1920," *North Carolina Historical Review* (April 1949): 198.

John Milton Cooper, Jr.

FOOL'S ERRAND OR FINEST HOUR?
WOODROW WILSON'S SPEAKING TOUR
IN SEPTEMBER 1919

NOTHING so became Woodrow Wilson's public career as the leaving of it, or so it seems. His last great public act was the whirlwind three-week speaking tour that he made in September 1919 on behalf of American membership in the League of Nations. That tour ended Wilson's public career because early in the morning of September 26, 1919, he suffered a stroke that forced him to cancel the remainder of his engagements and to return at once to the White House. There he suffered a second, massive stroke that left him so severely impaired that he never again functioned fully as President. In fact, the last address on the tour, at Pueblo, Colorado, on September 25, 1919, was the last real speech Wilson gave. On the fifth anniversary of the Armistice, on November 11, 1923, he did deliver a 500-word statement, which was broadcast over the radio, but that brief appearance witnessed the only public utterance he made with his own voice after September 1919.

Those late summer and early autumn days of stirring speeches, cheering crowds, and emotional encounters, climaxing in physical breakdown, evidently lent not only a dramatic close but also a fitting symbolism to Woodrow Wilson's public career. That was the prevailing view among friends and foes alike at the time—a view that has persisted among both sympathetic and critical historians during the last twenty years. Nearly all observers, regardless of their attitude toward him, have professed to find the essence of his character epitomized in that speaking tour.

For Wilson's admirers, this was his finest hour. They have depicted his tour as a noble act of self-sacrifice. In their view, he put such a premium on the attainment of world peace through the League of Nations and he felt such a deep obligation, especially to his country-

men who had just fought and died in World War I, that he willingly, knowingly risked his health, indeed his life, in the effort to persuade Americans to adopt his program. To those who have esteemed him, this speaking tour has represented the purest and best in Woodrow Wilson.[1]

For Wilson's detractors, by contrast, this was a fool's errand at best. They have depicted his tour as a willful, ill-conceived act of vanity and desperation. In their view, he was so filled with self-righteous egotism, bordering on a messiah complex, and he took such a rigid stand toward his critics and opponents that he fell prey to delusions of grandeur about his own persuasive powers and even to a wish for martyrdom in a holy cause. To those who have disesteemed him, this speaking tour has represented the least and worst in Woodrow Wilson.[2]

The unanimity in viewing this as the greatest and most revealing event in Wilson's public career, combined with the sharp conflict about the value placed on the event and, by extension, the career, presents both a challenge and an obstacle to interpreting what he said and did during those three weeks in September 1919. Does this event really deserve to be judged on the exalted scale of apotheosis or damnation that interpreters have persistently invoked? On one side, was this speaking tour so noble a gesture or so heroic a gamble as to be deemed the finest hour in a career fraught with great ventures on the domestic and international stage? On the other side, was this speaking tour so futile and ill-conceived, did it promise so little reward at so great cost as to be deemed a fool's errand that perhaps needlessly doomed a great cause? On a less exalted scale of judgment, questions arise about why the speaking tour ever took place and how well its author appraised the perils and opportunities that he faced. These are some of the questions that need to be addressed in interpreting Wilson's actions in September 1919.

Both of the usual ways of viewing the event encompass an incorrect assumption. Although nearly all interpreters have regarded Wilson's decision to take his case to the country as deeply revealing, they have also assumed that he was doing something special and unusual mainly in response to a difficult predicament. In fact, the reverse is true. Wilson, it appears, never considered not making a public effort to explain the peace settlement and to justify membership in the League of Nations. Starting in February 1919, during the early days of the peace conference in Paris, he was instructing his secretary, Joseph P. Tumulty, back in Washington to start making arrangements for a speaking tour. Wilson originally wanted to begin the tour immediately after his return from the peace conference at the beginning of July. It is

important to recall this long-standing resolve to go to the public with his peace program because it casts Wilson's action in a different light.[3]

He did not make his speaking tour on behalf of the peace program because of senatorial opposition. Wilson probably would have made some kind of tour even if he had encountered less opposition and criticism on Capitol Hill. The desire for contact with the people sprang from his deepest convictions about the nature of democratic government and the nature of leadership. Even before he entered politics, Wilson had believed that education of the public formed the essential task of leadership in a democracy and that such education was a two-way process in which the leader both instructed and learned from the led. As a politician he had transformed those convictions into a near mystical faith in the efficacy of informed public opinion and an Antaeus-like yearning to renew his strength periodically by getting in touch with the people. On the tour, when he told a small crowd at Mandan, North Dakota, "I am glad to get out to see the real folks, to feel the touch of their hands," Wilson was not just indulging in a rhetorical gesture. Since his entry into politics in 1910, he had made seven extensive speaking tours. Five of those tours had occurred in his campaigns for election and reelection as governor of New Jersey and as president. The other two, in support of his state reform program in 1911 and his military preparedness program in 1916, had come in response to legislative opposition. But both campaigning and combatting opposition had only offered Wilson excuses for doing what he wanted to do anyway.[4]

What was unusual about the speaking tour in September 1919 and where opposition did play a critical part lay in the timing and possibly the scope of Wilson's actions. In view of his own predilections, he behaved out of character in not going out to meet the public earlier. Indeed, some critics have faulted him for not taking his case to the people sooner, before the lines of battle with elements in the Senate became too sharply drawn. The criticism has some merit, although not in the way that it is presented. The stronger of the two main reasons for delaying the tour was that the President made prolonged efforts to negotiate with various factions among the senators. Contrary to the often repeated depiction of an obdurate, irascible executive dealing grudgingly with the legislators, Wilson displayed patience, good humor, and flexibility when he met with individual senators and on August 19 with the Foreign Relations Committee as a group at the White House. To castigate him, therefore, for not taking to the hustings earlier in order to facilitate his dealings with the Senate smacks of damned-if-you-do-and-damned-if-you-don't. Besides negotiations with the senators, the other main reason for delaying the speaking

tour may have been quiet resistance mounted by his wife, Edith Bolling Galt Wilson, and his physician, Admiral Cary T. Grayson. Both
Mrs. Wilson and Grayson feared for the President's health if he subjected himself to the rigors of what would in effect be a presidential
campaign.[5]

The chief merit in the charge that Wilson hurt his cause by delaying
the tour comes from two different considerations. First, he lost opportunities for educating people about his work at the peace conference
and about the meaning and advantages of the League of Nations. Second, because he had spent so much time and energy in Washington's
enervating summer climate dealing with senators and with pressing
domestic problems, he made the speaking tour with diminished physical strength and intellectual resiliency and perhaps with less adequate preparation than he would have done earlier. Because these
criticisms bear on Wilson's actual performance and on broader questions, the proper place to consider them is in the context of his arguments on the tour. What needs to be considered immediately about
the delayed decision to make the tour is why he finally made it. What
weighed uppermost in his mind at the moment? What did he think he
could accomplish? How well aware was he of the risks he was running?

The only contemporary evidence about the actual decision to make
the tour comes in two sentences in Secretary of State Robert Lansing's
desk diary. "Prest very angry at Senators for proposed amendment as
to Shantung," Lansing recorded on August 25, 1919. "Told me most
confidentially that he planned to go to the people at once, and that if
they [his senatorial opponents] wanted war he'd give them a belly
full." Both Wilson's evident tone in that statement and the earlier on-
again-off-again references to a speaking tour have led the editors of
The Papers of Woodrow Wilson to conclude, "Wilson's decision to go to
the country was obviously made without much thought, in anger, and
on the spur of the moment. The decision was, we have to say, irrational." It was irrational, they add, particularly because a "swing
around the circle" held out no real prospect of influencing the critical
group of Republican senators whom he needed to win over.[6]

As further testimony to the basically emotional character of the decision, the Wilson Papers editors cite Grayson's later recollection, which
may not be totally reliable, that he tried to dissuade Wilson from making the tour on grounds of health. "I know what you have come for,"
the doctor allegedly recalled the President telling him. "I do not wish
to do anything foolhardy, but the League of Nations is now in its crisis,
and if it fails, I hate to think what will happen to the world. You must
remember that I, as Commander in Chief, was responsible for sending our soldiers to Europe. In that crucial test in the trenches they did

not turn back—and I cannot turn back now. I cannot put my personal safety, my health in the balance against my duty—I must go."[7]

Moreover, according to the editors, the essentially impulsive character of the decision affected the nature and scope of the tour. They believe that Tumulty and his staff had to work "frantically" to make arrangements. Three days later, on August 28, Tumulty announced to the press that the President would begin a twenty-five day, ten-thousand-mile journey on September 3, with the first speech to be delivered in Columbus, Ohio, on September 4. The editors imply, therefore, that the speaking tour became more extensive and less well planned because Wilson had decided to make it so suddenly and impulsively. This implicit criticism has a point. In undertaking such an extensive tour, with over forty speeches, Wilson would be doing much more speaking than he had ever done before, even during presidential campaigns. In addition, his itinerary took him through the West, mainly to sparsely populated states, and it gave no indication of having been targeted toward either reaching the largest numbers of people or swaying critical senators.

Despite that point, however, is this interpretation of Wilson's decision correct? The itinerary does not, in fact, appear to have been hastily arranged. According to Tumulty's biographer, John M. Blum, the President's secretary had been making tentative plans for a speaking tour, and he had drawn upon the previous experiences of the League to Enforce Peace, the principal pro-League organization, in arranging trips for its head, former President William Howard Taft. In an apparent effort to duck blame for having caused the President's collapse, Tumulty later claimed that the decision to make the tour came at the urgent insistence of the Democratic senators who supported the treaty and League membership.[8]

Actually, the main impetus arose from Wilson himself, abetted by Tumulty. Both men set the location, extent, and pace of the trip. Tumulty also alleged afterward that he had suggested a week's break for a vacation at the Grand Canyon, which Wilson had rejected because "the people would never forgive me if I took a rest on a trip such as the one I contemplate taking." In fact, Tumulty designed the campaign-style schedule and would have included still more whistle-stop appearances and meetings with local politicians had not Mrs. Wilson and Dr. Grayson objected. As for the western focus, Wilson himself evidently chose that. His sweep of those states had played a big part in his reelection in 1916, and, like his friend Frederick Jackson Turner and many domestic reformers of the day, he regarded westerners as more democratic and "real Americans." Furthermore, according to Tumulty, this tour may have been only the first of several

projected speaking ventures. The secretary recalled that the western trip was "so successful that we planned . . . to invade the enemy's country, Senator [Henry Cabot] Lodge's own territory, the New England States and particularly Massachusetts." Whether or not the western tour was well-conceived or wisely planned, therefore, it did not spring from haste or impulsiveness.[9]

But what of the decision itself on August 25, 1919? The *Wilson Papers* editors' interpretation of an emotional response to senatorial opposition undoubtedly contains an element of truth. Wilson almost certainly felt balked and frustrated when, after having tried so hard to explain his position, the Republican senators on the Foreign Relations Committee seemed bent on amending the treaty to nullify the cession to Japan of Germany's previous rights in the Chinese province of Shantung. That apparent rebuff almost certainly undermined his previous resolves to stay in Washington and try to work things out with the senators. But is their larger interpretation, which leans toward the "fool's errand" side, correct? The critical considerations are what Wilson may have hoped to accomplish by making the tour and whether he may have been courting martyrdom by ignoring his doctor's warning.

There is no ready answer to the question of what Wilson hoped to accomplish with the speaking tour. The closest that he came to explaining his purpose occurred on August 19 in the meeting with the Foreign Relations Committee. In a somewhat testy exchange, Frank Brandegee, a sharp-tongued Republican from Connecticut and an announced opponent of League membership, pressed the President about the possibility of making peace with Germany without joining the international organization. "We could, sir," answered Wilson; "but I hope the people of the United States will never consent to do it." Brandegee fired back, "There is no way by which the people can vote on it." That exchange posed the problem precisely. Why, if only the Senate could consent to the peace treaty, was Wilson so intent on taking his case to the people? Did he seriously believe that he could foment so much pressure from public opinion that wavering or opposing senators would come to heel, especially when many of them would not be up for reelection until 1922 or 1924?[10]

Wilson often talked in his speeches in September 1919 as if popular pressure would overcome senatorial opposition. Later, in January 1920, he called for making the next presidential election "a great and solemn referendum, a referendum as to the part the United States is to play in completing the settlements of the war and in the prevention" of future wars. But when he began the speaking tour, he never said that he was trying to achieve any particular result. Instead, he was

doing something that he wanted to do, and seems to have believed that taking his case to the people was simply a good thing. Wilson may also have been engaging in a defensive partisan maneuver. Leading supporters in the Senate such as Gilbert Hitchcock of Nebraska and Key Pittman of Nevada had warned that many of their fellow Democrats might defect to Lodge's position of attaching reservations to the instrument of ratification. At the least, then, a demonstration of the President's popularity in the western states—which had proven indispensable to the Democrats' narrow victory in 1916 and that seemed to offer the best hopes of future national success—would shore up support in his own party.[11]

Conversely, the question needs to be asked, what would Wilson have accomplished by not making a speaking tour? Critics of his decision have either argued or implied that he missed opportunities for further negotiation with the senators that might have laid the basis for compromise. Perhaps so. Earlier, in the prolonged debates and negotiations over banking reform in 1913 and 1914, Wilson had stayed in Washington and kept Congress in session for months, patiently worked out differences with the men on Capitol Hill, and finally gotten most of what he wanted in the Federal Reserve Act. But in 1919 the prospects of successfully repeating such a feat seemed far less promising. The President himself had taken a much firmer stand on a specific program, and he felt much more deeply committed on the issue. Likewise, the congressional situation was much less fluid, involving only one house of Congress, the necessity for a two-thirds vote to gain consent to the treaty, and the presence of only four more or less hardened factions on the question of League membership. In those circumstances, Wilson may not have acted so irrationally in thinking that he could accomplish little by remaining in Washington.

But there is a more critical aspect of what might have occurred if he had not gone on the tour. Nearly every critic of the decision has suggested that he would not have suffered a major stroke and, thereby, he would have obviously been far better equipped to deal with the Senate. This is the most haunting speculation that hangs over the speaking tour and the whole controversy over the peace treaty and League membership. But it is only a speculation. Obvious as it seems, this argument—that the stresses of the speaking tour brought on Wilson's stroke—is not airtight. He might well have suffered a stroke anyway in the fall of 1919 even if he had not made his journey westward. Would such a stroke have occurred sooner or later? Would it have been more or less severe? Would it have affected his role in the political controversy the same way? None of these questions can ever receive answers that are anything more than wild guesses.[12]

What is less speculative about the risks of the tour for Wilson's health is how he regarded the matter himself. All interpreters of his decision seem agreed that he gladly faced the danger to his person. Not only Grayson, but also Mrs. Wilson, Tumulty, and the journalist H. H. Kohlsaat later recalled him making statements about setting aside personal considerations in order to take his case to the people. Mrs. Wilson and Tumulty likewise remembered him alluding to his having sent young men to fight and die in the war and likening himself to them. These recollections have formed the basis for both the argument that the speaking tour was a noble act of self-sacrifice and the contention that it was a vainglorious flirtation with martyrdom. These views have some plausibility. Grand gestures and flamboyant risks were not beyond Wilson's ken. The style of heroic leadership was something that he had long envied in his great rival, Theodore Roosevelt. Lonely suffering for principle was a posture that he had long admired in his erstwhile ideological confrere and now bitter enemy, Robert M. La Follette. Given the probable effects of deteriorating health on his emotional state in the summer of 1919, such motives may have swayed Wilson more than they would have done at other times.[13]

But that is not likely. Viewing Wilson primarily as a hero or martyr on his speaking tour misreads the man and the action. Soldier-like resignation was apparently not the only response that he gave to warnings about his health. Secretary of the Navy Josephus Daniels remembers him as replying to such warnings, "You are mistaken. It will be no strain on me—on the contrary, it will be a relief to me to meet the people. No, the speeches will not tax me. The truth is, I am saturated with the subject and spoiling to tell the people about the Treaty. I will enjoy it." That sounds more like Wilson. He relished contact with the public, and his characteristic response to physical illness or limitations was to deny them. When his wife, doctor, secretary, and others tried to dissuade him from making the trip by warning about risks to his health, they were barking up the wrong tree. By making the speaking tour, Wilson was neither heroically facing peril nor vainly sacrificing himself. Rather, he was doing what came naturally both by choosing a pleasanter alternative than staying in Washington and by brushing aside concern about his physical well-being.[14]

Predictably perhaps, with the stakes apparently so high and the risks presumably so great, the speaking tour itself turned out to be neither triumph nor tragedy. Although it was Wilson's most extended and unrelieved public performance, the trip in September 1919 was not his best appearance on the hustings. His first presidential campaign in 1912 probably deserves to be judged his finest virtuoso per-

formance, although that campaign also had a few less-than-sparkling moments. Wilson had also shone better on his brief swings during his reelection campaign in the fall of 1916. On a tour to promote a program, such as he was doing now, he had done a more masterly job in selling his military preparedness program to the public at the beginning of 1916. Wilson did not do so well in 1919 as he had done earlier for two reasons. First, the effects of age and ill health told on his performance. Second, the more complicated nature of his message and greater difficulty of his political task hampered his effectiveness.

How much Wilson's health hurt him on the hustings must also remain a matter of speculation. The only putatively direct testimony to his physical condition comes from the diary that his physician allegedly wrote during the journey. Even taken at a discount for some later self-serving additions, Grayson's diary paints an unmistakable portrait of a man in discomfort and distress throughout the tour. From the time the presidential train left Washington on the night of September 3, Wilson complained of headaches. Those headaches persisted during the first few days of the trip and then recurred and grew worse during the last ten days. Also, according to Grayson, as soon as the party entered higher altitudes on the way west, Wilson began to have difficulty breathing, which the doctor attributed to asthma. The breathing difficulty, Grayson recounted, forced the President to try to sleep sitting in a chair and gave him sleepless nights. Finally, by the midpoint of the trip, the physician recorded that he "was doing everything possible to prevent a breakdown. . . ." Grayson did not specify what he did, but he was almost certainly administering painkilling drugs, probably morphine.[15]

Clearly then, Wilson's public performance in September 1919 took place against the backdrop of grave physical limitations. Some who accompanied him on the tour recognized this, and, despite his bent toward psychological denial, Wilson himself seems to have been aware of how his health affected his speaking. Thanks to his having been a student at Princeton while Wilson was president of the university, David Lawrence knew him best of any of the journalists on the presidential train. Lawrence later judged Wilson's early speeches on the tour below his usual standard because they were all "extemporaneous. That was a tremendous strain." Tumulty likewise recalled, "never have I seen the President look so weary as on the night we left Washington for our swing into the West." The secretary also remembered the President complaining to him that night, ". . . I have not had a single minute to prepare my speeches. I do not know how I shall get the time for during the past few weeks I have been suffering from daily headaches; but perhaps tonight's rest will make me fit for the work of tomorrow."[16]

These are telling observations. For either an intimate acquaintance or the president himself to complain about his lack of preparation was extraordinary. Except on the most formal occasions, Wilson always spoke extemporaneously or from the sketchiest of notes. Indeed, he prided himself on that ability, and observers marveled at the feats of complex organization and polished expression that he wrought without benefit of written texts. Nor were the circumstances of the tour unusual aside from its length. The physical arrangements of the train and the public appearances were the same as on his earlier campaign swings. As before, Wilson found time both to seclude himself and to mix with the reporters, sometimes holding informal press conferences. Between the heat of the late summer on the Great Plains and in the Rockies and the jarring nature of rail travel, the hours off the hustings were rarely restful, but they were no different from conditions that Wilson had often endured earlier without ill effect. What was different was the state of his health from the beginning of the trip to its end.

Wilson's speechmaking in September 1919 had its ups and downs. Some speeches were more effective than others; some phases of the tour made greater impact than others. By most accounts, Wilson did not start out well. Strikes in Columbus, Ohio, held down the crowds for his first appearance on September 4, and his opening speech seemed to lack punch. The President appeared, however, to hit his stride by the time he crossed the Mississippi. He made stirring speeches and drew big, enthusiastic crowds in Missouri and Iowa. But after he reached Minnesota and moved on toward the West Coast he seemed to wander a bit and get flatter and more abstract. Tumulty began making suggestions, especially urging the President to be more specific, to deliver more of an emotional appeal, and to eschew all appearances of partisanship. In San Francisco, Wilson conferred with Gavin McNab, a former California Progressive and now a League supporter, who offered further suggestions about making the issues of the peace settlement compelling to ordinary people. Partly in response to their advice, he appeared to catch fire with his audiences in California, and he continued to strike sparks as he returned eastward through the Rocky Mountain states.[17]

Curiously, the ups and downs of Wilson's speechmaking do not appear to have matched the variations in his physical condition. Often, as in the case of some early speeches and the last ones, he staged some of his best performances in spite of extreme fatigue and nearly incapacitating headaches. By common report, Wilson showed the effects of ill health, probably premonitory symptoms of the first stroke, in the final speech at Pueblo, Colorado, on September 25. He reportedly staggered as he mounted the platform, spoke at first in a weak voice,

and appeared to lose his train of thought, but he rallied to finish the address with a moving peroration that left few dry eyes in the audience. That final burst of eloquence has led some interpreters to compare Wilson implicitly to the light bulb that burns brightest just before it goes out. Actually, other speeches on the tour offered better examples of argument and appeal than the Pueblo address. The apparent disparity between the state of Wilson's health and his public performances may also reflect the scanty and sometimes questionable record that Grayson kept.[18]

More clearly than health, variations and shortcomings in presidential speechmaking in September 1919 sprang from political conditions. Wilson devoted the great majority of the speeches to explanations of the peace treaty and the Covenant of the League of Nations. He gave special attention to three provisions, Articles X and XI of the Covenant and the Shantung settlement. In part, the emphasis reflected Wilson's long-standing convictions about education of the public as the essential task of a democratic leader. These portions of the speeches resembled his earlier performances in 1912 and 1916. "Professor" Wilson, the "schoolmaster" in politics, was once more discharging a congenial duty and often doing it as ably as he had done it earlier. But there was a more compelling reason why he spent so much time explaining provisions of the treaty and the Covenant. It was because he had no choice.

"One of the most unexpected things that I have found on my journey," Wilson declared in his speech in San Diego, "is that the people of the United States had not been informed as to the real character and scope and contents of the great treaty of peace with Germany." That was a damning admission. If the American people did not know, as he put it, "the real meaning of this great human document," the President had no one but himself to blame. He was paying the price for nearly three years of neglect of the task of cultivating public support for his foreign policies. Not since the 1916 election had he made an extended speaking tour outside Washington. He had not ventured out on the hustings primarily because from April 1917 to November 1918 he had been the commander-in-chief of a nation at war and from December 1918 though June 1919 he had been the world's peacemaker-in-chief at Paris. Still, those circumstances did not completely explain or excuse his conduct. During the war, Wilson's workload had not increased appreciably, thanks to his orderly habits and ability to delegate authority in every critical area except diplomacy with the belligerents. Even without making speaking tours, he could have devoted more time and attention to explaining his war aims and peace program through addresses to Congress and cultivation of the

press. At Paris in 1919, he had vexed his press advisor Ray Stannard Baker with his unwillingness to share information with reporters and take them into his confidence.[19]

The need to explain his program to an ignorant and apparently misled public placed Wilson too much on the defensive in his speeches in September 1919. On the "fool's errand" side, it can be argued that he was doing too little too late, that in seeking to repair the damage caused by his own neglect the game was lost before he started. But that argument carries the observation too far. Even if Wilson had built up more popular support earlier, he almost certainly would have used considerable portions of the speeches to elucidate the settlement. The difference would have been one of degree. With a better informed public, he could have devoted more time to pleading his case and rallying support. He could have become more of an advocate and less of an educator.

These two roles were not mutually exclusive. Wilson accomplished some of his best advocacy in the course of his explications of the treaty's provisions. For example, his defense of the Shantung settlement, which he admitted he disliked, allowed him to argue that American disavowal would not help China in any effective way, whereas membership in the League could prevent future Shantungs. Likewise, his elucidation of the six votes awarded to the League's Assembly to the self-governing Dominions of the British Empire permitted him both to underline the difference between the League Council's veto-protected enforcement powers and the debating functions of the Assembly and to praise the Canadians, Australians, New Zealanders, and South Africans for their gallant part in winning the war. Still, it is undeniable that Wilson could have made a more ringing appeal for support if he had not felt so often compelled to dispel error and ignorance.

To make the case for the treaty and the League similarly required difficult choices. Should Wilson appeal more to the head or to the heart? Should he make a rational and at least partly self-interested argument? Or should he play on people's emotions, high and low, and tap feelings left over from the war? The appeal to reason was Wilson's forte, long perfected in both his academic and political careers, and no one in American public life matched him at opening and moving minds. Yet the appeal to emotion was not alien to him either, despite his longstanding regret that his late rival Roosevelt had done better in that department. Especially since 1917, as he had intermittently addressed the issues of the war, the President had demonstrated that he too could stir his countrymen's deepest feelings.

Like any good politician, Wilson tried to have it both ways on the

hustings in September 1919. Making a reasoned case for League membership dovetailed nicely with defending the treaty and the organization, and Wilson often scored points by knocking down misapprehensions about the League. He was especially anxious to dispel the notion that the United States would be involved in frequent future wars in faraway places. The League was not, he argued in a speech in St. Louis early in the tour, "a combination of the world for war," but rather "a combination of the world for arbitration and discussion." He stressed Article XI, which provided for compulsory delay and arbitration efforts, even more than Article X because he believed that article provided the foundation for a new international system. "War is a process of heat," he explained in the same speech. "Exposure is a process of cooling; and what is proposed in this is that every hot thing shall be spread out in the cooling air of the opinion of the world. . . ." If such cooling failed, then the League would act like a fire department. "If you want to put out a fire in Utah," Wilson asserted late in the tour in his speech at Salt Lake City, "you do not send to Oklahoma for the fire engine. If you want to put out a fire in the Balkans, if you want to stamp out the smouldering flame in some part of central Europe, you do not send to the United States for troops."[20]

Those down-to-earth explanations, illustrated with homely analogies, demonstrated that Wilson had not lost his touch as an educator of the public. Nor had he forgotten how to appeal to enlightened self-interest. In the earlier speeches of the tour, the President advanced two kinds of interested motives for joining the League. One was business. "What is our business?" he asked in St. Louis. "Is there any merchant present here or any manufacturer or any banker who can say that our interests are separate from the interests of the rest of the world, commercially, industrially, financially?" Americans had a concrete economic stake, he maintained, in "the great problem of the rehabilitation of Germany industrially. I say the problem of her rehabilitation because unless she is rehabilitated she cannot pay her reparation," and without those reparations international trade could not flow again through channels of prosperity. The other interested motive that Wilson advanced was the desire to get back to "normal" prewar American ways. Without the League, he declared, the United States would have to "be physically ready for anything that comes. We must have a great standing army," universal military training, great stores of munitions and weapons. "And what does that mean? Reduction of taxes? No." It meant not only higher taxes, he argued, "but something very much more serious than that." It meant having a government like Imperial Germany's, "the only sort of government that could handle an armed nation."[21]

From the beginning of the tour, however, Wilson went beyond reasoned, self-interested arguments to make an emotional pitch for membership in the League of Nations. He closed his first speech, in Columbus, with a salute to the "youngsters in Khaki" and with the pledge that "men in khaki will not have to cross the seas again." In his second speech, at Indianapolis, he declared, "I can look all the mothers of this country in the face and all the sisters and the wives and the sweethearts and say, 'The boys will not have to do this again.'" In his third speech, at St. Louis, he warned that without the League "the glory of the Armies and Navies of the United States is gone like a dream in the night, and there ensues upon it, in the suitable darkness of the night, the nightmare of dread which lay upon the nations before this war came; and there will come sometime, in the vengeful Providence of God, another struggle in which, not a few thousand fine men from America will have to die, but as many millions as are necessary to accomplish the final freedom of the peoples of the world." Against that calamity, Wilson affirmed in his fifth speech, at Kansas City, that he had pledged himself, following the example of his ancestors, those "troublesome Scotch . . . known as Covenanters," to the Covenant of the League of Nations, and he avowed, "I am a Covenanter!" [22]

Those early speeches set the tone for the appeals to the heart that Wilson continued to make throughout the tour. They also established the rough mixture of rational and emotional elements in his appearances. Because he often shifted, sometimes abruptly, from calm exposition to impassioned exhortation, many of his earlier speeches assumed a rambling, disorganized character. In one of his appearances, in St. Louis, Wilson apologized for "these somewhat disjointed remarks." Such an admission, which he had never made before in any speech, indicated how far off his top form he felt. Later in the trip, thanks in part to Tumulty's and McNab's advice, the speeches gained greater measures of clarity and consistency. Even then, discordant notes remained. The main disparity lay not so much between rational and emotional appeals as among several sorts of emotional appeals. In his search for the best route to Americans' hearts, Wilson faced choices both between a low road and a high road and between the past and the future. Again, after the fashion of a canny politician, he tried a bit of everything, but the results were frequently less than satisfying. [23]

As the early speeches indicated, the most readily available, perhaps inescapable reservoir of sentiment to tap was popular feeling left from the World War. But the question arose immediately—which feelings? If Wilson sought to sell the peace treaty and the League as

fulfillment of the war effort, should he draw upon vengeful or mag-
nanimous sentiments? The early speeches showed that he was torn
between two roles. The evocation in St. Louis of a future conflict recalled Abraham Lincoln's Civil War addresses, especially the famous
vision in his second inaugural speech of God's judgment on slavery.
The self-enlistment in Kansas City in a righteous cause echoed Theodore Roosevelt's rhetoric, especially his famous depiction of himself
in 1912 standing at Armageddon and battling for the Lord. For Wilson, those alternatives represented the high road and low road in appeal to war-time attitudes.

Throughout the tour, he resorted to both kinds of arguments, although not in equal measure. Invocations of belligerence occupied
much less of his time and attention, although they figured in his
speeches until close to the end of the tour. It was a standing tempta-
tion to present the peace settlement as Germany's deserved punishment and the League as perpetuation of an armed coalition to keep
Germany down. That route may have seemed especially alluring because Roosevelt had apparently favored that kind of program at the
time of his death in January 1919. Furthermore, Roosevelt's intimate
friend Senator Lodge continued to favor such a settlement, particularly the collateral American security pact with Britain and France
that had been negotiated at Paris. Wilson did bow toward such appeals in his frequent characterization of the treaty as "harsh" but just
toward the Germans, his repeated praise for the Allies, and some of
his warnings about another world war.

A similar and equally tempting argument for League membership
lay in erecting an international bulwark against Bolshevism. Fears of
radicalism were rising in the United States, most notably after the general strike in Seattle in February 1919 and the wave of bombings in
late April and early May. Thanks also to further labor unrest, particularly the Boston police strike in September and the activities of Attorney General A. Mitchell Palmer, antiradical sentiment was about to
explode into the infamous "Red Scare" of late 1919 and early 1920.
At the beginning of the tour, Wilson condemned the Bolsheviks as
"government by terror, government by force, not government by
vote." Further on, he warned against the "poison" that was "running
through veins of the world." He also deplored domestic disorder and
condemned the striking policemen in Boston. But those references
largely disappeared by the time the presidential party reached the
West Coast. During the last half of the trip, almost the only gestures
that Wilson made toward vindictiveness lay in repeated observations
that Germany wanted the United States not to join the League and
insinuation that "disloyal" elements were working to keep the nation out.[24]

But appeals to belligerent and antiradical sentiments engaged Wilson far less than appeals to loftier emotions. From the beginning of the tour, two approaches to the heart dominated. One was the twin evocation of the sacrifices made by fallen soldiers and of the memories that their loved ones held of them. The other was conjuring up visions of a future world war. In addition to references to the "boys in Khaki" in the early speeches, as he went westward, Wilson dwelled increasingly on mothers who had lost sons. "A woman came up to me the other day," he recalled in his speech at Billings, Montana, "and grasped my hand and said, 'God bless you,' and then turned away in tears." A bystander explained that she had lost her son in France. Wilson reflected that in her blessing "was the love of her boy, the feeling of what he had done, the justice and the dignity and the majesty of it, and then the hope that through such instrumentality as men like myself could offer that no other woman's son would be called upon to lay down his life for the same thing." Soon afterward, on the West Coast he started to comment on the children who turned out in the crowds and to avow, as he did in Tacoma, ". . . we are making decisions now that will mean more to the children than they mean to us and that as we care for future generations we will be careful to make the right decisions as to the policy of the United States as one of the factors in the peace of the world."[25]

Warning about another, more terrible global conflict also formed a staple in Wilson's appeals as he moved westward. In Mandan, North Dakota, he observed that soldiers would tell people "that job" was not finished, "that unless we see to it that peace is made secure they will have to do the job all over again" and Americans "may have to sacrifice the flower of their youth again." On the West Coast, Wilson blended predictions of another war with facts and figures about the death and destruction of this war, to brew a potent rhetorical concoction. In San Francisco, after reciting statistics about the World War, he observed that more men had been killed between 1914 and 1918 than in all the wars of the preceding century. "We cannot realize that," he asserted, but Americans must grasp that "it is not so much the present generation but the next generation that goes maimed off the stage or is laid away in obscure graves upon some battle field; and that great nations are impaired in their vitality for two generations. . . ." The next day, at San Diego, in perhaps the most affecting appeal of the entire tour, Wilson declared, "Why, my fellow citizens, nothing brings a lump into my throat quicker on this journey I am taking than to see the thronging children . . . because I know if by any chance we do not win this great fight for the League of Nations it would be their death warrant. They belong to the next generation which would then have to fight the final war, and in that final war there would not be merely seven

and a half million men slain. The very existence of civilization would be in the balance."[26]

In all, Wilson showed that he could reach Americans' hearts. But the ultimate effect of these appeals remains questionable. Despite Wilson's predilections, taking his case to the people and arousing popular enthusiasm were not ends in themselves. Presumably, they were means to influence the Senate. All the while that Wilson was speaking to audiences on the tour, he was also indirectly addressing the Senate. The need to persuade senators introduced further complications into the President's task. Having to explain his position on the various reservations proposed by the Republicans on the Foreign Relations Committee inevitably diverted him from making a straightforward case for the treaty and the League on his own terms. Answering senatorial critics likewise posed choices between approaches. Should he follow the proposition that a good attack was the best defense and take a defiant stance? Or should he be conciliatory and open to suggestions? Further, what role should partisan considerations play?

Not surprisingly perhaps, Wilson never took a consistent position on the speaking tour toward the senators. Often he sounded defiant, even petulant, in alluding to critics of the peace settlement and League membership. An exact correlation cannot be drawn between Wilson's health and his posture toward his critics, but he does seem to have made more inflammatory statements about reservations and opposition when he showed signs of fatigue and was probably suffering most from headaches. His worst outburst came near the end of the tour when he spoke at the Mormon Tabernacle in Salt Lake City. Mrs. Wilson remembered the heat and stuffiness of the huge, unventilated building, packed with 15,000 people. "To this day," she wrote later, "I cannot conceive how the President spoke under such conditions." The two-hour speech left him exhausted, and his suit jacket was soaked with perspiration. With hindsight, it also seems likely that he was suffering from premonitory symptoms of the stroke that occurred two and a half days later. The speech was filled with defiance and highlighted by flashes of anger. After reading a proposed reservation to Article X, Wilson charged, "That is a rejection of the Covenant. That is an absolute refusal to carry any part of the same responsibility that other members of the League carry." Wilson tried intermittently to control his temper, and he calmly explained the obligations under Article X. But he also, uncharacteristically for the last part of the tour, once more raised the specter of Bolshevism and insinuated that pro-German influences lay behind the opposition to League membership.[27]

Wilson likewise failed to assume a clear posture toward senators,

either supporters, critics, or opponents. The most explicit mention he made of any of them came early in the tour, in his speech in Omaha on September 8, when he affirmed "how proud I have been to stand alongside Senator Hitchcock in this fight. I would be just as glad to stand by Senator [George W.] Norris if he would let me." That was a nice touch. The President had not only named both of Nebraska's senators, but he had also praised a leading supporter from his own party and reached out to a possibly persuadable member of the other party. Unfortunately, Wilson did almost nothing like that again on the tour. The closest he came was the next day in a speech in St. Paul, when he absolved Minnesota's two senators from his indictment of "downright ignorance." But he did not refer to them, Knute Nelson and Frank B. Kellogg, both Republican "mild reservationists," by name, and he said nothing more about them. The only other implicit reference that he made to any senator was the comment on September 12 in Coeur d'Alene, Idaho, "I must confess that I have been amazed that there are some men in responsible positions who are opposed to the ratification of the treaty of peace altogether." Everyone assumed that he meant Idaho's senior senator, William E. Borah, the most outspoken "irreconcilable" opponent of League membership and a scathing critic of other aspects of the settlement.[28]

Partisan considerations added still more complications. At first blush, Wilson's partisan task seemed simple. Because the Republicans held a majority in the Senate and because such prominent Republicans as ex-President Taft strongly supported the League, eschewal of party politics appeared an obvious course. In fact, the President compiled a good record of nonpartisanship on the tour. "Forget that I am a Democrat," he asked in one of his speeches at St. Louis early in the tour. "Forget that some of you are Republicans. Forget all of that. That has nothing to do with it." Yet such disclaimers, repeated throughout the tour, fell short of what was needed. As Tumulty and others recognized, the President had to reach out openly to Republicans. Following Tumulty's suggestions, Wilson began to emphasize past Republican support for an international peace-keeping organization. In addition to the 1916 Republican platform plank endorsing a league in principle, he quoted statements by Roosevelt in 1914 and by Lodge in 1915 and 1916 supporting a league of nations, together with more recent endorsements by other Republicans. He also praised William McKinley and John Hay on several occasions for their championship of Chinese sovereignty and Roosevelt for his mediation of the Russo-Japanese War.[29]

Welcome as these gestures were, they did not suffice. The situation required full-fledged bipartisanship, and that was a stance that Wilson

persistently shrank from taking. He was too good a student of parliamentary coalitions and too experienced an adapter of parliamentary practices to the American scene not to appreciate that true bipartisanship entailed genuine sharing of power, influence, and credit. But there seems to have been an emotional barrier that he could not surmount. Just as he had previously declined to include prominent Republicans in the delegation to the peace conference, now he held back from making substantive and symbolic gestures to the most important Republicans who might support the treaty and the League. Wilson mentioned Taft's name only once, cursorily, during the entire speaking tour. He likewise referred only once, even more cursorily, to the League to Enforce Peace. The oblique reference to Senators Nelson and Kellogg was the sole overture in any speech toward the mild reservationists. For example, when he spoke in Bismarck and Mandan, North Dakota, he said nothing about the state's senior senator, Porter J. McCumber, the mildest of all the reservationists and the most strongly pro-League Republican in the chamber.

Wilson committed no overt acts of partisanship, either. Hitchcock was the only Democratic senator whom he mentioned. When he spoke in Montana, California, and Nevada, he let such loyal Democrats as Thomas J. Walsh, James D. Phelan, and Key Pittman go unnamed in their home states. Furthermore, although the President dwelled so extensively on Article XI of the Covenant and its provision for compulsory delay, he never mentioned the man who had originated this idea of "cooling off" and who had negotiated a series of treaties that embodied it—former Secretary of State William Jennings Bryan. It was true that a nonpartisan posture ruled out taking too much partisan credit; it was also well known that Wilson harbored hard feelings toward Bryan for his resignation in 1915. But properly balanced by frequent bows to the opposition, praise for members of his own party would not have been amiss. The tour apparently did accomplish Wilson's purpose of keeping the Democratic senators in line, but that success seems to have come in spite of any cultivation of his party.

If partisanship clearly presented Wilson with his biggest obstacle it also raised his greatest potential opportunity. There was one move that he could have made which would have rendered partisan questions moot and might have greatly enhanced the chances for League membership—Wilson could have promised not to run again in 1920. Twice he seemed to be on the verge of making that gesture. In his speech to the Minnesota legislature early in the tour, he declared, ". . . I should be ashamed of myself if I permitted any partisan thought to enter into this great matter. If I were a scheming politician and anyone wanted to present me with the peace of the world as a campaign

issue, it would be very welcome, because there could be no easier issue to win on; but everybody knows that this is not a worthy thought, everybody knows that we are all Americans." Three days later, speaking at Spokane, Washington, he avowed, "I leave the verdict with you, and I beg, my Republican fellow citizens, that you will not allow yourselves for one moment, as I do not allow myself for one moment, as God knows my conscience, to think of 1920 when thinking about the redemption of the world." Those were pregnant words. A pledge not to run in 1920 would have followed easily, logically from those pleas.[30]

Whether Wilson ever contemplated making such a gesture is not known. It would have been a risky move. Inasmuch as he was both the incumbent President and the most popular, effective living politician in America, the possibility of his candidacy in 1920 constituted the most powerful weapon in his political armory. Still, a dramatic divorce of the peace treaty from his own and his party's political fortunes would have transformed the whole complexion of the debate. What better concession could he have made to bipartisanship than to give the opposition a better shot at winning the next election and a greater opportunity to implement the peace program themselves? True, such a move could have backfired. The Democratic senators might have broken ranks, and the Republicans might have become even less willing to seek compromises. But the move might have worked. A younger, bolder Wilson might well have gambled this way for the biggest stakes, as he had often done as governor, presidential candidate, and president before mid-1918. In the past year, however, he had shown less inclination to take imaginative leaps, and diminished boldness may also have stemmed from his deteriorating physical condition.

The assessment of Wilson's speaking tour comes, then, full circle, back to his health. Just as his physical condition and its psychological consequences have raised questions about how and why he decided to make the tour, so the same considerations continue to impinge upon his performance on the tour and his failure to complete the enterprise. A stronger, healthier Wilson would almost certainly have done a better job of balancing the myriad tasks of persuasion that he faced. It was a tribute to his intellectual and oratorical powers that he performed as well as he did. For all their flaws, his speeches in September 1919 sparkled with eloquence and advanced compelling arguments for his program.

Yet even if Wilson had been in better health, he would have had great difficulty in touching all the bases of support and in trying to fend off all kinds of criticism with which he had to deal. The still more poignant speculation about the tour and Wilson's health is what might

have happened if he had returned to Washington unimpaired, fit to deal with the senators in the final confrontation over the treaty. His previous record during the summer of 1919 offered examples of both conciliation and intransigence, and the impact of reports of his tour on various senators remains hard to judge.

Moreover, Wilson did not have the best of luck with technology. The only public address that he delivered after September 1919 was broadcast over the radio, and several interpreters have speculated that he could have taken his case to the people more successfully a few years later, when radio was well developed. Perhaps so, although earlier development of radio would have laid a heavier burden on him to educate the public about his programs sooner. As with health, technology introduces imponderables that can never be resolved.

In the final analysis, Wilson's speaking tour in September 1919 was neither a fool's errand nor his finest hour. He went on a political errand that he had long wanted to pursue. His decision to pursue the errand was not the smartest political move he ever made. Neither was it devoid of promise of reward, much less a sign of irrationality or desperation. Wilson behaved heroically on the hustings, but he did not mount the finest political performance of his life in September 1919. The effects of age, deeply exacerbated by failing health, held him well below the exalted standard of performance that he had long since set for himself. The tour was too late, but it was not too little. It was too much. It was too varied, too scattered, too disordered. It was intermittently magnificent, but it was not Wilsonian politics at their best. Dramatic and spectacular as it was, the leaving of his public career really did not become Woodrow Wilson.

Notes

[1] For the finest statement of this view of Wilson's tour, see Arthur S. Link, *Woodrow Wilson: Revolution, War and Peace* (Arlington Heights, Ill., 1979), pp. 113–121. For an earlier statement, see Dexter Perkins, "Woodrow Wilson's Tour," in Daniel Aaron, ed., *America in Crisis: Fourteen Critical Episodes in American History* (New York, 1952), pp. 245–265.

[2] The classic statement of this view is Thomas A. Bailey, *Woodrow Wilson and the Great Betrayal* (New York, 1945), pp. 90–121. For a more recent statement, see Lloyd Ambrosius, *Woodrow Wilson and the American Diplomatic Tradition: The Treaty Fight in Perspective* (New York, 1987), pp. 178–189.

[3] On Tumulty's role, see John M. Blum, *Joe Tumulty and the Wilson Era* (Boston, 1951), pp. 208–209.

[4] WW speech at Mandan, N. Dak., Sept. 10, 1919, in Ray Stannard Baker and William E. Dodd, eds., *The Public Papers of Woodrow Wilson* (New York, 1927). VI, 101 [hereafter cited as *PPWW*].

[5] See Cary T. Grayson, *An Intimate Memoir* (New York, 1960), pp. 94–95; Edith Bolling Wilson, *My Memoir* (Indianapolis, 1936), p. 273.

[6] Robert Lansing Desk Diary, Aug. 25 [1919], in Arthur S. Link *et al.*, eds., *The Papers of Woodrow Wilson* (Princeton, N.J., 1990), LXII, 504, [hereafter cited as *PWW*]; *ibid.*, n. 2.

[7] Grayson, *WW*, 94–95.

[8] Blum, *Tumulty*, 209–210.

[9] Joseph P. Tumulty, *Woodrow Wilson as I Know Him* (Garden City, N.Y., 1921), pp. 438, 446; Edith B. Wilson, *My Memoir*, pp. 280–281; Cary T. Grayson Diary, Sept. 6, 1919, *PWW*, LXIII, 140.

[10] Transcript of WW meeting with Foreign Relations Committee, Aug. 19, 1919, *PWW*, LXII, 406.

[11] WW to Homer S. Cummings, Jan. 8, 1920, *PPWW*, VI, 455. For the warnings of possible Democratic defections, see Rudolph Forster to Tumulty, Sept. 8, 12, 1919, *PWW* (MS of forthcoming volume LXIII), 256–257, 531–532. The second telegram conveyed this warning from Vance McCormick; "Some Democratic Senators are not going to follow the President any further than they have to, to preserve their party standing." McCormick therefore urged trying "to bring pressure on the Senate from the folks back home." *ibid.*, 531.

[12] For medical speculation about possible effects of the tour, see Edwin A. Weinstein, *Woodrow Wilson: A Medical and Psychological Biography* (Princeton, N.J., 1981), 353–355, and Bert Edward Park, *The Impact of Illness on World Leaders* (Philadelphia, 1986), pp. 45–48.

[13] For these allusions, see Grayson, *WW*, 94–95; Edith B. Wilson, *My Memoir*, 273–274, and H. H. Kohlsaat, *From McKinley to Harding: Personal Recollections of Our Presidents* (New York, 1923), pp. 218–219.

[14] Josephus Daniels, *The Life of Woodrow Wilson* (Philadelphia, 1924), pp. 326–327.

[15] Grayson Diary, Sept. 7, 1919, *PWW*, LXIII, 700. See also *ibid.*, 1, 337, 541–542, 754, 883, 993, 1043, 1086, 1144. The entry in Grayson's diary describing the first stroke after the Pueblo speech shows unmistakable signs of having been written later. That entry also contains Grayson's first and only reference to Wilson's "asthma" and his having had to sleep sitting up. Such discrepancies cast doubt on the reliability of at least some of what Grayson allegedly wrote on the days listed in his diary. This document must be used with great care, but because it is the only putatively contemporary, intimate private record of the tour it remains an indispensable source.

[16] David Lawrence, *The True Story of Woodrow Wilson* (New York, 1924), p. 275; Tumulty, *WW*, 439.

[17] For Tumulty's suggestions, see Tumulty memoranda, Sept. 12, 20., 1919, *PWW*, LXIII, 525–529, 885. See also Blum, *Tumulty*, 211–212.

[18] On Wilson's condition during the Pueblo speech, see Edmund W. Starling and Thomas Sugrue, *Starling of the White House* (New York, 1946), 151–152, and Edith B. Wilson, *My Memoir*, 283.

[19] WW speech at San Diego, Sept. 19, 1919, *PPWW*, VI, 277. For Baker's account see Ray Stannard Baker, *Woodrow Wilson and the World Settlement* (Garden City, N.Y., 1922), I, 116–160.

[20] WW speech at St. Louis, Sept. 5, 1919, *PPWW*, V, 626- 627; speech at Salt Lake City, Sept 23, 1919, *ibid.*, VI, 351.

[21] WW speeches at St. Louis, Sept. 5, 1919, *ibid.*, V, 624- 625, 638; speech at Columbus, *ibid.*, 604.

[22] WW speech at Indianapolis, Sept. 4, 1919. *ibid.*, 619; speech at St. Louis, Sept. 5, 1919, *ibid.*, 633; speech at Kansas City, Sept. 6, 1919, *ibid.*, VI, 13.

[23] WW speech at St. Louis, Sept. 5, 1919, *ibid.*, V, 631.

[24] WW speech at Des Moines, Sept. 6, 1919, *ibid.*, VI, 15.

[25] WW speech at Billings, Mont., Sept. 11, 1919, *ibid.*, 108.

[26] WW speech at Mandan, N.Dak., Sept. 10, 1919, *ibid.*, 161; speech at San Francisco, Sept. 18, 1919, *ibid.*, 262; speech at San Diego, Sept. 19, 1919, *ibid.*, 291- 292.

[27] Edith B. Wilson, *My Memoir*, 282; WW speech at Salt Lake City, Sept. 23, 1919, *PPWW*, VI, 350.

[28] WW speech at Omaha, Sept. 8, 1919, *ibid.*, 43; speech at St. Paul, Sept. 9, 1919, *ibid.*, 63; speech at Coeur d'Alene, Ida., Sept. 12, 1919. *ibid.*, 139.

[29] WW speech at St. Louis, Sept. 5, 1919, *ibid.*, V, 643.

[30] WW speech at St. Paul, Sept. 9, 1919, *ibid.*, VI, 65; speech at Spokane, Sept. 12, 1919, *ibid.*, 163.

PART IV
WOODROW WILSON REASSESSED

John M. Mulder

"A GOSPEL OF ORDER"
WOODROW WILSON'S RELIGION AND POLITICS

By his own testimony, from the observation of contemporaries, and according to the analysis of subsequent historians, a major key to understanding Woodrow Wilson's political thought and activity was his conspicuous fusion of religion and politics. Wilson himself remarked that "my life would not be worth living, if it were not for the driving power of religion, for faith, pure and simple." At a time of adversity during his presidency, he confessed, "If I were not a Christian, I think I should go mad, but my faith in God holds me to the belief that He is in some way working out His own plans through human perversities and mistakes."[1]

Early Wilson biographers and observers, in a display of rare unanimity, similarly noted the importance of Wilson's religious faith. Ray Stannard Baker, Wilson's contemporary and first major biographer, maintained that Wilson's "career can in no wise be understood without a clear knowledge of [his] profound religious convictions. . . . Religion was never incidental with him; it was central." He flatly concluded that "no one can understand Woodrow Wilson without knowing his deep religious foundations."[2]

Other contemporaries agreed with Baker but took a less felicitous view of the effect of Wilson's religion on his political thought and activity. For example, John Maynard Keynes, disillusioned with Wilson's efforts at the Paris peace conference, described the American President's "theological or Presbyterian temperament" which "wove the web of sophistry and jesuitical exegesis that was finally to clothe with insincerity the language and substance of the whole Treaty." Similarly, Harold Nicolson described Wilson as a "descendent of the Covenanters" and argued that the "spiritual arrogance which seems inseparable from the harder forms of religion had eaten deep into his soul."[3]

More recent historians have also focused on the importance of the

relationship between Wilson's religious faith and his political thought and activity. Arthur S. Link has maintained that "the foundations of all of Wilson's political thinking were the religious and ethical beliefs and values that he inherited from the Christian tradition and from his own Presbyterian theology." John M. Blum concurred but insisted that Wilson's faith made him rigid and inflexible. "All issues were for him primarily moral and personal. Given his manner of thought and his intensity of purpose, resistance was bound to make him an obdurate, pertinacious foe."[4]

And so the historiographical battle seemed to be pitched—those who saw Wilson's religion as a source of moral and political vision versus those who saw Wilson's religion as a deleterious influence on his politics and policies. During the last two decades, however, two developments have helped historians gain a richer and more nuanced understanding of Wilson, his times, and the religious and cultural factors which influenced him.

The first has obviously been the publication of the *Papers of Woodrow Wilson*, superbly edited by Arthur S. Link, David W. Hirst, John E. Little, and their colleagues. This series is not only the best documentary of any President of the United States but is likely to be the last for any twentieth-century President.

The editors have been able to recover material about Wilson, particularly during his prepolitical life and career, which sheds new light on his thinking, including his religious thought. The publication of Wilson's papers has spawned a number of new works which significantly expand our understanding of the development of Wilson's thought and personality.[5]

The formative period in Wilson's development was the years prior to his entry into politics in 1910. Although his political ideas changed to some degree during his political career, his basic assumptions, or "principles" as he called them, were forged before he became a candidate for governor of New Jersey. Wilson himself wrote of Abraham Lincoln that he could "be known only by a close and prolonged scrutiny of his life before he became President. The years of his presidency were not years to form, but rather years to test character." Similarly, Baker has written of Wilson, "The first fifty-four years of Wilson's life were all preparatory; when he came to the New Jersey campaign, . . . he was made, intellectually and morally."[6]

The second development to enrich our understanding of Wilson and particularly his religion has been a series of studies that have explored the epochal changes in American Protestantism during the late nineteenth and early twentieth centuries.[7] In addition, new research has also explored the moral and religious influences that deci-

sively shaped so much of American political and cultural life during the same period.[8] Historians may continue to debate the constructive or detrimental role that Wilson's religion played in his politics, but the nature of that religious influence is now much clearer and can be described much more accurately.

Thomas Woodrow Wilson was born near midnight on December 28, 1856, in the Presbyterian manse of Staunton, Virginia. He later expressed his "unspeakable joy of having been born and bred in a minister's family." His first memory was of Lincoln's election and the news of war, and the South and southern Presbyterianism left a deep and abiding imprint on Wilson's thought and personality. The foremost influence on his early intellectual and religious life was his father, Joseph Ruggles Wilson, a transported northern Presbyterian minister, who was one of the founders of the southern Presbyterian Church in 1861 and its Stated Clerk of the General Assembly for nearly forty years. Wilson called him "my incomparable father" and remained devoted to him until his father died in 1903.[9]

Equally important in shaping Wilson's personality was his mother, Janet or Jessie Woodrow Wilson, the daughter of a distinguished Presbyterian ministerial family with roots in the Church of Scotland. Nearly thirty years after her death, Wilson found it difficult to talk about her. He declared, "It is very hard for me to speak of what my mother was without colouring the whole estimate with the deep love that fills my heart whenever I think of her. . . . She was one of the most remarkable persons I have ever known. . . . I seem to feel still the touch of her hand, and the sweet steadying influence of her wonderful character. I thank God to have had such a mother!" A former butler in the Wilson house concluded, "Outside Mr. Tommy was his father's boy, but inside he was his mother all over."[10]

Spending his early life in the South, Wilson knew at first hand the devastation and suffering brought by the Civil War. Coupled with it was family tragedy. Nearly all of Wilson's father's family remained in the North, and there is no evidence of any reconciliation between them until Woodrow Wilson met some of the relatives after the death of his parents. Wilson's mother's family was shocked by the famous heresy trial of her brother, James Woodrow, who was attacked for his favorable views on evolution. Wilson's father seemed to be a rising star in the southern Presbyterian Church until the 1870s, when he had to resign a professorship at Columbia Theological Seminary in the midst of a rancorous and highly embarrassing controversy over his judgment. Though he returned to the pastorate and remained a southern Presbyterian leader, Wilson's father loved teaching most, and he resented his rebuff by the Presbyterian church. It seems evident that

both parents turned toward their son for the realization of their frustrated hopes and the restoration of the family's reputation.[11]

The impact of Wilson's parents on his personality has been the subject of lively psychohistorical debate, complicated by his later cardiovascular disease, which surely affected his behavior at critical moments of his life. Obviously, Wilson did appropriate the hopes of his parents, which contributed to his extraordinary drive and ambition. Whether he also retained a suppressed resentment of his parents is at least dubious and an insufficient explanation for the complexity of his personality and intellect, shaped by both of his parents, his subsequent marriages, and the culture of late Victorian America.[12]

The religiosity of the Wilson family, especially the particular Calvinistic theology and ethos of southern Presbyterianism, left a deep mark on Wilson and shaped his views of society and government. His training in Presbyterianism came from his father, who was deeply influenced by the covenant or "federal" theology of nineteenth-century southern Presbyterianism. This theology envisaged God's relationship to human beings in covenantal terms. God established two covenants, one of grace and another of nature. Within the covenant of grace, God offered forgiveness in exchange for obedience to divine laws. The covenant of nature, in turn, was a form of constitution. God ruled the affairs of the world by the moral law, and governments were responsible for organizing society on the basis of that moral or natural law. This theology was essentially a comprehensive "theology of politics" in its conception of the distribution of power, divine and human, in the world.[13]

Joseph Ruggles Wilson drew heavily on this theological tradition, preaching on themes such as "Family Government," and declaring slavery to be "an organizing element in that family order which lies at the very foundation of Church and State." He emphasized adherence to the moral law—"that law which determines the *principles* of divine administration over men—a law which constitutes the very *constitution* of that royal kingdom whose regulations begin and end in the infinite holiness of Jehovah, and whose spread through the universal heart of the race is the aim of all Scripture." Furthermore, the covenant theology, through its conception of history and the doctrine of election, provided a creed calling the Christian to vigorous moral exertion in the world. "The *inactive* Christian is the doubting Christian," declared the elder Wilson and confidently maintained that God presided over and through "all truly successful enterprise."[14]

When his son's devotion to his studies waned, his father advised, "Through this work success comes—and comes as a matter of law—therefore, *must* come." The covenant theology also left its imprint on both father and son in its emphasis that life was a struggle in the world

to fight for good and combat evil. "Christianity came . . . as a 'sword,'"
Wilson's father proclaimed, "to set men at 'variance' on the field of a
great fight between evil and good." The Christian's mission summoned him to enlist as a soldier of God in a difficult battle. "It is often
uphill," Wilson's father warned. "It is through an enemy's country. It
is a running fight all along." [15]

Wilson's life is striking in how he, like so many late nineteenth-century American Protestants, appropriated the values and ideas of his
religious training. It was a typical Protestant work ethic that the son
inherited, a preoccupation with success, moral endeavor, and activistic
assertion to realize moral principles in an evil world. "In order to advance," Wilson believed, "the Christian must strain every muscle." In
an oration to his fellow students at Princeton, he admonished, "Let
me again remind you that it is only by working with an energy which
is almost superhuman and which looks to uninterested spectators like
insanity that we can accomplish anything worth the achievement." In
one of his first published essays, written when he was nineteen years
old, Wilson described "Christ's Army," fighting for supremacy against
"the Prince of Darkness." "Surely in this great contest there is a part
for every one," he wrote, "and each one will be made to render a strict
account of his conduct in the day of battle. Will anyone hesitate as to
the part he shall take in this conflict? Will any one dare to enlist under
the banners of the Prince of Lies, under whose dark folds he only
marches to the darkness of hell? For there is no middle course, no
neutrality." [16]

Although Wilson later achieved a greater appreciation of the ambiguity of moral decisions, the tendency to make a simplistic division
between right and wrong and to fight for moral ideals stayed with him
throughout his life. It gave to Wilson's political speeches the atmosphere of a moral and religious crusade, and he was fond of using
military and moral imagery to describe political issues. The conclusion to Wilson's first inaugural address is a fine example. "This is not
a day of triumph; it is a day of dedication," he declared. "Here muster,
not the forces of party, but the forces of humanity. Men's hearts wait
upon us; men's lives hang in the balance; men's hopes call upon us to
say what we will do. Who shall live up to the great trust? Who dares
fail to try? I summon all honest men, all patriotic, all forward-looking
men, to my side. God helping me, I will not fail them, if they will but
counsel and sustain me!" [17]

In addition to the inclination to reduce issues to moral categories,
Wilson's Presbyterian background encouraged the application of
moral ideals through involvement in society—what he frequently
called "disinterested service." Wilson gave explicit recognition to this
connection between religious faith and political commitment in his

famous address, "Princeton in the Nation's Service," delivered at the University's sesquicentennial celebration in 1896. He drew on the legacy of John Witherspoon and "the spirit of practical piety in the revolutionary doctrines which Dr. Witherspoon taught" and declared, "We can easily hold the service of mankind at arm's length while we read and make scholars of ourselves, but we shall be very uneasy, the while, if the right mandates of religion are let in upon us and made part of our thought." If education gave students "no vision of the true God," Wilson believed, "it has given them no certain motive to practise the wise lessons they have learned."[18]

Wilson's Presbyterian heritage interacted with his political thought in deeper and more subtle ways than his obvious tendency to moralize. At the heart of the Calvinistic covenant tradition was a concern with order, structure, and wholeness. Wilson was scarcely aware of the intricacies of this theological tradition, candidly admitting, "I am no theologian," and maintaining that he preached nothing "not written on the face of life and of providence."[19] Yet the heritage of covenant theology gave him a comprehensive view of the world in which the individual, society, and God were given definite roles and responsibilities. Its advantage for Wilson and his appealing proclamation of what his father called "a gospel of order" for American society reduced the capriciousness of human life and helped resolve the disintegration of society by giving it structure.[20]

Wilson frequently used the covenant theological emphasis on order and structure to deal with personal turmoil in his own life and the disintegration of society around him. The most common device was a covenant or constitution. As a boy in Augusta, Wilson reportedly organized his fellow baseball players into an association known as the Lightfoot Club. Even more significant is the fact that one of the earliest Wilson documents, which he saved throughout his life, is a constitution for an imaginary yacht club. The document was written by Wilson when he was eighteen years old in the midst of a family crisis and his own religious and vocational turmoil.[21] It not only demonstrates Wilson's "passion, even at an early age, for constitutional order,"[22] but it is also revealing and symptomatic of how Wilson used the covenant as a response to disorder.

Later as a student at Princeton he again utilized the covenant theological tradition as he confronted graduation and the question of his vocational and professional future. With a classmate he established "a solemn covenant" regarding the values which they vowed to establish in society. In a letter to his fiancee, Wilson recalled the event:

> I had then, as I have still, a very earnest political creed and very pronounced political ambitions. I remember forming with Charlie Talcott (a

class-mate and very intimate friend of mine) a solemn covenant that we would school all our powers and passions for the work of establishing the principles we held in common; that we would acquire knowledge that we might have power; and that we would drill ourselves in all the arts of persuasion, but especially in oratory (for he was a born orator if any man ever was), that we might have facility in leading others into our ways of thinking and enlisting them in our purposes. And we didn't do this in merely boyish enthusiasm, though we were blinded by a very boyish assurance with regard to the future and our ability to mould the world as our hands might please. It was not so long ago but that I can still feel the glow and pulsations of the hopes and purposes of that moment—nay, it was not so long ago but that I still retain some of the faith that then prompted me.[23]

This was essentially Wilson's covenant for his entire life, pledging himself to a career in public life in which his moral principles would be realized.

Basically moral in character and preoccupied with power, the covenant represents Wilson's attempt during his senior year to establish a structure for his life, a goal for his ceaseless work, a duty which he must fulfill. From his Presbyterian father, Wilson had learned that God's relationship to individuals and to all of creation was a contractual, covenanted order ruled by a moral law contained in the Bible. In that order God reserved divine sovereignty but made people agents of divine will, giving them power and responsibilities for the accomplishment of God's work. In his covenant with Talcott, Wilson once again used this covenant view of the world and individualized it for himself. Like all of creation, he placed himself in a relationship to God with definite responsibilities and clear-cut goals. The order of the covenant became the answer to his uncertainties and anxieties about his future.

Similarly, Wilson turned to the covenant theological tradition to understand his relationship with his wife, Ellen. He appropriated the liturgical synonym for "covenant"—"compact"—and in constitutional terms described their relationship. "I long to be made your master," he wrote her before they were married, "only, however, on the very fair and equal terms that, in exchange for the authority over yourself which you relinquish, you shall be constituted supreme mistress of me. That seems to be a fair compact. Besides, having studied constitutions of various sorts, I have not failed to observe that the constitution of the great and ancient State of Matrimony is Love." He also jokingly suggested that during their separation they should establish "an inter-State *Love* League (of two members only, in order that it may be of manageable size)" and he, of course, would draw up the constitution.[24]

Throughout his long career in academia, Wilson also used constitutions to structure his favorite extracurricular activity—debating
clubs. At Davidson, Princeton, the University of Virginia, Johns Hopkins, and Wesleyan, Wilson either founded and drafted or joined and
redrafted the constitutions for these organizations.[25] Debating clubs
enjoyed a vogue of extensive popularity during the late nineteenth
and early twentieth centuries, and it is hardly surprising that Wilson
shared many of the same interests as other students of his era. In addition, his father's interest in training his son's forensic abilities
spurred Wilson's desire to participate in debates and orations. But it
is not stretching the issue to point to the pervasive influence of Wilson's Presbyterian and covenant theological heritage as a factor in encouraging Wilson's participation.

In terms of church polity, the covenant theology argued that God's
will could be determined for the church by the discussion and debate
of elders and ministers under the guidance of the Holy Spirit. Wilson's reverence for discussion, or "common counsel," as a means of
determining political issues is in part a mark of his Presbyterian faith.
In addition, his reliance upon constitutions for these debating societies is indicative of his desire to have that discussion take place within
a well-defined structure.

Duly constituted debating societies also made his interaction with
others less threatening and more susceptible to his control. He once
observed that it was "characteristic of my whole self that I take so
much pleasure" in the writing of constitutions. In a revealing statement, he confessed that the covenanted order of a debating society
gave him a feeling of authority over others without making himself
vulnerable to them. "I have a sense of power in dealing with men collectively which I do not feel always in dealing with them singly," he
said. "In the former case the pride of reserve does not stand so much
in my way as it does in the latter. One feels no sacrifice of pride necessary in courting the favor of an assembly of men such as he would
have to make seeking to please one man."[26]

If Wilson's covenant background aided in defining his goals, struc-
turing his marriage, and ordering his activities with friends, it left an
even more pervasive mark on his conception of society and politics. In
his first speech at Princeton as a student, Wilson revealed what would
be a primary concern throughout his entire life of studying and prac-
ticing politics—the structure of government and its constitutional
framework. The nation's primary genius, the nineteen-year-old student proclaimed, was "the Constitution, the main-spring of the
Union, [which] has been the love and theme of our greatest statesmen
in their youth, their guide and word in their old age."[27]

As Niels Aage Thorsen has pointed out, Wilson's commitment to

the Constitution and the Union are remarkable for a young man whose formative years were spent in the South during the Civil War and Reconstruction.[28] However, Wilson's attitude toward the Constitution was hardly the uncritical worship of much popular opinion in late nineteenth-century America. His first line of criticism was an attack on American constitutional government by comparing it to the British parliamentary model. In his first scholarly article after his graduation from Princeton, Wilson damned the two major American political parties for their "want of unifying and vitalizing principles" and described Congressmen as "scheming, incompetent, political tradesmen whose aims and ambitions were merely personal." His solution was to make the cabinet into a body of ministers directly responsible to Congress.[29]

In a series of subsequent essays, Wilson refined this prescription for American politics and completed his criticisms in his first book, *Congressional Government*, published in 1885. In analyzing the weaknesses of American legislative government, Wilson depended heavily on the ideas and even the literary style of Walter Bagehot, whose study of the English constitution attempted to go beyond constitutional theory to the actual functions of political institutions. Measuring the ineptness of Congress against the British parliament, Wilson argued that the answer to political manipulation was parliamentary debate, the common determination of policy by the contractual give-and-take of differing opinions. Animating his entire analysis was a desire to synthesize political interests, to bring order and unity out of the divisions of power between the executive and legislative branches. Basically Wilson insisted that the competing interests of various groups and sections of the country could be brought together by contractual, constitutional order, governed by reasoned debate.[30]

Congressional Government was submitted *ex post facto* as Wilson's doctoral dissertation at Johns Hopkins University. The decision to enter the Hopkins came after studying law at the University of Virginia and a brief and thoroughly dissatisfying legal practice in Atlanta. Wilson believed he had to escape from what he described as the "hum-drum life down here in slow, ignorant, uninteresting Georgia" and the depressing "atmosphere of broken promises, of wrecked estates, of neglected trusts, of unperformed duties, of crimes and of quarrels." He resolved to make teaching and writing his profession, albeit with the same goal—political service. "My natural, and therefore predominant, tastes every day allure me from my law books; I throw away law reports for histories, and my mind runs after the solution of political, rather than legal, problems, as if its keenest scent drew it after them by an unalterable instinct," he told a friend. "I want to make myself an *outside force in politics*."[31]

During his first semester at the Johns Hopkins, Wilson outlined the contours of his later academic teaching and writing with remarkable prescience. "My predilections, ever since I had any that were definite," he wrote his fiancee,

> have always turned very strongly towards a literary life, notwithstanding my decided taste for oratory, which is supposed to be the peculiar providence of public men. With manhood came to me an unquenchable desire to excel in two distinct and allmost opposite kinds of writing: political and imaginative. I want to contribute to our literature what no American has ever contributed, studies in the philosophy of our institutions, not the abstract and occult, but the practical and suggestive, philosophy which is at the core of our governmental methods; their use, their meaning, "the spirit that makes them workable." I want to divest them of the theory that obscures them and present their weakness and their strength without disguise, and with such skill and such plentitude of proof that it shall be seen that I have succeeded and that I have added something to the resources of knowledge upon which statecraft must depend.[32]

"The political and the imaginative" and "studies in the philosophy of our institutions" which would be "practical and suggestive"—these characteristics dominated Wilson's subsequent contributions to political science and his historical and literary writing.

When Wilson entered Johns Hopkins, the university was in the initial stages of one of the most creative and exciting periods in its history. Wilson joined a cadre of bright young intellectuals attracted by Herbert Baxter Adams and Richard T. Ely. There he was introduced to German scientific historical methods and German political theorists, and his reaction was violently negative. He complained about the minutiae he was forced to investigate in historical research and found the political philosophers he read to be too abstract. "My chief interest," he declared, "is in politics, in history as it furnishes object-lessons for the present."[33] Adams released Wilson from the recommended path of research, and the result became *Congressional Government*, his Ph.D. degree, and his entry into American academic life.

As Thorsen has argued, despite Wilson's rebellion against his Hopkins training, Wilson did recognize the importance of the social sciences that would transform the understanding of American society, economics, and politics.[34] Furthermore, the organicism of German thought was congenial to the covenantal styles of thinking that Wilson inherited from his religious background, and the combination of the two can be seen in Wilson's long and tedious textbook, *The State*, published in 1889. Here Wilson attempted to trace the development of political institutions from Greek society to the present. The result was

a compilation of facts, based upon extensive research, but sometimes undigested, and of theories, some rather thinly plagiarized from German scholars.[35]

Wilson's own vision of government and politics came through clearly. Picking up the popular Social Darwinism of the time, Wilson insisted that government was a process of evolution, which reached its highest form in democratic states. The chief characteristic of government was its contractual basis, but Wilson insisted that this was not an artificial or static Lockean compact made in a state of nature but one rising out of society itself. The contract between the governors and the governed, he said, arose out of "the common habit, an evolution of experience, an interlaced growth of tenacious relationship, a compact, living, organic whole, structural, not mechanical." But Wilson differed from the Social Darwinists in two important respects, paving the way for his emergence later as a leader of progressivism and reform. First, he saw a positive role for government, not the severely limited force which merely insured individual freedom, but the agency that created the conditions for progress in society. Second, he insisted that political development was not governed by deterministic forces but by human choice, which brought change and growth to society.[36]

Given Wilson's concern with order, structure, and democratic change, it was perhaps inevitable that he would turn his energies to the study of administration. During the late 1880's and 1890's he offered a regular course at Johns Hopkins on public administration. He was, in fact, probably the first American academic to take seriously the problems of public administration in an industrial society. His approach was characteristic in emphasizing the moral purposes and efficient order of administrative action. "The object of administrative study," he declared, "is to rescue executive methods from the confusion and costliness of empirical experiment and set them upon foundations laid deep in stable principle." Order based on principles—this was Wilson's primary theme in the study of administration, and constitutionalist that he was, he maintained that it was "closely connected with the study of the proper distribution of constitutional authority." In these lectures, Wilson outlined a conception of the state that embraced all of society and gave it a positive function and inclusiveness that assumed the state's mediation of all social conflict. What his Calvinist forebears had reserved for the church, Wilson bequeathed to politics, declaring, "The State . . . is the eternal, natural embodiment and expression of a higher form of life than the individual. . . . [It] makes individual life possible and makes it full and complete."[37]

Throughout the 1890's, most of Wilson's writing was historical or

literary in character. As Wilson confronted the escalating social and economic crises of the decade, he again used covenant modes of thought to order his thinking about politics. Law, he told the Princeton undergraduates, was "an *organic product*, the result of the association of men with each other and the consequent institution of certain definite relationships between them." Always stressing the contractual relationship of individuals in society, Wilson described the various sources of public law but insisted they were "reduced to one, namely *Compact*." Constitutions were essential for the stability of society, especially the American constitution. "It should be reverenced as the Solemn Covenant of a People," he said. Gradually Edmund Burke emerged as a powerful influence on his thought. In 1893 Wilson noted "the grave social and economic problems now thrusting themselves forward," and stated, "Under such circumstances, some measure of legislative reform is clearly indispensable. . . . We must look and plan ahead. We must have legislation which has been definitely forecast in party programs and explicitly sanctioned by the public voice." [38]

It was also during his professorship at Princeton from 1890 to 1902 that Wilson struggled with what his family called his "POP" or "Philosophy of Politics," designed to be his magnum opus. The most complete expression of Wilson's ideas for this work came in an early essay, "The Modern Democratic State," written in 1885 and published in revised form in 1889. In it Wilson proposed to construct the basis of democratic government out of a synthesis of moral principles, which he confidently expected to read out of the history of political institutions. Many of the themes of "The Modern Democratic State" endured throughout his later writing: the insistence upon the organic character of society balanced against the need for individual self-expression, especially in political leaders; the emphasis upon the moral basis of democracy—its "principles"; democracy as the fullest expression of political life; and a faith in the progressive evolution of societies to democratic forms of government. [39]

Wilson's essay reflected many of the themes and emphases of the covenant theological tradition. It embodied the tension between a severe individualism (the election by God of individuals) and an emphasis upon the corporate character of all human affairs (the covenant of God in nature and with the people of God in the church). Wilson's view of society as an organism was reinforced by the covenant theology's attempt to see the world in inclusive, comprehensive terms. As Wilson rejected a formalist understanding of constitutions, he moved away from the narrow contractualism of the covenant theology only to embrace it again by trying to formulate a unity of society forged by common allegiance to moral values.

"The Philosophy of Politics" was never completed, largely because Wilson seemed to realize that the moral synthesis could not be achieved in theoretical terms but only by leadership.[40] "The most helpful service to the world awaiting the fulfillment of its visions," he declared in 1899, "would be an elucidation, a real elucidation of the laws of leadership." By 1902 he had his opportunity—the presidency of Princeton. He regretted turning aside from the task of finishing the work but also realized that the project was "too problematical and distant to be handled now."[41] His growing awareness of the role of leadership, his experience as the president of Princeton, and the increasing power of the American presidency itself combined to alter Wilson's analysis of the role of the nation's chief executive in *Constitutional Government of the United States*, his primary contribution to political theory during his Princeton presidency.[42]

The covenant theological tradition left its imprint on Wilson's educational reforms at Princeton—from reorganizing the curriculum to establishing a graduate college. They were animated by the ideal of the university as an organic community, unified by clear lines of authority, shared ideals, and leadership. Education became the means of providing students with an inclusive vision of the world that defined an individual's place and mission. "My conception . . . of the higher education is a conception broad enough to embrace the whole field of thought, the whole record of experience," Wilson declared. Relying once again on geographical imagery to describe the individual's relationship to the world, he added, "[Education] is a process by which the young mind is, so to say, laid alongside of the mind of the world, as nearly as may be, and enabled to receive its strength from the nourishing mother of us all, as Anteus received strength from contact with the round earth."[43]

Education became the means for creating the moral basis for a democratic society and the forum for breaking down the special interests that made such a moral synthesis impossible. "Learning knows no differences of social caste or privilege. The mind is a radical democrat," Wilson believed. ". . . And that, too, is the spirit of American life. It recognizes no privilege or preference not bestowed by nature herself. . . . [A true American college] will recognize uncompromisingly the radical democracy of the mind and of truth itself, will rank its men according to their native kinds, not their social accomplishments, and bestow its favours upon immaterial achievement."[44]

The covenant tradition also played a role in Wilson's policies as governor of New Jersey and President of the United States, ranging from reorganizing the government of New Jersey cities with commissions to centralizing the banking system of the country to establishing an international organization to guarantee peace. At the root of Wilson's

political programs, even when he changed directions, was an attempt to motivate individuals and groups to transcend self-interest in behalf of ideals, persuasively proclaimed by a leader. Wilson's politics were driven by the effort to tame the disintegrating forces of industrialized America through social and political change and adaptation within a constitutional order.

Eventually these values shaped his vision of the post-war world, which left the old order of Europe in shambles. During the negotiations at Paris over the Covenant of the League of Nations, Wilson gave tribute to the covenant tradition in Calvinism that had helped shape his understanding of the treaty. "I wish that it were possible for us to do something like some of my very stern ancestors did, for among my ancestors are those very determined persons who were known as the Covenanters," he told a British audience in 1918. "I wish we could not only for Great Britain and the United States, but for France and Italy and the world, enter into a great league and covenant, declaring ourselves, first of all, friends of mankind and uniting ourselves together for the maintenance and the triumph of right." [45] Wilson's dream was ultimately frustrated, but his views have decisively shaped American foreign policy and the twentieth century's understanding of world order.

Historians have widely agreed on the importance of religion in Woodrow Wilson's life. In this essay, I have tried to identify more specifically the nature of that religious influence as coming primarily from the Calvinist, covenant tradition of southern Presbyterianism. At the same time, no claim is made here for the exclusive or even predominant role which religion and the covenant theological tradition played in shaping Wilson's thought. It is abundantly clear that Wilson was influenced by a wide variety of intellectual influences throughout his life, and the growth in Wilson scholarship increasingly reveals the complexity of his thought and his indebtedness to many crosscurrents in late nineteenth- and early twentieth-century America. [46]

At least three lines of criticism of this interpretation have been suggested. First, Thorsen argues that the covenant has been both exaggerated and distorted as an influence in Wilson's thought. "The term *covenant*," he writes, "appears in Wilson's writings very few times before 1910." Thorsen takes particular exception to stressing the importance of the "solemn covenant" which Wilson formed with his classmate Charles Talcott and to the linkage of the covenant tradition with Wilson's political thought. [47]

Although it is possible to overemphasize the importance of the Talcott-Wilson covenant, the literary evidence of Wilson's appropriation of the covenant tradition in various ways is so strong that an em-

phasis on the importance of Calvinism is warranted. It is not only Wilson's use of the term covenant and its various synonyms but also the covenantal, contractual, and constitutional forms of his thinking that bear out the influence of Calvinism. Obviously, other intellectual influences in nineteenth- and early twentieth-century America coincided with this religious tradition, just as they had in forging conceptions of politics in the eighteenth century.[48] But to acknowledge the importance of Calvinism as an important tradition in the forming of American revolutionary thought and then deny its continuing significance for an obviously committed Presbyterian like Wilson living a century later seems mistaken, if not historically obtuse. Furthermore, Thorsen's critique of a connection between Calvinism and democratic forms of political thought contradicts a substantial body of previous scholarship.[49]

A second, more compelling critique has been advanced by John Milton Cooper, who argues: "Despite what many interpreters have contended, specifically Calvinist doctrines and viewpoints had comparatively little impact on Wilson. He never took any interest in theology or metaphysical speculation, although exposure to ideas about predestination probably reinforced his personal fatalism."[50] Although it is true that Wilson almost instinctively resisted abstract forms of thought[51] and that there is no evidence that Wilson read much theology, even that of John Calvin, one cannot ignore the influence of his home and particularly his father. Cooper himself concedes that "the greatest influence" on Wilson's early years "was not war or politics but religion," and that "for Wilson, Presbyterianism was a faith and a way of life."[52] My argument tries to identify the nature of Wilson's Presbyterianism and its relationship to his political thought without making him a political theologian or a theological politician.

A third critique argues that Wilson's religious thought was less distinctively Calvinist than a product of late nineteenth-century evangelical Protestantism.[53] There are two salient points to be made in response to this critique. First, Wilson was not a generic Protestant but was nurtured in a religious tradition that was self-conscious about its Presbyterian and Calvinist identity. Second, historians of American religion easily acknowledge the importance of the Calvinist heritage as one of the important influences shaping not only evangelical Protestantism but also the generally Protestant tone of turn-of-the-century American culture.[54] To point out the role of Calvinism in Wilson's development is not a case of special pleading but a recognition of the significance of a particular religious tradition, which joined with other forces in molding American politics and the thought of one of its most prominent figures, Woodrow Wilson.

However, this critique does have merit in encouraging an examina-

tion of the diverse influences which affected Wilson. Although I have stressed the importance of the Calvinist tradition on the development of Woodrow Wilson's thought, it is perhaps instructive to try to place Wilson within the broader context of American religion and society. Indeed, there were influences—including some within American Presbyterianism—that had little or no effect on him and some which he appropriated from the larger context of American Protestantism of his age.

The late nineteenth and early twentieth centuries were "a critical period in American religion," to use Arthur M. Schlesinger, Sr.'s phrase. As he described it, the dominant Protestant ethos of America was challenged on two fronts. First, it confronted the questions raised by German biblical criticism, the awareness of world religions, Darwinism, and later the new social sciences, including psychology. Second, its programs were affected by the corrosive effects of immigration, industrialization, and urbanization. The period has been described as "the spiritual crisis of the Gilded Age"; in effect, it was American Protestantism's delayed confrontation with modernity, and it eventually produced the "second disestablishment" of religion in American culture.[55]

It is safe to say that Wilson had virtually no reaction to these epochal changes taking place in American Protestantism and the nation's religious life. While his contemporaries wrote and read novels of people plagued by religious doubt, Wilson remained serenely confident in his own Christian faith. He wrote in his journal in 1889, "I used to wonder vaguely why I did not have the same deep-reaching spiritual difficulties that I read of other young men having. I *saw* the intellectual difficulties but I was not *troubled* by them: they seem to have no connection with my faith in the essentials of the religion I had been taught. Unorthodox in my reading of the standards of the faith, I am nevertheless orthodox in my faith. I am capable it would seem, of being satisfied spiritually without being satisfied intellectually."[56] Doubt or lack of faith was both a psychological and religious impossibility for this particular child of the Presbyterian manse. "My life would not be worth living," Wilson declared as President, "if it were not for the driving power of religion, for *faith*, pure and simple. I have seen all my life the arguments against it without ever having been moved by them. . . . There are people who *believe* only so far as they *understand*—that seems to me presumptuous and sets their understanding as the standard of the universe. . . . I am sorry for such people." His faith was evident to those who heard him conduct religious services. One minister recalled that Wilson "prayed like a man who knew God not only as a fact in history or a doctrine in theology or an ideal in ethics, but as an experience in his own soul."[57]

Wilson's acceptance of Darwinian science was partly a matter of family allegiance to his embattled uncle, James Woodrow, whose espousal of Darwinism rocked the southern Presbyterian church. In all likelihood, it was also due to the influence of James McCosh, who embraced Darwinism. Wilson greatly admired McCosh as president of Princeton, and during his own presidency Wilson tried to recover McCosh's vision of Princeton as a major American university.[58] Wilson was critical of some of the influences of science in American society. In "Princeton in the Nation's Service," he declared that "the scientific spirit of the age" was producing "a certain great degeneracy," which made people "credulous of quick improvement, hopeful of discovering panaceas, confident of success in every new thing." But these warnings never affected his commitment to superior scientific scholarship during his years as president of Princeton nor his overall positive evaluation of the constructive impact of science.[59]

Wilson distanced himself from the doctrinal wars breaking out in American Presbyterianism during the late nineteenth and early twentieth centuries which finally culminated in the fundamentalist controversy of the 1920s and 1930s. He was disdainful of rigid dogmatism, naively believing that "the day of the battle of the creeds" was over and that "it was spiritual amusement for us to split hairs." He had no patience with the fundamentalist leanings of his predecessor at Princeton, Francis Landey Patton, and took the firm position that "between the ages of eighteen and twenty-two you create doubt by ramming dogma down the throat." In fact, Wilson was so eager to put distance between Princeton University and the fundamentalism of the Presbyterian church that he eliminated the teaching of Bible for the first three years of his presidency and then only reinstated it outside the departmental structure of the curriculum.[60]

Similarly, Wilson's appointment of William Jennings Bryan as Secretary of State can be explained partly in terms of expedient Democratic politics but also their common affinity to a foreign policy based on moral principles.[61] Mercifully Wilson was spared the sight of his fellow Presbyterian Bryan as the prosecutor of the Scopes trial of the 1920's.[62]

On the other hand, Wilson also showed little interest in or support for the social gospel movement of his day. Richard T. Ely's contributions to the social gospel movement served as no inspiration or model for Wilson. As vehemently as Wilson preached that religion ought to drive individuals toward social service, he resented the fact that "our novels have become sociological studies, our poems vehicles of criticism, and our sermons political manifestos." He strongly believed that "*the object of the church* as an organization [is] the *salvation of souls*—only indirectly *the purification of Society. That it must effect indirectly, by ex-*

ample, not by organizing vs. particular vices but by kindling a light in which no vice can live." Only occasionally would he acknowledge that individual salvation was connected with the transformation of the structures of society. In 1909, he declared, "Christianity came into the world to save the world as well as to save individual men, and individual men can afford in conscience to be saved only as part of the process by which the world itself is regenerated." For Wilson, the role of religion was to transform and inspire individuals in behalf of service to the world, and he resisted the intrusion of the church into the political realm.[63]

Wilson's attitude toward religion in politics or the church's involvement in political action may be traced to the southern Presbyterian tradition which emphasized "the spirituality of the church" and eschewed political pronouncements or political involvement.[64] But Wilson also shared the more general evangelical Protestant view that religion was for individuals and the church was the forum for the cultivation of religious faith, not the arena for mobilizing political action.

In one other notable respect, Wilson remained unaffected by a significant movement in American Presbyterianism and American Protestantism during his lifetime. Recent scholarship has uncovered the tremendous debate about millennialism in American Protestantism, dating back to the colonial period and extending into the twentieth century. As the lines were drawn between modernists and fundamentalists, each side took opposing views of the millennium. Modernists adopted a view of the Kingdom of God gradually being ushered into history with Christ returning in victorious culmination of the progressive improvement of human life. Fundamentalists saw history as steadily deteriorating and Christ's dramatic return as a necessity to redeem history from sin. The fundamentalist wing of the Presbyterian church slowly picked up premillennialism and fused it with the Princeton theology, while modernists retained the optimistic postmillennialism that seemed to capture so much of progressivism's faith in progress in the late nineteenth and early twentieth centuries.[65]

There is no evidence that Wilson was even aware of the tortured debates about millennialism in the Presbyterian church and in American Protestantism generally. However, the influence of millennial thought on Wilson has been a neglected dimension of the relationship between Wilson's religion and politics. It would be easy to ascribe to him a general acceptance of postmillennialism, particularly given his faith in progress and his acceptance of evolutionary theories of human history. For Wilson, political progress was not inevitable but depended upon governmental direction and wise leadership. As Thorsen has put it, Wilson "conceived of progress as an idea and as

governmental practice that would restrain both the liberal belief in economic individualism and the belief in majoritarian democracy." Such is the assumption that lies behind Wilson's belief that "*Progress is a march, not a scamper.* It is achieved by advance *in hosts and under discipline*, not by running hither and thither of inquisitive crowds. It is a slow thing, of *movement together* and in united masses, a movement of *states.*"[66]

And yet, to see the influence on millennialism on Wilson's political thought coming only from postmillennialism obscures the evangelical impulses in his religion that were more heavily indebted to premillennialism. At the heart of Protestant millennialism in both of its forms was the idea of conversion—the acceptance of God's grace and salvation, the individual's radical turn to God, the turning point in individual history. Postmillennialism tended to undermine the doctrine of conversion in favor of more gradualist understandings of grace. The sense of immediacy and urgency to choose and act was replaced by a concern with process, nurture, and even inevitability.[67]

Wilson never abandoned the evangelical call to action and human responsibility. It is a persistent theme from his earliest religious essays to his perorations on the Western tour. In September, 1919, Wilson issued an evangelical call to decision with the imagery of the covenant tradition. "If [the world] must know that the future is going to be one of disorder and of rivalry and of the old contests of power, let it know at once so it can make its arrangements and its calculations and lay its taxes and recruit its armies and build its ship for the next great fight," Wilson proclaimed; "but, if, on the other hand, it can be told that it will have an insurance against war, that a great body of powerful nations has entered into a solemn Covenant to substitute arbitration and discussion for war, . . . then men will know that we have the opportunity to do that great, that transcendent duty that lies ahead of us, sit quietly in council chambers and work out the proper reforms of our own industrial and economic life."[68]

One of the central features of American life in the twentieth century has been an erosion of the faith in progress shared by Wilson and so many of his contemporaries and nurtured by postmillennialism. The devastation of two world-wars, the ravages of industrialization and urbanization, the threat of a nuclear holocaust, the growing pluralism of the population, and other factors combined to eat away at the basis of what Ralph Henry Gabriel called the American democratic faith and what others describe as America's civil religion.[69] Thorsen and John Milton Cooper have argued that the final effect of Wilson's political thought and programs was the development of American political life as "a system," in which the contending self-

interests of American society are moderated and mediated by government through leadership. According to Cooper, Wilson was a supreme "realist" in recognizing the degree to which self-interest shaped political attitudes and sought to create institutions and political processes in which the contending interests could be contained and marshalled for progress.[70] But what has been seriously damaged is the moral core of American culture that lies at the heart of Wilson's understanding of political life and progress. What has seemingly triumphed is process alone.[71]

Debate will continue about the wisdom and the results of Wilson's appropriation of religious symbols and ideas into the political sphere. His moral imperialism shaped not only his foreign policy but also continues to define many of the issues surrounding America's role in world affairs. His conception of the role of government in a pluralistic society has left an enduring legacy that influences government programs and policies today.[72] In one sense, the sheer endurance of Wilson's ideas is testimony to the "higher realism" which Arthur S. Link so well described.[73] And yet, the Wilsonian mix of religion and politics may be fatally flawed, a noble yet finally tragic attempt. Ironically, by combining religious and political values as he did, Wilson may have contributed to the secularization of religion, the sacralizing of politics, and the relativizing of the moral order which he knew was the foundation of democracy.[74]

In any case, Wilson acknowledged that "the stern Covenanter tradition that is behind me sends many an echo down the years."[75] The echoes can be heard in Wilson's proclamation of "a gospel of order," and they resound across the decades of the twentieth century since his death.

Notes

[1] Mrs. Crawford H. Toy, "Second Visit to the White House," diary, January 3, 1915 (R. S. Baker Collection, Library of Congress); Cary Grayson, *Woodrow Wilson: An Intimate Memoir* (New York, 1960), p. 106.

[2] Ray Stannard Baker, *Woodrow Wilson: Life and Letters*, 8 vols. (Garden City, N.Y., 1927-39), I, 68, 49. Hereinafter cited as *WWLL*.

[3] John Maynard Keynes, "The Economic Consequences of the Peace," *Woodrow Wilson at Versailles*, Theodore P. Green, ed. (Boston, 1957) pp. 29, 32-33; Harold Nicholson, "Peacemaking 1919," *Ibid.*, p. 39.

[4] Arthur S. Link, *Wilson the Diplomatist* (Chicago, Quadrangle ed., 1965), p. 12; John M. Blum, *Woodrow Wilson and the Politics of Morality* (Boston, 1956), p. 36. See also the important essays by Link, "Woodrow Wilson: Presbyterian in Government," *Calvinism and the Political Order*, George L. Hunt, ed. (Philadelphia, 1965), pp. 157-74; "The Higher Realism of Woodrow Wilson," *Journal*

of Presbyterian History, XLI (1963), 1–13; "Woodrow Wilson and His Presbyterian Inheritance," Essays in Scotch-Irish History, E. R. R. Green, ed. (London, 1969), pp. 1–17. The last two essays have been reprinted in Link's book, The Higher Realism of Woodrow Wilson (Nashville, Tenn., 1971).

⁵ Arthur S. Link, David W. Hirst, John E. Little, et al., eds., Papers of Woodrow Wilson, (Princeton, N. J., 1966–). Hereinafter cited as PWW. Among the biographical studies benefitting from this magnificent editorial project are John M. Mulder, Woodrow Wilson: The Years of Preparation (Princeton, N. J., 1978); Edwin A. Weinstein, Woodrow Wilson: A Medical and Psychological Biography (Princeton, N. J., 1981); Frances Saunders, Ellen Axson Wilson: Between Two Worlds (Chapel Hill, 1985); John Milton Cooper, Jr., The Warrior and the Priest: Woodrow Wilson and Theodore Roosevelt (Cambridge, Mass., 1983); Niels Aage Thorsen, The Political Thought of Woodrow Wilson, 1875–1910 (Princeton, N.J., 1988).

⁶ WWLL, xxxiii–xxxiv.

⁷ See for example, the seminal essay by Arthur M. Schlesinger, "A Critical Period in American Religion, 1875–1900," Massachusetts Historical Society Proceedings, LXIV (1930–32), 523–46, Reprinted in John M. Mulder and John F. Wilson, Religion in American History: Interpretive Essays (Englewood Cliffs, N. J., 1978), pp. 302–17; and more recently Sydney E. Ahlstrom, A Religious History of the American People 2 vols. (Garden City, N.Y., Image Books ed., 1975), II, 191–407.

⁸ See, for example, David B. Danbom, "The World of Hope": Progressives and the Struggle for an Ethical Public Life (Philadelphia, 1987), and Robert M. Crunden, Ministers of Reform: The Progressives' Achievement in American Civilization, 1889–1920 (New York, 1982). Jean B. Quandt, From the Small Town to the Great Community: The Social Thought of Progressive Intellectuals (New Brunswick, N.J., 1970); Thomas Bender, Toward an Urban Vision: Ideas and Institutions in Nineteenth-Century America (Lexington, Ky., 1975); Peter J. Frederick, Knights of the Golden Rule: The Intellectual as Christian Social Reformer in the 1890s (Lexington, Ky., 1976); Arthur J. Vidich and Stanford M. Lyman, American Sociology: Worldly Rejections of Religion and Their Direction (New Haven, Conn., 1985); Paul Boyer, Urban Masses and Moral Order in America, 1820–1920 (Cambridge, Mass., 1978); Allen F. Davis, Spearheads for Reform: The Social Settlements and the Progressive Movement, 1890–1914 (New York, 1967); Morton Keller, Affairs of State: Public Life in Late Nineteenth-Century America (Cambridge, Mass., 1977); Arthur S. Link and Richard L. McCormick, Progressivism (Arlington Heights, Ill., 1983).

⁹ "The Minister and the Community," March 30, 1906, PWW, XVI, 350; "Abraham Lincoln: Man of the People," Feb. 12, 1909, ibid., XIX, 33; Woodrow Wilson to Joseph Ruggles Wilson, Dec. 16, 1888, ibid., VI, 30. The following abbreviations for individuals will be used in the notes: WW—Woodrow Wilson; JRW—Joseph Ruggles Wilson; JWW—Janet Woodrow Wilson; ELA—Ellen Louise Axson; EAW—Ellen Axson Wilson. Wilson's father's life is treated at length in Mulder, Woodrow Wilson, pp. 3–28.

¹⁰ WW to the Rev. William J. Hampton, Sept. 13, 1917; quoted in WWLL, I, 34; William Allen White, Woodrow Wilson (Boston and New York, 1924), p. 259.

[11] For the story of the Wilson family, see Mulder, *Woodrow Wilson*, pp. 3–58.

[12] Alexander L. George and Juliette L. George, *Woodrow Wilson and Colonel House* (New York, 1956); Robert C. Tucker, "The Georges' Wilson Reexamined: An Essay on Psychobiography," *American Political Science Review*, LXXI (1977), 606–18; Edwin A. Weinstein *et al.*, "Woodrow Wilson's Political Personality: A Reappraisal," *Political Science Quarterly*, XCIII (1979): 585–88; Alexander L. George and Juliette L. George, "Woodrow Wilson and Colonel House: A Reply to Weinstein, Anderson, and Link," *Political Science Quarterly*, XCVI (1982), 641–65; Weinstein, *Woodrow Wilson: Medical and Psychological Biography*; Dorothy Ross, "Woodrow Wilson and the Case for Psychohistory," *Journal of American History*, LXIX (1982), 659–68.

[13] The most helpful study of Calvinism and its political implications is Michael Walzer's *Revolution of the Saints* (Cambridge, Mass., 1965). For discussions of covenant theology, see Leonard J. Trinterud, "The Origins of Puritanism," *Church History*, XX (1951), 37–57; Sidney A. Burrell, "The Covenant as a Revolutionary Symbol, 1596–1637," *Church History*, XXVII (1958), 338–50; H. Richard Niebuhr, "The Idea of the Covenant and American Democracy," *Church History*, XXIII (1954), 126–37. James B. Torrance, "'Covenant or Contract' A study of the theological background of worship in seventeenth century Scotland," *Scottish Journal of Theology*, XXIII (1970), 51–76; Perry Miller, *The New England Mind*, 2 vols. (New York, 1939 and 1953), and *Errand into the Wilderness* (Cambridge, Mass., 1956). For the character of Presbyterian theology and American Protestantism in the South during the late nineteenth century, see R. Brooks Holifield, *The Gentlemen Theologians: American Theology in Southern Culture, 1795–1860* (Durham, N.C., 1978); Lefferts A. Loetscher, *Facing the Enlightenment and Pietism: Archibald Alexander and the Founding of Princeton Theological Seminary* (Westport, Conn., 1983); Theodore Dwight Bozeman, *Protestants in an Age of Science: The Baconian Ideal and Antebellum American Religious Thought* (Chapel Hill, N.C., 1977); E. T. Thompson, *Presbyterians in the South*, 3 vols. (Atlanta, 1963–73); Samuel S. Hill, ed., *Encyclopedia of Religion in the South* (Macon, Ga., 1984); James O. Farmer, *The Metaphysical Confederacy: James Henley Thornwell and the Synthesis of Southern Values* (Macon, Ga.: 1986); Charles Regan Wilson, *Baptized by Blood: The Religion of the Lost Cause, 1865–1920* (Athens, Ga.: 1980); Regan, ed., *Religion in the South* (Jackson, Miss., 1985).

[14] *Mutual Relation of Master and Slaves as Taught in the Bible* . . . (Augusta, Ga., 1861), pp. 7, 15; sermon on Genesis 47:8, written sometime during 1878 (J. R. Wilson Papers, Historical Foundation, Montreat, N. C.); *The True Idea of Success in Life, An Address Delivered before the Union and Philanthropic Societies of Hampden-Sidney College, June 10, 1857* . . . (Richmond, Va., 1857), p. 29.

[15] JRW to WW, Jan. 26, 1876, *PWW*, I, 346: *Mutual Relation of Masters and Slaves* . . . , p. 10; sermon on Mark 14:50, n. d. (Woodrow Wilson Papers, Library of Congress).

[16] News report of a speech to the Philadelphian Society, May 20, 1898, *PWW*, X, 533; "The Ideal Statesman," Jan. 30, 1877, *ibid.*, 244–45; "Christ's Army," Aug. 17, 1876, *ibid.*, 181.

[17] "First Inaugural Address," *The Public Papers of Woodrow Wilson: The New*

Democracy, R. S. Baker and W. E. Dodd, eds., 2 vols. (New York and London, 1926), I, 5–6.

[18]"Princeton in the Nation's Service," Oct. 21, 1896, *PWW*, X, 21–22, 20.

[19]Baccalaureate address, June 12, 1904, *ibid.*, XV, 369.

[20]JRW to WW, March 6, 1889, *ibid.*, VI, 137.

[21]Constitution for the Royal United Kingdom Yacht Club, ca. July 1, 1874, *PWW*, I, 54–56; Mulder, *Woodrow Wilson*, pp. 12–23, 37–43.

[22]Constitution for the Royal United Kingdom Yacht Club. ca. July 1, 1874, *PWW*, I, 56, n. 1.

[23]WW to ELA, Oct. 30, 1883, *ibid.*, II, 499–500.

[24]WW to ELA, February 21, 1884 and July 15, 1884, *ibid.*, III, 38, 248.

[25]Mulder, *Woodrow Wilson*, pp. 38–39, 51–53, 64–66, 82–83, 102.

[26]WW to ELA, Dec. 18, 1884, *PWW*, III, 552–53.

[27]"The Union," Nov. 15, 1876, *ibid.*, I, 226.

[28]Thorsen, *The Political Thought of Woodrow Wilson*, pp. 3–16.

[29]"Cabinet Government in the United States," August 1879. *PWW*, I, 493–510.

[30]*Congressional Government* is reprinted in *ibid.*, IV, 13–179.

[31]WW to R. H. Dabney, May 11, 1883, *ibid.*, II, p. 350; WW to R. Bridges, April 29 and May 13, 1883, *ibid.*, p. 343–44, 354–58.

[32]WW to ELA, Oct. 30, 1883, *ibid.*, pp. 501–502.

[33]WW to ELA, Nov. 13, 1884, *ibid.*, III, 430; October 16, 1883, *ibid.*, II, 479–80.

[34]Thorsen, *The Political Thought of Woodrow Wilson*, pp. 41–88.

[35]Editorial Note, Wilson's "The State," *PWW*, VI, 244–52.

[36]*The State*, June 3, 1889, *ibid.*, pp. 256–83. See Thorsen, *The Political Thought of Woodrow Wilson*, p. 217: "This step [toward an interior, tolerant point of view], in which mind becomes conscious of its ability to anticipate social events, was the crucial step that brought Social Darwinism into an evolutionary phase, where the ability to anticipate implied the ability to modify and turn to social advantage, as Edward S. Corwin pointed out in 1950." See also Thorsen, *idem.* pp. 89–116.

[37]"The Study of Administration," ca. Nov. 1, 1886, PWW, V, 370, 373; Notes for Lectures on Administration, ca. Jan. 26, 1891–Feb. 27, 1894, *ibid.*, VII, 124. See also the bibliographical note in Thorsen, *The Political Thought of Woodrow Wilson*, p. 119, n. 6.

[38]Lecture notes, "Place of Law in the General Theory of Society," Sept. 26, 1891, *PWW*, VII, 304; Lecture notes on Public Law, "Written Constitutions," ca. Sept. 22, 1894–Jan. 20, 1895, *ibid.*, IX 23; Lecture notes on American constitutional law, "The Constitution as an Administrative Instrument," March 9, 1894, *ibid.*, VIII, 520; "Government under the Constitution," ca. June 26, 1893, *ibid.*, p. 270.

[39]"The Democratic State," ca. Dec. 1–20, 1885, *ibid.*, pp. 61–92; cf. pp. 58–61 and the editorial note, "Wilson's First Treatise on Democratic Government," pp. 54–68.

[40]See Thorsen's interesting discussion about why Wilson failed to complete "The Philosophy of Politics" in *The Political Thought of Woodrow Wilson*, pp. 220–ff.

41 WW to F. J. Turner, Jan. 21, 1902, *PWW*, XII, 240; WW to Richard Watson Gilder, Oct. 31, 1902, *ibid.*, XIV, 190.

42 *Constitutional Government in the United States* (New York, 1908), published in *PWW*, XVIII, 69–216.

43 "The Statesmanship of Letters," Nov. 5, 1903, *ibid.*, XV, 40–41.

44 "The Country and the Colleges," ca. Feb. 24, 1910, XX, 160–61.

45 Speech in Manchester, England, Dec. 30, 1918, *Public Papers of Woodrow Wilson: War and Peace*, I, 355–56.

46 Cooper, *The Warrior and the Priest*; Thorsen, *The Political Thought of Woodrow Wilson*; Mulder, *Wilson: The Years of Preparation*.

47 Thorsen, *Ibid.*, pp. 45, n. 18, 237–38.

48 The literature on religion and the American Revolution is voluminous; see for example, Bernard Bailyn, *The Ideological Origins of the American Revolution* (Cambridge, 1967); Gordon S. Wood, *The Creation of the American Republic, 1776–1787* (Chapel Hill, N.C., 1969); Nathan O. Hatch, *The Sacred Cause of Liberty: Republican Thought and the Millennium in Revolutionary New England* (New Haven, 1977); Alan Heimert, *Religion and the American Mind from the Great Awakening to the Revolution* (Cambridge, Mass., 1966); Harry S. Stout, *The New England Soul: Preaching and Religious Culture in Colonial New England* (New York, 1986); Robert E. Shalhope, "Republicanism and Early American Historiography," *William and Mary Quarterly*, 3rd series, XXXIX (1982), 334–56; Donald Weber, *Rhetoric and History in Revolutionary New England* (New York, 1988).

49 See, for example, James Hastings Nichols, *Democracy and the Churches* (Philadelphia, 1951); A. S. P. Woodhouse, *Puritanism and Liberty* (London, 1958); Ralph Barton Perry, *Puritanism and Democracy* (New York, 1944).

50 Cooper, *The Warrior and the Priest*, p. 19.

51 See note 19.

52 Cooper, *The Warrior and the Priest*, pp. 17, 18.

53 This is Cooper's point in *ibid.*, p. 19, and was also made by Daniel Rodgers in a response to this paper when it was originally presented at the conference in honor of Arthur S. Link at Princeton in May 1989.

54 See note 7; see also the new collection of essays edited by Mark A. Noll, *Religion and American Politics* (New York: Oxford University Press, 1990).

55 Schlesinger, "A Critical Period in American Religion"; Carter, *The Spiritual Crisis of the Gilded Age*; Handy, "The American Religious Depression" and *A Christian America*, pp. 134–84.

56 Confidential Journal, Dec. 28, 1889, *PWW*, VI, 462.

57 Diary of Mrs. Crawford H. Toy, Jan. 3, 1915 (R. S. Baker Coll., Library of Congress); The Rev. John J. McDowell to R. S. Baker, quoted in *WWLL*, I, 71.

58 Mulder, *Woodrow Wilson*, p. 105; J. David Hoeveler, Jr., *James McCosh and the Scottish Intellectual Tradition: From Glasgow to Princeton* (Princeton, N. J., 1981).

59 "Princeton in the Nation's Service," October 21, 1896, *PWW*, X, 29; Mulder, *Woodrow Wilson*, pp. 162, 172, 173.

60 *New York Tribune*, Dec. 2, 1902; Mulder, *Woodrow Wilson*, pp. 177–178.

61 Crunden, *Ministers of Reform*, pp. 225–73.

[62] Lawrence W. Levine, *Defender of the Faith – William Jennings Bryan: The Last Decade, 1915–1925* (New York, 1965).

[63] Mulder, *Woodrow Wilson*, p. 85, 150–51, 255–56; "On an Author's Choice of Company," Nov. 10, 1895, *PWW*. IX, 343; notes for a religious address, Jan. 17, 1900, *ibid.*, XI, 376; "The Present Task of the Ministry," May 26, 1909, *ibid.*, XIX, 221.

[64] Ernest Trice Thompson, *The Spirituality of the Church: A Distinctive Doctrine of the Presbyterian Church in the United States* (Richmond, Va., 1961).

[65] See Sandeen, *The Roots of Fundamentalism*; Marsden, *Fundamentalism and American Culture*; James H. Moorhead "Between Progress and Apocalypse: A Reassessment of Millennialism in American Religious Thought, 1800–1880," *Journal of American History*, LXXI (1984), 524–42, and "The Erosion of Post-millennialism in American Religious Thought, 1865–1925," *Church History*, LIII (1984), 61–77.

[66] Thorsen, *The Political Thought of Woodrow Wilson*. p. 160; *PWW*. "Democracy," VII, 365. See Ernest C. Tuveson, *Redeemer Nation: The Idea of America's Millennial Role* (Chicago, 1968).

[67] Moorhead, "The Erosion of Postmillennialism in American Religious Thought in American Religious Thought, 1865–1925."

[68] Speech at Cheyenne, Wyoming, Sept. 24, 1919, *Public Papers of Woodrow Wilson: War and Peace*, II, 384.

[69] Ralph Henry Gabriel, *The Course of American Democratic Thought: An Intellectual History since 1815* (New York, 1940); Robert A. Nisbet, *A History of the Idea of Progress* (New York, 1979). The literature on civil religion is extensive. Helpful introductions to the issues and the debate are Robert N. Bellah, "Civil Religion in America," *Daedalus*, XCVI (1967), 1–21; Russell E. Richey and Donald G. Jones, *American Civil Religion* (New York, 1973); John F. Wilson, *Public Religion in America* (Philadelphia, 1979); Robert E. Stauffer, "Bellah's Civil Religion, Review Symposium on the Sociology of Robert N. Bellah, *Journal of the Scientific Study of Religion* XIV (1975), 390–95; Michael W. Hughey, *Civil Religion and Moral Order: Theoretical and Historical Dimensions* (Westport, Conn., 1983); Richard V. Pierard and Robert D. Linder, *Civil Religion and the Presidency* (Grand Rapids, Mich., 1938). A helpful bibliographical essay is Gerald Robert McDermott, "Civil Religion in the American Revolutionary Period: An Historiographic Analysis," *Christian Scholars Review*, XVIII (1989), 346–62.

[70] Cooper, *The Warrior and the Priest*, pp. 217–21; Thorsen, *The Political Thought of Woodrow Wilson*, pp. 214–34.

[71] Robert Bellah,. et al., *Habits of the Heart: Individualism and Commitment in American Life* (Berkeley, Calif., 1985).

[72] Cooper, *The Warrior and the Priest*, pp. 346–61.

[73] Link, "The Higher Realism of Woodrow Wilson."

[74] Robert Booth Fowler, *Unconventional Partners: Religion and Liberal Culture in the United States* (Grand Rapids, Mich., 1989).

[75] Speech at the Mansion House in London, Dec. 28, 1918, *Public Papers of Woodrow Wilson: War and Peace*, I, 346.

Charles E. Neu

WOODROW WILSON
AND COLONEL HOUSE
THE EARLY YEARS, 1911–1915

IN recent years the relationship between Woodrow Wilson and Colonel House, one of the most famous and well-documented friendships in American political history, has received considerable attention. Building on the archival research of Arthur S. Link in his biography of Wilson and on the new material brought together in the *Papers of Woodrow Wilson*, scholars such as Inga Floto, Edwin A. Weinstein, and John Milton Cooper, Jr., have offered a more penetrating description of the friendship than that of earlier writers and a more skeptical assessment of House's role in the domestic and foreign policy achievements of the Wilson administration.[1] Most scholars, however, have been more concerned with Wilson than with House, leaving many questions unanswered about this elusive and controversial man and his relationship with Wilson. They have not closely studied the voluminous evidence on the friendship in House's diary or carefully traced the evolution of the long collaboration between the two men. This essay will begin rather than complete that task, focusing on the early phases of the friendship, from the first meeting on November 24, 1911 until the end of 1915, when Wilson's marriage to Edith Bolling Galt marked a decisive break in the two men's relationship.

The friendship between Wilson and House was slow to develop. After House gave up hope for the presidential candidacy of Mayor William J. Gaynor of New York in early 1911, he was in no rush to jump on the Wilson bandwagon. House and Wilson did not meet until November 24, 1911, and while the two men were strongly drawn to one another, on December 9 House left New York for a long stay in Texas. In January and February 1912 he was busy writing his utopian novel of the future, *Philip Dru: Administrator*, and remained on the margin of Wilson's drive for the Democratic nomination. Although

House and his political allies in Texas helped Wilson win that state's primaries in May 1912, as the Wilson presidential movement faltered in the late spring and early summer of 1912 House sought to avoid identifying himself too closely with it. On June 25, on the opening day of the Baltimore convention, he left for a leisurely tour of northern Europe, traveling all the way to Moscow. Returning to the United States on August 14, he lingered on the North Shore of Boston until September 14, when he finally moved to New York and began to play a minor part in the campaign. It was only after Wilson's election that House's energies were fully engaged and that he became totally absorbed in the selection of the new cabinet.[2]

It was not, therefore, until late 1912 and the early months of 1913 that the intimacy between Wilson and House was firmly established and that House became the new President's most trusted and influential adviser. As such, he played three distinct roles.

First, during the period of cabinet selection House established his role as a high-level political intermediary. He dealt with all kinds of people the President-elect did not want to see and with squabbles within the Democratic party that Wilson wished to avoid. Despite his extraordinary political gifts, Wilson was a political leader, as John Milton Cooper, Jr., observes, of solitary habits, one who did not thrive on day-to-day contact with politicians and reporters. He needed someone like House who could serve as a buffer. Wilson's personal secretary, Joseph P. Tumulty, also served as an intermediary, but on a lower level, for Tumulty's political connections were far more limited than those of House. In short, Wilson's weakness was House's genius. House knew how to win the confidence of individuals, to share their aspirations and soothe their anxieties. His days were filled with conferences, phone calls, and all sorts of political tasks that the President found distasteful.[3]

House began to assume a second role as Wilson's leading foreign policy adviser as early as May 21, 1913, when he left for Europe to consult with British and French leaders. He was eager to broaden his horizons and, especially after the outbreak of World War I, House's influence on Wilson's foreign policy grew rapidly. He established his expertise on European affairs, maneuvered to curb Secretary of State William Jennings Bryan's influence, and sought to dominate the advice that the President received. House became not just an intermediary, but a formulator of policy as well.[4]

A third role underlay House's activity in both domestic and foreign affairs. This was his friendship with Wilson, for without the President's confidence and trust House's influence would have been negligible. Among all the politicians around Wilson, House was unique.

Others wanted political office and preferment, but House was content to serve as a confidential adviser and seemed to offer Wilson availability, expertise, and unselfish devotion.[5]

Wilson was a brilliant, intense man, a spellbinding orator whose ambition and sense of destiny had carried him far. He had, however, paid a physical price for his remarkable academic and political success, entering the White House in 1913 with a complex medical history. He suffered from cerebral vascular disease, which may have appeared as early as 1896, when he was only thirty-nine, and which brought a series of strokes of varying intensity prior to 1913. Coupled with this progressive disease, the nature of which Wilson never clearly understood, was a cluster of other ailments, such as headaches and digestive troubles, with which he had to contend over the course of his life. Wilson compulsively described the details of his various ailments to those he loved, and these discussions of illness formed a bond between him and his close friends.[6]

Despite a wonderful marriage and a warm, happy family life, Wilson was highly vulnerable to emotional stress. He often felt lonely and depressed, and sometimes feared the loss of emotional control and of control over his strong sexual drives as well.[7] With his election to the presidency, he faced extraordinary political pressures and increased personal isolation. More than ever before, he was in need of skilled advisers and of male companionship.[8]

House appeared at the right time with a combination of personal and political qualities that strongly appealed to Wilson. House's gentle, deferential manner, his lack of an assertive masculinity, put the President at ease. His apparently fragile health elicited the President's sympathy and concern, and his frequent assurances of affection and esteem helped to satisfy one of Wilson's deepest needs. Moreover, House had impressive political skills that complemented those of the President. His many years in Texas politics had made him a patient and crafty political infighter, experienced in dispensing patronage and in attempting to maintain harmony among the many factions within the Democratic party. He was a thoughtful political adviser and an amiable, urbane companion, one with whom the President could discuss political issues and with whom he could also share his inner thoughts and feelings. During the winter of 1912–1913, House joined that circle of intimates around the President who were dedicated both to advancing his political career and to maintaining his physical health and emotional stability.[9]

As Wilson and House spent more time together, their conversation ranged far beyond the political concerns of the moment. They shared favorite poems, occasionally reading them out loud to one another,

discussed religion and the "imagination of man," worried over the low wages of women, calculated how much of his salary Wilson could save, talked of innovative political leadership, and lamented the rarity of true, disinterested friendship.[10]

In *Philip Dru: Administrator*, House had expressed his concern with America's spiritual regeneration and his belief that inspired leadership could solve the nation's problems.[11] Now he found in Wilson a leader who embodied his moral values and who could move the American people toward this larger goal. On January 17, 1913, House's diary reveals that he told Wilson that he

> was glad that the dominant note throughout his administration was to be the giving of equal opportunity to all classes, thereby leavening the entire social fabric; that it was better worth while to do something for your fellow men than it was to do something for yourself. I believed that this had never been done, as far as I knew, and he said 'no not since Jefferson.' This pleased me greatly for I am more interested in that *motif* than in anything. I pointed out that it could not be accomplished by law, but if he would say it often enough, it would set people to thinking who had never thought along these lines before, and that it would make them feel ashamed of their selfishness and their lack of thought for their fellow man. I thought it would do untold good.[12]

Thus House formed a deep and genuine admiration for Wilson's political leadership; he wanted the dominant theme in the President's public addresses to be that the "strong should help the weak, that the fortunate should aid the unfortunate, and that business should be conducted upon a higher and more humane plane." On February 13, when Wilson read to House his inaugural address, House thought it a "masterpiece of its kind. It is off the beaten track and is full of spirituality." Four days later, defending Wilson at a dinner with financial leaders, House claimed that he was a leader of exceptional moral and physical courage, one who sought "to raise the moral stamina of the Nation."[13]

During a visit to Washington on April 1, when Wilson and House had finished their political business, they drove around the city and stopped at Rock Creek Cemetery, where Wilson wanted to show his friend the statue commemorating the wife of Henry Adams by Augustus Saint-Gaudens. "We walked across the Cemetery," House recorded, "and sat upon a granite bench in front of the marvelous figure depicting Grief. He [Wilson] called attention to the beautiful outlines and the look of resolution upon the face. I thought she seemed of the kind to send sons to the wars and bear with fortitude the news of their death." After discussing Greek and modern sculp-

tors, Wilson and House "sat for a long while before the statue, which affected me much as some mournful strain of music would." The two men had achieved a rare degree of closeness.[14]

For a man of allegedly frail health, House had displayed a remarkable degree of stamina during the winter of 1912–1913. He had worked long hours, beginning generally around 9:00 A.M. and often continuing late into the evening, screening applicants, collecting information, conferring with aspiring politicians, and advising the President. He made many trips to Washington, where his schedule was equally arduous, and missed his annual winter stay in Texas. His only regular escape from the constant pressure of patronage and cabinet-making was evenings at the theater. Nevertheless, his health was remarkably good. Twice he complained in his diary that he was "worn out," and in early January he was in bed with a fever and cold for five days. All in all, however, he thrived on this intense political activity, excited by the fact that at last he was "playing a part on so large a stage."[15]

House realized, however, that the arrival of warm weather would bring a change in his routine, and as early as April 23 warned Wilson that "the weather will soon begin to grow warm which warns me that I am not to see much more of you until the Autumn." He confided to his close friend and brother-in-law Sidney E. Mezes, the president of the University of Texas, that the "demands upon me are growing absolutely unbearable" and that "I just simply have to quit for awhile [*sic*] now that the weather has grown warm." Breaking away for his annual trip to Europe would provide a much-needed rest.[16]

During his last visit to Washington on May 11, House noted that the President "spoke of the loneliness of his position in a way that was saddening. He expressed again and again his regret at my departure. I said I felt like a deserter and that I would not go excepting that it had come to the point where I could no longer serve him, for I was broken down and it was absolutely necessary for me to get away for a few weeks." House urged Wilson "to keep up his courage," and House left convinced that the President "will carry himself like a brave and gallant gentleman."[17]

Wilson was sympathetic with House's European journey, urging him not to worry "after you have once stepped on board." "I do not think you can ever know, my great and good friend," House wrote Wilson the day before he left, "how much I appreciate your kindness to me. . . . I go only because of my desire to conserve my strength in order that I may serve you the better. I shall believe that you will be successful in all your undertakings for, surely, no one is so well equipped as you to do what you have planned. My faith in you is as

great as my love for you – more than that I cannot say." Wilson responded in kind, telegraphing House that "my affectionate thoughts go with you and my prayers for your strength, refreshment and happiness." On May 21 House sailed on the *Mauretania* for England.[18]

House traveled to Europe not only for rest and diversion, but also to advance a vague idea of a "sympathetic understanding" between Germany, Great Britain, Japan, and the United States. During his stay in London he talked with government leaders and met, for the first time, British Foreign Secretary Sir Edward Grey.[19] Returning on July 16, he retreated to Boston's North Shore to escape the heat until September 19, when he felt it safe to leave for New York. He had last seen Wilson in Washington on May 11, and did not resume the relationship by traveling to the capital until mid-October. The two friends had, of course, corresponded, but House was absent during a critical period, when Wilson was holding the Congress in session to push through tariff and banking reform and when the inner circle of advisers around the President was crystallizing. Alone in the White House while his family escaped the heat in Cornish, New Hampshire, Wilson leaned heavily on the companionship of Tumulty and of the young, personable White House physician, Cary T. Grayson.[20]

Not until October 14 did House travel to Washington to reestablish his ties with the President. The President, House noted in his diary, "greeted me very warmly, taking both hands to shake mine," and House learned from Grayson, with whom he had forged a close alliance, that Wilson "had a deep affection for me and often during the summer while I was gone he would say 'my Grayson, but how I wish that dear fellow House was here.'" The two men discussed Wilson's health, the progress of banking legislation, relations with Mexico, and a variety of lesser matters, but did not exchange the sort of intimacies that had marked many of their earlier meetings. Only gradually did Wilson resume his earlier practice of confiding his deepest fears and feelings to House. On December 12 he told his friend that "he had not slept well the night before; that he had nightmares, and that he thought he was seeing some of his Princeton enemies." "Those terrible days," House observed, "have sunk deep into his soul and he will carry their marks to his grave."[21] The passage of the Federal Reserve Act in December 1913 produced more fears than elation in the President. As Wilson had earlier confided to House, "he always lacked any feeling of elation when a particular object was accomplished." On December 22, during his last visit of the year, House sought to encourage Wilson, speaking of his great success and the place he had already made for himself in the history of the nation. But Wilson was not to be easily consoled, for he worried about his early successes and said

that "his Princeton experience hung over him sometimes like a nightmare; that he had wonderful success there, and all at once conditions changed and the troubles . . . were brought about. He seemed to fear that such a denouement might occur again." House could only console the President by observing that "there was a difference in dealing with the American peoples and a small clique of selfish millionaires." It was nearly midnight before they left the President's study for bed. Wilson was, House recorded, "solicitous of my welfare and came into my room to see that everything was properly arranged. He said he enjoyed talking with me because he did not have to think about what he was saying." "He was," House concluded, "at his best tonight and was most affectionate in his manner."[22]

Inevitably House's intimacy with Wilson pulled him into controversies within the inner circle around the President, particularly the growing tension between William G. McAdoo and Tumulty. During the winter of 1912–1913 he had grown close to McAdoo, supporting his appointment as Secretary of the Treasury, listening to his anxieties and aspirations, and helping him maintain the emotional equilibrium essential for his success.[23] Prior to Wilson's election, House had not known Tumulty well, but in the aftermath of victory he came to appreciate Tumulty's frank manner and political skills. Despite Wilson's reservations about Tumulty's parochial perspective, Catholic faith, and social background, House had strongly urged his appointment as the President's personal secretary. House anticipated that Tumulty would be a valuable ally, but from the start he felt that Tumulty's "main trouble is talking too much" and was uncertain of his loyalty, sensing that with Tumulty, in contrast to McAdoo, he did not have any special rapport.[24]

Tumulty was jealous of House's access to the President and sometimes tactless in dealing with others. After his return from Europe in late July 1913, House began hearing complaints from McAdoo, Grayson, and others over the behavior of the President's secretary. By December 1913 House felt "somewhat humiliated when I think of my warm advocacy of Tumulty for Private Secretary. The President desired a man of refinement and discretion and of broad vision. He has instead just the opposite and almost wholly at my instance. . . . Tumulty has good sense, but it is becoming warped by his growing egotism and jealousy concerning everyone near the President." For House to record a mistake of this magnitude in his diary, his distress must have been acute.[25]

Tumulty's behavior was erratic: at one moment he accused House of lacking confidence in him; at another he assured House that "I had been like a father to him; that I was his friend when he had none."

House had moved, however, beyond the point where he could be appeased, and on January 22, 1914, noted with pleasure news from Grayson that "there seems enough trouble brewing for Tumulty to drown him. The irony of all is, he is bringing destruction upon himself by his jealousy, his egotism and his garrulous tongue." Nevertheless, House continued to consult with Tumulty, concealing the extent of his hostility. In early May Tumulty unwisely told House that he was thinking of resigning because he could not live on his salary; four days later House conveyed the news to Wilson, adding that he believed Tumulty was "sincere." If House sought to test Wilson's feelings toward Tumulty, he must have been disappointed, for Wilson was fond of his young secretary and "upset" over the idea of losing him. House's animosity toward Tumulty remained intense, but he knew that he would have to bide his time before making another move against him.[26]

In early 1914 House and Wilson remained close. Just prior to House's departure for Texas on January 30, Wilson wrote that "it grieves me to see you go to even to the distance of Texas. My thought and affection go with you. I thank God every day that I have so generous and disinterested a friend." House replied: "I never forget that but for you I should not have had the supreme joy that comes from effort in such a glorious cause. I am thankful, too, that when I first met you some inspiration gave me your full measure, and in this I cheated the rest of the world, for it is only now that it has come to them."[27]

House left Texas on March 20, 1914, stopping in Washington on his way to New York. Wilson was in a lonely mood and insisted that House spend a second night in Washington so that they might have "a more connected talk." House was pleased with the results, commenting that Wilson "literally thinks aloud with me and it is exceedingly delightful and interesting. He was never kinder or more confidential with me than on this visit."[28]

During this visit House received disturbing news about the President's health. From the start of the friendship with Wilson, he had known that his health was fragile. Now he learned from Grayson, who "tells me everything concerning the President in the most minute detail in order to get my advice," that Wilson's medical problems were serious. Grayson, House recorded, "alarmed me somewhat by saying that the Philadelphia oculist, Dr. Swinehart [sic] . . . told him, Grayson, that there was some indication of the hardening of the arteries. The President does not know this, neither does any member of his family."[29]

As House learned more about Wilson, his assessment of the President became more complex. He had no doubts about Wilson's intellec-

tual gifts. "I am impressed," he recorded on April 17, "by the analytic qualities of his mind and the clearness with which he expresses his thoughts. I have come in contact with minds of greater initiative and imagination, but never one that had more analytical power and comprehension." Increasingly, however, he complained about Wilson's reluctance to consult with his cabinet and with congressional leaders, and occasionally he encouraged Wilson to broaden his range of advisers. After emphasizing George Washington's dependence on Alexander Hamilton, House told Wilson "that all the really big men I had known had taken advice from others, while the little men refused to take it. The fact that a man took advice did not lessen his greatness because, after all, he had to judge for himself finally, as to what was good and what was bad." Wilson not only agreed, but made the mistake of remarking "that he always sought advice." House responded in his diary with what was almost contempt, noting that "I almost laughed at this statement." Apparently House had wanted the President to agree on the need to change the way in which he made his decisions.[30]

House's trip to England and France in June and July of 1913 had stimulated his interest in international affairs. By December of that year he was convinced that he should undertake another trip to Europe, this time beginning in Germany, to promote his plan for the reduction of armaments and the easing of tension among the great European powers. Wilson agreed, and on May 11, 1914, when House visited Wilson shortly before his departure, the President said that "his heart misgave him to think I was going so soon, but he added, 'it is worth while for you to go upon a great mission.'" Armed with the President's approval and his letter of introduction, on May 16 House left for Germany on the *Imperator*. Full of enthusiasm and anticipation, he wrote his long-time private secretary Frances B. Denton that "I am ready for Berlin and the great adventure. No matter how unsuccessful, not even an Emperor can take from me the joy I have had in looking at the stars."[31]

House spent two months in Europe, stopping in Berlin, Paris, and London, where he sought to promote negotiations between Germany and Great Britain and to encourage the leading nations of Europe to cooperate in guiding the "underdeveloped countries of the world." Two days after arriving in Berlin, House wrote Wilson that the situation in Europe was "extraordinary." "It is," he continued, "jingoism run stark mad. Unless someone acting for you can bring about a different understanding, there is some day to be an awful cataclys." After a conversation with Emperor William II, however, he became more optimistic, informing Wilson that "I have been as successful as I antic-

ipated [in Germany] and I have ample material to open negotiations in London." "It is my plan," he concluded, "to get Sir Edward Grey to go with me to Kiel at the end of the month, ostensibly to attend the regatta, but really for the purpose of the three of us getting together so there may be no go-betweens or misunderstanding."[32]

In London House's talks with Sir Edward Grey and other British leaders were rambling and inconclusive; he raised, but did not push, the idea of a meeting between himself, the Kaiser, and Grey, only noting that "this was not gone into further." Although the British had, in effect, rejected House's single concrete proposal, the same day House wrote that "it is difficult for me to realize that the dream I had last year is beginning to come true. I have seen the Kaiser, and now the British government seem eager to carry on the discussion." House already displayed serious weaknesses as a negotiator.[33]

Another purpose of House's "great adventure" was to explain to European leaders Wilson's purposes and policies. In Germany he spoke of Wilson's "character and courage," warning Grand Admiral Alfred von Tirpitz, the Navy Minister, that Wilson, unlike Bryan, was "a man of iron courage and inflexible will." In Britain he argued that Wilson, although lacking Theodore Roosevelt's flamboyance and physical robustness, would in the end accomplish more. "I have a keen desire," House wrote the President from London, "for you to become the world figure of your time. Never again can the old order of statesman hold sway, and you are, and will continue to be, the prophet of a new day." While Wilson was not ready to assume such a role, he praised House's efforts effusively, describing the "thrill of deep pleasure" which his letters gave him.[34]

When House landed in Boston on July 29, the crisis had already erupted in Europe that would soon bring the outbreak of World War I. As his vague peace plans collapsed, House also had to contend with the most severe personal crisis of the President's life, the death of his wife Ellen on August 6. "I am grieved beyond measure," he recorded in his diary, "that I am heat-bound and cannot go to Washington, for it is now that I might comfort the President most. . . . Her death will be a grievous blow to the President for she was one of the elect, and has been of more help to him than even he realizes." The death of his wife, House wrote to the President, "leaves me unnerved and stunned. It only proves again how near to us the Angel of Death hovers." Reminding Wilson of his great destiny and "splendid courage," House encouraged the President to visit him on the North Shore. Instead, Wilson retreated to Harlakenden near Cornish, New Hampshire, where on August 30 House joined him for two days.[35]

The two friends talked of the war in Europe and of other political

matters, but essentially they grieved together over Ellen's death. On the second afternoon, as they sat on a terrace overlooking the Connecticut River valley, Wilson "began to talk of Mrs. Wilson and of what her loss meant to him personally. Tears came into his eyes, and he said he felt like a machine that had run down, and there was nothing left in him worth-while. As far as he could see, he was still doing good work and his mental capacity had not been impaired by the trouble he had gone through, and yet, he looked forward to the next two years and a half with dread. He did not see how he could go through with it [the remainder of his first term]." Wilson showed House "photographs of her, read poems written about her, and talked of her as freely as if she were alive." [36]

In mid-September, after House moved from the North Shore to New York, he concentrated on talks with the ambassadors of Germany and Great Britain that would lay the groundwork for a future peace move. His interest in domestic politics waned as his conviction hardened that the European war presented great opportunities for the Wilson administration. He now complained about the burdens of patronage, lamenting that "I have tried my utmost to keep out of national and state politics and devote myself to international affairs, but I seem doomed to the treadmill for awhile longer." [37]

House was eager to return to Europe in pursuit of peace. During a visit to Washington in late September, however, he found that both the British Ambassador, Cecil Spring Rice, and the President did not think the time was ripe for a trip to Europe. House disagreed, complaining in his diary that he found Wilson "singularly lacking in appreciation of the importance of this European crisis. He seems more interested in domestic affairs, and I find it difficult to get his attention centered upon the one big question." [38]

Try as he might, House could not easily disengage from domestic politics or from the intrigues swirling around the President. Prior to arriving in Washington on September 27, his first visit since early May, he had learned from Grayson that the President was "suffering from indigestion and he thought one cause of it was that McAdoo and Tumulty persisted in talking business to him during his meals." House accepted the unenviable task of urging both to exercise restraint. House could also not avoid the question of whether or not Wilson would run for a second term, a question that was complicated by uncertainties about the President's health. Still depressed by his wife's death, Wilson freely shared his doubts with his confidential adviser, claiming that "if he knew that he would not have to stand for re-election two years from now, he would feel a great load had been lifted from him." House wondered what Wilson could do with his life that would be so interesting; Wilson had no answer but feared that the

people would expect the future accomplishments of his administration to be as great as those in the past. House did not believe the nation expected additional domestic achievements, suggesting that Wilson could add to his fame through a foreign policy that "would bring him world-wide recognition."[39]

The question of Wilson's second term was complicated by McAdoo's growing presidential ambitions. McAdoo's great abilities had made him a powerful member of the President's cabinet, and even before his marriage to Eleanor Wilson on May 7, 1914, he had enjoyed informal access to the President. But McAdoo was restless and ambitious, and on October 20 House concluded that "McAdoo has the Presidential bee firmly fixed." House sought to discourage McAdoo, but McAdoo was convinced that Wilson would not run again. House, whose emotions were less engaged, was a far wiser observer, noting that he was certain Wilson "would be a disappointed man if anything should arise to make a second term impossible." House concluded that McAdoo could best advance his political and financial fortunes if he accepted an offer for the presidency of the Metropolitan Life Insurance Company. House was tiring of the constant turmoil generated by the Secretary of the Treasury.[40]

House sought to convince the President that McAdoo could be easily replaced, but in early November he found Wilson upset by the prospect of McAdoo's loss and convinced that McAdoo's presidential ambitions would be best advanced if he stayed within the administration. The President struck House as "thoroughly weary and heartsick" and more emotionally fragile than before. House told Wilson of the "trouble brewing between McAdoo and Tumulty," repeating McAdoo's criticisms of Tumulty's machinations. Confronted by the simmering conflict between two close advisers, "the President became flushed and excited and wanted to know if McAdoo had gone crazy. That kind of talk sounded to him more like McCombs than McAdoo. His face became grey and he looked positively sick. I was unable to lift him out of this depression before bedtime." The President's tolerance for controversy was so low that the next evening after dinner Wilson avoided retreating to his study with House, fearful that his friend would raise the McAdoo-Tumulty feud again. House, of course, avoided the subject, instead encouraging Wilson to read poems and to recite limericks. The next day he sought to modify the impression he feared that he had left, reassuring Wilson that McAdoo was not consciously a candidate for president. Wilson's trust in House seemed undiminished. "'We know one another so well,'" he replied, "'that even if something is said in the course of a conversation we did not quite mean, we each of us would understand it.'"[41]

During the fall and early winter of 1914 Wilson leaned heavily on

House for companionship and emotional support. The burden was substantial. Wilson complained that "he was broken in spirit by Mrs. Wilson's death, and was not fit to be President because he did not think straight any longer, and had no heart in the things he was doing." Moreover, during House's visits to Washington Wilson became more demanding, pressing House to take an automobile ride in an open car in cold weather and even asking him to accompany him to church. House evaded the invitation by having his wife go in his place. At the end of House's visit on November 8, Wilson "asked me to come as often as I could. He was exceedingly solicitous and affectionate, and promised to come over to me at this week end if it was at all possible."[42]

Wilson was true to his word, and on November 14, only six days after he had returned from Washington, House returned to his apartment from the theater to learn that the President would arrive at 6:00 A.M. the following morning and would expect to see him at 6:30 A.M. for breakfast. House had to stay up past midnight to prepare for the sudden presidential visit, complaining that "the matter of entertaining a President within such confined quarters as our little apartment is not an easy undertaking." Nevertheless, House tried hard to please, taking Wilson to the Pipping Rock Club on Long Island for golf and arranging for a quiet dinner in his apartment.[43]

While House sought to ease Wilson's grief and to remind him of the great challenges ahead, he also sought to reorder his priorities. On November 25 he told the President that his greatest domestic achievement, the Federal Reserve Act, was now behind him. The time had come, House continued, "to pay less attention to his domestic policy and greater attention to the welding together of the two Western Continent[s]." House now was not only pursuing a peace plan for the European war, but was also proposing a pact setting ground rules for the nations of the hemisphere. During his December 3 visit to Washington, the President seemed to agree on these general goals, telling House that "we were right in our conclusions that he would be judged from now almost wholly by the way our foreign affairs were conducted."[44]

As Wilson focused more on foreign policy, he was reminded of Bryan's weaknesses as secretary of state. He and House agreed that Bryan "had served his usefulness" as secretary of state and that he should not be involved in any peace moves toward the European belligerents. Wilson decided that he would use House "to initiate peace unofficially" without telling his Secretary of State. House was pleased that the President had "placed this problem squarely up to me."[45]

House was eager to press ahead. On December 16 he arrived in

Washington for a four-day stay, an unusually long one for him. He and Wilson quickly outlined the major points of a new Pan-American treaty. The President also agreed that the time had come for House to travel to Europe to pursue peace negotiations. In fact, Wilson was now so enthusiastic that he "wanted to know whether I could go to Europe as early as the coming Saturday. . . . He said he needed me on two Continents, but thought before I left we could button up our South American matters so as to leave me free." "He spoke in feeling terms," House continued, "and expressed again and again his gratitude for my assistance. . . . I have never known him so appreciative or more affectionate."[46]

A Christmas day message from Wilson confirmed the accuracy of House's diary. "I wish I could see brought into your life," Wilson wrote, "some happiness and blessing equal to those you have brought into mine by your wonderful friendship. You have kept faith and strength in me."[47]

For all of his ambitions, House found it a strain to stay in the White House with the President, adjusting to Wilson's rigid schedule and dealing with his complicated and shifting moods. When he was only a day into his four-day stay, he confided to Fanny Denton that "I do not know when I can leave but I hope by tomorrow night. I ought to stay longer, but I cannot bring myself to do so." And once he had decided to prolong his trip, he wrote: "My how disappointed I am that I am compelled to stay until at least Monday night!"[48]

Twice in late December 1914, and twice again in January 1915, House traveled to Washington to advance his plans for hemispheric solidarity and peace in Europe. As House busied himself with last minute preparations, the grandiosity of his plans and his sense of superiority over even the President, began to surface again. He planned to stay in Europe six months, although the goals of his trip were vague, and now, having shifted the President's attention to the foreign arena, he complained that Wilson did not appreciate the importance of improving conditions among the unemployed at home. "If I did not," he continued, "have so much to do, and had not undertaken so much in connection with our foreign affairs, I would ask him [Wilson] to turn the whole matter over to me so that I might work it out as expeditiously as possible. My heart is strongly in such work, and when I am through with public affairs, it is my purpose to give my time almost wholly to it." House now saw himself as the indispensable man in both foreign and domestic affairs.[49]

Long before meeting Wilson, House had fantasized about masterminding great domestic and international reforms. The more power he achieved, the more his fantasies expanded and his sense of reality

weakened. And Grayson's frequent news about the President's deteriorating health intensified House's sense of urgency, forcing him to ponder how long his "dear friend" would remain in office. On January 13, 1915, Grayson, House recorded, "alarmed me somewhat by saying that the President's kidneys were not acting as well as they should. There was nothing serious as yet, but he was watching him closely." Wilson's accumulating ailments were beginning to have ominous implications.[50]

On January 24, 1915, House arrived in Washington for a final visit before his departure for Europe. Wilson asked House "to tell Sir Edward Grey his entire mind so he would know what his intentions were about everything, and he wished me to mention his relations with Mr. Bryan and the conduct of the State Department under him. He said, 'Let him know that while you are abroad I expect to act directly through you and to eliminate all intermediaries.' He approved all I had in mind to say to Sir Edward and to the Germans. He said: 'There is not much for us to talk over for the reason we are both of the same mind and it is not necessary to go into details with you.'" Excited about his impending departure and over the extent of the authority the President had vested in him, House asked Wilson "if it would be possible for him to come over to Europe in the event a peace conference could be arranged and in the event he was invited to preside over the conference. He thought it would be well to do this and that the American people would desire it." Both men had allowed their hopes to run far ahead of the realities of the European war.[51]

On January 25 the two friends said good-bye. House recorded the scene carefully for posterity:

> The President's eyes were moist when he said his last words of farewell. He said: 'Your unselfish and intelligent friendship has meant much to me,' and he expressed his gratitude again and again, calling me his 'most trusted friend.' He declared I was the only one in all the world to whom he could open his entire mind.
>
> I asked if he remembered the first day we met, some three and a half years ago. He replied 'yes, but we had known one another always, and merely come in touch then, for our purposes and thoughts were as one.' I told him how much he had been to me; how I had tried all my life to find someone with whom I could work out the things I had so deeply at heart, and I had begun to despair, believing my life would be more or less a failure, when he came into it, giving me the opportunity for which I had been longing.[52]

Even such an emotionally intense farewell did not leave House entirely satisfied. Back in New York, he wrote Wilson: "My! How I hated

to leave you last night. Around you is centered most of the interest I have left in life and my greatest joy is to serve you. Your words of affection at parting touched me so deeply that I could not tell you then, and perhaps never can tell you, just how I feel."

As if this letter was not enough, the day before his departure for England on the *Lusitania* on January 30, House wrote Wilson a final farewell: "Goodbye, dear friend, and may God sustain you in all your noble undertakings. When I think of the things you have done, of the things you have in mind to do, my heart stirs with pride and satisfaction. You are the bravest, wisest leader, the gentlest and most gallant gentleman and the truest friend in all the world."[53]

House's first official trip to Europe in 1913 had lasted eight weeks; his second, in 1914, had lasted ten; his third, in 1915, lasted nineteen. As his absorption in the European war deepened, so too did the length of his stays there. Initially House had planned to leave London for Berlin on February 15, only nine days after his arrival in England, but Grey convinced him to prolong his stay. Despite Wilson's warning that he should not "go too far in allowing the English Government to determine when it is best to go to Germany," House identified with the Allied cause so strongly that he did not leave for Paris until March 11 and for Berlin until March 17. After nine days in Berlin, he returned to France and eventually to England on April 28. In London he rented a small house, obviously planning to stay for some time.[54]

House's conversations with prominent Europeans gave him vivid, detailed impressions of virtually every phase of the war, and he wrote Wilson long letters filled with valuable information. Wilson appreciated House's efforts, writing on April 19 that "your letters, added to your cables, make me independent of rumours and irresponsible informants in general, and constantly serve to steady my thinking and clarify it, too. They are an incalculable help, even though the situation alters as they cross the ocean." Wilson accepted House's judgment that the belligerents were not ready for peace negotiations and were instead "settling down for a long war," one that might "last through another winter." On May 25 House informed Wilson that he would return home in early August, possibly only for a short time, in order "to go over the situation in person"; five days later he was convinced that the crisis between the United States and Germany, stemming from the sinking of the *Lusitania* on May 7, made war inevitable and that he ought to return sooner. Wilson was content to let House set the date of his departure.[55]

On June 13 House arrived in New York and immediately went to his son-in-law's summer house in Roslyn, Long Island, where he lingered for nearly two weeks before heading for the North Shore. During his long absence, the German submarine decree, the sinking of

the *Lusitania*, and Wilson's stern response had led to Bryan's resignation and had brought the United States and Germany to the brink of war. Wilson was eager to talk to House and urged him to travel to Washington, but House refused because of the heat. He also preferred to consult with McAdoo, Attorney General Thomas W. Gregory, and other friends, so that he would be fully prepared when he finally met with the President.[56]

On June 24 Wilson took the initiative, stopping by Roslyn on his way to Cornish. The President, House recorded, "greeted me with warmth and affection, placing both hands over mine," and during a three-hour conversation the two friends covered a wide range of public and personal matters. House reported at length on his European journey, assuring Wilson that he had laid the groundwork for future peace efforts and that the leaders of the belligerent governments would let him know when it was best to return. Wilson, House noted, "seemed delighted with the work done," and continued to give House extraordinary leeway, telling him that he should go back "whenever you consider the time propitious." The two friends also discussed Robert Lansing as Bryan's successor as Secretary of State, but most of all Wilson wanted House's opinion on an "intimate personal matter."[57]

In March 1915 Wilson had met Edith Bolling Galt. The relationship developed rapidly, and in early May Wilson had proposed marriage. Deeply in love and impatient to remarry, Wilson wanted House's advice. "What would you think," the President asked his trusted adviser, "of my getting married again? Since you left I have met a delightful woman and I am thinking of asking her to marry me [Wilson did not reveal that he had already done so.] Do you believe I would lessen my influence with the American people by taking such a step? And when do you think I could do it?"[58]

Both Grayson and Gregory had already told House of Wilson's love for Edith Galt, so he was not caught unprepared and quickly approved the marriage. As House explained in his diary, "I feel that his health demands it and I also feel that Woodrow Wilson today is the greatest asset the world has. If he should die or become incapacitated, it is doubtful whether a right solution of the problems involved in this terrible conflict and its aftermath would be possible." Throughout his life House had been preoccupied with death and afflicted by the premature deaths of those he loved; now he worried that Wilson, too, might leave him too soon. Telling his friend "how much depended on him and how anxious I was that he might maintain his health and strength," House asked the President how he thought Vice President Thomas R. Marshall would hold down the presidency in the event of his death. Wilson's response was quick and pointed: "'The situation would hold him down and sit on his neck.'"[59]

During the remainder of the summer of 1915 the two men corresponded intensively, trying to sort through the diplomatic thicket
brought by the sinking of the *Lusitania*, by the growing irritation over
British maritime practices, and by the sinking of still another British
passenger liner on which American lives had been lost, the *Arabic*, on
August 19. House sought to protect America's relationship with the
Allies and to respond firmly to Germany's provocations; in the end he
approved of the notes the President sent. Even so, he complained,
claiming that "The trouble with the President is that he does not move
at time with sufficient celerity. . . . I am afraid that the President's
characterization of himself as 'a man with a one track mind' is all too
true, for he does not seem able to carry along more than one idea at a
time. I say this regretfully because I have the profoundest admiration
for his judgment, his ability, and his patriotism. The thing I regret
most is that with me each summer is so much time lost. From the first
of May until the first of October I see him practically not at all, and I
find that I cannot stir him to action unless I am with him in person
and undertake the prosecution largely myself." [60]

Long frustrated by Wilson's deliberateness, House now had to contend with a love-sick President and worry about the political implications of an early remarriage. According to Grayson, House wrote, the
President "is wholly absorbed in this love affair and is neglecting practically everything else. Grayson says the President is using my approval as an excuse." "I am sorry," House concluded, "the President
has fallen in love at this time, for he will be criticized for not waiting
longer after Mrs. Wilson's death." [61]

As the summer drew to a close, Wilson eagerly anticipated another
meeting with House, carefully following his migration from the North
Shore to Roslyn, hoping that the heat would lift so that House could
venture as far south as Washington. "It's jolly," Wilson wrote on September 7, "that you are making your way in this direction. I am very
eager to see you." House replied that he was "daily hoping for a
change in weather so I may go to you," while Wilson wished "with all
my heart that this heat would pass." At last, on September 22, the
weather turned cool, and House telegraphed Wilson that he was leaving for Washington that very day. Once again, the ever-faithful Grayson prepared House for the trip, describing "both the President and
McAdoo as terribly upset because of their personal affairs." "The
President," House learned, "is anxious to have his engagement announced and is waiting for me to come in order to discuss it with me.
Grayson says it is clearly up to me to decide this question." [62]

Members of the cabinet, along with some other prominent Democrats in Washington, feared that the President's remarriage prior to
November 1916 might bring a Democratic defeat. Only McAdoo,

however, was impetuous enough to approach the President. On September 18, four days before House arrived in Washington, McAdoo told Wilson, in an attempt to get him to discuss his remarriage, that he had received an anonymous letter from Los Angeles informing him that Mary Allen Hulbert (with whom Wilson had had an affair prior to his presidency) was publicizing his letters. Wilson did not respond to McAdoo's bait, but was terribly upset by the revelation of Mrs. Hulbert's apparent disloyalty and by its political implications. His first move was to go to Edith Galt, revealing his relationship and asking for her forgiveness. His next was to await the arrival of House.[63]

On September 22, when House arrived in Washington, he first saw McAdoo, who was "terribly concerned about the President's private affairs" and told him what he had done. Prior to dinner at the White House, Wilson and House discussed diplomatic affairs, but after dinner they retreated to Wilson's study, where "the President at once took up his most intimate personal affairs. I could see he did it with reluctance, but with a determination to have it over." Wilson told House the story of his relationship with Mrs. Hulbert. According to the President, "there had never been anything between them excepting a platonic friendship, though afterward he had been indiscreet in writing her letters rather more warmly than was prudent." Wilson informed House that he had also told Edith Galt, and "he expressed the desire, if any trouble were to come to him because of this indiscretion, he would like it to come now, and he would not, in any circumstances, allow anyone to blackmail him." House was impressed with his friend's "honesty and splendid courage." Knowing that an anonymous letter did not really exist, House advised Wilson "not to worry about it, for I was sure she was not showing his letters or attempting in any way to blackmail him." House was convinced that "no trouble was brewing," that McAdoo was "entirely wrong," and that his behavior was "cruel." House had managed both to reassure the President and to protect McAdoo.

The two friends then went on to discuss the President's remarriage, the timing of the announcement, and other details concerning the wedding. "The decision," House recorded, "was placed squarely up to me and upon my shoulders the responsibility was set. . . . We tentatively agreed upon the middle of October for the announcement and for the wedding to follow before the turn of the year."

House then sought to justify his advice. "I wish to explain here," he wrote for posterity,

> while I am upon this extremely delicate subject that I believe the President's affection for Mrs. Wilson has not lessened. I have never seen a man

more dependent upon a woman's companionship. He was perfectly happy and contented with his wife. They had an ideal married life, as all her relatives will readily testify and have, indeed, to me. But his loneliness since her death has oppressed him, and if he does not marry, and marry quickly, I believe he will go into decline. Dr. Grayson shares this belief. None of his family are with him, and his loneliness is pathetic. With the weight of the burdens upon him, it seems but a small concession which public opinion might make in behalf of this man not to criticize him too much for doing what one in a humbler station of life would be able to do without comment.

House had dealt with Wilson's personal crisis with compassion and sensitivity.[64]

On September 23 House met Edith Galt at lunch, claiming in his diary that "she and I became friends immediately." Each sought to charm the other. The President, Edith told House, "spoke of me with affection and said that 'his mind is so lucid that when I bring matters to him, it is like a clearing house. Things were assorted, placed in their proper niches and the situation cleared of its complexities.'" "She seems," he observed, "delightful and full of humor, and it makes me happy to think the President will have her to cheer him in his loneliness." And House sought to captivate her with a vision of Wilson's future greatness. "I thought," he confided, "if our plans carried true, the President would easily outrank any American that had yet lived; that the war was the greatest event in human history excepting the birth of Christ, therefore, if the President were able to play the part I hoped for, I was in favor of his retiring at the end of the present term."[65]

Initially House did not realize that the President's second wife was a much different person than his first. Ellen Wilson was a woman of learning and artistic talent, one with a keen insight into her husband's emotional needs and a wise tolerance of his political associates. She had welcomed House into her family, seeking his advice on both personal and political matters and thanking him, on one occasion, for "'being so good to us all.'"[66] Edith Galt was lively and attractive, but poorly educated and intolerant of some of the President's closest advisers. Wilson had imprudently drawn her into his work, showing her House's letters and many important state papers and encouraging her to believe that her judgment was as good as that of his experienced advisers. Excited by her collaboration with the President, she counted on receiving a "big envelope" nearly every day full of secrets of state.[67]

Well before Edith and House met, Wilson sought to encourage a friendship between them. Writing to her on August 13, Wilson quoted

Grayson as observing "'that probably no man ever had in a life-time more than one such friend as Col. House, if he were fortunate enough to have one,' and so, when we fell to speaking of you, I said that you were another such friend as Col. House, and he agreed very heartily. . . . I feel about your character and the disinterested loyalty of your friendship just as I have so often told you I felt about House." Despite Wilson's efforts, Edith was not inclined to share her love for him with another person and was skeptical of House's value. "I hope if Col. House comes to Washington," she observed, ". . . I will see him. I know I am wrong but I can't help feeling he is not a very *strong* character. I suppose it is in comparison to you, for really every other man seems like a dwarf when I put them by you in in [*sic*] my thoughts. I know what a comfort and staff Col. House is to you Precious One and that your judgment about him is correct, but he does look like a weak vessel and I think he writes like one very often." [68]

Wilson responded with the fullest assessment of House that he ever wrote. "And, then," he replied,

> dear House. About him . . . you are no doubt partly right. You have too keen an insight and too discerning a judgment to be wholly wrong, even in a snap judgment of a man you do not know! House *has* a strong character – if to be disinterested and unafraid and incorruptible is to be strong. He has a noble and lovely character, too, for he is capable of utter self-forgetfulness and loyalty and devotion. And he is wise. He can give prudent and far-seeing counsel. He can find out what many men, of diverse kinds, are thinking about, and how they can be made to work together for a common purpose. He wins the confidence of all sorts of men, and wins it at once – by deserving it. But you are right in thinking that intellectually he is not a great man. His mind is not of the first class. He is a counsellor, not a statesman. And he has the faults of his qualities. His very devotion to me, his ardent desire that I should play the part in the field of international politics that he has desired and foreseen for me, makes him take sometimes the short and personal view when he ought to be taking the big and impersonal one – thinking, not of my reputation for the day, but of what is fundamentally and eternally right, no matter who is for the time being hurt by it. We cannot require of every man that he should be everything. You are going to love House some day, – if only because he loves me and would give, I believe, his life for me, – and because he loves the country and seeks its real benefit and glory. I'm not afraid of the ultimate impression he will make on you, because I know you and your instinctive love and admiration for whatever is true and genuine. You must remember, dear little critic, that sweetness and *power* do not often happen together. You are apt to exact too much of others because of what you are yourself and mistakenly suppose it easy and common to be. [69]

Confronted with Wilson's remarkable analysis of House's strengths and weaknesses, Edith relented slightly. "I am almost sorry," she quickly replied, "I wrote you what I did yesterday about Col. House, but I can no more keep things from you than I can stop loving you – and so you must forgive me. I know he is fine and true, but I don't think him vigorous and strong – am I wrong?" A wiser person would not have questioned Wilson's judgment of those who, like House, had served him for years.[70]

House was pleased with the results of his visit, writing his wife Loulie after his return to New York that "I had a wonderful time in Washington. The President has never shown so much confidence and affection." "You can never know," he wrote, "what a happy time I had in Washington. I feel that life will soon have a more splendid outlook for you and that your days of loneliness will be something of the past. I wish I could tell you too of my deep affection and of my appreciation of your confidence and friendship."[71]

Wilson, too, was pleased with House's visit, for their conversation had cleared away the last obstacle to an early marriage. On the morning of September 23, Wilson wrote Edith that "I had a *fine* talk with House last night, which cleared things wonderfully. . . . He is really a wonderful counsellor. His mind is like an excellent clearing house through which to put one's ideas and get the right credits and balances. I am sure that the first real conversation you have with him, about something definite and of the stuff of judgment, you will lose entirely your impression that he lacks strength. It is quiet, serene strength, but it is great and real. I am impatient to have you know him. . . ." After her first conversation with House, Edith seemed to soften her earlier judgment of him. "I did have," she wrote Wilson, "such a nice talk with Col. House, and he is just as nice and fine as you pictured him, and his admiration for you is sufficient to establish my faith in his judgment and intelligent perceptions."[72]

Wilson was relieved that two people he loved so much had finally met and become friends. More eager than ever to bring them together, he wrote Edith that

it was a joy to see House afterwards and talk to him about you. I never saw him so enthusiastic about anything as he was about you. He said he had not words in which to express his admiration for you, – that the sum of the matter was that you were a wonderful and delightful person and that it seemed to him that it was the best and most fortunate thing that could have happened, for me or for the country, that I had won such a partner and comrade and helper. I wish I could give you some impression of the way in which his face glowed when he spoke of you. . . . I love

him more than ever – the true, loyal friend – because he has become, from the moment of seeing and knowing you, as much your friend and partisan as mine. I hope you liked and admired and trusted him a tithe as much as he did you![73]

Despite Wilson's somewhat strained efforts, it seemed that the friendship of Edith Galt and House was off to a good start. After receiving a copy of Wordsworth's poems from House, Edith wrote: "I can't resist sending just a line to tell you how happy your friendship has made me. . . ." House quickly replied: "May I tell you here how happy I am that you have come into the life of my friend. I thank you in my heart every time I look into his dear face and see what you have brought there. It means much to him and even more to humanity. Because of you he will be eager and better fitted to do the big work before him, and when the final story of his life is told your part in it will be a noble one."[74]

On October 6 Wilson and Edith Galt announced their engagement; two days later they arrived in New York for their first visit with House and his wife. Dropping Edith off at the St. Regis Hotel, Wilson and House drove on to his apartment. Before the two men dressed for dinner, House, who was eager to undertake another mission to Europe, briefly explained to the President the mediation scheme that was eventually to result in the House-Grey memorandum. Given the precariousness of American neutrality, House advised that "we should do something decisive now – something that would either end the war in a way to abolish militarism or that would bring us in with the Allies to help them do it." He then went on to outline his plan for an Allied-approved American demand that the war should end. "The Allies," he went on, "after some hesitation, could accept our offer or demand, and if the Central Powers accepted, we would then have accomplished a master stroke in diplomacy. If the Central Powers refused to acquiesce, we could then push our insistence to a point where diplomatic relations would first be broken off, and later the whole force of our Government, and perhaps the force of every neutral, might be brought against them." "The President," House observed, "was startled by this plan. He seemed to acquiesce by silence." House was so absorbed in this complex diplomatic initiative that he raised it with Wilson while the latter was in New York on a vacation; he would have to wait to determine Wilson's more considered reaction.[75]

Only four days after Wilson left New York, House was in Washington, explaining his plan for American intervention to Secretary of State Lansing and talking about it further with the President, who agreed with House's views and left only the question open "as to when

and how it should be done." "I now have the matter," House recorded with satisfaction, "in my own hands, and it will probably be left to my judgment as to when and how to act."[76] Returning to New York, House composed a letter to Grey that would prepare the way for another mission to Europe. Wilson made only a few changes, noting that "I do not want to make it inevitable quite that we should take part to force terms on Germany, because the exact circumstances of such a crisis are impossible to determine."[77]

As House pondered the complexities of the European war, he concluded on November 17 that "it is all very clear in my mind now what this country should do. The question is can the President do it unmolested." More than ever before, House's hopes rested on Wilson's leadership. He was increasingly critical, however, of Wilson's alleged inattention to both small details and large policies. "The reports from Washington that I am getting," he noted on November 22, "tell of a curious inertia everywhere. It is largely due, of course, to the President. He is so engrossed with his fiancee that he is neglecting business. I would go to Washington, but I know I would not be very welcome at this time, particularly, if I attempted to stir him to action." Once again House noted the President's tendency to dodge trouble and his "intense prejudices against people." "He likes a few," House continued, "and is very loyal to them, but his prejudices are many and often unjust."[78]

Despite a discouraging reply from Grey, House sought to reassure British leaders through informal channels of America's determination to see the Allies through to victory and to convince them that his mediation scheme deserved serious discussion. On December 15 House arrived in Washington, convinced that the nation was drifting into war and that the time had come for decisive measures. House was, however, disappointed with Wilson's view of the war. "I found the President," he recorded, "not quite as belligerent as he was the last time we were together. He seemed to think we would be able to keep out of the war. . . . I cannot quite get him up to the point where he is willing to take action. By action, I mean not to declare war, but to let the Allies know we are definitely on their side and that it is not our intention to permit Germany to win if the strength of this country can prevent [it]. The last time we talked he was quite ready to take this stand, but he has visibly weakened."[79]

Given the gap between his views and those of the President, House was now inclined to delay his mission. Both House and Lansing agreed that it would be better to wait, since the diplomatic impasse with Germany might draw the United States into the war and make American disputes with the Allies irrelevant. "But I do not," House

explained, "like to present my thoughts upon this subject strongly to the President for fear he may think I do not wish to go. As a matter of fact, it is the breaking up of our plans for the winter. Loulie is not well and I dread the trip at this time. I do not feel able to leave our apartment without renting it, and that in itself, involves no end of annoyance." Although House dismissed such considerations as trivial, the fact remained that he preferred to delay a trip abroad. Wilson, however, wanted House to go immediately, reasoning that he could give the British government a much better sense of America's position, especially over Allied violations of American neutral rights.[80]

Once in Washington, House could not escape family gossip and details of the impending wedding. For half an hour Grayson plied him with "family and household matters." "I seem to be the receptacle," House complained, "for everything and everybody when I am in Washington. It is tiresome, though in a way, gratifying." Wilson showed him presents that had come for Edith, and Wilson and House visited her for half an hour of "intimate personal conversation." "She expressed regret," House noted cryptically, "that we were going to Europe and also that I was not to be at the wedding. She said it did not seem right, but I made it clear that it would be an impossibility on account of the hurt feelings it would engender."[81]

House's statement to Wilson and Edith on December 15, only three days before their wedding on December 18, that he would be unable to attend is puzzling. He was not leaving for Europe until December 28; his explanation that his attendance was impossible because "of the hurt feelings it would engender" is unconvincing. The wedding was, to be sure, a small one, including only thirty-eight relatives and close friends, but House had a unique relationship with Wilson and had been instrumental in clearing away the obstacles to an early marriage. Apparently he could not overcome his growing resentment over Wilson's transference of affection to Edith and over the extent to which she was changing his relationship with the President. On November 4 House had learned from Edith that she was reading portions of his correspondence with the President; later in the month he recorded a desire to go to Washington, but added that "I know I would not be very welcome at this time." Realizing that Edith had now become a part of the inner circle of advisers around the President, in late November House sought to guide her, advising that she ignore the importunities of the President's friends and that she "let [sic] the President alone to think out his problems in the future as he has done in the past."[82]

Whatever House's apprehensions, his refusal to attend the wedding revealed a curious lack of self-control, for he disappointed both Edith

and Wilson. It is hardly surprising that, when House left Washington late on the evening of December 15, Wilson's good-bye must have been so perfunctory that he did not bother to record it. Less than a year earlier, when Wilson and House had parted before his journey to Europe, the good-bye of the two men had been long and effusive. This time Wilson telegraphed that "our loving thoughts will follow you across the sea and in all your generous labors on the other side the good wishes that go with you from us are too many and too deep to express." Wilson's terse farewell was a harbinger of a lessening of the intimacy between the two men.[83]

During the period between Wilson's election to the presidency and the end of 1915, House had, by and large, served his friend well. He had played a major, constructive role in the selection of Wilson's cabinet, and had served as an intelligent and versatile high-level intermediary, sifting through people and issues and helping to rally various constituencies behind the President's legislative program. With the outbreak of war in Europe, House had been the first member of the administration to inform himself about the complexities of the struggle and to grapple seriously with the dangers and opportunities that the war poised for the United States. And throughout these years he had devoted himself to maintaining Wilson's physical and emotional health.

House faltered in part because he had underestimated the tasks that he had undertaken. By the close of 1912, when he finally became engaged with Wilson's new administration, he had been away from the strife of Texas politics for many years and was blandly optimistic about his emerging role as Wilson's unofficial, confidential adviser. On January 24, 1913, House confided to Mezes that "I understand the jealousies that would be engendered ordinarily in Washington, towards one occupying such a position as I have in mind, but I think I shall try it out. In the first place a great many of the members of the Cabinet will be my warm personal friends and it is my belief that I can aid them in many ways and push their political fortunes to such as extent, that they will be glad to co-operate with me."[84] It was a pleasant, painless vision, but House should have anticipated the clashes of personality and ambition that would inevitably break out within the President's inner circle of advisers. As these developed, House got caught in a cycle of intrigue and deception, occasionally with the encouragement of Wilson himself, from which there was no escape.

Nor did House anticipate the differences between his role as a confidential adviser to Texas politicians and to the President. In Texas, House either conferred with his political allies and protégés in his Austin home or returned to his home at the end of a day in the gov-

ernor's office. With Wilson's election, however, he found himself tied to a political leader of intellectual brilliance and emotional intensity. House wisely maintained his distance from Washington, but during his visits there, and during Wilson's visits to New York, he found himself subjected to the idiosyncracies and rigidities of Wilson's daily routines. And coping with the President's emotional outpourings, knowing what to say and when to say it, was a far more complex task than House had ever encountered before. He thrived on the power that he had acquired, but also found more than a day or two of the President's companionship oppressive.

In Texas, House had cared little about the issues, content to advance the interests of his faction within the Democratic party. Prior to Wilson's election in 1912, however, House had become a progressive, and had proposed in *Philip Dru: Administrator* radical solutions to the nation's domestic problems. Wilson's progressivism appealed deeply to House, who was eager to collaborate with the President in implementing his reform program. Wilson's legislative success, and the outbreak of war in Europe, allowed House to shift his energies to international affairs. As he did so, he gradually realized that he and the President differed substantially over America's relationship to the European war. By the close of 1915, House was beginning to confront the question of loyalty, of the extent to which he would pursue his own views on America's relationship to the war or subordinate them to those of the President. Had the President been less convinced of the mystical union of feeling and thought with his friend, he might have been more careful in analyzing differences and in delegating authority, and might early on have realized some of House's weaknesses as a negotiator. By giving him so much authority, Wilson nourished House's fantasies of international glory and made it more likely that House would misrepresent him and misperceive the realities of the European struggle. If House eventually became a "dangerous man to have close to any president," Wilson must share a part of the blame.[85]

The remarkable intimacy that the two men established resulted from a unique combination of circumstances. These were bound to change. The completion of Wilson's reform agenda, the growing involvement of the United States in the conflict in Europe, and Wilson's marriage to Edith Galt, brought a shift in House's role, serious differences with the President over foreign policy, and a loosening of the emotional ties between the two men. They would remain dependent on one another, but the extraordinary closeness of these years would gradually fade away.

Notes

[1] Inga Floto, *Colonel House in Paris: A Study of American Policy at the Paris Peace Conference 1919* (Princeton, 1980). Floto provides an excellent analysis of the literature on House in her Introduction, while Arthur S. Link's Foreword sums up the controversy still surrounding him; Edwin A. Weinstein, *Woodrow Wilson: A Medical and Psychological Biography* (Princeton, 1981), pp. 265–78; John Milton Cooper, Jr., *The Warrior and the Priest: Woodrow Wilson and Theodore Roosevelt* (Cambridge, Mass., 1983), pp. 240–45, 291–96. On p. 398, Cooper shrewdly assesses House's diary. The first draft of this essay was written in the summer of 1988, when I was a Guest Scholar at the Woodrow Wilson International Center for Scholars. I am grateful to the Wilson Center and its staff for providing such a stimulating environment for my work.

[2] Neu, "In Search of Colonel Edward M. House: The Texas Years, 1858–1912," *Southwestern Historical Quarterly*, 93 (July 1989), 20–23; Lewis L. Gould, *Progressives and Prohibitionists: Texas Democrats in the Wilson Era* (Austin, 1973), pp. 71–84, 97–102.

[3] Cooper, *Warrior and the Priest*, pp. 241–44.

[4] *Ibid.*, pp. 244–45.

[5] *Ibid.*, p. 243.

[6] Weinstein, *Wilson*, pp. 107–244; Bert Edward Park, *The Impact of Illness on World Leaders* (Philadelphia, 1986), pp. 3–7, 331–42; Edwin A. Weinstein, James William Anderson, Arthur S. Link, "Woodrow Wilson's Political Personality: A Reappraisal," *Political Science Quarterly*, 93 (Winter 1978), 585–98.

[7] Weinstein, *Wilson*, pp. 79–81, 111–116; Dorothy Ross, "Review Essay: Woodrow Wilson and the Case for Psychohistory," *The Journal of American History*, 69 (Dec. 1982), 659–68.

[8] Cooper, *Warrior and the Priest*, pp. 241–43.

[9] *Ibid.*, pp. 243–45; Weinstein, *Wilson*, pp. 265–78.

[10] House Diary, Feb. 28, March 25, April 1, 1913, House Papers, Yale University Library.

[11] *Philip Dru: Administrator, A Story of Tomorrow, 1920–1935,* (N.Y., 1912), pp. 8–9, 42, 44–45, 155–57.

[12] House Diary, Jan. 17, 1913, House Papers.

[13] House Diary, Jan. 22, Feb. 13, 26, 1913, House Papers.

[14] Ernest Samuels, *Henry Adams: The Major Phase* (Cambridge, Mass., 1964), pp. 22, 63, 86–90; House Diary, April 1, 1913, House Papers.

[15] House Diary, Dec. 15, 1912, Jan. 1–5, March 20, April 15, 1913, House Papers.

[16] House to Wilson, April 23, 1913, to Mezes, May 8, mid-May, 1913, House Papers.

[17] House Diary, May 11, 1913, House Papers.

[18] Wilson to House, May 17, 1913, House to Wilson, May 20, 1913, Wilson to House, May 20, 1913, House Papers.

[19] House Diary, May 9, July 3, 1913, House Papers.

[20] Arthur S. Link, *Wilson: The New Freedom* (Princeton, 1956), pp. 72–73, 177–227; Frances Wright Saunders, *Ellen Axson Wilson: First Lady Between Two*

Worlds (Chapel Hill, N.C., 1985), pp. 248–60; Hugh C. Wallace to House, July 10, 1913, House Papers.

[21] House Diary, Oct. 14, 16, Nov. 12, 13, 29, Dec. 12, 1913, House Papers.

[22] House Diary, Oct. 16, Dec. 22, 1913, House Papers.

[23] John J. Broesamle, *William Gibbs McAdoo: A Passion For Change, 1863–1917* (Port Washington, N.Y., 1973), pp. 34, 76–77; House Diary, Dec. 11, 19, 21, 23, 1912, House Papers.

[24] House Diary, Dec. 15, 18, 1912, Jan. 15, March 7, 1913, House Papers; John M. Blum, *Joe Tumulty and the Wilson Era* (Boston, 1951), pp. 51–52.

[25] House Diary, July 20, Sept. 26, Nov. 29, 30, Dec. 18, 19, 20, 1913, House Papers.

[26] House Diary, Dec. 11, 12, 1913, Jan. 22, April 15, May 7, 11, 1914, House Papers; Hugh C. Wallace to House, Feb. 17, 1914, House Papers; Blum, *Tumulty*, pp. 115–22.

[27] Wilson to House, Jan. 9, 28, 1914, House to Wilson, Jan. 29, 1914, House Papers.

[28] House Diary, March 24, 25, 1914, House Papers.

[29] *Ibid.*, March 25, 1914.

[30] *Ibid.*, April 15, 17, 1914.

[31] *Ibid.*, Dec. 2, 12, 1913, April 9, 18, 28, May 11, 1914; House to McAdoo, May 12, 1914, House Papers.

[32] Link, *Wilson: The New Freedom*, pp. 314–18; House to Wilson, May 28, June 3, 1914, House Papers. In the letter-press copy House used the word "militarism," but changed it to "jingoism" in the original that he sent to the President. Link, *Wilson: The New Freedom*, p. 315. House Diary, May 26, 27, June 1, 21, 1914, House Papers.

[33] House Diary, June 27, 1914, House Papers.

[34] *Ibid.*, May 26, July 2, 19, 1914; House to Wilson, July 1, 1914, Wilson to House, June 16, 1914, House Papers.

[35] House Diary, Aug. 6, 1914, House Papers; House to Wilson, Aug. 7, to Grayson, Aug. 12, 1914, House Papers.

[36] House Diary, Aug. 30, 1914, House Papers.

[37] Link, *Wilson: The Struggle for Neutrality, 1914–1915* (Princeton, 1960), pp. 200–06; House Diary, Sept. 5, 9, 14, 18, 20, 26, Oct. 3, 1914, House Papers.

[38] House Diary, Sept. 28, 1914, House Papers.

[39] *Ibid.*, Sept. 26, 28, 1914.

[40] Broesamle, *McAdoo*, pp. 114, 120–24, 138–42; Link, *Wilson: The New Freedom*, pp. 114–16; House Diary, Sept. 30, Oct. 20, 27, 1914, House Papers.

[41] House Diary, Oct. 29, 30, Nov. 2, 4, 6, 7, 8, 1914, House Papers.

[42] *Ibid.*, Sept. 28, Nov. 6, 7, 8, 14, 1914.

[43] *Ibid.*, Nov. 14, 1914.

[44] *Ibid.*, Nov. 25, Dec. 3, 1914; House to Wilson, Nov. 30, 1914, House Papers; Link, *Wilson: The New Freedom*, pp. 324–25.

[45] House Diary, Dec. 3, 1914, House Papers.

[46] Link, *Wilson: The Struggle For Neutrality*, pp. 207–17; House Diary, Dec. 14, 16–20, 1914, House Papers.

[47] Wilson to House, Dec. 25, 1914, House Papers.

[48] House to Denton, Dec. 17, 18, 1914, House Papers.

[49] House to Wilson, Jan. 5, 1914, House Papers; House Diary, Jan. 4, 25, 1914, House Papers.

[50] Neu, "In Search of Colonel Edward M. House," 41–42; House Diary, Jan. 13, 1915, House Papers.

[51] House Diary, Jan. 24, 1915, House Papers.

[52] *Ibid.*, Jan. 25. 1915.

[53] House to Wilson, Jan. 26, 29, 1915, House Papers.

[54] House Diary, Jan. 30, Feb. 13, 17, House Papers; Wilson to House, Feb. 20, 1915, House to Wilson, Feb. 18, 21, 1915, to Mezes, March 1, 1915, House Papers; House Diary, April 29, 1915, House to Gordon Auchincloss, April 30, 1915, House Papers.

[55] Link, *Wilson: The Struggle For Neutrality*, pp. 217–31; Wilson to House, April 19, 1915, House to Wilson, May 25, 1915, House Papers; House Diary, May 30, 1915, Wilson to House, June 1, 1915, House to Gordon Auchincloss, June 1, 1915, House Papers.

[56] House Diary, June 16, 19, 20, 1915, House Papers.

[57] *Ibid.*, June 24, 1915.

[58] Tom Shachtman, *Edith & Woodrow: A Presidential Romance* (N.Y., 1981), pp. 73–99; House Diary, June 24, 1915, House Papers.

[59] House Diary, June 24, 1915, House Papers; House engaged in a life-long quest to overcome his fear of death. His beloved brother Jimmie had died when he was nine, his mother when he was twelve, and his father when he was twenty-one. Of the eight House children, only four survived beyond 1900. Throughout his childhood and youth death and violence were always close at hand, and in the early years of this century House was unsettled by the death of family and friends. In 1902 his brother-in-law, Clarence Hunter, died, "at a time," House recalled "[when] I needed him most." In 1904 Joe Lee Jameson, "my political right hand," died, and his brother John's wife followed him. In February 1905 John H. B. House, one of the heroes of his youth, died at the age of fifty-six. Of House's five brothers only the eldest, T. W., Jr., still lived. In March 1906 former governor James Stephen Hogg, House's political mentor, died from injuries sustained in a train collision. Neu, "In Search of Colonel Edward M. House," 40–41.

[60] Link, *Wilson: The Struggle For Neutrality*, pp. 438–55, 551–87; House Diary, July 10, 1915, House Papers.

[61] House Diary, July 31, 1915, House Papers.

[62] Wilson to House, Sept. 7, 1915, House to Wilson, Sept. 13, 22, 1915, House Papers; Grayson to House, Sept. 10, 1915, House Papers; House Diary, Sept. 22, 1915, House Papers.

[63] Link, *Wilson: Confusions and Crises, 1915–1916* (Princeton, 1964), pp. 3–7; In *My Memoir* (Indianapolis, 1939), pp. 75–78, Edith Bolling Wilson claims that House later admitted collaborating with McAdoo. Link dismisses Mrs. Wilson's account (*Wilson: Confusions And Crises*, 5), while Weinstein (*Wilson*, 290) suggests that House may have been involved in McAdoo's scheme. It is inconceivable that House encouraged McAdoo's clumsy approach to the President. Prior to his arrival in Washington on September 22, he had not seen

McAdoo since August 10. Moreover, he believed Wilson's early remarriage was essential to his physical and emotional well-being. Shachtman, *Edith & Woodrow,* pp. 108–16, gives a full account of this curious episode.

[64] House Diary, Sept. 22, 1915, House Papers.

[65] *Ibid.,* Sept. 23, 24, 1915.

[66] Saunders, *Ellen Axson Wilson,* p. 246; House Diary, Jan. 22, 1914, House Papers.

[67] Weinstein, *Wilson,* pp. 279–89; Wilson to Edith Bolling Galt, Aug. 13, 1915, Edith Bolling Galt to Wilson, Aug. 13, 1915, *The Papers of Woodrow Wilson* (Princeton, 1980), XXXIV, 190–95.

[68] Wilson to Edith Bolling Galt, Aug. 13, 1915, Edith Bolling Galt to Wilson, Aug. 26, 1915, *PWW,* XXXIV, 190, 338.

[69] Wilson to Edith Bolling Galt, Aug. 28, 1915, *PWW,* XXXIV, 352–53.

[70] Edith Bolling Galt to Wilson, Aug. 25, 1915, *PWW,* XXXIV, 356.

[71] House to Loulie House, Sept. 26, 1915, to Wilson, Sept. 26, 1915, House Papers.

[72] Wilson to Edith Bolling Galt, Sept. 23, 1915, Edith Bolling Galt to Wilson, Sept. 24, 1915, *PWW,* XXXIV, 510, 518.

[73] Wilson to Edith Bolling Galt, Sept. 25, 1915, *PWW,* XXXIV, 519–20.

[74] Edith Bolling Galt to House, Oct. 12, 1915, House to Edith Bolling Galt, Oct. 13, 1915, House Papers.

[75] House Diary, Oct. 8, 1915, House Papers.

[76] Link, *Wilson: Confusions and Crisis,* pp. 101–05; House Diary, Oct. 13, 14, 1915, House Papers.

[77] House to Wilson, enclosing draft of letter to Grey, Oct. 17, 1915, Wilson to House, Oct. 18, 1915, House Papers.

[78] House Diary, Nov. 17, 22, 1915, House Papers.

[79] Link, *Confusions And Crises,* pp. 105–14; House Diary, Nov. 25, 28, Dec. 8, 15, 1915, House Papers.

[80] House Diary, Dec. 15, 1915, House Papers.

[81] *Ibid.,* Dec. 15, 1915.

[82] *New York Times,* Dec. 19, 1915. McAdoo was the only cabinet member present, but he was, of course, the President's son-in-law. Grayson and Tumulty also attended; Shachtman, *Edith & Woodrow,* pp. 122–24; House Diary, November 4, 5, 22, 30, House Papers.

[83] Wilson to House, Dec. 27, 1915, House Papers.

[84] House to Mezes, Jan. 24, 1913, House Papers.

[85] Cooper, *The Warrior and the Priest,* p. 245.

PART V
THE WILSONIAN LEGACY

Dewey W. Grantham

THE PAPERS OF WOODROW WILSON
A PRELIMINARY APPRAISAL

In a recent essay on the work of documentary editors in the United States, an official of the National Historical Publications and Records Commission observed that "the Woodrow Wilson project is always mentioned as a positive example."[1] Indeed, *The Papers of Woodrow Wilson* may well be the best edited, the most successful, and the most critically acclaimed of all the American documentary series that took shape in the years after World War II. Reviewers have described the Wilson *Papers* as a model of historical editing and a "superb documentary history." Surely, one scholar asserts, "no series could have been edited with more care and thoroughness than [Arthur S.] Link and his colleagues have displayed over the years."[2] A leading diplomatic historian thinks that the editors are creating "a treasure trove that scholars will be mining for generations."[3] A Canadian historian concludes that *The Papers* "mark a major achievement and stand as a monument to both the career of President Wilson and the devoted scholarship of Arthur Link."[4] As the series nears completion,[5] it may be appropriate to undertake a tentative assessment of the project as a whole.

The success of the Wilson *Papers* can be explained, in the opinion of close observers, by a combination of favorable circumstances: the generous support of the Woodrow Wilson Foundation, Princeton University, and other foundations; a distinguished editorial advisory committee; an able, disciplined, and stable group of editors; and, in the words of Robert H. Ferrell, "the guiding hand of Arthur S. Link, not merely . . . [as] editor but the acknowledged master of Wilson scholarship."[6] Ferrell went on to describe the project's operation and what it produced: "The Wilson factory occupies a small suite in a corner of the Firestone Library, down a labyrinthine corridor designed,

one thinks, so that merely curious visitors get lost. There the staff comes in early each day and leaves late, and everyone works to turn out the books that are, physically, very appealing, handsomely designed and bound, nothing about them formal or celebratory but clearly for use, with colors of brown and gold, a nice brownish paper, each volume graced by a circled photograph of the president on dust jacket and title page."[7]

One aspect of *The Papers of Woodrow Wilson* is unmistakable: the series dominates historical documentaries devoted to twentieth-century Americans, and in some respects it towers above all of the documentary series now being published in the United States.[8] Large-scale printed documentary records for other twentieth-century presidents are limited in number and more modest in scope. *The Public Papers and Addresses of Franklin D. Roosevelt*, a thirteen-volume compilation of the thirty-second president's papers edited by Samuel I. Rosenman, is a valuable but selective collection containing no private letters or incoming material.[9] *Public Papers of the Presidents of the United States*, published by the Office of the Federal Register, is an annual compilation of the presidents' public messages and statements as released by the White House. Begun in 1957, the series extends from the administration of Harry S. Truman to the presidency of Ronald Reagan, plus that of Herbert Hoover.[10] Although these annual volumes provide a convenient source for the ideas and policies of recent presidents, they are limited to public documents and to the chief executives' own spoken and written words. Finally, in placing the Wilson *Papers* in the context of documentary works relating to twentieth-century presidents, several microform collections are available, including a comprehensive edition of the Woodrow Wilson Papers in the Library of Congress.[11]

Only two of the documentary projects devoted to modern presidents can be said to rival the Wilson *Papers* in scholarly influence and reputation. One of these is *The Letters of Theodore Roosevelt*, an eight-volume edition of Roosevelt's own letters published in the early 1950s.[12] Roosevelt was a great letter writer, and this edition makes a splendid selection of his letters accessible in a convenient and attractive format. The Roosevelt *Letters* illustrates TR's thought and action in all the major and many of the minor undertakings of his public and private life. They appeared at just the right time to help stimulate a revival of interest in the effervescent twenty-sixth president. The volumes were handsomely produced, provide reliable texts, and contain illuminating introductions and interpretive essays. They are, as a discerning reviewer noted, "one of the most important undertakings in American historical scholarship in the postwar era."[13] Yet, for all its

virtues, this sprightly series cannot and was not intended to satisfy the needs of all serious students of the Roosevelt era. The editors selected fewer than one of every ten letters available to them, and they decided against including incoming correspondence. Nevertheless, the scholarship of the editors, no less than the availability of *The Letters*, has had a profound and long-lasting effect on the study and interpretation of Theodore Roosevelt and his presidency.

A second series that might challenge the preeminence of the Wilson *Papers* among twentieth-century presidential documentary editions is *The Papers of Dwight David Eisenhower*, a project that has just reached the presidential years.[14] The series is intended "to provide a set of volumes complete enough to present a detailed record of Eisenhower's thought and action and yet not so voluminous as to make them cumbersome." The coverage of this documentary work effectively begins with Eisenhower's role in World War II, and the editors define "papers" to include "only those documents which he himself had written or dictated or which he had taken a direct part in preparing."[15] Since incoming documents are not included, the record is one-sided. On the other hand, the Eisenhower *Papers* are liberally annotated and extensive bibliographies of secondary works, notes on primary sources, glossaries, and detailed chronologies are provided. This series, contrasting so sharply in purpose and scope with *The Papers of Woodrow Wilson*, will constitute a major biographical and historical documentary, one second only to the Wilson *Papers* in its importance for the modern period. It is likely to have a significant influence on American scholarship and to emerge as a competing model to the Wilson *Papers* in the editing of presidential documents.

Arthur S. Link, the editor of the Wilson *Papers*, and his associates set out to produce a definitive edition of Woodrow Wilson's "papers," which they defined quite broadly. They planned to include not only Wilson's own writings and speeches but incoming correspondence as well, in addition to many documents from collateral collections. The purpose announced in volume I was to "make available to readers all the materials essential to understanding Wilson's personality, his intellectual, religious, and political development, and his careers as educator, writer, orator, and statesman."[16] As the project proceeded the editors gradually adopted an even broader definition of purpose. Thus they decided to print most of Wilson's speeches, or accounts of them, although he seldom spoke from prepared texts. The more inclusive approach to "papers" was also reflected in the search for relevant newspaper and periodical accounts, a valuable source for Wilson's speeches, press releases, and daily activities. The editors turned as well to the memoranda, diaries, and letters of third parties

in which Wilson's friends and associates recorded his conversations with them. In short, by the time they reached Wilson's presidency, their objective had become the publication of a documentary record that would "illustrate the life and activities of the new President in all their aspects." [17]

The formulation of policies for the collection, selection, transcription, and annotation of Wilson "papers" presented difficult problems from the beginning of the project. How have the editors dealt with these problems? What editorial policies have guided them in the long and arduous process that extends from the search for Wilson documents to the publication of the finished record? How consistent have they been in adhering to the editorial standards announced in the early volumes? Have the editors' own views of their task changed over the years?

No doubt the most important editorial decisions were those outlined in the introduction to the first volume of the series. As Link and his colleagues noted at that time, no effort was being spared in gathering a comprehensive collection of documentary materials. They sifted through the voluminous Wilson Papers in the Library of Congress and the Princeton University Library, as well as the vast holdings of the National Archives. They combed scores of collateral manuscript collections in other libraries, in historical societies, and in private hands. They searched for pertinent documents in foreign archives and manuscript collections. They went through newspapers, periodicals, and other printed materials. By 1966 they had photocopied about 250,000 documents comprising more than half a million pages. In 1978 the editors reported that they had searched "all private manuscript collections and diaries that might conceivably contain materials shedding light upon our subject. . . . Moreover, our search continues and is particularly fruitful in the recovery of single items or small groups still in private hands and public repositories." [18] It would be hard to imagine a more thorough and resourceful quest for Wilson "papers."

In deciding what to print from this mass of materials, Link and his associates found their task becoming steadily more demanding as their chronological coverage moved forward. In the early volumes they were able to print all of Wilson's extant letters and a large proportion of his incoming correspondence, as well as a miscellany of other documents that included shorthand diary entries, class reports, lecture notes, course outlines and examinations, the minutes of debating societies, unpublished essays, newspaper and periodical articles about Wilson, and archival material on Johns Hopkins and Princeton. But as Wilson's stage grew larger—as he moved from college profes-

sor and author to college president, to the governorship of New Jersey, and then to the presidency of the United States—the selection of what to include in the documentary record became increasingly more complicated and more difficult. The war years made the situation even worse. As the editors remarked when they arrived at that point, "the volume of materials which fall within our definition of a 'Wilson paper' increases almost exponentially once the United States enters the World War."[19] In some respects the problem of selection was further exacerbated when the stage shifted to the Paris Peace Conference and the avalanche of contemporary materials it produced on the role of Woodrow Wilson.

For the presidential period the editors intended to publish the papers and records "that emanated directly or indirectly from Wilson and [that] shed significant light on his thoughts, purposes, and activities."[20] That objective provided the Link team with a broad but sensible guide to the thorny question of which documents to include and which ones to leave out. In general this approach has worked well. As might be expected, most of the ephemeral and trivial material in Wilson's correspondence is excluded. The editors include little of the routine mail, correspondence with department heads and agencies, and the like that involved the normal operation of the government, and they publish only a limited amount of the president's substantial correspondence pertaining to patronage—only enough to illuminate the important aspects of Wilson's patronage policies and problems. Inevitably, thousands of "interesting and important" documents in the Wilson Papers, in collateral collections, and in the National Archives are not published in this edition. Indeed, it may not be possible "to find and publish every important record of Wilson's thoughts and purposes without concern for the form in which the records have been preserved."[21] Since deciding what to publish is at least in part a subjective judgment, the editors would have strengthened their series if they had called attention more frequently to the character and volume of "papers" confronting them at different stages in Wilson's experience, as well as pointing out the special problems they faced in selecting the most appropriate documents to print.[22]

Specialists in the Wilson period may occasionally find the documentary record too thin, even when viewed narrowly from the perspective of Wilson's own activities and attitudes. Thus the coverage of Wilson's role in Democratic party politics, especially as it related to state and regional developments in 1913 and 1914, might have been more fully revealed. Also, the twenty-eighth president's central part in the enactment of the great legislative measures of the New Freedom, as well as some of the less notable reform accomplishments, should perhaps

have received more attention. The objectives of the series might have been more fully realized had greater care been taken to throw light on Wilson's relationship with congressional leaders, on congressional opinion of the president, on the shaping of administration proposals, and on the influence of public opinion on the legislative process. It is not altogether clear why some diaries are used as sources and others are not. Although the editors' decision to publish only contemporary documents follows precedent in the editing of documentary works of this kind, an exception might have been made in a few instances, such as Stockton Axson's unpublished memoir and interviews conducted by Ray Stannard Baker.

In some respects the Wilson *Papers* may be more inclusive than they need to be. Were the editors right in their decision to reprint Wilson's *Congressional Government* and *Constitutional Government in the United States*, given the fact that both books are readily available? The seminal place of those volumes in Wilson's political thought and development probably justify their inclusion in *The Papers*. On the other hand, perhaps only a few examples of the numerous reviews of Wilson's books should have been included, with a checklist of the others. One wonders about the decision to print approximately seventy-five pages of congratulatory messages following Wilson's election as governor of New Jersey in 1910. Some of the material on Wilson's role in the Paris Peace Conference could have been omitted on the ground that it had already been published in *Papers Relating to the Foreign Relations of the United States*. Yet exclusions of this kind would have violated the editors' commitment "to bring together in one series" all important documents that throw light on Woodrow Wilson and the larger arena in which he acted.[23] Editors of future documentary series may not have that luxury. Gordon S. Wood has remarked that all editors of large-scale documentary projects today are apparently reluctant to omit from their volumes important documents, even when they have been reprinted elsewhere in modern scholarly editions. It seems that the editors "view their particular papers project as akin to a complete biographical narrative of their subject that can be read and enjoyed essentially within the covers of their volumes."[24] Wood doubts the wisdom of that assumption.

According to Link and his colleagues, their most important task is "the presentation of a reliable Wilson text."[25] While making some concessions to the practical need for clarity and uniformity in their texts, they have tried to reproduce documents exactly as they appeared in the original. They adopted a policy of "printing documents *verbatim et Liberatim*, spelling and typographical errors and all," and of repairing "words and phrases in square brackets only when absolutely necessary

for the sake of clarity." Even so, they made some silent alterations in letters: changing periods in salutations to commas, substituting periods for dashes when the latter would ordinarily be read as periods, and lowering superior letters to the regular line. Ellen Axson Wilson's letters presented "extraordinary problems" of this kind, and the editors "felt obliged" to eliminate "excessive punctuation, the capitalization of words that Ellen obviously meant to be read as capitalized, the substitution of periods for dashes and semicolons when she obviously ended a sentence, etc." In general the editors silently corrected words with transposed letters, corrected obvious typographical errors in typed copies of telegrams and other typed documents, and modernized archaic spelling in contemporary transcripts of Wilson's speeches. While promising not to exclude a text because it was too long, they tended as the series progressed to excise passages of ephemeral interest from letters and other documents more frequently than in the past.[26] In all of these practices *The Papers* followed "rather scrupulously" the editorial methods employed by modern historical editors.[27]

Transcribing Wilson "papers" in a variety of forms has been one of the distinguishing features of this project. One example was the transcription of the voluminous shorthand material scattered through the Wilson *Papers*. Woodrow Wilson, who learned shorthand as a youth and made extensive use of it in later years, was the author of much of this material: drafts of letters, speeches, lectures, articles, state papers, and marginal notes in books and on documents. The Graham shorthand system that Wilson learned was no longer in use when work on *The Papers* began, but the editors were able to locate surviving experts and to have some two thousand pages of shorthand notes transcribed.[28] These transcripts became an invaluable source for the series. Since Wilson seldom spoke from written texts, the recovery and reconstruction of his political speeches posed another major challenge to the enterprise. Link and his associates enjoyed great success in reconstructing the speeches on the basis of surviving transcripts, shorthand notes, and newspaper accounts. Their procedures resulted from an elaboration of the methods used by John Wells Davidson, one of the editors, in *A Crossroads of Freedom: The 1912 Campaign Speeches of Woodrow Wilson* (1956). They began with the transcripts and shorthand notes of Charles L. Swem, Wilson's personal stenographer. They compared all known parallel texts (usually newspaper accounts) with each other and with old and new transcriptions of extant shorthand notes, while also testing doubtful phrases against Wilson's characteristic style.[29] The transcription of what many scholars had come to regard as unintelligible shorthand notes, the reconstruction of Wilson's

political addresses, and the identification of the early editorials he wrote for his father's newspapers and for Princeton publications represent what John Milton Cooper, Jr., has aptly called the "archaeological work" of the Wilson *Papers*.[30]

Concern for the reproduction of accurate and reliable texts was also reflected in other editorial procedures. The editors decided to print those portions of Wilson shorthand and Wilson typed documents that revealed the existence of significant changes between first and final drafts. They have tried to present the best possible translations of foreign-language documents, most notably perhaps in the case of Paul Mantoux's Paris Peace Conference transcripts, *Les Délibérations du Conseil des Quatre*.[31] The commitment to the principle of *verbatim et Liberatim* is also evident in the editors' decision to publish the decoded telegrams Wilson received during the peace conference, which were often garbled, just as the president *read* them, or in the case of Wilson's own typed messages, just as he *wrote* them.[32]

In outlining their policy of annotation, the editors stated that they would identify individuals, subjects, and events when necessary. Longer biographical notes would be provided for subjects "whose relationships with Wilson stretched over a number of years and were important to him." Well-known historical and literary figures, as well as writings and events, would not ordinarily be identified. Editorial notes would be supplied when the briefer and more specific footnotes failed to indicate the importance of the subject to Wilson or the context of the document.[33] The inclusion of longer notes—many of them illuminating essays in their own right—on such topics as "Wilson's Study and Use of Shorthand," "Wilson's Practice of Law," "Wilson's Teaching at Princeton," and "Wilson's History of the American People" gave a special character to the early volumes of the series.[34] At this stage the editors seem to have been strongly influenced by the tradition of historical editing that originated in the work of Julian P. Boyd and Lyman H. Butterfield—an assumption that they should provide explanatory notes that would enable their readers to understand a document in its historical context.

Editors of historical documentary series may well have concluded that it is impossible to meet the expectations of all their readers in the matter of annotating the documents they are publishing. As Dr. Johnson once said, "It is impossible for an expositor not to write too little for some, and too much for others. He can only judge what is necessary by his own experience; and how long soever he may deliberate, will at last explain many lines which the learned will think impossible to be mistaken, and omit many for which the ignorant will want his help."[35] In the case of the Wilson *Papers*, the editors were somewhat

inconsistent in their writing of notes around the documents, although they tended to become more sparing in their use of notes of identification and explanation. A reviewer of volumes 23 and 24 complained of unnecessary footnotes, citing a letter from one of Wilson's friends who had six children, whose full names were given in a note and each of whom was listed separately in the index![36] Other reviewers criticized the absence of notes, particularly historical notes.

When the series reached the presidential years, Link and his associates declared their intention of trying "to make the documents intelligible by appropriate identifications and explanatory notes." Since the biographical and historical literature on Wilson and his era was much more extensive for the presidential years than for the period before 1913, very few notes of biographical or historical character would be provided. That kind of work would be left to others; the editors had "neither the time nor the desire to write a history of the Wilson era."[37] Most of the historical documentary series were moving in the same direction. Although the value of the Wilson *Papers* has not been seriously diminished by this change in editorial policy, the utility and influence of the series might have been enhanced through a more liberal use of annotations. The illuminating editorial notes contained in the early volumes soon dwindled to one or two a volume, and they disappeared altogether by the time the coverage reached 1910. Though fewer in number, many of the notes for the presidential volumes are useful in providing needed context, in quoting from contemporary editorials and news reports, and in referring readers to authoritative books and articles. More adequate references to recent scholarship, where appropriate, would have strengthened the annotation of the series.

The editors have not embellished their volumes with interpretive essays or other peripheral features relating to Woodrow Wilson. Their introductions to the individual volumes, except for two or three comprehensive statements of editorial policy, have been brief and to the point. This editorial restraint was eventually reversed in one particular: the editors' growing interest in Wilson's health. Partly because of that interest, scholars seem to agree that Wilson "had a pronounced tendency to psychosomatic illness, suffered several physical traumas throughout his adult life, and was plagued by progressive vascular disease."[38] But controversy has developed over the findings of Dr. Edwin A. Weinstein, a retired neurologist, who argues that Wilson suffered from progressive arteriosclerosis and experienced a series of brain-damaging strokes before the massive, crippling attack that brought him down in October 1919. Weinstein asserts that these strokes resulted in marked behavioral changes and that Wilson's polit-

ical leadership was adversely affected as early as his Princeton presidency.[39] The editors of the Wilson *Papers* have generally endorsed Weinstein's interpretations and have collaborated with him on several occasions in responding to critics.

Among the critics of Dr. Weinstein—and of Arthur Link and his associates—are Alexander L. George and Juliette L. George, authors of *Woodrow Wilson and Colonel House*, a pioneering psychological study published in 1956.[40] The Georges, in collaboration with ophthalmologist Michael F. Marmor, argue against the existence of earlier "strokes." They also charge that "Link has permitted himself to state unequivocally" in the editorial apparatus of *The Papers* that Weinstein's stroke theory is valid, thereby misleading a number of writers. "We believe," they declare, that Link ". . . has thereby compromised the objectivity of that otherwise superb series and therefore compromised its value to historians. . . ."[41] Link and his colleagues agree that "the primary historical record [of *The Papers*] ought to be free from any tendency to steer interpretation," but they see an essential difference between primary sources and secondary historical writings such as the editorial notes that accompany the documents in the Wilson *Papers*. "We have tried to find and print the primary record of Wilson's life with scrupulous objectivity," they write. "We go to great efforts to make certain that our printed versions conform to the texts of the original documents." While acknowledging an obligation to Weinstein, they observe that "we would have concluded that Wilson had a long history of cerebrovascular disease and incidents characteristic of it had we never known Dr. Weinstein or read any of his works."[42]

Link and his associates have contributed to a new recognition of the nature and importance of Wilson's physical crises, but they could have made that contribution without identifying *The Papers* with a particular interpretation of his medical history. Kendrick A. Clements, a Wilsonian specialist, suggests, "Perhaps the editors may have gone out a little far on a limb in their notes about Wilson's health," but he adds that this "is arguable, and for the most part their annotations and especially their lengthy notes are significant contributions to scholarship in themselves."[43] Other scholars are more critical. One historian thinks the editors should not have tried "to pin down the nature of the illness" and that they were ill-advised to print "the essays thereon." Another student of the Wilson era agrees that including the medical essays as an appendix to volume 58 was "an egregious mistake," which violated Link's own principles of historical editing. In light of "the brevity, clarity, and balance" that characterize the annotation of the series as a whole, this historian thinks the treatment of Wilson's neurological illness "sticks out like the sorest of thumbs." At the same

time, he defends the editors against compromising "the integrity of the series in any way." A third scholar expresses keen disappointment that Weinstein's arguments were made a part of "the Wilson canon," since it led some students of Wilson to accept them as "a fact." It would have been far better had the editors presented Weinstein's interpretations as hypotheses, for that approach would "surely encourage further scholarship."[44]

Broadly construed, the debate between the Georges and Weinstein is concerned with the question of whether Wilson's behavior is best understood in terms of psychoanalysis or neurology. For the neurological case, most Wilsonian scholars will have to defer to medical specialists. The weight of the evidence thus far seems to lean toward Weinstein and Link. Although the Georges and Dr. Marmor are not persuaded by the stroke theory, they concede that "it is possible that vascular disease conditioned Wilson's abilities at the Paris Peace Conference, although we cannot attribute any specific difficulty to it."[45] The diverse body of literature on the nature of Wilson's personality and on his neurological problems has made clear the importance of psychological responses to organic illness in his case. Dorothy Ross has pointed out, moreover, that there is "a surprising degree of consensus about the quality of Wilson's behavior and about its causes."[46] The Wilson *Papers* have undoubtedly stimulated much of the research and writing that produced this broad consensus.

Although *The Papers of Woodrow Wilson* have encouraged important new research on the era of Woodrow Wilson, it is difficult to measure the scholarly influence of the series. Any attempt to evaluate the project at this stage must necessarily be preliminary; an authoritative assessment must await the completion of the series and the passage of enough time for additional research to reach fruition. Some historians admire the editing of the Wilson *Papers* but doubt that their publication has had a profound influence on Wilsonian scholarship, in part because serious researchers still find it necessary to use the unpublished papers. Some aspects of Wilson's career have not attracted the interest of recent scholars, despite the publication of *The Papers*. Wilson's first administration as president is a case in point, largely, one suspects, because of the earlier impact of Link's four biographical volumes on the interpretation of that period. The war years, which now offer many unexplored topics for research, have thus far elicited relatively little new investigation, and the coverage of the Paris Peace Conference is still too recent to have had much effect on scholarly inquiry into that great conclave. A few scholars are disappointed in a reinterpretation of Woodrow Wilson which they associate with the Wilson *Papers*. One historian concedes that the series has "temporarily

improved the general assessment of Wilson," but this scholar does not think it will last. Another writes that *The Papers* and related publications "have contributed to a positive presentation of and apology for Wilson's leadership in light of critical assessments."[47] These critics are disquieted by what they perceive as a protective attitude on the part of the Link team toward Wilson. As George W. Egerton writes, "Arthur Link and his associates have always been a major source of encouragement and hospitality; on the other hand their intense devotion to Wilson troubled me." Egerton concludes that on balance "this tension probably was positive as it made me think more deeply about the issues and controversies, even if the conclusions I reached were viewed tolerantly by Arthur as heretical."[48] Link's generosity toward other scholars is proverbial, and there is abundant evidence of how he and his colleagues have shared their files and their knowledge with other students of the period.

Whether or not *The Papers* have brought a reevaluation of Wilson, they have unquestionably served as a catalyst for significant historical research. "I think it's fair to say," observes one Wilson specialist, "that Wilson scholarship should forever after be divided *ante* and *post* Papers."[49] The most obvious evidence of the series' stimulative effect on new scholarship is more than a dozen works published as supplementary volumes to the Wilson *Papers*. These books deal with such diverse topics as Wilson's life prior to his entry into politics, his political thought, his medical history, executive management of public opinion in foreign affairs, and the American experience during the First World War.[50] John M. Mulder's *Woodrow Wilson: The Years of Preparation* (1978) supersedes all previous studies in its revealing treatment of Wilson's youth and academic career. Mulder says that his work would not have been possible without the Link series. "It formed virtually the mountain on which my book was built."[51] Another of the supplementary volumes, Niels A. Thorsen's *The Political Thought of Woodrow Wilson, 1875–1910* (1988), may do a good deal to restore Wilson's reputation as a scholar and political thinker. Thorsen has made good use of the Wilson *Papers*. One has only to compare his book with William Diamond's *The Economic Thought of Woodrow Wilson* (1943) to appreciate the far-reaching implications of its interpretation.

Some idea of the revitalization of Wilsonian scholarship can be gained from a sampling of recently published works on the period. Among these are John Milton Cooper, Jr., *The Warrior and the Priest: Woodrow Wilson and Theodore Roosevelt* (1983); Robert H. Ferrell, *Woodrow Wilson and World War I, 1917–1921* (1985); Frederick S. Calhoun, *Power and Principle: Armed Intervention in Wilsonian Foreign Policy* (1986); Kendrick A. Clements, *William Jennings Bryan: Missionary Iso-*

lationist (1982); and John A. Thompson, *Reformers and War: American Progressive Publicists and the First World War* (1987). *The Papers* have provided the basis for new perspectives on Wilson's leadership in these and other works. Lloyd C. Gardner, the author of a notable study of foreign affairs during the Wilson era, writes that the publication of the Wilson *Papers* had "a tremendous impact on my personal view of Woodrow Wilson." Gardner notes "the revelations of influences on Wilson that we had not really grasped fully" and "the many contributions that Link and his associates found in collateral collections." It was surprising, Gardner observes, how many "unanswered questions" there were about Wilson. "Some of these, indeed, we did not even know were questions, until the appearance of the papers."[52] Lawrence E. Gelfand writes that he is "depending increasingly on *the Papers* as I proceed towards completion of my large project on the American Commission to Negotiate Peace at the Paris Peace Conference of 1919."[53] Samuel F. Wells sums up a widely held belief among specialists when he declares, "The wider understanding of a more complex and more interesting Wilson is a splendid achievement."[54]

Arthur S. Link and his colleagues have gone a long way toward accomplishing their purpose of publishing "as complete a record as possible of the development of Wilson's significant thought and activities in all their varied aspects." That is an extraordinary achievement. Despite its selective character, the sheer scope of the series, something like seventy volumes when completed, is hard to comprehend. The editors have brought together and made accessible to scholars and general readers alike an incredibly rich documentary record of Wilson's public and private life. "For me," one historian declares, "the chronological ordering with the inclusion of correspondence to and from the President plus the informative editorial notes makes the collection invaluable."[55] The series as a whole reflects editorial skill, meticulous scholarship, and adherence to exacting standards for documentary publication. Not surprisingly, reviewers and commentators have been generous in their praise of the series. Whatever their reservations about the selection and annotation of documents, most scholars regard the Wilson *Papers* as a model of historical editing.[56]

Another impressive contribution of this documentary series is its illumination of many previously obscure or unknown aspects of Wilson's life. Most revealing is the understanding *The Papers* provide of the young Wilson: of his relationship with his parents, the importance of his health, recognition of his strong sexual drive, the development of his personality, and his intellectual growth. The Wilson *Papers* shed new light on Wilson's study of politics, on his contributions to the embryonic field of public administration, on the development of histori-

cal scholarship in the United States, on Wilson's ideas and leadership in the field of education, and on his brilliant and often embattled role as president of Princeton. "The material which now gives the early WW his stature," one historian remarks, "would simply not have been at hand for [earlier] researchers."[57] Another scholar suggests that the Wilson *Papers* have demonstrated two major themes. "First, the connection between Wilson's personal life and personal struggles and his public policies, thus linking the personal and the public; second, the struggle in Wilson's mind between the social conservatism of his background and American society and the progressivism and liberalism to which he was attracted by virtue of his background and the growing demands of and changes in American society."[58]

One of the striking things about the Wilson *Papers* is the context they create for an understanding of Wilson's thinking and behavior. The printed volumes show, for example, how the Mexican Revolution influenced Wilson's thinking about foreign policy in a revolutionary world. "Wilson's plan for a conference of all nations," Kurt Wimer writes, "emerges from a careful study of volumes 31–34 of *The Papers of Woodrow Wilson*."[59] When Wilson's correspondence and other documents are placed alongside entries from Edward M. House's famous diary, the seductive sway of House's writings is dispelled, and it becomes clear that he often provided a one-sided and unreliable account of what happened. Even more important is the way in which *The Papers* enable the student to trace the development of Wilson's thought on a variety of topics and to identify more precisely than ever before the influences that shaped his ideas and behavior.

On one occasion Arthur Link asserted, in speaking of documentary editors in general, that "our most important task is to reproduce accurate and trustworthy transcripts."[60] That is doubtless true, but it overlooks the way in which the editor of a documentary series gives meaning to his material through the selection, arrangement, and annotation of documents. Indeed, the modern documentary editions represent, as some commentators have pointed out, a new form of historical literature. *The Papers of Woodrow Wilson* demonstrate, as well as any of the great documentary projects, that at its best this kind of editing is a creative work of historical scholarship. Link and his colleagues are not "mere compilers of documents." They have created a work of history in the very act of editing—in the very process of collecting, arranging, and annotating their documents. As Burl Noggle once observed, "The editor is now his own historian, though obviously history can be—and is—written from the volumes he has compiled."[61]

Most historians who specialize in the Wilson period seem to agree that publication of the Wilson *Papers* in a comprehensive letterpress

edition is desirable.[62] A few scholars would have preferred a microfilm edition. One historian, who is complimentary of the series' "careful editorial work," considers *The Papers* too extensive to be "an attractive and manageable introduction" to Woodrow Wilson yet inadequate for the purposes of serious scholars. The series is not a sound investment, in the opinion of this critic, who adds: "I would rather see funds go toward a briefer, more accessible edition of papers, wider dissemination of microfilm or microfiche, and fellowship support for graduate students and scholars working on Wilson."[63] More typical is the comment of Samuel F. Wells: "I believe that in the case of extremely important leaders in our nation's history that an expensive, large-scale letterpress edition of this sort is justified."[64] But it would make sense to supplement the letterpress series with a comprehensive microfilm edition that would make available to researchers the full documentary richness of the unpublished material in the files of projects like the one on Woodrow Wilson.[65]

While scholars may differ in their assessment of the research potential of the Wilson *Papers*, they agree that the series has become the indispensable starting place for any serious investigation of Wilson and his administration. Although some scholars will find it necessary to go to the unpublished papers, the published volumes will meet the needs of a great many historians interested in the twenty-eighth president and the period he dominated. Because of the reliable record the series provides and the context it creates, the work is simply invaluable, even for the most authoritative interpreters of the Wilson period. *The Papers* are a boon to graduate students, and they are being used as a teaching tool in undergraduate seminars and honors courses. Other students of the Wilson era and early twentieth-century America, including social scientists, journalists, and writers of popular history and biography, should find the Wilson *Papers* an important source. Nor should the appeal of the series to foreign scholars and students be overlooked at a time when modern American politics, society, and culture are being increasingly studied abroad. Without documentary works like the Wilson *Papers*, an Australian scholar remarks, "American studies abroad would have ground to a halt years ago."[66] Woodrow Wilson's presidential papers, a West German historian writes, are no longer a part of American history *only*. "They cover an all-important segment of the general history of our contemporary world."[67]

We are not likely to see again anything like *The Papers of Woodrow Wilson*, certainly not involving a twentieth-century president. The concept is simply too audacious, the scope too large, the cost in financial support, time, and professional dedication too great. But if only a

single such project can be completed for a twentieth-century American, Woodrow Wilson may well be the best possible choice. For one thing, the Wilson *Papers* are remarkably complete; they constitute one of the truly great manuscript collections in the United States today. As Link and his associates pointed out in volume I of their series, Wilson "grew up during a generation that reverenced the raw materials of history, and he rarely threw away anything he thought to be of possible importance, at least after childhood."[68] A major component of the papers is the rich correspondence they contain. Wilson lived in an age when letter-writing was still one of the primary means of communication, and he and his correspondents expressed themselves freely and at length in their letters. Nor is that all. Wilson's extraordinary use of language—both in public expression and in private correspondence—makes him the preeminent literary stylist among modern American presidents. Equally important is the fact that Wilson was a modern, activist president, whose era was one of the most significant in our recent history. Many of his policies and programs—at home and abroad—are still meaningful in our lives. In a sense they represent the first part of our own times. How fortunate, then, that Arthur S. Link and his colleagues set out on their particular editorial odyssey more than thirty years ago.

Notes

[1] Mary A. Giunta, "The Routine of the Documentary Editor?" *OAH Newsletter*, 16 (November 1988), 15; I am indebted to John Milton Cooper, Jr., and Richard W. Leopold for their helpful criticisms of an earlier version of this paper.

[2] Lewis L. Gould to the author, September 17, 1988. A limited survey of scholars interested in the Wilson period, carried out by the author in the fall of 1988, asked a series of questions about the editing of *The Papers* and their influence on research and writing in the field. Approximately forty-three of some seventy questionnaires were returned. Several of the respondents indicated, in answer to the query "Are you willing to be quoted?", that they wished to preserve the confidentiality of their comments. Although the results of the survey would have greater significance if all authors of quoted passages in this paper were identified, it seems desirable to present a representative sample of the evaluations contained in the responses, even if proper attribution cannot always be made. It should be noted that in some cases scholars had not made enough use of the Wilson *Papers* to offer solid assessments. Even so, many of the responses are penetrating and thoughtful, and the returns as a whole are revealing and suggestive.

[3] Lloyd C. Gardner to the author, November 7, 1988.

[4] George W. Egerton to the author, September 30, 1988.

[5] By mid-1989 sixty volumes had been published, including four general index volumes, and the chronological coverage had almost reached the end of the Paris Peace Conference of 1919. Beginning with the appearance of the first volume in 1966, the editors have published an average of two and a half volumes a year, a rate of publication far surpassing that of any other major historical series.

[6] Robert H. Ferrell, review in *American Historical Review*, 88 (October 1983): 1091; Ferrell to the author, September 15, 1988.

[7] Ferrell, review in *American Historical Review*, 88 (October 1983): 1092.

[8] The Wilson *Papers* have superseded two older and once-useful documentary works: Ray Stannard Baker and William E. Dodd, eds., *The Public Papers of Woodrow Wilson*, 6 vols. (New York, 1925–1927), and Ray Stannard Baker, *Woodrow Wilson and World Settlement: Written from His Unpublished and Personal Material*, 3 vols. (Garden City, New York, 1922).

[9] Samuel I. Rosenman, comp., *The Public Papers and Addresses of Franklin D. Roosevelt*, 13 vols. (New York, 1938, 1941, 1950). Several specialized documentary projects have extended the coverage of the Rosenman series. These include Edgar B. Nixon, comp. and ed., *Franklin D. Roosevelt and Conservation*, 2 vols. (Hyde Park, New York, 1957); Edgar B. Nixon, ed., *Franklin D. Roosevelt and Foreign Affairs*, 3 vols. (Cambridge, Mass., 1969); Donald B. Schewe, ed., *Franklin D. Roosevelt and Foreign Affairs*, second series, vols. 4–17 (New York, 1979–1983); and Warren F. Kimball, ed., *Churchill and Roosevelt: The Complete Correspondence*, 3 vols. (Princeton, 1984).

[10] See Warren R. Reid, "Public Papers of the Presidents," *American Archivist*, 25 (October 1962), 435–39.

[11] In addition to the Wilson Papers, the Library of Congress has produced microfilm editions of the papers of three other twentieth-century presidents: Theodore Roosevelt, William Howard Taft, and Calvin Coolidge. The Ohio Historical Society has prepared a microfilm edition of the Warren G. Harding Papers. University Publications of America has produced numerous microfilm collections of recent presidents that are organized on the basis of particular issues or presidential files. See, for example, *The Diaries of Dwight D. Eisenhower, 1953–1961*; *President John F. Kennedy's Office Files, 1961–1963*; and *The War on Poverty, 1964–1968: White House Central Files*.

[12] Elting E. Morison, John M. Blum, and Alfred D. Chandler, Jr., eds., *The Letters of Theodore Roosevelt*, 8 vols. (Cambridge, Mass., 1951–1954).

[13] Arthur S. Link, "Theodore Roosevelt in His Letters," *Yale Review*, 43 (Summer 1954): 589.

[14] Alfred D. Chandler, Jr., Stephen E. Ambrose, Louis Galambos, and others, eds., *The Papers of Dwight David Eisenhower*, 13 vols. to date (Baltimore, 1970–1989). Twenty-three volumes are projected for the completed series.

[15] *Ibid.*, I, xiv.

[16] Arthur S. Link, John Wells Davidson, David W. Hirst, T. H. Vail Motter, and John E. Little, eds., *The Papers of Woodrow Wilson*. Volume I: *1856–1880* (Princeton, 1966), xiv. Hereinafter cited as *PWW*, with the date of publication for particular volumes provided in initial references. There has been, as might be expected, considerable turnover among junior members of the edi-

torial staff. In addition to the editors listed above, the following individuals have worked on *The Papers* at one time or another: Fredrick Aandahl, Manfred F. Boemeke, Sylvia Elvin, Ann Dexter Gordon, Robert C. Hilderbrand, Edith James, William M. Leary, Jr., Margaret D. Link, Jean MacLachlan, Phyllis Marchand, John M. Mulder, M. Halsey Thomas, and Denise Thompson.

[17] *PWW*, XXVII (1978), vii, xxi.

[18] *Ibid.*, I, xiii-xiv., XXVII, x.

[19] *PWW*, XLII (1983), viii.

[20] *Ibid.*, XXVII, xiv.

[21] *Ibid.*, viii, xiv-xvii.

[22] The editors note in their introduction to volume 10, for instance, that the number of news reports of Wilson's addresses has increased substantially. They then describe their method of selecting the addresses to be printed. *PWW*, X (1971), viii.

[23] *PWW*, LIII (1986), xv.

[24] Gordon S. Wood, "Historians and Documentary Editing," *Journal of American History*, 67 (March 1981): 871–77 (quotation on p. 876).

[25] *PWW*, I, xvi.

[26] *Ibid.*, II (1967), ix., XXVII, xvii, LIII, xii-xiii.

[27] Mary-Jo Kline, *A Guide to Documentary Editing* (Baltimore, 1987), pp. 113–66; Arthur S. Link to the author, July 17, 1989. G. Thomas Tanselle, "The Editing of Historical Documents," *Studies in Bibliography*, 31 (1978), 1–56, criticizes historical editors for their textual policies of partial modernization and silent alteration, which, he argues, may subtly distort the character and content of the texts.

[28] *PWW*, I, xv-xviii. The Graham shorthand experts were Clifford P. Gehman and Marjorie Sirlouis.

[29] *Ibid.*, XXIV (1977), viii-xiii; XXV (1978), viii-xiii. The same basic methodology was used in editing Wilson's press conferences. See *PWW*, Vol. L: *The Complete Press Conferences*, edited by Robert C. Hilderbrand (Princeton, 1985).

[30] John Milton Cooper, Jr., to the author, January 4, 1988.

[31] In an effort to save space, beginning with volume 44, foreign-language documents were printed only in translation (or, where appropriate, by printing them verbatim, without translations). In earlier volumes the practice had been to print original texts and translations of such documents.

[32] *PWW*, LIII, x.

[33] *Ibid.*, I, xvi-xvii.

[34] Another editorial feature, an index for each volume, was skimpy in the early volumes. Beginning with volume IV they were improved. Subentries are organized within each main entry in the order in which a reference first occurs in the volumes. Each volume of the series also includes a useful analytical table of contents, itself a quasi-index that locates specific documents through subject listings. In the prepresidential volumes the indexes provide cross references to the fullest earlier identification of persons, institutions, and events. The decision to discontinue this practice was unfortunate, since individuals and events are not usually reidentified in later volumes. It should be noted

that the cumulative contents-and-index volumes, published after every twelve volumes of *The Papers*, are excellent finding aids.

[35] Quoted in Reid, "Public Papers of the Presidents," 439.

[36] Seward W. Livermore, review in *American Historical Review*, 83 (December 1978): 1356–57.

[37] *PWW*, XXVII, xviii-xix.

[38] David M. Kennedy, "The Wilson Wars," *The New Republic* (March 17, 1982), 38.

[39] See Edwin A. Weinstein, *Woodrow Wilson: A Medical and Psychological Biography* (Princeton, 1981). For a balanced review of this study, see Charles E. Neu, "The Search for Woodrow Wilson," *Reviews in American History*, 10 (June 1982): 223–28.

[40] Alexander L. George and Juliette L. George, *Woodrow Wilson and Colonel House: A Personality Study* (New York, 1956).

[41] Juliette L. George and Alexander L. George, "*Woodrow Wilson and Colonel House*: A Reply to Weinstein, Anderson, and Link," *Political Science Quarterly*, 96 (Winter 1981–82), 641–65 (quotation on pp. 642–43). See also Juliette L. George, Michael F. Marmor, and Alexander L. George, "Issues in Wilson Scholarship: References to Early 'Strokes' in the *Papers of Woodrow Wilson*," *Journal of American History*, 70 (March 1984), 845–53; and George, Marmor, and George to the Editor, *Journal of American History*, 71 (June 1984), 198–212, in which the authors assert that "Link and his coeditors of the *Papers of Woodrow Wilson* have compromised the objectivity of that series by including numerous unequivocal references in editorial matter of several volumes to 'strokes' that Wilson allegedly suffered in 1896, 1906 and 1907, as if that diagnosis were established fact" (198).

[42] Arthur S. Link, David W. Hirst, John Wells Davidson, and John E. Little to the Editor, *Journal of American History*, 70 (March 1984), 945–55 (quotations on 945–47). The editors seem to rely increasingly on the findings of Dr. Bert Edward Park, a neurosurgeon and trained historian. See his contribution to "Wilson's Neurologic Illness at Paris," an appendix to *The Papers of Woodrow Wilson*, LVIII (1988), 607–40, and his book, *The Impact of Illness on World Leaders* (Philadelphia, 1986), which contains a chapter on Wilson.

[43] Kendrick A. Clements to the author, undated (September 1988).

[44] Confidential sources, September 21, October 3, December 12, 1988.

[45] George, Marmor, and George to the Editor, *Journal of American History*, 71 (June 1984), 212. See also Michael F. Marmor, "Wilson, Strokes, and Zebras," *New England Journal of Medicine*, 307 (August 26, 1982), 528–35.

[46] Dorothy Ross, "Woodrow Wilson and the Case for Psychohistory," *Journal of American History*, 69 (December 1982): 661.

[47] Confidential sources, undated (September 1988), September 30, 1988.

[48] George W. Egerton to the author, September 30, 1988.

[49] John Milton Cooper, Jr., to the author, January 4, 1988.

[50] See, for example, John M. Mulder, *Woodrow Wilson: The Years of Preparation* (Princeton, N.J., 1978); Niels Aage Thorsen, *The Political Thought of Woodrow Wilson, 1875–1910* (Princeton, N.J., 1988); Weinstein, *Woodrow Wilson: A Medical and Psychological Biography*; Kendrick A. Clements, *Woodrow Wilson:*

World Statesman (Boston, 1987); Robert C. Hilderbrand, *Power and the People: Executive Management of Public Opinion in Foreign Affairs, 1897–1921* (Chapel Hill, N.C., 1981); Frances Wright Saunders, *Ellen Axson Wilson: First Lady Between Two Worlds* (Chapel Hill, N.C., 1985); and Stephen Vaughn, *Holding Fast the Inner Lines: Democracy, Nationalism, and the Committee on Public Information* (Chapel Hill, N.C., 1980).

[51] John M. Mulder to the author, October 19, 1988.

[52] Lloyd C. Gardner to the author, November 7, 1988; Gardner, *Safe for Democracy: The Anglo-American Response to Revolution, 1913–1923* (New York, 1984).

[53] Lawrence E. Gelfand to the author, September 26, 1988.

[54] Samuel F. Wells, Jr., to the author, November 3, 1988.

[55] David F. Trask to the author, October 5, 1988.

[56] The comments of Lloyd E. Ambrosius reflect this appreciative view: "The extensive search for pertinent documents, the wisdom in selection, the reliability of the printed texts, and the useful addition of notes and annotations, all make *The Papers* a model of historical editing." Ambrosius to the author, undated (October 1988). Most of the respondents to the questionnaire referred to in note 2 emphasize the impressive quality of the editing and the value of the series in making easily accessible an incomparable documentary record for Wilson and his era.

[57] Niels A. Thorsen to the author, October 12, 1988.

[58] John M. Mulder to the author, October 19, 1988.

[59] Kurt Wimer, "Woodrow Wilson and World Order," in Arthur S. Link, ed., *Woodrow Wilson and a Revolutionary World, 1913–1921* (Chapel Hill, N.C., 1982), p. 169.

[60] Arthur S. Link, "Where We Stand Now and Where We Might Go," *Newsletter* of the Association for Documentary Editing, 2 (February 1980), 2.

[61] Burl Noggle, "A Note on Historical Editing: The Wilson *Papers* in Perspective," *Louisiana History*, 8 (Summer 1967), 292–93.

[62] The survey cited above elicited a large majority in favor of the letterpress edition.

[63] Michael McGerr to the author, November 9, 1988. It should be noted that the commission created by Congress to celebrate the centennial of Wilson's birth was not interested in fellowship support. The Woodrow Wilson Foundation wanted another Jefferson *Papers* enterprise, not a microfilm edition. Such ideas were still a decade in the future. The Ford and Rockefeller foundations would probably not have contributed substantially to the publication of "a briefer, more accessible edition." Nor is it likely that Princeton University would have provided logistical support for a lesser undertaking.

[64] Samuel F. Wells, Jr., to the author, November 3, 1988. Another scholar is convinced that the Wilson *Papers* "would not receive one-tenth of their current use, by both scholars and students, in a microfilm or microfiche edition." Ralph B. Levering to the author, September 12, 1988.

[65] A new microfilm edition of Wilson materials might be designed, not to duplicate the Library of Congress edition, but to make accessible to scholars the many documents collected and assembled by the editors but not included in the Wilson *Papers*.

[66] Joseph M. Siracusa, "A Reply to Professor Etzold," *SHAFR Newsletter*, 8 (June 1976), 14.

[67] Klaus Schwabe, quoted in *Inaugurating the Presidential Years of The Papers of Woodrow Wilson*, an undated brochure apparently published by the Princeton University Press.

[68] *PWW*, I, ix.

Thomas J. Knock

KENNAN VERSUS WILSON

IN the eyes of virtually all diplomatic historians, George Frost Kennan occupies a position of central (most would say seminal) importance in the evolution of the Cold War. By many, the author of the doctrine of "containment" is esteemed as something more than just a major figure in the history of Soviet-American relations. He has been assigned by Richard Ullman, for instance, "a unique place in American life and letters—the rare practitioner who is able to delineate the full significance of the events he helped shape, and in writing of the highest quality."[1] Louis Halle once attributed to the body of Kennan's work as a diplomatist the quality of "Shakespearian insight and vision."[2] In an otherwise harsh characterization, Paul Seabury wrote in the *New Republic* that Kennan belongs "in a special class of 20th century American intellectuals first exemplified by Henry Adams—men ill at ease with their times and their countrymen, men both eminently civilized and deeply troubled by vulgarity. . . ."[3]

As for this latter-day Henry Adams's initial contribution to American foreign policy—his famous "Long Telegram" of February 22, 1946—no less an authority than Henry Kissinger has written that "George Kennan came as close to authoring the diplomatic doctrine of his era as any diplomat in our history."[4] Daniel Yergin has designated Kennan's subsequent elaboration of containment—"The Sources of Soviet Conduct," published under the pseudonym, "X," in *Foreign Affairs* in 1947—"arguably the single most famous magazine article in American history."[5] Among manifestos on American foreign policy it is probably now safe to say that the document has acquired a station comparable to Washington's Farewell Address, the Monroe Doctrine, the Open Door Notes, and the Fourteen Points. And, if evidence is required to substantiate such a claim, one need only gauge the current of the stream of studies on Kennan published in the past

decade alone—by John Lewis Gaddis, Barton Gellman, Walter Isaacson and Evan Thomas, David Mayers, Anders Stephanson, and Walter L. Hixson.[6]

Yet Kennan's significance endures not because of any success that he enjoyed as an architect of American foreign policy (for he remains in fact a frustrated diplomatist) but rather because of his impress as searching critic—as the brilliant and misunderstood proponent of the balance of power and "realism" in the conduct of international relations. And, in this respect, the permanence of his footing on the high summit of statesmanship rests in considerable measure upon the force of his intellectual antagonism toward the policies and philosophy of Woodrow Wilson.

As champions of presumably antithetical concepts of diplomacy, Wilson and Kennan, in retrospect, may well be each other's chief historical antagonist. To be sure, they were inimitably well-matched adversaries. Each was possessed of a uniquely inclusive comprehension of the repercussions of the United States in world politics; and each, with a keen sense of the relationship between past, present, and future, devoted a considerable portion of his life to the writing of history—a fact which no doubt enhances the continuing interest in the two statesmen.[7] Then, too, whereas Kennan appears "on any short list of influential thinkers on American foreign policy," Wilson has been pronounced "the prophet and pivot of the twentieth century" by his distinguished biographer, Arthur S. Link, while Lloyd Gardner has declared it "beyond dispute" that "Wilson represents the beginning point for scholars of all 'schools'."[8] Moreover, Wilson's hold on historians, like Kennan's, shows no sign of lessening even in the 1980s, as affirmed by the contributions to the field by Link, Gardner, David M. Kennedy, John Milton Cooper, Jr., Robert H. Ferrell, Lloyd E. Ambrosius, and Niels Thorsen, to name a few.[9]

Like the major works of the ongoing Kennan renaissance, the recent studies on Wilson have plumbed their subject primarily, though not exclusively, from the liberal perspective; yet, if one were to draw a single, general conclusion from them all (with perhaps one exception), it would be that the weary cliche, "Wilson the Impractical Idealist," is simply not a serious proposition. For example, in the judgment of Lloyd Gardner, a historian steeped in the radical tradition, "Wilson proves to be a far more astute student of the workings of American society than those who come to see him as a dangerous idealist, a chronic missionary intervener in the affairs of other nations."[10] If Gardner is correct—and, again, most of the aforementioned scholars would agree with him—then one is confronted with the task of examining anew both the genesis and the soundness of Kennan's strictures as well as the essential properties of Wilson's internationalism. A

comparative analysis of the turns in Kennan's and Wilson's thought reveals, in both subtle and conclusive ways, elements of idealism and realism exerting constant pull against one another within a common center of gravity. At the same time, by virtue of the distinctive trajectory that he has followed, Kennan, particularly in the latter stages of his career, has evidenced a certain striking affinity for Wilson—an "irony of fate" which he surely would not have foreseen forty years ago.

At least since the 1960s, Kennan's endeavors to provide American foreign policy with a measure of intellectual coherence have, to paraphrase Kennan himself in another context, run "like a red skein" through the historiography of the Cold War. There is no need to review in detail the impressive corpus of his writings on that subject, or to assess the merits of the innumerable attempts by historians to interpret just what he meant by "containment."[11] A few generalizations about the basic thrust of his argument, and the assumptions that informed it, will suffice here. Kennan's analysis of Soviet behavior, his prescriptions for containment, and his case on behalf of the balance of power and realism were grounded not only in his years of first-hand experience in Eastern Europe and the Soviet Union, but also in his reading of nineteenth-century European and twentieth-century American diplomatic history. It is at this point—and especially in his estimation of the balance of power—that he crossed swords with Woodrow Wilson.

Kennan has noted in his memoirs that as a recent college graduate in 1925, he felt "the promptings of a vague Wilsonian liberalism; a regret that the Senate had rejected . . . the League of Nations."[12] With one notable exception in the 1970s, this recollection remains the most explicit expression of approval of Wilson that he has ever committed to print. Indeed, Theodore Roosevelt and Henry Cabot Lodge notwithstanding, no one ever took sharper aim at Wilson than Kennan. As he contended in his celebrated Walgreen Lectures at the University of Chicago in 1951, in the Wilsonian legacy lay "the most serious fault of our past policy formation."[13] This he described as the "legalistic-moralistic approach" to international relations, which manifested itself in "the inordinate preoccupation with arbitration treaties, the efforts toward world disarmament . . . and illusions about the possibilities of achieving a peaceful world through international organization and multilateral diplomacy, as illustrated in the hopes addressed to the League of Nations and the United Nations." Kennan believed that the "vainglorious and pretentious assertions of purpose" characteristic of Wilsonian rhetoric failed to provide sound foundations for foreign policy.[14] The Wilsonian conception of international order, Kennan wrote in his memoirs, simply could not "replace power as the

vital force for a large part of the world." And, he added, "We are being almost criminally negligent of the interests of our people if we allow plans for an international organization to be an excuse for failing to occupy ourselves seriously and minutely with the sheer power relationships of the European peoples."[15]

Kennan illustrated this point in a Walgreen lecture on the First World War. He harshly criticized the nature of Wilson's policies of neutrality and the tone and substance of his subsequent war address. The country would have been better served, Kennan argued, if the President had recognized that, from the start of the conflict, the United States clearly had a stake in the victory of the Entente powers; if he had earlier perceived the need to build up the armed forces; and if he had led the country into war for the avowed practical purposes of saving Great Britain from defeat and of ending hostilities "with a minimum prejudice to the future of the Continent."[16] Instead, Wilson permitted "war hysteria and impractical idealism to lie down together," thus contributing demonstrably to the shattering of the former European equilibrium. The result, as Kennan put it, "Was a peace which had the tragedies of the future written into it by the Devil's own hand"—that is, a second terrible war which, like the first, failed to restore the balance of continental forces and also rendered western Europe "dangerously, perhaps fatefully, vulnerable to Soviet power."[17]

Kennan was not alone in scoring Wilson for a lack of realism; nor was he the first to do so. As early as 1943, Walter Lippmann anticipated this interpretation as well as its language. His criticisms are especially interesting because he had served as one of Wilson's bright young men. "He failed," Lippmann wrote of the President in *U.S Foreign Policy: Shield of the Republic*,

> because in leading the nation to war he had failed to give the durable and compelling reasons for the momentous decision. The reasons he did give were legalistic and moralistic and idealistic reasons, rather than the substantial and vital reason that the security of the United States demanded that no aggressively expanding imperial power, like Germany, should be allowed to gain the mastery of the Atlantic Ocean. . . . The legalistic, moralistic, and idealistic presentation of the war and of the League obscured the realities. . . . It was made to seem that the new responsibilities of the League flowed from President Wilson's philanthropy and not from the vital necessity of finding allies to support America's existing commitments in the Western Hemisphere and all the way across the Pacific to the China Coast.[18]

Then, too, around the time that Kennan composed his Walgreen lectures, the laying of the foundations of a "realist" school by other learned masons was already getting underway. Reinhold Niebuhr,

Hans J. Morgenthau, and Robert E. Osgood published fairly similar critiques of what they considered the misguided, unrealistic aspects of American foreign policy, with Morgenthau and Osgood singling out Wilson's neutrality and his concept of collective security as negative object lessons.[19] A good case could be made for either Niebuhr, Morgenthau, or Kennan as the single most important proponent of "realism." Kennan himself has referred to Niebuhr as "the father of us all," and Niebuhr once called Morgenthau "the most brilliant and authoritative political realist."[20] Yet, it does not diminish the significance of either Niebuhr's or Morgenthau's intellectual legacy to suggest a more compelling case for Kennan. Unlike his colleagues, who accomplished their work more or less in the circumstances of academic quietude, Kennan recycled the past while directly participating in the making of contemporary foreign policy, beginning in the late winter and early spring of 1946.

As *chargé d'affaires* in Moscow from 1944 to 1946, Kennan's frustrations with what he perceived to be the unfortunate cast of American diplomacy developed, on one level, within the context of the vicissitudes of Wilsonian historiography. By 1943–44, Wilson's stock on the historian's and pundit's exchange, notwithstanding Walter Lippmann, had recovered dramatically from the all-time lows to which it had fallen during the interwar years of disillusionment and withdrawal. The new wisdom, for a season of three or four years, held that the Second World War somehow might have been averted if only the United States had joined the League of Nations. This view was implicit in Wendell Willkie's best seller, *One World* (1944), in Thomas A. Bailey's two widely read volumes on Wilson and the League, and in a variety of other books and popular media, including a spectacular Hollywood motion picture on the subject. The theme was, of course, manifest in virtually all forms of wartime propaganda on behalf of the United Nations as well.[21] More alarming from Kennan's point of view, it suffused the rhetoric that President Roosevelt employed in his public statements on the future of American foreign policy in general and of Soviet-American relations in particular.[22]

Disturbed by Roosevelt's apparent Wilsonian predilections in his dealings with Stalin and by the utopian expectations that publicists for the United Nations had raised, Kennan disputed the notion that even a significantly modified peacekeeping organization—one dominated by the "Four Policemen"—took into account either the fundamental differences between the two senior partners of the Grand Alliance or the basic security interests of the United States. To his good friend and fellow Soviet specialist Charles Bohlen he complained in January 1945: "If we insist at this moment in our history in wandering about

with our heads in the clouds of Wilsonian idealism and universalistic conceptions of world collaboration . . . [and] on staking the whole future of Europe on the assumption of a community of aims with Russia . . . then we run the risk of losing even that bare minimum of security which would be assured to us by the maintenance of humane, stable and cooperative forms of human society on the immediate European shores of the Atlantic." [23] Once the Soviet Union "had been permitted" to overrun Eastern and Central Europe, Kennan dispatched his famous "Long Telegram" of February 22, 1946. In the atmosphere of confusion and recrimination which by then had overtaken Soviet-American relations, Kennan's treatise could not have been better timed. His analysis of the nature of the Soviet threat to American interests quickly "went the rounds" at the highest levels within the Truman administration and reverberated for many months. By the following year, as Director of the new Policy Planning Staff in Washington, Kennan had become the acknowledged mastermind behind the developing doctrine of containment. [24]

Throughout the period of his greatest influence, in lectures at the National War College and in unpublished papers prepared for the new Policy Planning Staff, Kennan continued to reinforce his arguments on behalf of containment—on behalf of the concept of the balance of power and realism—with implicit condemnations of Wilsonian idealism and the impulse toward "universalism" in American foreign policy. [25] "A real community of interest" he maintained, ". . . is to be found only among limited groups of governments and not . . . [in] the abstract formalism of universal international law or in international organization." "Perhaps the whole idea of world peace," he said to the Policy Planning Staff on another occasion, "has been a premature, unworkable grandiose form of day-dreaming and that we should have held up as our goal: 'Peace if possible, and insofar as it affects our interest.'" [26] Moreover, the interests of the United States and the Soviet Union were palpably irreconcilable, he warned readers of *Foreign Affairs* in the summer of 1947. "Soviet policies," said Mr. X, "will reflect no abstract love of peace and stability, no real faith in the possibility of a permanent happy coexistence of the Socialist and capitalist world." [27]

Kennan nonetheless was ever sensitive to the limitations of American power—probably more so than any other member of the administration. He urged caution and restraint, emphasizing the political and economic components of containment. The United States would have to conserve its limited resources and set its priorities accordingly. In the process of restructuring international relations, the State Department would have to develop a sensible policy based not on the

rhetoric of "universalism" but on "particularism"—that is, a spheres of influence arrangement, a strategy fundamentally grounded in the concept of the balance of power which resisted communist expansion only in those areas of particular and vital importance to the interests of the United States. "[A] 'balance of power policy,'" he explained some years later, "means using American influence, wherever possible, to assure that the ability to develop military power on the grand scale is divided among several governmental entities and not concentrated entirely in any one of them."[28] Hence, Kennan advocated plans to reconstruct the economy of Western Europe as well as to exploit tensions within the communist bloc as the best means of restoring the geopolitical balance and of reducing the capacity of the Soviet Union to project its influence beyond the Yalta demarcation. Moreover, by employing "counter-pressures," or proper rewards and penalties for Soviet actions, he hoped that the United States in time might be able to induce the Kremlin to modify communist universalism, even to the point of tolerating diversity.[29]

Thus, through adroit and persistent efforts "to establish a balance among the hostile or undependable forces of the world," Americans could find a reasonable measure of security while ensuring "that the constructive forces, working for world stability, may continue to have the possibility of life."[30]

By the end of 1947, Kennan could lay claim to having put the Wilsonian genie back into the bottle from which it had escaped during the war. He had become ghost writer for the Secretary of Defense, and had the ear of the Joint Chiefs of Staff and the Secretary of State who frequently quoted him to the President. In April 1947, the Joint Chiefs had concluded: "Faith in the ability of the United Nations as presently constituted, to protect, now or hereafter, the security of the United States . . . could quite possibly lead to results fatal to that strategy." Seven months later, Secretary of State George C. Marshall summed up for President Truman a recent Kennan memorandum in the following way: "[T]he object of our policy from this point would be the restoration of [a] balance of power in both Europe and Asia and . . . all actions would be viewed in light of that objective."[31]

Kennan's single greatest achievement as Director of the Policy Planning Staff was the decisive role he played in the drafting of the Marshall Plan. In its application of the political and economic components of containment, the Marshall Plan conformed more closely to his prescriptions than any other major manifestation of early Cold War strategy.[32] Yet his usefulness to the government was short-lived. Even

before the Marshall Plan was unveiled, the Truman Doctrine had raised in Kennan's mind the possibility of a new incarnation of universalism. The President seemed to have written "a blank check to give economic and military aid to any area in the world where the communists show signs of being successful" he admonished Dean Acheson.[33] The decisions to form the NATO alliance, to develop the hydrogen bomb, and to rearm Germany—all aimed against the Soviet Union—he regarded as egregious mistakes that virtually eliminated the prospects for the *political* resolution of the Soviet-American confrontation. The crowning blow came in 1950. National Security Council Report 68 advanced a monolithic interpretation of international communism and failed to differentiate between independent communist movements and Soviet expansionism. It also stressed the new Soviet military capacity rather than Soviet intentions, thus implying that American global interests required huge defense expenditures and an unlimited strategy of containment. NSC-68 was the stuff that Kennan's nightmares were made of.[34]

Once the new predication of military considerations had thus become institutionalized—containment would now be an unlimited strategy—Kennan was "out of step" with the administration and ceased further to exert any real influence on policy. He soon accepted Robert Oppenheimer's invitation to take up residence at the Institute for Advanced Study at Princeton and write history. "Only the diplomatic historian, working from the leisure and detachment of a later day will be able to unravel this incredible tangle and to reveal the true aspect of the various factors and issues involved," Kennan recorded in his diary in August 1950. "[N]o one in my position can contribute very much more . . . unless he first turns historian, earns public confidence and respect through the study of an earlier day, and then gradually carries the public up to a clear and comprehensive view of the occurrences of these recent years."[35] As one student of Kennan's ouster has observed, "If he could not persuade those who would shape the future, then perhaps he would have better luck persuading those who interpret the past."[36]

Kennan became a greater source of controversy after his retirement from public service. Even before turning full-fledged historian, he had become perhaps the first Cold War "revisionist." Returning to government service for a brief and unhappy tour of duty as Ambassador to the Soviet Union in 1952, he dispatched from the American Embassy in Moscow a document, "The Soviet Union and the Atlantic Pact," which could be termed his "Second Long Telegram," but one with a mission considerably different from the first. In it he suggested, among other things, that the present state of affairs between the

Kremlin and the Western powers amounted to a "cosmic misunder-standing." The NATO military program, he argued, was based on the erroneous assumption—in large measure perpetrated by the United States, he implied—that the Soviet Union planned "an overt and un-provoked invasion of Western Europe" and utterly distorted "the real delimitations both of Soviet intentions and of Soviet strength."[37] With respect to its influence on American NATO policy, Kennan noted a generation later, the document might "just as well never have been written."[38]

Then, in 1957, when the BBC invited him to deliver the prestigious Reith Lectures, Kennan made a spirited case on behalf of German unification and gradual military disengagement in Europe. For his efforts, he was denounced in Western Europe for "neutralism" and in the United States for advocating a "new isolationism." Dean Acheson was moved publicly to protest that Kennan actually had "never grasped the realities of power relationships," but was possessed of a "rather mystical attitude toward them." At this pass Kennan now held the curious distinction of having been declared *persona non grata* not only by the Soviet Union (in 1952), but also by the American foreign policy establishment.[39] Growing increasingly disillusioned and pessi-mistic about the gyrations of American domestic politics and the dec-adence of American mass culture and materialism, he began seriously to wonder, in the mid-1950s, whether the United States had "reached the limit of the international role allowed to it by the state of its own habits and its own mentality to date."[40]

The travails of the "father of containment" were not yet behind him. By the late 1960s and early 1970s, when Vietnam exposed the grievous shortcomings of American Cold War foreign policy, Kennan came under fire from New Left historians. These revisionists, as criti-cal of anticommunist realism as Kennan was of Wilson and his cam-paign for the League, cast him in the role of intellectual progenitor of a most grotesque kind of American universalism. Such were the wages of ambiguity and of the numerous inconsistencies in his analyses of Soviet motivations and his blueprints for containment.[41]

In his two volumes of memoirs (and elsewhere) Kennan tried to clear up some of the misunderstanding about his position by explain-ing that he had intended containment to be limited both in its geo-graphical application and in its duration.[42] By the 1970s, he had not only abjured containment, but also seemed to have given up hope that the American system could be reformed. Both political parties time after time had presented the electorate with "a choice of deplorable mediocrities" who pushed the country "into taking actions in the for-eign field, not for their effectiveness in the matters with which they

purport to deal, but for their ulterior function here at home." Americans were unfitted for world leadership and ought to withdraw from far-flung foreign involvements, he told an interviewer, because "we have nothing to teach the world" and because "the kind of government we have does not permit, even if we *had* a valid message to impart, the shaping of that message into a consistently pursued foreign policy." [43]

Perhaps more cogently than Kennan himself could have done, however, John Lewis Gaddis's influential *Strategies of Containment* has isolated and clarified the areas of divergence between Kennan's views and the policies pursued by the Truman administration and its successors. Nonetheless, there was (and is) good cause for confusion over just what Kennan had meant to say. Gaddis's fine work and Kennan's protests notwithstanding, the published and private record raises certain questions about his intentions at the time, the means he employed in his advocacy of realism and the balance of power, and the legitimacy of his condemnations of the moralistic aspects of Wilson's formulations.

Kennan has never directly acknowledged the degree to which his commitment to containment was grounded in his own sense of moral values; nor, despite his capacity for self-criticism, has he ever conceded his appreciable role in abetting, wittingly or not, the anticommunist paranoia which permeated the highest reaches of the government as he strove to alert his superiors to the necessity of shelving the UN and of playing hard ball with the Russians. What, for example, *was* one to make of Mr. X's call for "a *long-term*, patient, but firm and vigilant containment," or his assertion of "the basic unfriendliness of purpose" of the Soviet Union?[44] How was it possible to mistake the message, in the campaign for public support for the Marshall Plan, when he warned one audience, in February 1948, of the Soviets' "dreams of the smashing of our society and the domination of the world"?[45] To the Policy Planning Staff he said, in January 1949, the Soviets "are seized in the vice-like grip of an iron logic of history which makes the preservation of their rule in Russia dependent on the destruction of freedom in the western world."[46] Then too, it is equally difficult to square Kennan's aversion to Wilson's moralism and idealism with "Mr. X's" sweeping summons to Americans to shoulder "the responsibilities of moral and political leadership that history plainly intended them to bear,"[47] or with the observation a year later at the National War College: "[I]f we ever get to the point . . . where we cease having ideals in the field of foreign policy, something very valuable will have gone out of our internal political life."[48]

The foregoing record, in view of the forces which Kennan (perhaps

inadvertently) helped to set in motion, surely invites inquiry into the merits of his criticism of "the inordinate preoccupation with arbitration treaties, the efforts toward world disarmament . . . and illusions about the possibilities of . . . the League of Nations and the United Nations"—or, in short, a comparison of Kennan's balance of power strategy with Wilson's advocacy of a concert of power as the best means of achieving diversity, peace, and stability in the world, not to mention the best interests of the United States. What, then, one must ask after all, was the nature of Wilson's so-called "universalism," which served as Kennan's point of departure for the advancement of realism?

To begin, it must be pointed out that Wilson was not unmindful or heedless of the practical uses to which the concept of the balance of power could be put in the international situation that confronted him in 1914–1918. For instance, he realized fully the implications of American neutrality in his decision not to break the British blockade, which otherwise in all probability would have resulted in the victory of Germany. Later, during the prearmistice negotiations of October 1918, the timing of his submission of the German request for an armistice to the British and French was aimed at putting the brakes on the accelerating demands which the latter had made at each stage of those negotiations. Wilson counted heavily on using Germany—until its unanticipated military and political collapse—as a diplomatic lever against some of the more extreme objectives of the Allies.[49]

Even so, Wilson harbored grave doubts about foreign policies guided by the precepts of *realpolitik*. Whereas Kennan believed that the balance of power during the century before 1914 had both provided stability and prevented a major continental war,[50] Wilson believed that the fragile structure of European alliances, as a system, was inherently self-destructive, lacking as it did any instrumentalities to defuse potential conflict among the major powers, or to redirect it into safer, more prudent forms of rivalry. For Wilson, the cataclysm of the war was evidence enough in support of the conclusions one might come to about "a balance which was determined by the unstable equilibrium of competitive interests."[51] As he declared before the Italian Parliament in January 1919, "We know that there cannot be another balance of power. That has been tried and found wanting, for the best of all reasons that it does not stay balanced inside itself, and a weight which does not hold together cannot constitute a makeweight in the affairs of men. Therefore, there must be something substituted for the balance of power. . . ." A league of nations, he added, "once considered theoretical and idealistic[,] turns out to be practical and necessary."[52]

Wilson had come to this conclusion and had formulated his most salient ideas for a postwar "community of nations" during the period of American neutrality. These ideas included the settlement of international disputes by means of arbitration and conciliation; general disarmament; a decent respect for the principle of the equality of states and the right of peoples to self-determination; and, of course, collective security. By January 1917, shortly before the United States entered the war, he had synthesized his ideas into a unified program grounded in a "League of Peace." In the "Peace Without Victory" address to the Senate, perhaps his most withering indictment of the old diplomacy and the pronouncement which marked his ascent to a position of central importance in the history of international relations in this century, Wilson launched a penetrating critique of European imperialism, militarism, and balance-of-power politics. These, he said, were the root causes of the war and related disturbances. His solution stemmed from his own observations and analysis of the basic structural causes behind the European conflict. As he put it in a series of questions in his address, "Is the present war a struggle for a just and secure peace, or only for a new balance of power? If it be only for a new balance of power, who will guarantee, who can guarantee, the stable equilibrium of the new arrangement? There must be, not a balance of power, but a community of power; not organized rivalries, but an organized common peace."[53]

Kennan might easily have pointed to certain passages of the "Peace Without Victory" address as prime examples of Wilsonian universalism: for instance, Wilson's references to "the guarantees of a universal covenant," or his declaration that it was the destiny of the United States to lead the way toward a league of nations—although Kennan, as previously noted, also was wont to speak of "the responsibilities of moral and political leadership that history plainly intended [Americans] to bear."[54] To be sure, Wilson's conception of a community of nations reflected his idealism and tended toward the universal; but it did not seek the perfection of the international environment. In fact, one could characterize Wilson's proposals in the same words that Kennan once used to describe his own: "an indication of direction, not of final destination."[55]

Wilson's general approach to building the League—and a very gradual process, he believed, it should be—was roughly analogous to some of his early thought and writings on the developmental aspects of democracy and international law. In his treatise, "The Modern Democratic State" (1885), he had suggested that democracy was both a means and an end, "a stage of development . . . built by slow habit"; like international law, it was "not made," as such, but rather was the

result of organic maturation.[56] If an individual country could not attain democracy except by stages, then one could not expect the emerging community of nations to devise all at once the larger projection of a league until it had had time to apply new ideas to events as they unfolded. But, in the process, nations would find themselves bound together in "a humane jural society" which could secure for its members "a common protection of law for their general human and international rights."[57]

Wilson's views about the specific functions of the League also indicated a direction, a goal to be accomplished over the long term, and primarily though (to employ Kennan's terminology) "particularistic," rather than "universalistic," methods. Let us take collective security as one example. Throughout the entire period of active belligerency and in the subsequent public debate over the League, Wilson (in part owing to his preoccupation with the war effort and to partisan anxieties) utterly failed to explain himself adequately on this controversial matter, much as Kennan failed in some of his writings on containment. However, Wilson did set out his position many times in generally overlooked, but nonetheless revealing, private wartime correspondence. And its contents do not conform to the picture of unlimited military commitments and entanglements in European politics which his contemporary opponents painted from the start and for which the realists have often taken him to task.[58] To the contrary, they demonstrate an awareness of the limitations that the Constitution might impose upon American participation in international military action, and of the practical consideration that "the League must grow and not be made."[59]

Like Kennan, Wilson realized that a fundamental restructuring of international relations was a delicate business that could not be accomplished overnight. As he explained in March and August 1917 to Jean Jules Jusserand, the French ambassador to the United States, one should begin with simple covenants—for example, the obligation to submit disputes to arbitration. Then, "in the very process of carrying out these covenants into execution from time to time a machinery and practice of cooperation would naturally spring up which would in the end produce . . . a regularly constituted and employed concert of nations."[60] Therefore, the mutual guarantee of political independence and territorial integrity (provided for in Article X of the Covenant of the League of Nations) would not oblige every member of the League automatically to throw an army into the field every time the peace was disturbed. Whether or not the United States would employ military force would depend entirely upon the circumstances surrounding a particular incident. And, as Wilson repeatedly stressed in correspon-

dence with Colonel House, the method of carrying those mutual pledges out "should be left to develop by itself, case by case."[61]

Actually, Wilson did not think that military sanctions would need to be invoked often in the postwar period, in part because of the deterrent value of the threat of collective force, and especially because of the other provisions of the League—for disarmament, arbitration, and conciliation—all of which Wilson emphasized equally in his petition. To take just one example, no other single component of collective security was more critical, Wilson believed, than disarmament—because it would help to ameliorate, if not eliminate, the fundamental problems arising out of the quest for national security in the first place. This was the most perspicacious indication of direction that Wilson ever articulated. "There can be no sense of safety and of equality among nations if great and preponderating armaments are henceforth to continue here and there to be built up and maintained," he said in the "Peace without Victory" address (as well as on other occasions). "The question of armaments, whether on land or sea, is the most immediately and intensely practical question connected with the future fortunes of nations and of mankind."[62]

Ironically, it was Walter Lippmann who, in *The Stakes of Diplomacy* (1917), offered one of the most instructive terms for the kind of league that Wilson envisaged—"a temporary shelter after the storm." Lippmann was not uncritical of the league idea, even in 1917, but he still thought that it could serve an enormously salutary function. By itself, the League could not prevent conflict in every instance. But "what it may do," he wrote, "is keep Europe in equilibrium for a generation, [and] create a certain atmosphere of security and internationalism; it may allay fear and distrust." The best strategy for peace and security, therefore, was "to establish enough order for a few decades in order to release some of the more generous forces of mankind," to bring about a sufficient measure of tranquility for a few years to explore the potential for generosity, diversity, rationality, and enlightened self-interest—to see whether collective security, in tandem with arbitration procedures, disarmament, and the principle of the equality of states stood a reasonable chance of acceptance in the conduct of international relations.[63] For Wilson, then, the League of Nations was a compass rather than the final destination itself. Could such a league, formed under specific covenants and subject to a broad construction, really work in actual practice? That, Wilson frankly admitted, was a good question. But, as he said to Jusserand, "it would be an experience to try it."[64]

The realists of his own time did not agree. But only partly because of that circumstance did Wilson fail in the grand endeavor. This is not

the place to engage the historiography on the struggle over the ratification of the Treaty of Versailles. Yet, it is worth pointing out two factors behind Wilson's failure, factors which contributed to Kennan's failure as well. To the first Kennan himself once referred, albeit in another context: that Wilson did in fact permit wartime hysteria to lie down beside idealism. Whereas he usually leavened his remarks with sincere expressions of sympathy for the German people (much as Kennan frequently talked and wrote about the Russian people), Wilson also employed the most vivid of exhortatory rhetoric, aimed against the German government, in the campaign to galvanize support for the war effort.[65] His ultimate objective was overwhelmed and subverted, even before the Paris Peace Conference convened, at least in part by the intense patriotism and political intolerance which many of his own words had appeared to sanction.[66] In this respect, Kennan sinned almost as greatly. At the same time, Wilson, like Kennan, failed to clarify the generality. During the months of belligerency, he made only a single speech about the League of Nations, at the end of September 1918, and would not follow up in any sustained way for yet another year—long after it was too late to do any good.[67]

Wilson rarely wavered in his faith that some day the United States would embrace a foreign policy that would strive toward an ultimate community of nations. In retirement, he confided to his daughter, Margaret: "I think it was best after all that the United States did not join the League of Nations. . . . Now, when the American people join the League it will be because they are convinced it is the right thing to do, and then will be the *only right* time for them to do it."[68] Harry S. Truman stated in the summer of 1945 that the Charter of the United Nations had at last vindicated Wilson.[69] And, by the late 1960s, the New Left would point out that Wilson "established the main drift toward an American liberal globalism," with the suggestion of continuity between Wilson and those, like Kennan, who had, ironically, shunned his example. "Ultimately, in the post–World War II period," N. Gordon Levin concluded in his influential study, *Woodrow Wilson and World Politics* (1968), "Wilsonian values would have their *complete triumph* in the bi-partisan Cold War consensus."[70]

Yet, it is somewhat doubtful whether Wilson himself would have accepted either Truman's fine tribute or Levin's verdict. For, if Wilson was the father of internationalism, then his children—those who fashioned Cold War globalism after creating and then deliberately undermining the UN—were all bastards. In certain crucial respects, the New Left interpretation falls wide of the mark. What triumphed in the postwar period was at best a mutant form of Wilson's internationalism, and Wilson almost certainly would have denied paternity. For

example, Franklin Roosevelt's concept of the United Nations, overtly based as it was on the idea of the "Four Policemen," hardly conformed to the Wilsonian version.[71] Moreover, it would be difficult to make the case that the architects of the Cold War ever attempted, as a matter of either policy or principle, forthrightly to find peaceful solutions to international disputes or to reduce the dangers of "preponderating armaments." Finally, the ostensible inspiration behind the United Nations soon gave way to opposing systems of collective security—NATO and the Warsaw Pact—at least in part because Kennan, despite his ambivalence about NATO itself, had given such forceful intellectual validation to the balance of power. These developments would seem to suggest that Wilson's community of nations, indeed, had not prevailed.

In all of this, it would not be accurate or fair to imply that Kennan was responsible for the unfortunate course that American foreign policy took in the Cold War. Admittedly, many of his writings do cause one to ask: "How else could the foreign policy establishment have interpreted his words except to mean that the Soviet Union was the implacable foe and that the United States should undertake to thwart it at every point?" Nevertheless, if they had had the desire to do so, his colleagues were fully capable of discerning and responding to the subtleties of his recommendations, imperfections and all. (Many did, of course, discern the subtleties, and when he persisted in them, he was eased out.) In the same way, it is just as uncharitable of Kennan to dismiss Wilson's strategy (especially since it, like Kennan's, was never in fact systematically implemented), or to condemn Wilson's approach as having made "violence more enduring, more terrible, and more destructive to political stability than did the older motives of national interest."[72]

It is doubtful whether, today, Kennan would still hold steadfastly to that reproach. Over the years—even since the publication of his memoirs—his thinking about many things has changed, and in ways that disclose a belated appreciation of Wilson. In 1974, he was called upon to deliver a commemorative address marking the fiftieth anniversary of Wilson's death. "I have never been an admirer of all of Woodrow Wilson's political philosophy," he said candidly. But Wilson's "intuitive judgments on points of principle were very often, in the light of history, extremely perceptive and accurate . . . [and] by no means unreasonable or impractical or unconstructive. . . . Fifty years later, a great many people would come to understanding, in the light of the development of nuclear weapons, that the vision he put forward might be not just the dream of an idealist but was the price for the survival of civilization."[73]

Kennan's most recent collection of essays and public addresses, *The Nuclear Delusion* (1982) in a sense constitutes an elaboration of his commentary on Wilson and further illustrates the shift in emphasis in his thinking.[74] The publication of the volume took on profound moment when, in the light of the incalculable, potential grief confronting the West and the communist bloc, leading members of the Reagan administrations openly discussed the feasibility and survivability of a "limited" nuclear war. And here it is important to emphasize that Kennan's timely compulsion to write on the futility of modern warfare—that is, his perception of impending apocalyptic catastrophe—is acutely similar to the compulsion that animated Woodrow Wilson, who witnessed a holocaust of the sort humankind had never previously imagined possible. Wilson never more eloquently revealed his thoughts in this regard than in a lengthy, unpublished prolegomenon to his peace note to the belligerents in December 1916. "War, before this one," he wrote, "used to be a sort of national excursion . . . with brilliant battles lost and won, national heroes decorated, and all sharing in the glory accruing to the state. But can this vast, gruesome contest of systematized destruction . . . be pictured in that light . . . wherein the big, striking thing for the imagination to respond to was untold human suffering? . . . Where is any longer the glory commensurate with the sacrifice of the millions of men required in modern warfare to carry and defend Verdun?"[75]

Likewise, Kennan's chief concerns, particularly in the past ten years, have been fixed upon the universalistic assertion that the paramount national interest of the United States is to prevent war. In the introduction to *The Nuclear Delusion* he has flatly stated: "War itself, as a means of settling disputes among the great industrial powers, will have to be in some way ruled out; and with it there will have to be dismantled . . . the greater part of the vast military establishments now maintained with a view to the possibility that war might take place."[76] In the closing essay, "Why, Then, Not Peace?", he has declared: "[A] new effort must be undertaken, a more serious, realistic, consistent, and determined effort than anything put forward in the past, to eliminate war in general as a conceivable possibility for Europe. . . . [W]hat I am talking about here means instilling in a number of governments and peoples the realization that war, . . . this long-established and accepted sanction of national interest and national inspiration, is simply no longer a rational means of affecting the behavior of other governments."[77]

The views expressed in the foregoing lines are a far cry from Kennan's former, cynical oath, "'Peace if possible, and insofar as it affects our interest.'"[78] Indeed, they not only speak to both the particularistic

and universalistic aspects of Wilson's program; many of the essays in *The Nuclear Delusion* could easily have been recited by Wilson himself in his swing around the circle for the League of Nations in the autumn of 1919. It would seem, then, that the cumulative perversions of his original ideas about containment by diplomatists of narrow vision—"crackpot realists," C. Wright Mills once called them—have compelled Kennan, the "realist," to take a significant step in the direction of the "higher realism" of Woodrow Wilson.

In a review of *The Nuclear Delusion*, Lloyd Gardner wrote, "George Kennan has rendered his country—and humanity—an important service: he has written difficult truths sparing no one."[79] Thus, whereas his critics on the right may not have relented, Kennan's writings on contemporary issues have gone a long way toward rehabilitating him in the eyes of critics to his left. Moreover, and perhaps because of an ever-growing readership as well as the honors and tributes which continue to come his way, his sense of despair is no longer as pronounced as it was. Indeed, both the steadiness of his literary output and his choice of subjects themselves represent an affirmation of faith in redemption. To be sure, he continues to point to the defects and shortcomings of American society and politics, but now as "the reverse side of the great coin of the liberties we so dearly cherish." If this, the American political system with all its faults, he avers in the recent, expanded edition of *American Diplomacy*, "is the only way such a mass of people can be governed without the sacrifice of their liberties—then so be it; and let us be thankful that such a possibility exists at all, even if it is not a perfect one."[80] Whether this note of cautious optimism is warranted or not, the public side of Kennan's career has entered a new and decidedly Wilsonian phase. And, in the end, what stands out not only in his more recent work, but also in the whole of his life's endeavors is the quality that he attributed to Wilson in his commemorative address. "[W]hat we can respect and hold in memory and draw wisdom from, was primarily the texture of the effort of itself," Kennan said of the President. "It was an effort more important in its intrinsic quality and in its eloquence as an example than in its tangible and visible results."[81]

Of course, the Kennan-Wilson convergence—even the area of mutual comprehension concerning disarmament and the abolition of war—has a limited range. In the final analysis, it may be impossible to reconcile Wilson's pursuit of a community of nations with Kennan's brief on behalf of the "delicate balance." If his two most recent works of history are any indication, then "in George Frost Kennan the Presbyterian elder [still] wrestle[s] with the Bismarckian politician," to paraphrase Lloyd Gardner's observation of some twenty years ago.[82] In

The Decline of Bismarck's European Order, Kennan stoutly defends his protagonist against the reproach that he cultivated "a system of alliances too complex and intricate to be useful—a system that no one but himself could understand or manage." He maintains, perhaps with his own painful experiences in mind, that Bismarck's aims were simple and logical, but that he became "the victim of the mistakes of the Prussian military leaders whom he had used, in earlier years, as instruments to the attainment of his *political* ends."[83] What Kennan deplores, then, as ever, is not the concept of the balance of power, but the ineptitude of Bismarck's epigones, not the system that nurtured calamity, but the crucial missteps in the big game. Therein lies the rub. It does make one wonder whether the propositions which Wilson asked Americans to consider in 1919 could have possibly proved any more perilous than the commitment to the balance of power in the nuclear age.

Notes

[1] Richard Ullman, "The 'Realities' of George F. Kennan," *Foreign Policy*, 28 (Fall 1977): 139. The author would like to acknowledge his debt and express his gratitude to the following people for their good will and for their helpful criticisms of this essay: David F. Schmitz, John Milton Cooper, Jr., Charles E. Neu, Richard D. Challener, Gary Gerstle, Lloyd C. Gardner, Justus Doenecke, Peter S. Onuf, Louis H. Rose, James S. Amelang, Manfred F. Boemeke, David F. Hirst, Daniel T. Orlovsky, John S. Long, Richard W. Leopold, and Arno J. Mayer.

[2] Louise Halle, *The Cold War As History* (New York, 1967), p. 116.

[3] Paul Seabury, "George Kennan vs. Mr. 'X': The Great Container Springs a Leak," *The New Republic*, (Dec. 16, 1981), 17.

[4] Henry Kissinger, *The White House Years* (Boston, 1979), p. 135.

[5] Daniel Yergin, *The Shattered Peace: The Origins of the Cold War and the National Security State* (Boston, 1977), p. 322.

[6] See Gaddis, *Strategies of Containment: A Critical Appraisal of Postwar American National Security Policy* (New York, 1982); Gellman, *Contending With Kennan* (New York, 1984); Isaacson and Thomas, *The Wise Men: Six Friends and the World They Made* (New York, 1986); Mayers, *George Kennan and the Dilemmas of US Foreign Policy* (New York, 1988); Stephanson, *George Kennan and the Art of Foreign Policy* (Cambridge, Mass., 1989); Hixson, *George F. Kennan: Cold War Iconoclast* (New York, 1989).

[7] Wilson, of course, spent most of his career in the academy before entering politics at the age of fifty-four, whereas Kennan served for some twenty-five years in the diplomatic corps and did not publish his first work of history until the age of forty-seven. Their respective first books, *Congressional Government* (1885) and *American Diplomacy: 1900–1950* (1951) each became practically in-

stant classics, to be followed by a prodigious outpouring of other distinguished books—another ten volumes for Wilson and, thus far, seventeen for Kennan—not to mention, between them, literally hundreds of articles and reviews. Kennan, in part because he has been blessed with longevity, is the more prolific of the two. At the age of eighty-six, he continues to write incisive pieces for the *New Yorker*, the *New York Review of Books*, and *Foreign Affairs*, and is at work on the third volume of his monumental study of the origins of the First World War. The best and most exhaustive examinations of Wilson's career before 1910 are Henry W. Bragdon, *Woodrow Wilson, The Academic Years* (Cambridge, Mass., 1967); John Mulder, *Woodrow Wilson: The Years of Preparation* (Princeton, N.J., 1978); and Niels Thorsen, *The Political Thought of Woodrow Wilson* (Princeton, N.J., 1988). No historian thus far has subjected Kennan's scholarly output to comprehensive analysis, but for a brief overview, see Gellman, *Contending With Kennan*, pp. 14–15; for a thorough, though selective, bibliography, see Mayers, *George Kennan*, pp. 376–78.

⁸Link, *Woodrow Wilson, Revolution, War and Peace* (Arlington Hts., Ill., 1979), p. 128; Gardner, "The Impact of the New Left," (paper delivered at the 1984 convention of the American Historical Association), 18. The estimation of Kennan is from Gellman, *Contending With Kennan*, xv.

⁹See Link, *Woodrow Wilson: Revolution, War and Peace*; Gardner, *Safe for Democracy: The Anglo-American Response to Revolution, 1913–1923* (New York, 1984); Kennedy, *Over Here: The First World War and American Society* (New York, 1980); Cooper, *The Warrior and the Priest: Woodrow Wilson and Theodore Roosevelt* (Cambridge, Mass., 1983); Ferrell, *Woodrow Wilson and World War I* (New York, 1985); Ambrosius, *Woodrow Wilson and the American Diplomatic Tradition: The Treaty Fight in Perspective* (New York, 1987); and Thorsen, *The Political Thought of Woodrow Wilson*.

¹⁰Gardner, "The Impact of the New Left," 18.

¹¹For his own account, see Kennan's *Memoirs, 1925–1950* (Boston, 1967), pp. 216–367. Gaddis's *Strategies of Containment* (in particular, 25–126) is generally regarded as the best contextual rendering of Kennan's recommendations for containment, but it should be supplemented by three more recent studies which, unlike Gaddis's, also scrutinize Kennan's career before and after the period from 1945 to 1950: Michael Joseph Smith, *Realist Thought from Weber to Kissinger* (Baton Rouge, Louisiana, 1986), pp. 165–91; Mayers's *George Kennan*, pp. 105–88 and 219–44; and Stephanson, *George Kennan*, pp. 51–103, 111–49, and 168–97. Gaddis, Mayers, and Stephanson elucidate the extensive historiography on Kennan.

¹²*Memoirs, 1925–1950*, p. 16.

¹³"Diplomacy in the Modern World," in *American Diplomacy, 1900–1950* (Chicago, 1951; expanded ed., 1984), p. 95. (All page citations refer to the 1984 edition.)

¹⁴Kennan, *Memoirs, 1950–1963* (Boston, 1972), p. 71. See also, in *American Diplomacy*, "America and the Orient," pp. 45–49, and "Diplomacy in the Modern World," pp. 95–103.

¹⁵*Memoirs, 1925–1950*, p. 219.

¹⁶"World War I," in *American Diplomacy*, pp. 57–58 and 63–64.

[17] *Ibid.*, pp. 61 and 51.

[18] Lippmann, *U.S. Foreign Policy: Shield of the Republic* (Boston, 1943), pp. 37, 39; see also, 33–36 and 71–77, and a companion volume, *U.S. War Aims* (Boston, 1944), pp. 157–82. For a discussion, see Ronald Steele, *Walter Lippmann and the American Century* (New York, 1980), pp. 405–10. Twenty-six years earlier, Lippmann's views were considerably different. He wrote: "Our debt and the world's debt to Woodrow Wilson is immeasurable. Any mediocre politician might have gone to war futilely for rights that in themselves cannot be defended by war. Only a statesman who will be called great could have made America's intervention mean so much to the generous forces of the world, could have lifted the inevitable horror of war into a deed so full of meaning" ("The Great Decision," *The New Republic*, April 7, 1917, 297–80). See also Lippmann to Wilson, April 3, 1917, in Arthur S. Link *et al.* eds., *The Papers of Woodrow Wilson*, 63 volumes to date (Princeton, N. J., 1966–), XLI, 537–38 (hereinafter cited as *PWW*).

[19] See, for example, Niebuhr's classic, *The Children of Light and Darkness: A Vindication of Democracy and a Critique of Its Traditional Defense* (New York, 1944); Morgenthau's *Politics Among Nations: The Struggle for Power and Peace* (New York, 1948) and *In Defense of the National Interest* (New York, 1951), pp. 3–7, 23–33; and Robert E. Osgood, *Ideals and Self-Interest in American Foreign Relations* (Chicago, 1952,) *passim*. See also Osgood's "Woodrow Wilson, Collective Security, and the Lessons of History," in *Confluence*, 5 (Winter 1957), 341–54; and Roland Stromberg, *Collective Security and American Foreign Policy from the League of Nations to NATO* (New York, 1963), pp. 3–45 and 230–47 and Stromberg's "The Riddle of Collective Security, 1910–1920," in George L. Anderson ed., *Issues and Conflicts: Studies in Twentieth Century American Diplomacy* (Lawrence, Kansas, 1959), pp. 147–70.

[20] Kennan and Niebuhr are quoted in Smith, *Realist Thought from Weber to Kissinger*, pp. 99, 134. For excellent analyses of Niebuhr's and Morgenthau's contributions to the realist school, see *ibid.*, pp. 99–164.

[21] See Bailey's *Woodrow Wilson and the Lost Peace* (New York, 1944) and *Woodrow Wilson and the Great Betrayal* (New York, 1945). Scribner's bought out Doubleday's rights to Ray Stannard Baker's eight-volume *Woodrow Wilson, Life and Letters* (New York, 1927–1939) and published the "Potomac Edition" in 1946. Darryl F. Zanuck's 1944 production is examined in Thomas J. Knock, "'History With Lightning': The Forgotten Film, *Wilson*," *American Quarterly*, 27, No. 2 (Winter 1976), 523–43. For the campaign for the United Nations, see Robert A. Divine, *Second Chance: The Triumph of Internationalism in America during World War II* (New York, 1967).

[22] See Gaddis, *Strategies of Containment*, pp. 3–24, and *The United States and the Origins of the Cold War, 1941–1947* (New York, 1972), pp. 133–73; and Robert Dallek, *Franklin D. Roosevelt and American Foreign Policy, 1932–1945* (New York, 1979), pp. 283–84, 419–20, 482–84, and 506–08.

[23] Kennan to Bohlen, Jan. 25, 1945, quoted in Mayers, *George Kennan*, p. 96.

[24] For background on the origins and influence of the "long telegram," see Mayers, *ibid.*, pp. 89–102; Stephanson, *Kennan*, pp. 45–50; and Gaddis, *Strategies of Containment*, pp. 19–24. For Kennan's own account, see *Memoirs, 1925–1950*, pp. 271–97.

[25] Gaddis, *Strategies of Containment*, pp. 25–29.

[26] Paper prepared for the Policy Planning Staff, "Review of Current Trends: U.S. Foreign Policy," February 24, 1948; and Naval War College lecture, June 18, 1947, quoted in *ibid.*, pp. 28, 29.

[27] "The Sources of Soviet Conflict," *Foreign Affairs*, XXV, No, 4 (July 1947): 580–81.

[28] "An Interview With George Kennan," *Foreign Policy*, No. 7 (Summer 1972): 17.

[29] For a detailed discussion, see Gaddis, *Strategies of Containment*, pp. 30–53, 54–71. See also, Mayers, *Kennan*, pp. 105–31 and Stephanson, *Kennan*, pp. 174–76.

[30] Naval War College lecture, December 21, 1948, quoted in *Ibid.*, p. 27.

[31] Both quoted in Gaddis, *Strategies of Containment*, p. 57.

[32] See Kennan, *Memoirs, 1925–1950*, pp. 325–53; Mayers, *Kennan*, pp. 139–45; Gaddis, *The Long Peace: Inquiries into the History of the Cold War* (New York, 1987), pp. 152–57. The most recent study is Michael J. Hogan, *The Marshall Plan: America, Britain, and the Reconstruction of Western Europe, 1947–1952* (Cambridge, England, 1987).

[33] Kennan to Acheson, May 23, 1947, *Foreign Relations of the United States: 1947*, 3 (Washington, D.C., 1974), 229.

[34] For Kennan's perspective on these developments, see Gaddis, *Strategies of Containment*, pp. 71–106; Mayers, *Kennan*, pp. 152–60; and Stephanson, *Kennan*, pp. 132–43.

[35] Kennan, *Memoirs, 1925–1950*, p. 500.

[36] John F. Pauly, Jr., "Au Revoir, Mr. Kennan: George Frost Kennan's Estrangement and Ouster From American Foreign Policy-Making" (unpublished senior thesis, Princeton University, 1984), 103. This is the best and most detailed study of Kennan's retirement from government service.

[37] "The Soviet Union and the Atlantic Pact," Sept. 8, 1952, printed in Kennan, *Memoirs, 1950–1963*, pp. 327–51. See also, Smith, *Realist Thought from Weber to Kissinger*, pp. 177–79.

[38] Kennan, *Memoirs, 1950–1963*, p. 142.

[39] Kennan devotes an entire chapter to a discussion of the Reith Lectures and their reception, in *Ibid.*, pp. 229–66; for his troubled Moscow Ambassadorship, see *Ibid.*, pp. 105–67. Acheson is quoted in *Ibid.*, p. 250. See also, Walter L. Hixson, "From Containment to Neo-Isolation: George F. Kennan and the Early Cold War, 1944–1957" (paper delivered at the 1986 convention of the Society of Historians of American Foreign Relations), 25–27.

[40] From an address at Haverford College, April 1955, quoted in *Ibid.*, 30.

[41] The most compelling of these critiques is Lloyd C. Gardner, *Architects of Illusion* (Chicago, 1970), pp. 270–300. See also, William Appleman Williams, *The Tragedy of American Diplomacy* (New York, Norton ed., 1988), pp. 268–69; Barton J. Bernstein, ed., *Politics and Policies of the Truman Administration* (Chicago, 1970), pp. 53–55; and Walter La Feber, *America, Russia, and the Cold War* (New York, 5th ed. 1984), pp. 64–55. Walter Lippmann was the first writer to criticize the "X" article. In a series of newspaper columns in 1947, (published later that year as *The Cold War: A Study in U.S. Foreign Policy*), he called containment a potential "strategic monstrosity" (p. 18) and took Kennan to task on

some of the same points later argued by the New Left. For more recent, stimulating critiques of this aspect of Kennan's legacy, see Thomas G. Paterson's *Meeting the Communist Threat: Truman to Reagan* (New York, 1988), pp. 114–46; and Michael H. Hunt, *Ideology and U.S. Foreign Policy* (New Haven, Conn., 1987), pp. 5–8, 152–54, and 162–63.

[42] See, for example, the chapter on the "X" article, in *Memoirs, 1925–1950*, pp. 354–67.

[43] Kennan, quoted in "A Conversation," with George Urban, in Daniel Moynihan, ed., *Encounters With Kennan: The Great Debate* (London, 1979), pp. 18, 25, 28. For other examples of Kennan's disillusionment and pessimism, see *Memoirs, 1950–1963*, p. 321; and Kennan, *The Cloud of Danger: Current Realities of American Foreign Policy* (Boston, 1977), particularly, pp. 3–26.

[44] "The Sources of Soviet Conduct," 572, 575 (emphasis added).

[45] Address, Feb. 17, 1948, quoted in Mayers, *Kennan*, p. 143.

[46] Address, Jan. 19, 1949, quoted in Stephanson, *Kennan*, pp. 74–75.

[47] "The Sources of Soviet Conduct," 582.

[48] Naval War College lecture, September 17, 1948, quoted in Gaddis, *Strategies of Containment*, p. 32.

[49] See Arthur S. Link, *Woodrow Wilson, Revolution, War, and Peace*, pp. 34, 101. Link has expanded on these and related points about Wilson's neutrality and peacemaking in his essay, "The Higher Realism of Woodrow Wilson," in *Journal of Presbyterian History*, 41 (March 1963), 1–13. See also, Edward H. Buehrig, *Woodrow Wilson and the Balance of Power* (Bloomington, Ind., 1955), p. 275; Cooper, *The Warrior and the Priest*, pp. 338–39; and Whittle Johnson "Reflections on Wilson and the Problems of War and Peace," in Arthur S. Link, ed., *Woodrow Wilson and a Revolutionary World, 1913–1921* (Chapel Hill, N.C., 1982), pp. 192–93; and Klaus Schwabe, *Woodrow Wilson, Revolutionary Germany, and Peacemaking, 1918–1919* (Chapel Hill, N.C., 1985, translation of German edition, 1971), pp. 65–72, 112–14.

[50] Kennan, "The First World War," *American Diplomacy*, pp. 69–72.

[51] Address at Guildhall, Dec. 28, 1918, *PWW*, XLIII, 532.

[52] Address to the Italian Parliament, Jan. 3, 1919, *ibid.*, 599.

[53] Address to Senate, Jan. 22, 1917, *ibid.*, XL, 535–36.

[54] *Ibid.*, 534–35.

[55] Quoted in Gaddis, *Strategies of Containment*, p. 27. Herbert G. Nicholas has argued that, whereas Wilson was prone to overstating the transforming capacities of the League, he also "was right in erecting . . . it as a model of international society at which men of good will should be aiming." ("Woodrow Wilson and Collective Security," in Link, ed., *Woodrow Wilson and a Revolutionary World*, p. 183.) For a discussion of Wilson's synthesis of ideals and self-interest in the "Peace Without Victory" address, see Cooper, *The Warrior and the Priest*, pp. 312–14.

[56] "The Modern Democratic State," *PWW*, V, 59, 63, 71, 84, and 92.

[57] As Wilson put it in a lecture on international law at Princeton University, March 5, 1894. See Lecture Notes, Andre Clark Imbrie Papers, Princeton University Library.

[58] Osgood in "Woodrow Wilson, Collective Security, and the Lessons of His-

tory," 344, states: "[N]either the United States nor any other nation in its right mind is willing to subordinate its special security interests to a hypothetical general interest in maintaining a stable international order, especially if that subordination would impose a claim on its armed forces. The United States, like every nation, must choose the aggression it opposes and the method of opposition, according to the particular circumstances and calculated effect of alternative courses upon its power position. . . . [I]t must base this decision on the criteria of Realpolitik rather than of international law and universal moral principles, regardless of whether the two kinds of criteria happen to coincide."

[59] Wilson to Edward M. House, March 22, 1918, *PWW*, XLVII, 105.

[60] J. J. Jusserand to the French Foreign Ministry, March 7, 1917, *PWW*, XLI, 356–57, and Frank L. Polk to Jusserand, August 3, 1917, *ibid.*, XLII, 360.

[61] Wilson to House, March 22, 1918, *ibid.*, 105. See also, Wilson's "Bases of Peace," ca. March 1917, in which he outlined provisions for disarmament, equal trade opportunities, and the guarantee of political independence and territorial integrity. The document concluded: "It would in all likelihood be best to await the developments and suggestions of experience before attempting to set up any common instrumentality of international action" *ibid.*, XLI, 173–75; Article X of the Covenant of the League of Nations, as presented before a Plenary Session of the preliminary peace Conference in Paris on February 14, 1919, reads as follows: "The High Contracting parties undertake to respect and preserve as against external aggression the territorial integrity and the existing political independence of all States members of the League. In case of any such aggression, or in case of any threat or danger of such aggression, the Executive Council shall advise upon the means by which this obligation shall be fulfilled." *Foreign Relations of the United States, Paris Peace Conference*, 3 (Washington, D. C., 1942), 233.

[62] *PWW*, XL, 538.

[63] Walter Lippmann, *The Stakes of Diplomacy*, 2d ed. (New York, 1917), pp. xxi, xxii. See also Lippmann to Wilson, January 3, 1917, in Woodrow Wilson Papers, Library of Congress, and Wilson to Lippmann, February 3, 1917, *PWW*, XLI, 113, in which Wilson thanked Lippmann for sending him a copy of the book.

[64] Wilson to Jusserand, March 7, 1917, *ibid.*, 356–57.

[65] See, for example, Wilson's war address, April 2, 1917, *ibid.*, XLI, 523, or his Flag Day address of June 14, 1917, *ibid.*, XLII, 498–504.

[66] This view was held by a number of leading advocates of the League, including Herbert Croly, George Creel, Oswald Garrison Villard, and Max Eastman. See Croly's main editorial in *The New Republic*, 17 (Nov. 9, 1918), 26; Creel to Wilson, Nov. 8, 1918, *PWW*, XLI, 645–46; Villard to Joseph Tumulty, Nov. 8, 1918, *ibid.*, 646; and Eastman, "Twilight of Liberalism," *The Liberator*, 1 (February 1919), 5.

[67] This was Wilson's so-called "Fourth Liberty Loan" address, *ibid.*, LI, 127–33.

[68] Quoted in Edith Giddings Reid, *Woodrow Wilson: The Caricature, The Myth and the Man* (New York, 1934), p. 236.

[69] Harry S Truman, *Memoirs, The Year of Decisions* (New York, Signet ed., 1965), p. 326.

[70] N. Gordon Levin, *Woodrow Wilson and World Politics, America's Response to War and Revolution* (New York, 1968), p. 260. (Emphasis added).

[71] For a review of the contending interpretations of Roosevelt's attitude towards the United Nations, see William C. Widenor, "American Planning for the United Nations: Have We Been Asking the Right Questions?" in *Diplomatic History*, 6, No. 3 (Summer 1982): 11–13.

[72] *American Diplomacy*, p. 101.

[73] Kennan, "The Legacy of Woodrow Wilson," *Princeton Alumni Weekly*, (October 1, 1974), 11–13.

[74] *The Nuclear Delusion: Soviet-American Relations in the Atomic Age* (New York, 1982). The dilemma of nuclear weapons did not worry Kennan when he first developed the containment doctrine. Toward the end of his government service, however, he had become alarmed over the impending arms race. In January 1950, he submitted to Secretary of State Dean Acheson a lengthy memorandum which deprecated the integration of nuclear weapons into American strategic policy and articulated the doctrine of "no first use." See *Memoirs, 1925–1950*, pp. 471–76, and *Memoirs, 1950–1963*, pp. 244–48.

[75] Prolegomenon, ca. November 25, 1916, *PWW*, XL, 67–68, 70.

[76] *The Nuclear Delusion*, p. xxvii.

[77] *Ibid.*, p. 246.

[78] Quoted in Gaddis, *Strategies of Containment*, p. 29.

[79] Gardner, "Rethinking Our Soviet Policy," *In These Times* (December 22, 1983).

[80] Kennan, *American Diplomacy*, p. 177. In his latest book, *Sketches From A Life* (New York, 1989), Kennan has addressed the accusation that he is an expatriate. "I am not sure that I understand what the term means," he says. "Anyone who spent, as I did, nineteen out of the first twenty years of his active professional life in Europe would be very insensitive indeed if he were not affected by it. And to understand things beyond one's original cultural horizon is only to add them, in a sense, to what one already is. To do this does not mean that what one already is becomes discarded. Beyond which, if an American becomes 'expatriated,' he does so in a way which is itself an expression of his Americanism" (p. 363).

[81] Kennan, "The Legacy of Woodrow Wilson," 13.

[82] *The Decline of Bismarck's European Order: Franco-Russian Relations, 1875–1890* (Princeton, N. J., 1979) and *The Fateful Alliance: France, Russia, and the Coming of the First World War* (New York, 1984). The quotation from Gardner is from his exegesis of the "X" article, in *Architects of Illusion*, p. 285.

[83] Kennan, *The Decline of Bismarck's European Order*, pp. 421–22.

George Kennan

Comments on the paper entitled "Kennan versus Wilson" by Professor Thomas J. Knock

THE following comments are in no way intended as a rebuttal to Professor Knock's wholly admirable paper, for the comprehensiveness and fairness of which I am most appreciative, but rather as a few random observations on some of his points.

1. *The universalist approaches*, of Wilson and others of his time.

My distrust of these approaches arose from the difficulty I experienced in trying to generalize about the factors determining the behavior of the members of the international community, as it was emerging in the aftermath of the Second World War. In both the formative influences bearing upon the behavior of states, and in the effects of that behavior on the international community, there were such enormous variations and differences that I saw no possibility of treating all countries effectively under any single juridical or organizational framework. War, I thought, had really lost all rational function among the great industrialized powers; it was too destructive to serve any useful purposes; it had to be in some way ruled out. To be sure, the Stalin regime being what it was, I saw no way that ruling-out could be achieved in the case of Russia except by an adequate balance of opposing power, primarily political (because that was where the threat was) but also, in a defensive sense, military. And this opposing power, in the circumstances of that period, would have to be largely American. No multilateral organization, I thought, could achieve it.

But in the case of the small and new countries now coming into existence in such great numbers in consequence of decolonization, I saw little likelihood of ruling out wars, and indeed no apocalyptic danger even if war occurred. The regimes by which these new countries were governed were unsupported by any long tradition of independence; their leaders were inexperienced, often passionate, short-

sighted, and unrestrained. It was not to be expected that they could always be prevented from using force against one another. And the safety of the world could not be seriously endangered (at least not so long as the great powers handled themselves wisely) by their squabbles and skirmishes. What was important, I considered, was that the dream of world peace, of such great ultimate importance, should not be shattered by being saddled with the impossible task of trying to repress violence among these immature and relatively irresponsible minor political entities. No organizational system, in any case, could be devised that could be applied with equal effectiveness to all elements of so variegated a world community.

2. *The legalistic approaches.*

Similar reflections inspired my skepticism of that time about all schemes for achieving world peace by means of a rule of law, i.e., by treaties of arbitration and conciliation, etc. Wilson was of course by no means the initiator, or even the leading protagonist, of schemes of this nature. They had been an important preoccupation of the American statesmen, Republicans as well as Democrats, since the final decades of the nineteenth century. I may well have done Wilson an injustice in supposing that he leaned towards them.

All such schemes or devices seemed to me, in any case, to be predicated on an assumption that the status quo—the structure of international life, as it existed at any particular moment (i.e., the identity of states, their borders, their sovereignty, etc.)—was now permanent and fixed for all foreseeable time, so that if laws could only be established that would rule out any encroachment on these borders, these conditions, these institutions, world peace would be assured. These approaches, in other words, predicated an essentially static world.

I could never believe in the reality of such a world. It seemed to me that deep changes in the conditions of great masses of people—social, economic, psychological, etc.,—were constantly changing the demands to which the structure of international society would be obliged to respond, and that these demands would require adjustments in the entire pattern of international life: borders, sovereignties, names, even affiliations, of political entities. Any structure that attempted to rule out such changes, and made its success stand or fall with its ability to do just that, would, as I thought eventually destroy itself by the overweening quality of its commitment, and this would bring about the forfeiture of all that was valuable in it.

3. It was because most concepts of international organization (the League of Nations, the UN, etc.) seemed to me to be too deeply committed to one or the other of these impossible tasks: the ruling-out of violence or the ruling-out of change, that I was skeptical about them.

And the skepticism was greatest when the major aim seemed to be the assuring of international security on a global scale.

4. I would like to point out that those of my judgments about Wilson and the validity of his ideas that are usually referred to now were ones formed in 1950—in a period marked by three conditions that no longer apply.

First, this was the period of the Stalin regime in Russia. If there is any one feature of Professor Knock's paper to which I could take mild exception, it was the failure to point out that the severe judgments I made about the Soviet Union in the period prior to 1953 related precisely to that regime, not to what was to come after (which I could not foresee). They were not meant to arouse hatred, distrust and total rejection for the Russian people in their long-term personality.

Secondly, while we had, at that time, already developed and employed the nuclear fission bomb, I still hoped, fondly and naively, that the development of the nuclear weapon into a major element (or supposed element) of military strength, especially with the great powers, could be avoided. The fact that it has not been avoided, and that the danger it presents has now assumed global dimensions, creates a requirement for international action, and this on a global scale, that was never present in Wilson's time. This requirement gives new importance and significance to his dreams and hopes for a world order.

Thirdly, a similar requirement is now posed, but on an even more imperative and vast scale, by the global environmental crisis now so clearly advancing upon us. Wilson could not, of course, foresee this; nor could I, when lecturing at Chicago in 1950. But I attach greatest importance to it, precisely in its relationship to the question of international organization. It seems to me that it places demands on the international community, this time in the name of environmental protection, not dissimilar to those that Wilson would have liked to place upon it in the name of world peace.

I think it may well be (and all of you at the conference will be better able to judge this than I am) that Wilson, although he could not *know* these things I have just been mentioning, may have *sensed* them, and that they may have played a part in his reactions to the war and to the immediate post-hostilities period.

I must, however, add one word of caution. The more obvious becomes the necessity of widespread international collaboration in the interests of global environmental protection, the more acute will become the hitherto unsolved problem of decision-making among the members of a decidedly heterogenous international community. The principle of one government–one vote is, in view of the enormous disparities in what it is that a government represents, absurd and es-

sentially unworkable. A system of weighted values among the views of government leads, on the other hand, to invidious comparisons, and to suspicions of great-power domination. Neither the League of Nations nor the United Nations was able to find a fully satisfactory answer to this problem; but whoever tries to organize world society for a concerted response to the global environmental problem will have to do so. Whether Wilson's ideas, as cultivated by him within his lifetime, would have been adequate to this task, no one could say. But even if they had not been, who is to say that he, if confronted with this problem, would not have developed other ideas?

I now view Wilson, in any case, as a man who like so many other people of broad vision and acute sensitivities, was ahead of his time, and did not live long enough to know what great and commanding relevance many of his ideas would acquire before this century was out. In this sense, I have to correct or modify, at this stage of my own life, many of the impressions I had about him at an earlier stage. In his vision of the future needs of world society, I now see Wilson as ahead of any other statesman of his time.

Carol Bondhus Fitzgerald
Manfred F. Boemeke

BIBLIOGRAPHY OF WORKS BY ARTHUR S. LINK

From the author

Thinking back over my experiences as a historical writer, biographer, and editor, I am struck by the fact that I have always felt a good deal of tension while writing general history. My models of this genre have been Gibbon and Mommsen who, it seems to me, demonstrated that it is possible to organize huge bodies of historical evidence and to use a myriad of particular facts to construct narratives that tell a story that is significant because of the writers' powers of divination, historical imagination, and ability to differentiate between what is of ephemeral interest and what is of enduring significance.

I have enjoyed writing general history because it has compelled me to use all my knowledge and intellectual power to tell an extended story in compact form, but I have never been totally pleased with the product. To write general history, one has to generalize, and generalizations can convey only partial truth.

My long involvement with Woodrow Wilson has permitted me to do another and, to me, a more satisfying kind of historical work—to deal with a large subject with ever-increasing emphasis upon the particulars. I came to the study of Wilson and his time through the side door, so to speak. I was trained in Southern history at the University of North Carolina by the master, Fletcher Melvin Green. I was primarily interested in twentieth-century political history. The Wilson administration was the first since the Jackson administration in which Southerners had played a significant part in effecting a fundamental reform of basic national institutions and policies. I wanted to show how Southern reform impulses generated by Populism converged with national reform impulses to produce the New Freedom, the most comprehensive national reform program in American history to that date.

Two things happened to me in doing the research for my dissertation that changed my life in history. In doing the research for the background chapters, I gazed upon a political landscape that I had not known existed: a South

This bibliography originally appeared in *American History, A Bibliographic Review*, Vol. 5, 1989. Meckler Corporation, 11 Ferry Lane West, Westport, CN 06880. Reprinted with permission.

that was in tne vanguard of what is called progressivism, a region whose progressive (reformist, modernizing) leaders looked to Wilson as the most promising instrumentality in national politics. The story of the intersection of regional and national movements was enough for a dissertation, and I ended it with Wilson's election in 1912. Out of this work came my lifelong interest in progressivism.

Work on my dissertation also hooked me on Wilson, and, even before I received the Ph.D., I had begun work on what I thought would be a two-volume biography. But writing the first volume, *Wilson: The Road to the White House*, set me upon a longer road. Along that road, for about fifteen years, I wrote a general history of the first Wilson administration and four volumes in the still-unfinished biography. Then, in 1958, came the invitation of the Woodrow Wilson Foundation and Princeton University to undertake a comprehensive edition of the papers of Woodrow Wilson. Acceptance meant abandoning the biography for an indeterminate time, but I could not resist the challenge.

Work on *The Wilson Papers* has consumed most of my scholarly time and energy since the early 1960s, and that work has brought what has been to me ultimate satisfaction as a historian—of bringing together the documentary record, not only of one individual but also of an important period; of sifting out from among millions of documents those that I thought were of enduring historical significance; of providing an appropriate context of annotation; and of trying to produce a trustworthy printed record.

I have been blessed by help since my days as a graduate student. I could have accomplished little without the support of the Rosenwald, Guggenheim, and Rockefeller foundations and of Northwestern and Princeton universities. I could never have edited *The Wilson Papers* without the collaboration of a long line of editorial associates and the unflagging support of the Woodrow Wilson Foundation and Princeton University. And always at my side as my best editors have been my wife, Margaret Douglas Link, and my colleague and friend of forty-one years, Richard W. Leopold. I thank Carol Fitzgerald and Manfred Boemeke for bringing my bibliography together so handsomely.

Monographs: Books, Pamphlets and Papers

This section includes monographs written and edited by Arthur S. Link. All editions, and foreign translations, are listed.

1941

"A History of the Buildings at the University of North Carolina." [A thesis submitted to the faculty of the University of North Carolina in partial fulfillment of the degree of Bachelor of Arts, with honors, in the Department of History.] University of North Carolina, 1941

1942

"The Wilson Movement in the South: A Study in Political Liberalism." Master's thesis, University of North Carolina, 1942.

1945

"The South and the Democratic Campaign of 1910–1912." Ph.D. dissertation, University of North Carolina, 1945.

1947

Wilson: *The Road to the White House.* Princeton, NJ: Princeton University Press, 1947, (*Wilson*, Vol. I)
Wilson: *The Road to the White House.* Princeton, NJ: Princeton University Press, "First Princeton Paperback," 1968, 1947, (*Wilson*, Vol. I).

1952

Problems in American History. Edited with Richard W. Leopold. New York: Prentice-Hall, Prentice-Hall History Series, 1952.
Problems in American History. 2nd ed. Edited with Richard W. Leopold. Englewood Cliffs, NJ: Prentice-Hall, Prentice-Hall History Series, 1957.
Problems in American History. 3rd ed. Edited with Richard W. Leopold and Stanley Coben. 2 vols. Englewood Cliffs, NJ: Prentice-Hall, Prentice-Hall History Series, 1966. Each volume separately titled: Vol. I, *Through Reconstruction;* Vol. II, *Since Reconstruction.*
Problems in American History. 4th ed. Edited with Richard W. Leopold and Stanley Coben. 2 vols. Englewood Cliffs, NJ: Prentice-Hall, Prentice-Hall History Series, 1972. Each volume separately titled: Vol. I, *Through Reconstruction;* Vol. II, *Since Reconstruction.*

1954

Woodrow Wilson and the Progressive Era, 1910–1917. New York: Harper & Brothers, The New American Nation Series, 1954.
Woodrow Wilson and the Progressive Era, 1910–1917. London: H. Hamilton, The New American Nation Series, 1954.
Woodrow Wilson and the Progressive Era, 1910–1917. New York: Harper & Row, Torchbook Edition, The New American Nation Series, 1963.
Woodrow Wilson and the Progressive Era, 1910–1917. New York: Harper & Row, Harper Torchbook, TB 3023, The New American Nation Series, 1975, 1954.
Woodrow Wilson and the Progressive Era, 1910–1917. Norwalk, CT: The Easton Press, Collectors Edition, 1988.

1955

American Epoch: A History of the United States since the 1890s. New York: Alfred A. Knopf, 1955.
American Epoch: A History of the United States since the 1890s. 2nd ed., revised and rewritten. With the collaboration of William B. Catton. New York: Alfred A. Knopf, 1963.
American Epoch: A History of the United States since the 1890s. 3rd ed. With the collaboration of William B. Catton and the assistance of William M. Leary. New York: Alfred A. Knopf, 1967.

American Epoch: A History of the United States since the 1890s. 3rd ed. With the collaboration of William B. Catton and the assistance of William M. Leary. 3 vols. New York: Alfred A. Knopf, Borzoi paperback, 1967. Each volume separately titled: Vol. I, *1897–1920;* Vol. II, *1921–1941;* Vol. III, *1938–1966.*

American Epoch: A History of the United States since 1900. 4th ed. With William B. Catton. 3 vols. New York: Alfred A. Knopf, 1973. Each volume separately titled: Vol. I, *The Progressive Era and the First World War, 1990–1920;* Vol. II, *The Age of Franklin D. Roosevelt, 1921–1945;* Vol. III, *The Era of the Cold War, 1946–1973.*

American Epoch: A History of the United States since 1900. 5th ed. With William B. Catton, maps and charts by Theodore R. Miller. 2 vols. New York: Alfred A. Knopf, 1980. Each volume separately titled: Vol. I, *An Era of Economic Change, Reform, and World Wars, 1900–1945;* Vol. II, *An Era of Total War and Uncertain Peace, 1938–1980.*

American Epoch: A History of the United States since 1900. 5th ed. With William B. Catton. 2 vols. New York: Alfred A. Knopf, 1980. Each volume separately titled: Vol I: *An Era of Economic Change, Reform, and World Wars, 1900–1945;* Vol. II: *An Era of Total War and Uncertain Peace, 1938–1980.*

American Epoch: A History of the United States since 1900. 6th ed. With William B. Catton and William A. Link. 2 vols. New York: Alfred A. Knopf, 1987. Each volume separately titled: Vol. I: *An Era of Economic and Social Change, Reform, and World Wars, 1900–1945;* Vol. II: *An Era of War and Uncertain Peace, 1936–1985.*

Translations

História Moderna dos Estados Unidos. Com a colaboracão de William B. Catton. Traducão do Waltensir Dutra, Alvaro Cabral e Fernando de Castro Ferro. 3 vols. Rio de Janeiro: ZAHAR Editores, 1965. (Biblioteca de cultura históric.)

Beijing: China Social Science Publications, 1983.

1956

Wilson: The New Freedom. Princeton, NJ: Princeton University Press, 1956, (*Wilson,* Vol. II).

Wilson: The New Freedom. Princeton, NJ: Princeton University Press, Princeton paperbacks, 1968, 1956, (*Wilson,* Vol. II).

1957

Wilson the Diplomatist: A Look at His Major Foreign Policies. [The Albert Shaw Lectures on Diplomatic History, 1956] Baltimore: The Johns Hopkins Press, 1957.

Wilson the Diplomatist: A Look at His Major Foreign Policies. Chicago: Quadrangle Books, 1963, 1957.

Wilson the Diplomatist: A Look at His Major Foreign Policies. New York: New Viewpoints, 1974, 1957.

Translation

Tokyo: Tamagawa University Press, *1979.*

1959

President Wilson and His English Critics: An Inaugural Lecture Delivered before the University of Oxford on 13 May 1959. [Text of lecture delivered as the Harold Vyvyan Harmsworth Professor of American History] Oxford: Clarendon Press, 1959.
Der idealistische Realismus Woodrow Wilsons. [The final lecture in a series devoted to American Civilization, sponsored by the Freiburg University Commission for American Studies, this address was given in Frieburg/Breisgau on July 24, 1959.] [text in German and English] Hrsg. von der Kommission für Amerikastudien der Universität Freiburg in Verbindung mit dem Amerika-Haus Freiburg. Freiburg im Breisgau, Oktober 1959, (Schriftenreihe Amerika-Studien, No. 1).

1960

Wilson: The Struggle for Neutrality, 1914–1915. Princeton, NJ: Princeton University Press, 1960, (*Wilson,* Vol. III).

Translation

La Política de los Estados Unidos en América Latina, 1913–1916. [Traducción de Fernando Rosenzweig]. México City: Fondo de Cultura Económica, 1960. (Adapted from *Wilson: The New Freedom,* and *Wilson: The Struggle for Neutrality.*)

1962

With Katharine Edith Brand. *Edith Bolling Wilson: Tributes Given at a Memorial Service at the Woodrow Wilson Birthplace, Staunton, Virginia, January 28, 1962.* n.p., 1962?

1963

The Democratic Experience: A Short American History. With Louis B. Wright and others. Glenview, IL: Scott, Foresman and Co., 1963.
The Democratic Experience: A Short American History. Rev. Ed. With Louis B. Wright and others. Glenview, IL: Scott, Foresman and Co., 1968.
The Democratic Experience: A Short American History. 3rd ed. With Carl N. Degler and others. Glenview, IL: Scott, Foresman and Co., 1973.
Our American Republic. With David S. Muzzey. Boston: Ginn and Co., 1963.
Our American Republic. New Annotated Edition. With David S. Muzzey. Boston: Ginn and Co., 1966.
Woodrow Wilson: A Brief Biography. Cleveland and New York: World Publishing Co., American Presidents Series, 1963.
Woodrow Wilson: A Brief Biography. Chicago: Quadrangle Books, 1972, 1963.

Translations

Woodrow Wilson: Pequena Biografia. [Traducão de Nair Lacerda]. São Paulo: Livrária Martins, 1964.
Tokyo: Nanso Publishing Co., 1977.
Burmese ed.

1964

Wilson: Confusions and Crises, 1915–1916. Princeton, NJ: Princeton University Press, 1964, (*Wilson*, Vol. IV).

1965

Our Country's History. 1st revised ed. With David S. Muzzey. Boston: Ginn and Co. 1965.
Wilson: Campaigns for Progressivism and Peace, 1916–1917. Princeton, NJ: Princeton University Press, 1965, (*Wilson*, Vol. V).
Writing Southern History: Essays in Historiography in Honor of Fletcher M. Green. Edited with Rembert W. Patrick. Baton Rouge: Louisiana State University Press, 1967, 1965 (paperback).
Writing Southern History: Essays in Historiography in Honor of Fletcher M. Green. Edited with Rembert W. Patrick. Westport, CT: Greenwood Press, 1981, 1965.

1966

The Papers of Woodrow Wilson. [Sponsored by the Woodrow Wilson Foundation and Princeton University.] Edited by Arthur S. Link. Princeton, NJ: Princeton University Press, Vol. I, 1966– [63 vols. to date].

1967

The First Presbyterian Church of Princeton: Two Centuries of History. Princeton, NJ: The First Presbyterian Church, 1967.

1968

The Growth of American Democracy: An Interpretative History. Boston: Ginn and Co., 1968.
Woodrow Wilson: A Profile. Edited by Arthur S. Link. New York: Hill and Wang, American Profiles, 1968.

1969

The Progressive Era and the Great War, 1869–1920. With William M. Leary, Jr. New York: Appleton-Century-Crofts, Goldentree Bibliographies in American History, 1969.
The Progressive Era and the Great War, 1869–1920. 2nd ed. With William M. Leary, Jr. Arlington Heights, IL: AHM Publishing Corp. Goldentree Bibliographies in American History, 1978.

The Impact of World War I. Edited by Arthur S. Link. New York: Harper and Row, Interpretations of American History, 1969.

1970

The Diplomacy of World Power: the United States, 1889–1920. [Documents of Modern History] Edited with William M. Leary, Jr. New York: St. Martin's Press, 1970.
The Diplomacy of World Power, 1889–1920. Edited with William M. Leary, Jr. London: Edward Arnold, 1970.

1971

The Democratic Heritage: A History of the United States. With Stanley Coben. Waltham, MA: Ginn and Co., 1971.
The Democratic Heritage: A History of the United States. With Stanley Coben. 2 vols. Waltham, MA: Ginn and Co., 1971. Paperback edition. Each volume separately titled: Vol. I: *To 1877;* Vol. II, *Since 1965.*
The Higher Realism of Woodrow Wilson and other essays by Arthur S. Link. Foreword by Dewey W. Grantham. Nashville, TN: Vanderbilt University Press, 1971.

1972

Liberal Education in a Time of Revolution: An Address by Arthur S. Link, October 17, 1972, Hampden-Sydney College in Virginia. [Given during the official convocation signalling the inauguration of Bicentennial '76.] Hampden-Sydney, VA: Hampden-Sydney College, 1972.

1973

Crucial American Elections. With others. Philadelphia: American Philosophical Society, 1973.
Wilson's Diplomacy: An International Symposium. With others. Cambridge, MA: Schenkman Publishing, The American Forum Series, 1973.

1979

Woodrow Wilson: Revolution, War, and Peace. Arlington Heights, IL: Harlan Davidson, 1979. (Based in part on the author's *Wilson the Diplomatist,* first published in 1957.)

1981

The American People: A History. With Stanley Coben, Robert V. Remini, Douglas Greenberg, and Robert C. McMath, Jr. Arlington Heights, IL: AHM Publishing Corp., 1981.
The American People: A History. With Stanley Coben, Robert V. Remini, Douglas Greenberg, and Robert C. McMath, Jr. 2 vols. Arlington Heights, IL: AHM Publishing Corp., 1981, paperback. Each volume separately titled: Vol. I *To 1877;* Vol. II, *Since 1865.*
The American People: A History. 2nd ed. With Stanley Coben, Robert V. Remini, Douglas Greenberg, and Robert C. McMath, Jr. 2 vols. Arlington Heights,

IL: Harlan Davidson, 1987, paperback. Each volume separately titled: Vol. I *To 1877;* Vol. II, *Since 1865.*

A Concise History of the American People. [Revised and condensed edition of *The American People,* 1981] With Robert V. Remini, Douglas Greenberg, and Robert C. McMath, Jr. Arlington Heights, IL: Harlan Davidson, 1984.

A Concise History of the American People. [Revised and condensed edition of *The American People,* 1981] With Robert V. Remini, Douglas Greenberg, and Robert C. McMath, Jr. 2 vols. Arlington Heights, IL: Harlan Davidson, 1984, (paperback). Each volume separately titled: Vol. I: *To 1877;* Vol. II *Since 1975.*

1982

Woodrow Wilson and a Revolutionary World, 1913–1921. [Papers originally presented at an international symposium at Princeton University from October 10 through October 12, 1979.] Edited by Arthur S. Link. Chapel Hill: University of North Carolina Press, 1982. (Issued as a supplementary volume to *The Papers of Woodrow Wilson.*)

1983

Progressivism. With Richard L. McCormick. Arlington Heights, IL: Harlan Davidson, The American History Series, 1983.

The Twentieth Century: An American History. With William A. Link. Arlington Heights, IL: Harlan Davidson, 1983.

Articles in Journals, Newspapers and Yearbooks

Articles include essays, speeches, contributions to symposia, letters to the editor, and transcribed broadcasts which have been printed in serial publications. Reprints when identified have been listed with the original citation.

1944

"The Wilson Movement in Texas, 1910–1912." [Research on this article was made possible by a grant from the Julius Rosenwald Fund.] *Southwestern Historical Quarterly* 48 (Oct. 1944): 169–185.

"Correspondence Relating to the Progressive Party's 'Lily White' Policy in 1912." [The material for this contribution was obtained during the course of research under the auspices of a grant from the Julius Rosenwald Fund for a study of the presidential campaign of 1912 in the South.] *Journal of Southern History* 10 (Nov. 1944): 480–490.

1945

"The Underwood Presidential Movement of 1912." [Research for this article was made possible by a grant-in-aid from the Julius Rosenwald Fund.] *Journal of Southern History* 11 (May 1945): 230–245.

"The Baltimore Convention of 1912." [The author's research in this field, made possible by a grant from the Julius Rosenwald Fund, has been embodied in an unpublished doctoral dissertation, 'The South and the Democratic Campaign of 1912,' deposited in the Library of the University of North Carolina.] *American Historical Review* 50 (July 1945): 691–713.

"A Letter from One of Wilson's Managers." *American Historical Review* 50 (July 1945): 768–775.

"The Democratic Pre-Convention Campaign of 1912 in Georgia." [Research for this article was made possible by a grant-in-aid from the Julius Rosenwald Fund.] *Georgia Historical Quarterly* 29 (Sept. 1945): 143–158.

1946

"Democratic Politics and the Presidential Campaign of 1912 in Tennessee." [Research on this article was financed by grants from the Julius Rosenwald Fund.] *East Tennessee Historical Society's Publications* Nov. 18, 1946: 107–130.

"The Progressive Movement in the South, 1870–1914." [Research on this article was made possible by a grant from the Julius Rosenwald Fund.] *North Carolina Historical Review* 23 (Apr. 1946): 172–195; reprinted in Bobbs-Merrill Reprint Series in History, H-128; reprinted in *Myth and Southern History.* Edited by Patrick Gerster and Nicholas Cords. 2nd ed. Urbana: University of Illinois Press, 1989.

"The Federal Reserve Policy and the Agricultural Depression of 1920–1921." *Agricultural History* 20 (July 1946): 166–175.

"Theodore Roosevelt and the South in 1912." [Research on this article was made possible by a grant from the Julius Rosenwald Fund.] *North Carolina Historical Review* 23 (July 1946): 313–324.

"The Wilson Movement in North Carolina." [Research on this article was made possible by a grant from the Julius Rosenwald Fund.] *North Carolina Historical Review* 23 (Oct. 1946): 483–494.

1947

"The Negro as a Factor in the Campaign of 1912." [Paper read at the thirty-first annual meeting of the Association for the Study of Negro Life and History, in Philadelphia, October 26, 1946] *Journal of Negro History* 23 (Jan. 1947): 81–89.

"The Enigma of Woodrow Wilson." *American Mercury* 65 (Sept. 1947): 303–313.

1948

"A Decade of Biographical Contributions to Recent American History." [This essay is an amplification of a paper read at a joint session of the American Historical Association and the National Council for the Social Studies, at Cleveland, Ohio, Dec. 29, 1947.] *Mississippi Valley Historical Review* 34 (Mar. 1948): 637–652.

"Samuel Taylor Coleridge and the Economic and Political Crisis in Great Brit-

ain, 1816–1820." [Adapted from a paper written at Columbia University, 1945] *Journal of the History of Ideas* 9 (June 1948): 323–338.

1951

"The South and the 'New Freedom': An Interpretation." *American Scholar* 20 (Summer 1951): 314–324; reprinted in *Recent America: Conflicting Interpretations of the Great Issues.* Edited by Sidney Fine, 84–93. New York: Macmillan [1962] and subsequent editions; reprinted in *American History: Recent Interpretations.* Edited by Abraham S. Eisenstadt, II, 273–284. 2nd ed. New York: Thomas Y. Crowell, 1969.

1953

"The Middle West and the Coming of the First World War." [Given at the joint session on 'The Middle West and the Coming of the Two World Wars' at the forty-fifth annual meeting of the Mississippi Valley Historical Association held at Chicago, April 17–19, 1952.] *Ohio State Archaeological and Historical Quarterly* 62 (Apr. 1953): 109–121.

1954

"Theodore Roosevelt in His Letters." [Review essay of *The Letters of Theodore Roosevelt* edited by E. E. Morison, and *The Republican Roosevelt* by John M. Blum] 43 n.s. *Yale Review* (Summer 1954): 589–598.

1956

"Woodrow Wilson and the Democratic Party." [This article is drawn in part from the author's forthcoming *Wilson: The New Freedom,* which will be published by the Princeton University Press during the coming autumn.] *Review of Politics* 18 (Apr. 1956): 146–156.
"A Portrait of Woodrow Wilson." [Wilson Centennial Number] *Virginia Quarterly Review* 32 (Autumn 1956): 524–540.

1959

"What Happened to the Progressive Movement in the 1920's?" [This paper was read in a slightly different form before a joint meeting of the American Historical Association and the Mississippi Valley Historical Association in New York City, Dec. 28, 1957.] *American Historical Review* 64 (July 1959): 833–851; reprinted in *American History: Recent Interpretations.* Edited by Abraham S. Eisenstadt, II, 331–349. 2nd ed. New York: Thomas Y. Crowell, 1969; reprinted in Bobbs-Merrill Reprint Series in History H-129; reprinted in *Progressivism; the Critical Issues.* Edited by David M. Kennedy, 147–164. Boston: Little, Brown, 1971; reprinted in *Interpretations of American History: Patterns and Perspectives.* Edited by General N. Grob and George Athan Billias, II, 309–329. 2nd ed. New York: The Free Press, 1972.
"From Gettysburg to Little Rock." [Adapted from a BBC radio broadcast, Third Programme] *The Listener* 61, 21 May 1959, 871–873.

1962

"The Historian's Vocation." *Theology Today* 19 (Apr. 1962): 75–89; reprinted in *God, History and Historians: An Anthology of Modern Christian Views of History.* Edited by C. T. McIntire, 373–389. New York: Oxford University Press, 1977.

"President Wilson's Plan to Resign in 1916." *Princeton University Library Chronicle* 23 (Summer 1962): 167–172.

1963

"The Higher Realism of Woodrow Wilson." *Journal of Presbyterian History* 41 (Mar. 1963): 1–13; reprinted as "Wilson: Idealism and Realism," in *Woodrow Wilson: A Profile,* 163–177.

"Woodrow Wilson and the Life of Faith." [Article to commemorate the fiftieth anniversary of the inauguration of Woodrow Wilson] *Presbyterian Life* 16 (Mar. 1, 1963): 8–15.

1964

"The Church and Its Ministry: Crisis and Renewal." [Symposium on the Nature of Ministry] *McCormick Quarterly* 17 (Mar. 1964): 35–42.

"Woodrow Wilson: Christian in Government." [Essay based on a lecture delivered November 21, 1963, in Washington as part of the Woodrow Wilson Lecture Series sponsored by the Council for The National Presbyterian Church and Center] *Christianity Today* 8, 3 July 1964, 908–912; reprinted as "Woodrow Wilson, Presbyterian in Government." In *Calvinism and the Political Order.* Edited by George L. Hunt, 157–174. Philadelphia: Westminster Press, 1965.

1966

"Thomas Jefferson Wertenbaker (1879–1966)." [memorial] *Year Book of the American Philosophical Society* (1966): 202–206.

"The Proposed Confession of 1967: Another View." *Presbyterian Life* 19 (Mar. 15, 1966): 15–17, 35–38.

"Woodrow Wilson and Peace Moves." [adapted from a BBC radio broadcast, Third Programme] *The Listener* 75, 16 June 1966, 868–871; reprinted as "Wilson Moves to the Center of the Stage of World Affairs," in *The Impact of World War I,* 37–43.

"An Author Interprets His Own Work." *High School Social Studies Notes* No. 18, (1966–1967): 3.

1967

"The Case for Woodrow Wilson." [Review essay of *Thomas Woodrow Wilson* by Sigmund Freud and William C. Bullitt] *Harper's Magazine* 224 (Apr. 1967): 85–93.

1968

"Woodrow Wilson and the Study of Administration." [Paper read to the Society, April 18, 1968.] *Proceedings of the American Philospohical Society* 112 (Dec. 9, 1968): 431–433.

1970

"Woodrow Wilson: The American as Southerner." [This paper was delivered on October 30, 1969, as the presidential address at the annual meeting of the Southern Historical Association.] *Journal of Southern History* 34 (Feb. 1970): 3–17.

1971

"Woodrow Wilson and the Progressive Movement in New Jersey." *Princeton History* 1 (1971): 25–38.

1978

Weinstein, Edwin A. and James W. Anderson, joint authors. "Woodrow Wilson's Political Personality: A Reappraisal." *Political Science Quarterly* 93 (Winter 1978–1979): 585–598.

1979

"Letter from the President." *ADE Newsletter* (Association for Documentary Editing) 1 (Mar. 1979): 1.
"Verbatim et Literatim." *ADE Newsletter* (Association for Documentary Editing) 1 (May 1979): 1–2.

1980

"Where We Are Now and Where We Might Go." [Presidential address, Association for Documentary Editing] *Newsletter of the Association for Documentary Editing* 1 (Feb. 1980): 1–4.

1981

"The Historian and the World of Documents." [Fiftieth Anniversary of the Southern History Collection] *The Bookmark* (Friends of the University of North Carolina Library) No. 50 (1981): 8–21.
"'Enormous White House Staff' Weakens the Presidency: A Conversation with Arthus S. Link." [interview] *U.S. News & World Report* 95, 15 Aug. 1983, 43.

1984

Untitled. [Letter to the editor, written at the invitation of the editor, with David W. Hirst, John Wells Davidson, John E. Little] *Journal of American History* 70 (Mar. 1984): 945–955.

1985

"The American Historical Association, 1884–1984: Retrospect and Prospect."
[Presidential address, American Historical Association] *American Historical
Review* 90 (Mar. 1985): 1–17.
"That Cobb Interview." [This essay is the presidential address delivered to the
Organization of American Historians in Minneapolis, April 19, 1985.] *Journal of American History* 72 (June 1985): 7–17.

1988

"Woodrow Wilson [as Writer]." *Princeton History* 7 (1988): 11–29.

1990

"David Hunter McAlpin (1897–1989)." *Princeton University Library Chronicle* 94
(Winter 1990): 204–209.

Contributions by Arthur S. Link to Books by Others

This section includes original essays, speeches not previously published, and
extracts from books by Arthur S. Link that have been published in monographs edited by others.

1948

"Newspaper Reports of Woodrow Wilson's Speeches, Statements, and Papers,
1910–1912." In *Woodrow Wilson: A Selected Bibliography*. Edited by Laura S.
Turnbull, 137–143. Princeton, NJ: Princeton University Press, 1948; reprinted, Port Washington, NY: Kennikat Press, 1972, 1948.

1956

"The Progressive." In *The Greatness of Woodrow Wilson, 1856–1956*. Edited by
Em Bowles Alsop, 137–150. Introduction by Dwight D. Eisenhower. New
York: Rinehart & Co., 1956.
"Woodrow Wilson." [Adapted from a radio broadcast series organized by the
Society of American Historians] In *The American Story: The Age of Exploration
to the Age of the Atom*. Edited by Earl Schenck, 283–288. Great Neck, NY:
Channel Press, 1956.
"Wilson the Man and the Symbol." In *Lectures and Seminar at the University of
Chicago, January 30–February 3, 1956, in Celebration of the Centennial of Woodrow Wilson, 1856–1956*, 112–134, discussion, 135–159. Chicago: The University of Chicago in cooperation with The Woodrow Wilson Foundation,
1956.

1957

"The Cotton Crisis, the South, and Anglo-American Diplomacy, 1914–1915."
In *Studies in Southern History in Memory of Albert Ray Newsome, 1894–1951, by*

his Former Students at the University of North Carolina. [The James Sprunt Studies in History and Political Science, Volume 39] Edited by J. Carlyle Sitterson, 122–138. Chapel Hill: University of North Carolina Press, 1957.

"The Contributions of Woodrow Wilson." [Address given November 29, 1956, commemorating the centennial anniversary of the birth of Woodrow Wilson] *Woodrow Wilson Centennial Addresses Delivered at Miami University, Oxford, Ohio,* 12–19. Oxford, OH: Miami University, 1957.

"Woodrow Wilson: The Philosophy, Methods, and Impact of Leadership." In *Woodrow Wilson and the World of Today.* Edited by Arthur P. Dudden, 1–21. Philadelphia: University of Pennsylvania Press, 1957.

1958

"Houston, David Franklin." *Dictionary of American Biography,* XI (Supplement 1): 321–32. New York: Charles Scribner's Sons, 1958.

"Portrait of the President." [Excerpted from *Wilson: The New Freedom*] In *The Philosophy and Policies of Woodrow Wilson.* Edited by Earl Latham, 3–27. Chicago: University of Chicago Press, 1958.

"Wilson the Diplomatist." [Excerpted from *Woodrow Wilson: A Look at His Major Foreign Policies*] In *The Philosophy and Policies of Woodrow Wilson.* Chicago: University of Chicago Press, 1958.

1962

"Wilson, (Thomas) Woodrow." *Encyclopedia Americana* (1962) 29: 6–11; reprinted in subsequent editions.

"Wilson and American Neutrality, 1914–1917." [Excerpted from *Wilson the Diplomatist,* 31–90] In *Recent America: Conflicting Interpretations of the Great Issues.* Edited by Sidney Fine, 123–150. New York: Macmillan, 1962; 2nd ed., 1965, 303–329.

"Wilson, Woodrow." *World Book Encyclopedia* (1962) 19: 268–276; reprinted in subsequent editions.

1966

"Woodrow Wilson, 'Fourteen Points.'" [Text of Wilson's address to Congress, 8 January 1918, with introductory and concluding commentary by Arthur S. Link] In *An American Primer.* Edited by Daniel J. Boorstin, II, 772–781. Chicago: The University of Chicago Press, 1966.

Foreword to *Letters on the League of Nations, from the Files of Raymond B. Fosdick* by Raymond B. Fosdick. Princeton, NJ: Princeton University Press, 1966 (Supplementary volume to *The Papers of Woodrow Wilson*).

1967

"Daniels, Josephus." *Encyclopaedia Britannica* (1967) 7: 53; reprinted in subsequent editions.

1968

"Contemporary History." [panel discussion] in *The Challenge of Local History: A Conference Designed to Broaden the Interests of New York State Local Historians in Scholarly History*, 71–78. Albany: The University of the State of New York, The State Education Department, 1968.

"Wilson and the Ordeal of Neutrality." In *History of the Twentieth Century*. Edited by A. J. P. Taylor, V, 652–656. London: Purnell Publishers, 1968–1971.

1969

"Woodrow Wilson and His Presbyterian Inheritance." In *Essays in Scotch-Irish History*. Edited by E. R. R. Green, 1–17. London: Routledge & Kegan Paul, 1969.

1970

"Woodrow Wilson and American Traditions." [Paper delivered as lecture to the Society of Mayflower Decendants in Michigan.] In *Outstanding American Statesmen*. Edited by Russell H. Lucas, 17–33. Cambridge, MA: Schenkman Publishing, 1970.

"World War I." In *Interpreting American History: Conversations with Historians*. Edited by John A. Garraty, Part II, 121–144. New York: Macmillan Co., 1970.

1971

Leary, William M., Jr., joint author, "Election of 1916." In *History of American Presidential Elections, 1789–1968*. Edited by Arthur M. Schlesinger, Jr., and Fred L. Israel, III, 2245–2345. New York: Chelsea House Publishers, 1971.

"Thomas Woodrow Wilson." In *History of the First World War*. Edited by Barrie Pitt, V, 2001. London: Purnell Publishers, 1971.

"America Goes to War." In *History of the First World War*. Edited by Barrie Pitt, V, 2012–2020. London: Purnell Publishers, 1971.

"Wilson's 14 Points." In *History of the First World War*. Edited by Barrie Pitt, VI, 2545–2552. London: Purnell Publishers, 1971.

"World Wars—U.S. Opinion and Policy, 1914–February 1917." *Encyclopaedia Britannica* (1971), 23: 731–736; reprinted in subsequent editions.

1972

Untitled. [Excerpt from *Wilson the Diplomatist*] In *Interpretations of American History: Patterns and Perspectives*. Edited by Gerald N. Grob and George Athan Billias, II, 244–261. 2nd ed. New York: The Free Press, 1972.

1973

Foreword to *Crucial American Elections: Symposium Presented at the Autumn General Meeting of the American Philosophical Society, November 10, 1972*. Philadel-

phia: American Philosophical Society, 1973, (Memoirs of the American Philosophical Society, volume 99).

1974

"United States, History of—IV. Imperialism, the Progressive Era, and the Rise to World Power, 1896–1920." *Encyclopaedia Britannica, Macropaedia* (1974, 1984) 18:981–987.

1980

"The President as Progressive." In *Every Four Years.* Edited by Robert C. Post, 152–163. Washington, DC: Smithsonian Exposition Books, 1980.
Foreword to *Colonel House in Paris: A Study of American Policy at the Paris Peace Conference 1919,* by Inga Floto. Princeton, NJ: Princeton University Press, 1980 (Supplementary volume to *The Papers of Woodrow Wilson*).

1982

"Woodrow Wilson: Hinge of the 20th Century." In *Woodrow Wilson: A Commemorative Celebration,* 20–26. Washington, DC: The Woodrow Wilson International Center for Scholars, 1982.

1984

"Woodrow Wilson." In *The Presidents: A Reference History.* Edited by Henry F. Graff, 435–464. New York: Charles Scribner's Sons, 1984.
Foreword to *Politics and Administration: Woodrow Wilson and American Public Administration.* Edited by Jack Rabin and James S. Bowman. New York: Marcel Dekker, 1984.

1985

"Imperialism, the Progressive Era . . ." *The New Encyclopaedia Britannica, Macropaedia* (1985) 29:248–254

1987

Foreword to *Tales of the Phelps-Dodge Family: A Chronicle of Five Generations* by Phyllis Dodge. Princeton, NJ: Princeton University Press, 1987.

1989

Foreword to *Imperial Challenge: Ambassador Count Bernstorff and German-American Relations, 1908–1917* by Reinhard R. Doerries. Chapel Hill: University of North Carolina Press, 1989 (Supplementary volume to *The Papers of Woodrow Wilson*).

1990

"Woodrow Wilson as Commander in Chief." With John Whiteclay Chambers, II. In *United States Military Under the Constitution of the United States, 1789–1989.* New York: New York University Press, 1990. Forthcoming.

Book Reviews by Arthur S. Link

1946

Rev. of *Public Men In and Out of Office* by J. T. Salter. *North Carolina Historical Review* 23 (Oct. 1946): 583–584.

1948

Rev. of *Woodrow Wilson and American Liberlism* by E. M. Hugh-Jones. *American Historical Review* 54 (Oct. 1948): 219–220.

Rev. of *The Papers of Walter Clark,* Vol. I edited by Aubrey Lee Brooks and Hugh Talmage Lefler. *Journal of Southern History* 14 (Nov. 1948): 563–565.

1949

Rev. of *Lincoln's Herndon* by David Donald. *Pennsylvania Magazine of History and Biography* 73 (July 1949): 407–408.

Rev. of *Dry Messiah* by Virginius Dabney. *Journal of Southern History* 15 (Nov. 1949): 539–541.

1950

Rev. (unsigned) of *Incredible Tale: The Odyssey of the Average American in the Last Half Century* by Gerald Johnson. *U.S. Quarterly Book Review* 6 (Sept. 1950): 332–333; another review *American Historical Review* 56 (Oct. 1950): 215.

Rev. (unsigned) of *Generation on Trial; U.S.A. v. Alger Hiss* by Alistair Cooke. *U.S. Quarterly Book Review* 6 (Dec. 1950): 460.

1951

Rev. of *The Papers of Walter Clark,* Vol. II edited by Aubrey Lee Brooks and Hugh Talmage Lefler. *Journal of Southern History* 17 (Feb. 1951): 106–107.

Rev. (unsigned) of *Quakers and Slavery* by Thomas E. Drake. *U.S. Quarterly Book Review* 7 (Mar. 1951): 52.

"Of a Long Life." Rev. of *My First Eighty-Three Years in America* by James W. Gerard. *Saturday Review of Literature* 34, 10 Mar. 1951, 12–13, 31.

Rev. of *The British Press and Wilsonian Neutrality* by Armin Rappaport. *American Historical Review* 56 (July 1951): 941.

"An Adoring Friend." Rev. of *Joe Tumulty and the Wilson Era* by John M. Blum. *Saturday Review of Literature* 37, 14 July 1951, 20, 36; another review in *Mississippi Valley Historical Review* 38 (Dec. 1951): 532–533.

"Young Teddy Roosevelt." Rev. of *The Letters of Theodore Roosevelt,* Vols. I–II: *The Years of Preparation, 1868–1903* edited by E. E. Morison. *Yale Review* 41 (Autumn 1951): 157–159; another review (unsigned) in *U.S. Quarterly Book Review* 7 (Sept. 1951): 228.

Rev. of *The Negro and Fusion Politics in North Carolina, 1894–1901* by Helen G. Edmonds. *Phylon* (Fourth Quarter, 1951): 389–390; another review (unsigned) in *U.S. Quarterly Book Review* 7 (Sept. 1951): 269–270.

Rev. (unsigned) of *Midwestern Progressive Politics* by Russel B. Nye. *U.S. Quarterly Book Review* 7 (Sept. 1951): 276–277.

Rev. (unsigned) of *The Negro and the Communist Party* by Wilson Record. *U.S. Quarterly Book Review* (7 Sept. 1951): 279.

Rev. (unsigned) of *Agricultural Discontent in the Middle West, 1900–1939* by Theodore Saloutous and J. D. Hicks. *U.S. Quarterly Book Review* 7 (Sept. 1951): 280.

Rev. (unsigned) of *Reunion and Reaction* by C. Vann Woodward. *U.S. Quarterly Book Review* 7 (Sept. 1951): 282–283.

Rev. (unsigned) of *Here They Once Stood, the Tragic End of the Apalachee Missions* by Mark E. Boyd. *U.S. Quarterly Book Review* 7 (Dec. 1951): 376–377.

Rev. (unsigned) of *Bourbon Democracy in Alabama, 1874–1890* by Allen J. Going. *U.S. Quarterly Book Review* 7 (Dec. 1951): 378.

Rev. (unsigned) of *America's Colonial Experiment* by Julius W. Pratt. *U.S. Quarterly Book Review* 7 (Dec. 1951): 382.

1952

Rev. of *Charles Evans Hughes* by Merlo J. Pusey. *Annals of the American Academy of Political and Social Science* 280 (Mar. 1952): 172–173.

Rev. (unsigned) of *The Letters of Theodore Roosevelt*, Vols. III–IV: *The Square Deal, 1901–1905* edited by E. E. Morison. *U.S. Quarterly Book Review* 8 (Mar. 1952): 12.

Rev. (unsigned) of *Socialism and American Life* by Donald D. Egbert and Stow Persons. *U.S. Quarterly Book Review* 8 (Sept. 1952): 282–283.

Rev. (unsigned) of *The Letters of Theodore Roosevelt*, Vols. V–VI: *The Big Stick* edited by E. E. Morison. *U.S. Quarterly Book Review* 8 (Dec. 1952): 355.

1953

Rev. of *American History and American Historians* by H. Hale Bellot. *New Mexico Historical Review* 28 (Jan. 1953): 69–71.

Rev. of *Roosevelt and Daniels: A Friendship in Politics* by Carroll Kilpatrick. *North Carolina Historical Review* 30 (Jan. 1953): 116–117.

Rev. (unsigned) of *The American Socialist Movement, 1897–1912* by Ira Kipnis. *U.S. Quarterly Book Review* 9 (Mar. 1953): 24–25.

Rev. of *Woodrow Wilson's Own Story* by Donald Day. *American Historical Review* 58 (Apr. 1953): 710.

Rev. of *Franklin D. Roosevelt: The Apprenticeship* by Frank Friedel. *Journal of Southern History* 19 (May 1953): 256–258; another review (unsigned) *U.S. Quarterly Book Review* 9 (June 1953): 114.

Rev. of *Champion Campaigner: Franklin D. Roosevelt* by Harold F. Gosnell. *Mississippi Valley Historical Review* 40 (June 1953): 168–169.

Rev. of *Woodrow Wilson's China Policy, 1913–1917* by Tien-yi Li. *Pacific Historical Review* 22 (Aug. 1953): 315–316.

Rev. (unsigned) of *The Forging of American Socialism* by Howard H. Quint. *U.S. Quarterly Book Review* 9 (Dec. 1953): 408.

1954

"The Big Stick Stilled." Rev. of *The Letters of Theodore Roosevelt*, Vols. VII–VIII: *The Days of Armageddon* edited by E. E. Morison. *Saturday Review* 37, 27 Feb. 1954, 17, 36.

Rev. of *Franklin D. Roosevelt: The Ordeal* by Frank Freidel. *Journal of Southern History* 20 (May 1954): 291–292.

Rev. of *The Road to Safety* by Arthur Willert and *Decision for War* by Samuel R. Spencer, Jr. *Mississippi Valley Historical Review* 41 (June 1954): 159–160.

Rev. of *The Republican Roosevelt* by John Morton Blum. *Annals of the American Academy of Political and Social Science* 296 (Nov. 1954): 174–175.

Rev. (unsigned) of *The Roosevelt Family of Sagamore Hill* by Hermann Hagedorn. *U.S. Quarterly Book Review* 10 (Dec. 1954): 463–464.

1955

Rev. of *Red Scare: A Study in National Hysteria, 1919–1920* by Robert K. Murray. *Annals of the American Academy of Political and Social Science* 300 (July 1955): 142–143.

Rev. of *Bishop Cannon's Own Story* by James Cannon, Jr. Edited by R. L. Watson, Jr. *Journal of Southern History* 21 (Nov. 1955): 564–565.

"Intellectuals Victorious." Rev. of *Triumph of the Eggheads* by Horace Coon. *Saturday Review* 38, 5 Nov. 1955, 15.

1956

"Justice Hughes Profile's Superb." Rev. of *Charles Evans Hughes and American Democratic Statesmanship* by Dexter Perkins. *Chicago Sun-Times,* 22 July 1956, Sec. II, p. 5.

1957

Rev. of *Franklin D. Roosevelt: The Triumph* by Frank Freidel. *Journal of Southern History* 23 (Feb. 1957): 136–138.

1958

Rev. of *The University of North Carolina, 1900–1930* by Louis R. Wilson. *Social Forces* 36 (Mar. 1958): 282–283.

Rev. of *Wilson's Foreign Policy in Perspective* edited by Edward H. Buehrig. *American Historical Review* 63 (Apr. 1958): 756–57.

"Dimensions of a President's Greatness." Rev. of *The Ordeal of Woodrow Wilson* by Herbert Hoover. *New York Times Book Review,* 27 Apr. 1958, p. 7.

Rev. of *McIver of North Carolina* by Rose H. Holder. *Social Forces* 36 (May 1958): 391–392.

Rev. of *American Diplomacy in the Great Depression* by Robert H. Ferrell. *Indiana Magazine of History* 54 (June 1958): 193–194.

Rev. of *Woodrow Wilson,* Vol. I: *American Prophet;* Vol. II: *World Prophet* by Arthur Walworth. *Annals of the American Academy of Political and Social Science* 319 (Sept. 1958) 165–166.

1960

"The Man at the President's Side." Rev. of *Woodrow Wilson, An Intimate Memoir* by Cary T. Grayson. *New York Times Book Review,* 19 June 1960, pp. 3, 23.

Rev. of *Peace without Victory* by Lawrence W. Martin. *Political Science Quarterly* 75 (June 1960): 306–308.

"From Harding to Hoover, a Swirl of Events at Home and Abroad." Rev. of *Republican Ascendancy, 1921–1933* by John D. Hicks. *New York Times Book Review,* 10 July 1960, p. 3.

"Room Near the Top." Rev. of *Right-Hand Man: The Life of George W. Perkins* by John A. Garraty. *New York Times Book Review,* 16 Oct. 1960, pp. 6, 18.

1961

Rev. of *Josephus Daniels in Mexico* by E. David Cronon. *North Carolina Historical Review* 38 (Jan. 1961): 94–95.

"His History Was Current." Rev. of *The Autobiography of James T. Shotwell* by James T. Shotwell. *New York Times Book Review,* 24 Sept. 1961, pp. 10, 12.

"President's Helpmate." Rev. of *Edith Bolling Wilson, First Lady Extraordinary* by Alden Hatch. *New York Times Book Review,* 10 Dec. 1961, pp. 24, 26.

1962

Rev. of *The Enlargement of the Presidency* by Rexford G. Tugwell. *Annals of the American Academy of Political and Social Science* 339 (Jan. 1962): 198.

Rev. of *The United States in the Supreme War Council* by David F. Trask. *Mississippi Valley Historical Review* 48 (Mar. 1962): 728–729.

1963

Untitled. Rev. of *Mr. Wilson's War* by John Dos Passos. *New York Times Book Review,* 7 Apr. 1963, p. 41.

Rev. of *Josephus Daniels Says . . . : An Editor's Political Odyssey from Bryan to Wilson and F. D. R., 1894–1913* by Joseph L. Morrison. *Annals of the American Academy of Political and Social Science,* 349 (Sept. 1963): 193–194.

1964

Rev. of *The Inquiry: American Preparations for Peace, 1917–1919* by Lawrence E. Gelfand. *Journal of Modern History* 36 (Mar. 1964): 103–104.

"There Is No More Tragic and Searing Story." Rev. of *When the Cheering Stopped: The Last Years of Woodrow Wilson* by Gene Smith. *New York Times Book Review,* 9 Mar. 1964, p. 6.

Rev. of *The American Secretaries of State and Their Diplomacy,* Vol. XI: *Frank B. Kellogg-Henry L. Stimson* by Robert H. Ferrell. *Annals of the American Academy of Political and Social Science,* 354 (May 1964): 159.

Rev. of *The Cabinet Diaries of Jospehus Daniels, 1913–1921* edited by E. David Cronon. *Journal of Modern History* 36 (Dec. 1964): 473–474.

1966

Rev. of *Montaigne of Virginia: The Making of a Southern Progressive* by William Larsen. *Journal of Southern History* 32 (Aug. 1966): 409–410.

Rev. of *Politics is Adjourned: Woodrow Wilson and the War Congress, 1916–1918* by Seward W. Livermore. *American Historical Review* 72 (Oct. 1966): 322–323.

Rev. of *Letters from the Paris Peace Conference* by Charles Seymour, edited by Harold B. Whiteman, Jr. *American Historical Review* 72 (Oct. 1966): 323.

1968

Rev. of *The American Revisionists* by Warren I. Cohen. *New York Historical Quarterly* 52 (Jan. 1968): 111–112.

Rev. of *Woodrow Wilson: The Academic Years* by Henry W. Bragdon. *New England Quarterly* 41 (Mar. 1968): 118–121.

"Special Mission." Rev. of *Woodrow Wilson and World Politics: America's Response to War and Revolution* by N. Gordon Levin, Jr. *New York Times Book Review*, 28 Apr. 1968, p. 40.

Rev. of *The Negro in Virginia Politics, 1902–1965* by Andrew Buni. *Journal of Southern History* 34 (May 1968): 322–323.

1969

Rev. of *President Wilson Fights His War* by Harvey A. De Weerd. *Journal of American History* 56 (June 1969): 173.

1970

Rev. of *Heir to Empire: United States Economic Diplomacy, 1916–1923* by Carl P. Parrini. *Journal of Southern History* 36 (May 1970): 303–305.

Rev. of *Senator Robert F. Wagner and the Rise of Urban Liberalism* by J. Joseph Huthmacher. *Journal of American History* 57 (Sept. 1970): 474–476.

1971

Rev. of *The White Chief: James Kimble Vardaman* by William F. Holmes. *Journal of American History* 58 (June 1971): 189–190.

Rev. of *The Irreconcilables: The Fight Against the League of Nations* by Ralph Stone. *Journal of American History* 58 (June 1971): 204–205.

1972

Rev. of *A Mind of One Piece: Brandeis and American Reform* by Melvin I. Urofsky. *Business History Review* 46 (Spring 1972): 120–121.

Rev. of *The Republican Command, 1897–1913* by Horace S. and Marion G. Merrill. *Journal of Southern History* 38 (Aug. 1972): 495–496.

Rev. of *The New Citizenship: Origins of Progressivism in Wisconsin, 1885–1900* by David P. Thelen. *Journal of American History* 59 (Dec. 1972): 739–740.

1974

Rev. of *Progressives and Prohibitionists: Texas Democrats in the Wilson Era* by Lewis J. Gould. *Journal of Southern History* 40 (Feb. 1974): 154–155.

Rev. of *The Imperial Presidency* by Arthur M. Schlesinger, Jr. *Theology Today* 321 (Oct. 1974): 252–254, 256.

1975

Rev. of *The Hoover-Wilson Wartime Correspondence: September 24, 1914, to November 11, 1918* edited by Francis W. O'Brien. *Journal of American History* 62 (Sept. 1975): 449–451.

1976

Rev. of *The Shaping of Southern Politics: Suffrage Restriction and the Establishment of the One-Party South, 1880–1910* by J. Morgan Kousser. *Journal of Interdisciplinary History* 7 (Summer 1976): 178–181.
Rev. of *The Politics of American Individualism: Herbert Hoover in Transition, 1918–1921* by Gary Dean Best. *Journal of American History* 62 (Dec. 1976): 757–758.

1977

Rev. of *A Georgian at Princeton* by Robert Manson Myers. *Journal of American History* 64 (June 1977): 153–154.
Rev. of *Robert M. LaFollette and the Insurgent Spirit* by David P. Thelen. *Journal of American History* 64 (Dec. 1977): 820–821.

1978

Rev. of *Colonel House in Paris: A Study in American Foreign Policy at the Paris Peace Conference 1919* by Inga Floto. *Historisk Tidsskrift* (Denmark) 78 (1978): 335–337.

1981

Rev. of *World War I and the Origin of Civil Liberties in the United States* by Paul L. Murphy. *Journal of American History* 68 (June 1981): 165–166.
Rev. of *James McCosh and the Scottish Intellectual Tradition* by J. David Hoeveler, Jr. *American Journal of Education* 90 (Nov. 1981): 54–57.

1984

Rev. of *The American Style of Foreign Policy: Cultural Politics and Foreign Affairs* by Robert Dallek. *Pacific Historical Review* 53 (Aug. 1984): 414–415.

1987

Rev. of *Power and Principle: Armed Intervention in Wilsonian Foreign Policy* by Frederick S. Calhoun. *Political Science Quarterly* 102 (Spring 1987): 165.

1988

"Herbert Hoover's Finest Hour." Rev. of *The Life of Herbert Hoover: The Humanitarian, 1914–1917* by George H. Nash. *Washington Post Book World*, 4 Sept. 1988, p. 5.

1989

Rev. of *The New South Faces the World: Foreign Affairs and the Southern Sense of Self, 1877–1950* by Tennant S. McWilliams. *Georgia Historical Quarterly* 73 (Spring 1989): 163–166.

DOCTORAL DISSERTATIONS DIRECTED BY ARTHUR S. LINK

Northwestern University

George S. McGovern, "The Colorado Coal Strike, 1913–1914," (1953).

William H. Harbaugh, "Wilson, Roosevelt, and Interventionism, 1914–1917: A Study of Domestic Influences on the Formulation of American Foreign Policy," (1954).

Gerald N. Grob, "Trade Vs. Reform Unionism: The Emergence of the Modern American Labor Movement, 1865–1896," (1958).

Sidney I. Roberts, "Businessmen in Revolt: Chicago, 1874–1900," (1960).

James F. Findlay, Jr., "Dwight L. Moody, Evangelist of the Gilded Age: 1837–1899," (1961).

Daniel R. Beaver, "A Progressive at War: Newton D. Baker and the American War Effort, 1917–1918," (1962).

David W. Hirst, "German Propaganda in the United States, 1914–1917," (1962).

John E. Semonche, "Progressive Journalist: Ray Stannard Baker, 1870–1914," (1962).

Princeton University

John R. Lambert, "Arthur Pue Gorman: Politician," (1948).

David William Savage, "The Irish Question in British Politics, 1914–1916," (1963).

Justus Drew Doenecke, "American Public Opinion and the Manchurian Crisis, 1931–1933," (1966).

William M. Leary, Jr., "Smith of New Jersey: A Biography of H. Alexander Smith, United States Senator from New Jersey, 1944–1959," (1966).

Meyer J. Nathan, "The Presidential Election of 1916 in the Middle West," (1966).

355

Ralph B. Levering, "Prelude to Cold War: American Attitudes toward Russia during World War II," (1971).

Richard A. Harrison, "Appeasement and Isolation: The Relationship of British and American Foreign Policies, 1935–1938," (1974).

John M. Mulder, "The Gospel of Order: Woodrow Wilson and the Development of His Religious, Political, and Educational Thought, 1856–1910," (1974).

Frank A. Stricker, "Socialism, Feminism, and the New Morality: The Separate Freedoms of Max Eastman, William English Walling, and Floyd Dell, 1910–1930," (1974).

Walter M. Licht, "Nineteenth-Century American Railwaymen: A Study in the Nature and Organization of Work," (1977).

Gilbert Moore, "Poverty, Class Consciousness and Racial Conflict: The Social Basis of Trade Union Politics in the UAW-CIO, 1937–1955," (1977).

Grover F. Goodwin, "'A Mexican Army': The Democratic Party, 1924–1928," (1978).

Steven J. Ross, "Workers on the Edge: Work, Leisure, and Politics in Industrializing Cincinnati, 1830–1890," (1980).

James W. Berry, "Growing up in the Old South: The Childhood of Charles Colcock Jones, Jr.," (1981).

Christine A. Lunardini, "From Equal Suffrage to Equal Rights: The National Women's Party, 1913–1923," (1981).

Niels A. Thorsen, "The Political and Economic Thought of Woodrow Wilson, 1875–1902," (1981).

Thomas J. Knock, "Woodrow Wilson and the Origins of the League of Nations," (1982).

Anne Cipriano Venzon, "The Papers of General Smedley Darlington Butler, USMC. 1915–1918," (1982).

Manfred F. Boemeke, "The Wilson Administration, Organized Labor, and the Colorado Coal Strike, 1913–1914," (1983).

Peter Larsen, "Theodore Roosevelt and the Moroccan Crisis, 1904–1906," (1984).

Perry K. Blatz, "Ever-Shifting Ground: Work and Labor Relations in the Anthracite Coal Industry, 1868–1903," (1987).

Jun Furuya, "Gentlemen's Disagreement: The Controversy between the United States and Japan over the California Alien Land Law of 1913," (1989).

The Wilson Era: Essays in Honor of Arthur S. Link was copyedited by Andrew J. Davidson. Production Editor was Lucy Herz. The text was typeset by Graphic Composition, Inc., and printed and bound by McNaughton and Gunn, Inc.

Cover design by Vito DePinto Graphic Design.